# NORMAN ROCKWELL

## Drawings, 1911–1976

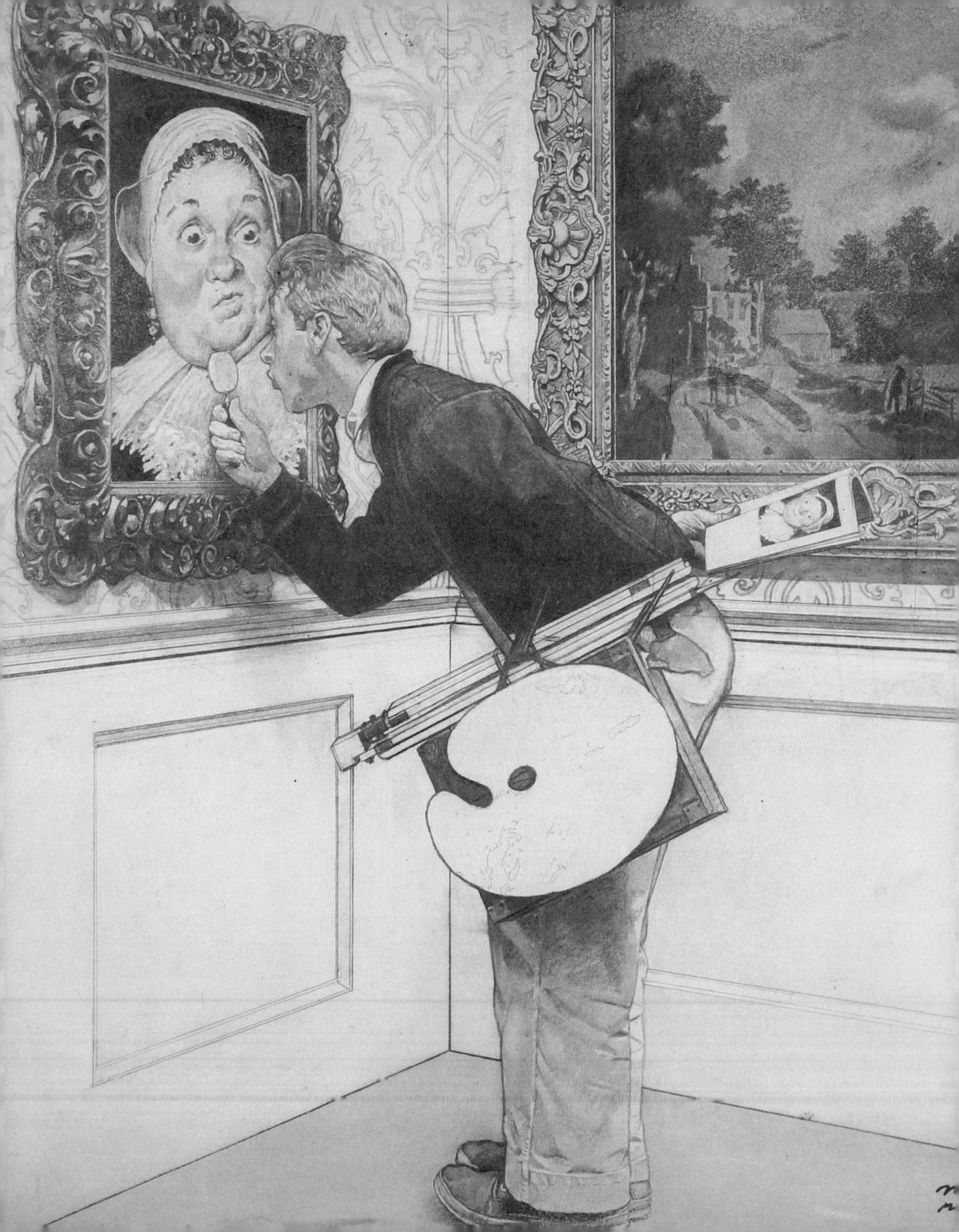

NORMAN ROCKWELL MUSEUM

# Norman Rockwell

## Drawings, 1911–1976

STEPHANIE HABOUSH PLUNKETT
AND JESSE KOWALSKI

FOREWORD BY
LOUIS HENRY MITCHELL

ABBEVILLE PRESS PUBLISHERS
New York London

A NOTE ON THE CAPTIONS

Unless otherwise noted, the works illustrated herein are held at the Norman Rockwell Museum in Stockbridge, Massachusetts. Accession numbers are given at the end of the captions.

FRONT COVER
Charcoal drawing for *The Problem We All Live With*, 1963. See plate 3.12.

BACK COVER
*Left top and bottom:* Drawings for *My Adventures as an Illustrator*, 1960. See plates 8.18 and 8.23.
*Right:* Study for *Couple in Rumble Seat*, 1935. See plate 4.10.

PAGE 2
Detail of a study for *Art Critic*, 1955. See plate 1.8.

PAGE 256
*The Gossips*, 1948
Pencil and charcoal on paper, 31 × 28¼ in. (78.7 × 71.8 cm)
Cover study for the *Saturday Evening Post*, March 6, 1948
NRACT.1973.011

PROJECT EDITORS: Lauren Bucca and David Fabricant
COPY EDITOR: Stephanie Baker
PRODUCTION MANAGER: Louise Kurtz
DESIGNER: Misha Beletsky

PHOTOGRAPHY CREDITS
Copyright © Art Students League of New York: p. 51; copyright © Sam Calder: p. 106; copyright © Chester Kronfeld: pp. 170; copyright © Bill Scovill: p. 126 left; copyright © Peter Willi/Bridgeman Images: p. 40



First edition
10 9 8 7 6 5 4 3 2 1

ISBN 978-0-7892-1410-2

Library of Congress Cataloging-in-Publication Data available upon request

For bulk and premium sales and for text adoption procedures, write to Customer Service Manager, Abbeville Press, 655 Third Avenue, New York, NY 10017, or call 1-800-ARTBOOK.

Visit Abbeville Press online at www.abbeville.com.

This book is published in conjunction with the exhibition
NORMAN ROCKWELL: DRAWINGS, 1911–1976
Norman Rockwell Museum, Stockbridge, Massachusetts
September 2, 2022, through January 7, 2023

## ABOUT THE NORMAN ROCKWELL MUSEUM

The Norman Rockwell Museum's mission is to illuminate the power of American illustration art to reflect and shape society, and to advance the enduring values of kindness, respect, and social equity portrayed by Norman Rockwell. Dedicated to the art of illustration in all its variety, the Museum, located in Stockbridge, Massachusetts, holds the largest and most significant collection of art and archival materials relating to the life and work of Norman Rockwell. The Museum also preserves, interprets, and exhibits the Stockbridge studio where Rockwell painted for his last twenty-one years, and a growing collection of original illustration art by noted American illustrators working in many genres. The Norman Rockwell Museum's Art and Archival Collections inspire a vibrant exhibition program, national and international traveling exhibitions, arts and humanities programs, and wide-ranging Virtual Museum experiences. The Museum's collections, made accessible worldwide, are a comprehensive resource relating to Norman Rockwell, the art of illustration, and the role of published imagery in society.

Since its inception in 1969, the Museum has explored the impact of published images and their ability to shape and reflect our world. Dedication to a deepened understanding of the art of illustration within historical, literary, and cultural contexts has led to the formation of the Rockwell Center for American Visual Studies. The first of its kind in the nation, this research institute supports sustained scholarship relating to published imagery and the emerging field of Illustration Studies through fellowships, symposia, and an ever-growing Illustration History website, accessed at illustrationhistory.org and at rockwellcenter.org.

The Museum places humanitarian compassion, equality, and inclusion at the center of its work as Rockwell did. We acknowledge with humility the systemic authority systems in published illustration that have for centuries denied subordinated groups and citizens their rightful dignity, expression, and representation. To redress centuries of structural inequity and historical prejudice, the Museum commits to being a learning organization and to deconstructing and reconstructing a just and equitable representative visual narrative for America through the art of illustration.

*Norman Rockwell Museum, 9 Glendale Road, P.O. Box 308, Stockbridge, MA 01262, 413-298-4100, nrm.org*

# CONTENTS

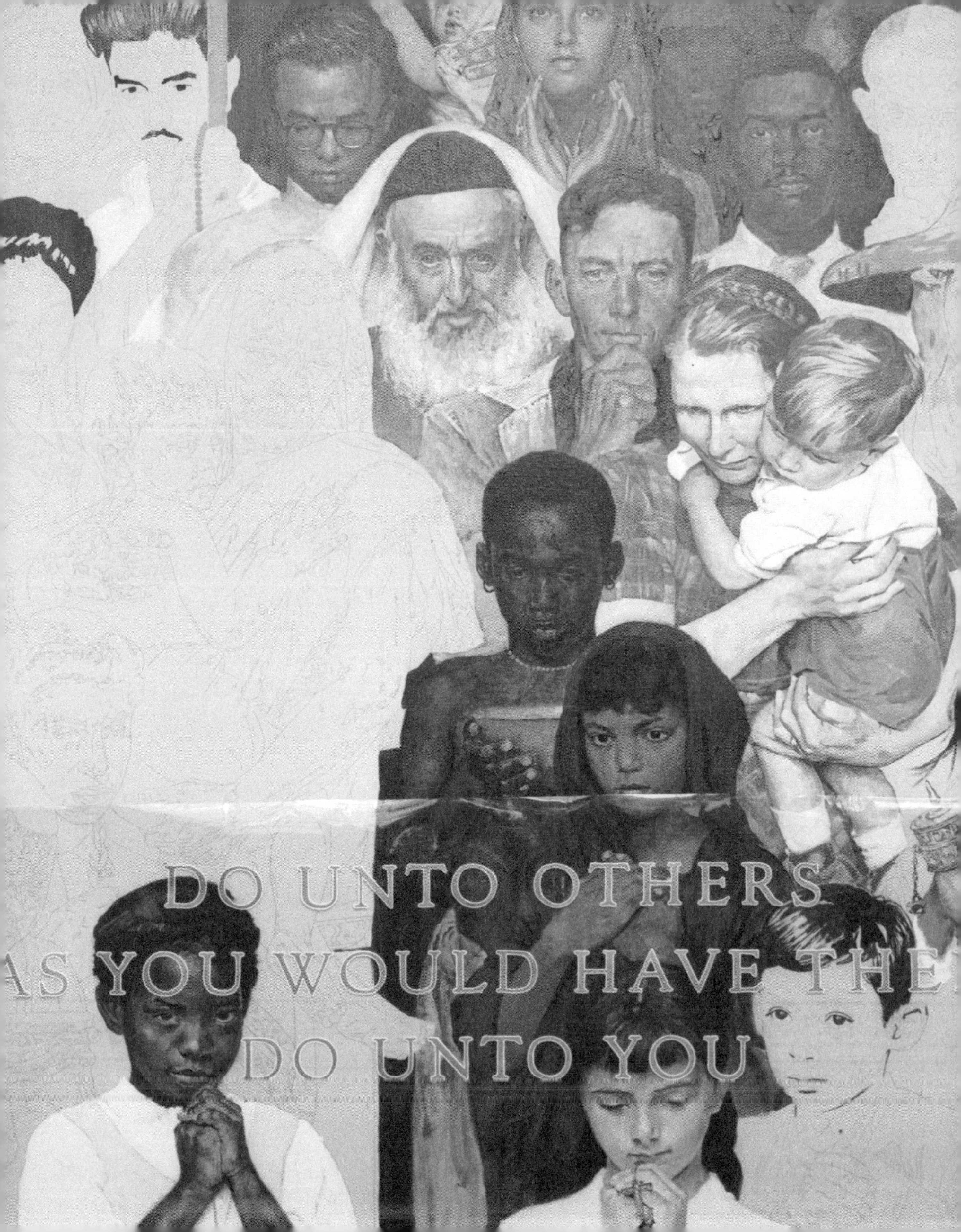

DO UNTO OTHERS
AS YOU WOULD HAVE THE
DO UNTO YOU

FOREWORD

# Learning to Draw with Norman Rockwell

LOUIS HENRY MITCHELL
CREATIVE DIRECTOR OF CHARACTER DESIGN, SESAME WORKSHOP

In 1976, the door of a modest little bookstore became the threshold to an amazing journey for a sixteen-year-old art student after the very first day of high school. I wandered through this treasure trove that I happened upon as I explored the new neighborhood that brought me into Manhattan, on my own, for the very first time. I asked the kind, elderly man who owned the bookstore where the art books were, and he led me up the narrow, tiered stairs. I had never seen so many art books in one place. So many different artists expressing themselves uniquely, in an endless vari-

Detail of *Golden Rule*, 1961, in progress
See plate 4.43.

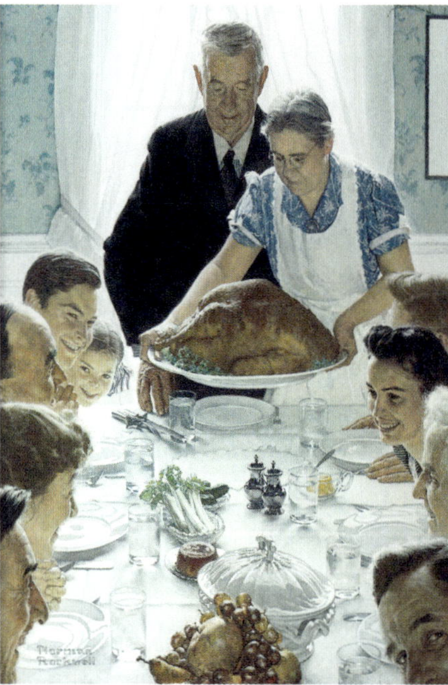

1. *Freedom from Want*, 1943
Oil on canvas, 45¾ × 35½ in. (116.2 × 90.2 cm)
Illustration for the *Saturday Evening Post*, March 6, 1943
NRACT.1973.022

ety of ways: my mind was being opened as never before. And then, there it was—*Norman Rockwell: Illustrator*, the book that would catapult my creative mind to another level and change my very life!

On the book's cover was Rockwell's famous 1943 Thanksgiving dinner painting, *Freedom from Want* (plate 1). In seeing this work and in leafing through the book's pages, I felt that my art education had truly begun, in that very bookstore, which I visited each and every day after attending classes at Manhattan's High School of Art and Design. I was feeding upon the brilliant renderings and the astounding compositions that I saw within this book, which I couldn't afford to buy at the time. The kindness of that bookstore owner went above and beyond my ability to even notice it because of how mesmerized I was by Rockwell's artwork. It moved me so much that I was compelled to read the written words, hoping I could somehow understand how his work was being accomplished. It just so happened that I started at the very back of the book. What I read still resonates within me to this day:

> Neither time nor effort nor materials should be spared if worthy work is to be expected. Even if it is necessary to give up something—something outside of the studio—in order to get the right things in the studio, I think it is almost criminal not to do it that way.

From those words during those wonderful days in the presence of that bookstore owner, I graduated to a career that has given me so much joy. I received opportunities I could never have imagined. Yes, I had my aspirations, but in my mind they were unattainable fantasies. I grew up an African American in East Flatbush, Brooklyn, where dreams like mine were laughed at and, worse, sorely discouraged. But my dear mother, Justa C. Mitchell, always knew what to say to me in the face of all that discouragement: "Don't pay attention to all of that. Just keep going!" Those simple yet powerful words are how I stayed the course and obtained my dream job as Creative Director of Character Design for Sesame Street (plates 2 and 3). As wonderful as this was, I could never have imagined it would be the channel through which I received one of the greatest honors of my life. A request to give a lecture about my Sesame Street work at the Norman Rockwell Museum led to an invitation to partner on several Rockwell projects and become a member of the museum's board. My experiences at Sesame Workshop ultimately brought me full circle, as through my work with the company and the museum, I came to discover Rockwell's art again, in a new way. Now, I am privileged to write the foreword to another book celebrating his

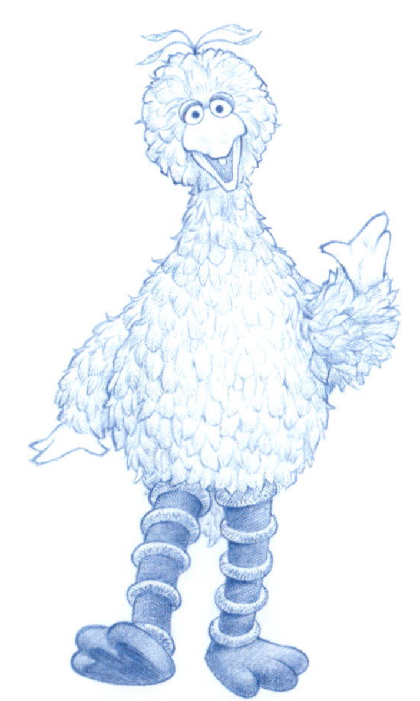

2. Louis Henry Mitchell (b. 1960)
*Big Bird*, c. 2014
Blue pencil on paper
17 × 11 in. (43.2 × 27.9 cm)
NRM.2019.16.02 (Louis Henry Mitchell)

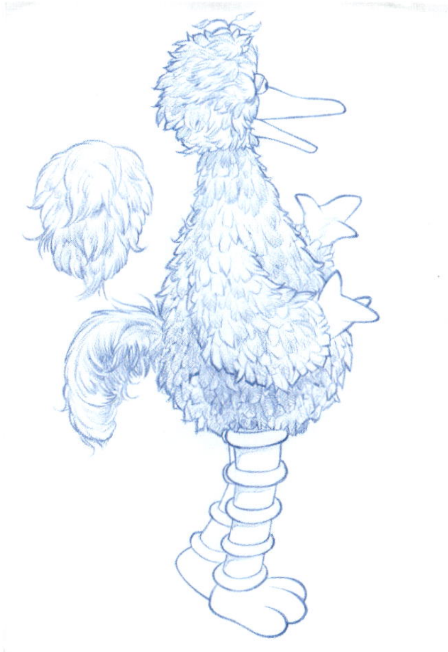

3. Louis Henry Mitchell (b. 1960)
*Big Bird* side view, c. 2014
Blue pencil on paper
17 × 11 in. (43.2 × 27.9 cm)
NRM.2019.16.03 (Louis Henry Mitchell)

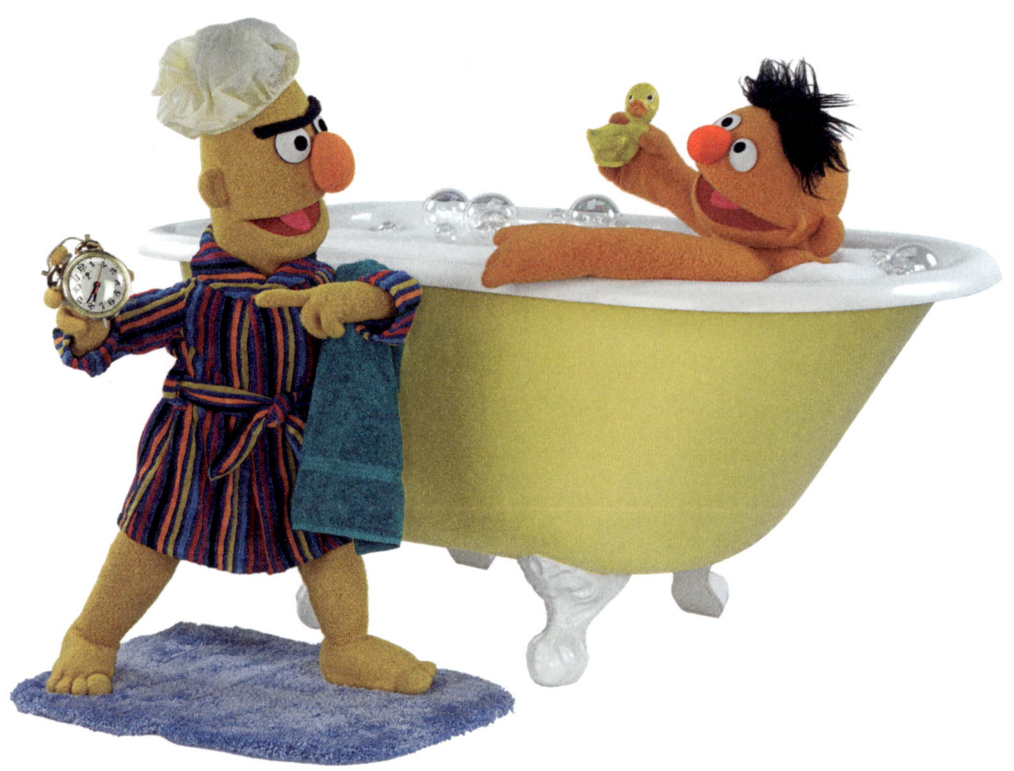

4. Untitled [Bert and Ernie], 2008
Digital photograph
Sesame Workshop, New York

inner sanctum—his drawings, which form the underpinning of his finished illustrations but stand strongly on their own.

Among the many things I have been privileged to do at Sesame Workshop, the nonprofit educational organization behind Sesame Street, is direct the still-photo shoots for products, packaging, and promotion, among other uses. Although I spend most of my time drawing them, I also work with the actual Sesame Street Muppets, which have been fitted with aluminum armature wire so I can put them in various poses to be photographed. In practice, I consider what I do a "still performance," as I become the character that I am performing in a still moment of time. I work toward convincing the viewer that Elmo, Cookie Monster, Big Bird, and all the others are alive and actually doing whatever I am tasked with delivering based upon specific educational initiatives. In addition, I must also consider composition and how the characters are being placed in the scene. Ultimately, though, the storytelling element expressed in the posing of each character,

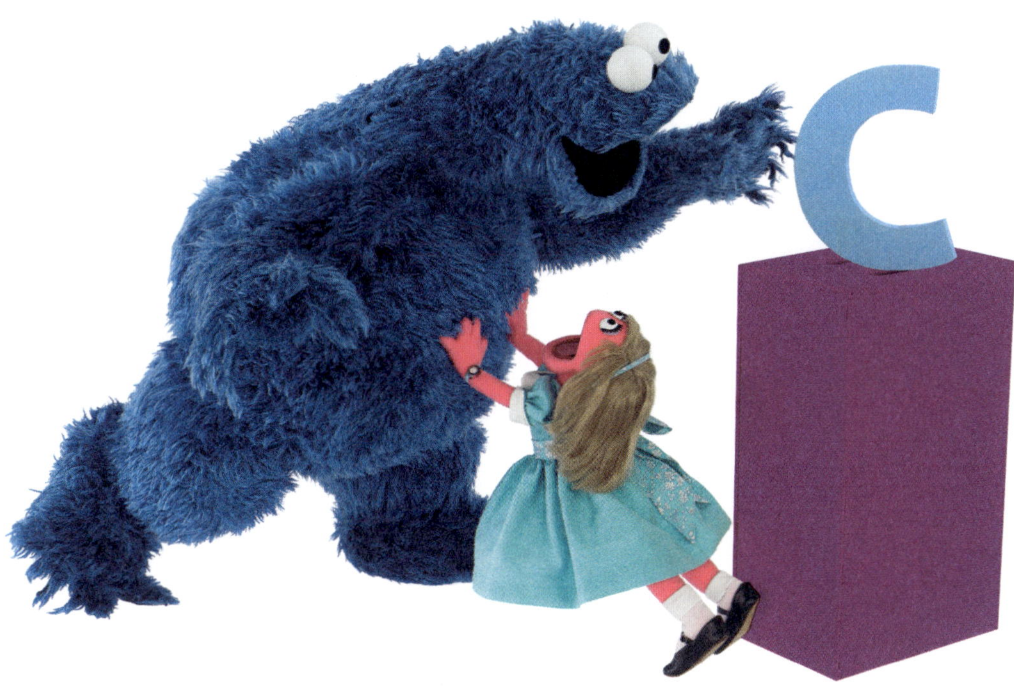


5. Untitled [Prairie Dawn and Cookie Monster], 2008
Digital photograph
Sesame Workshop, New York

independently and in relation to the others, serves as my motivation. These three fundamental areas—posing, composition, and storytelling—along with many intangible processes, came to me over the course of many years spent studying how Rockwell created his images.

I was aware of how influential Rockwell was to me. But only in retrospect did I realize that he was also a mentor, virtually leaning over my shoulder as I drew and posed the Sesame Street Muppets. Rockwell's way of composing an image, convincing the viewer that the characters are alive, and making the story the most important element is my perpetual guide. In one photo, I depicted best friends Bert and Ernie, who share one bathroom in their home. Bert is alerting Ernie of how long he has been in the tub, and Ernie is gesturing toward him, happily taking his time with his favorite toy, Rubber Duckie (plate 4). In another, little Prairie Dawn hopelessly attempts to prevent Cookie Monster from eating "the letter of the day," which is the letter *C* (plate 5).

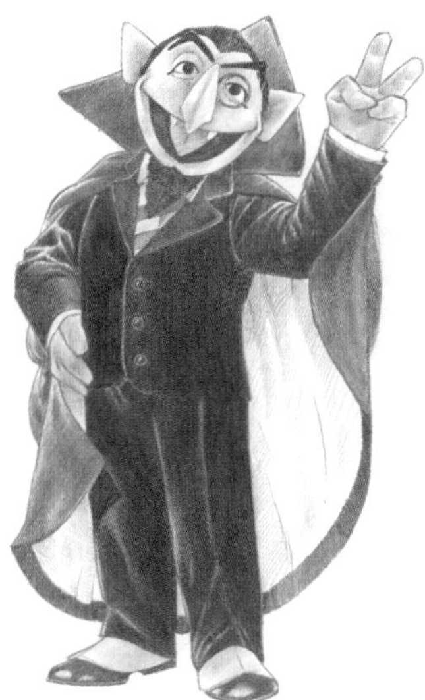

6. Louis Henry Mitchell (b. 1960)
*Count von Count*, 2014
Pencil on paper, 17 × 11 in. (43.2 × 27.9 cm)
NRM.2019.16.13 (Louis Henry Mitchell)

As I aspire toward the excellence of Rockwell's compositions, his continued influence has helped me create successful imagery that has moved people to joyful tears. His art has taught me to become one with my subjects, inspiring me to see and feel their emotions. And, in a real way, each character is me, a kind of self-portrait. I become Grover and Count von Count (plate 6) and even Oscar the Grouch, an experience made possible through my love and respect for each character's unique qualities and inner "life." As I continue to immerse myself in Rockwell's art, I am grateful for the generous teachings he has left me and all of us.

However, Rockwell's influence impacts my work and life beyond Sesame Street. Even before my professional aspirations were realized, I was reaching for all I could learn from Rockwell, through books and interviews that revealed his enthusiasm, working methods, and professionalism. Rockwell appreciated and studied the work of many artists, including Rembrandt, an exceptional draftsman whom he identified as a favorite. His attention to art history and the artwork that inspired him opened my eyes to the importance of studying other artists and their work. Among them were Andrew Wyeth, whose drawing *The Bed* (a study for *Chambered Nautilus*, 1956) inspired attention to detail, and Michelangelo, who created my favorite single drawing of all time, the main figure in the *Studies for the Libyan Sibyl* (c. 1510–11), for the Sistine Chapel (plate 7). I was honored to view the orig-

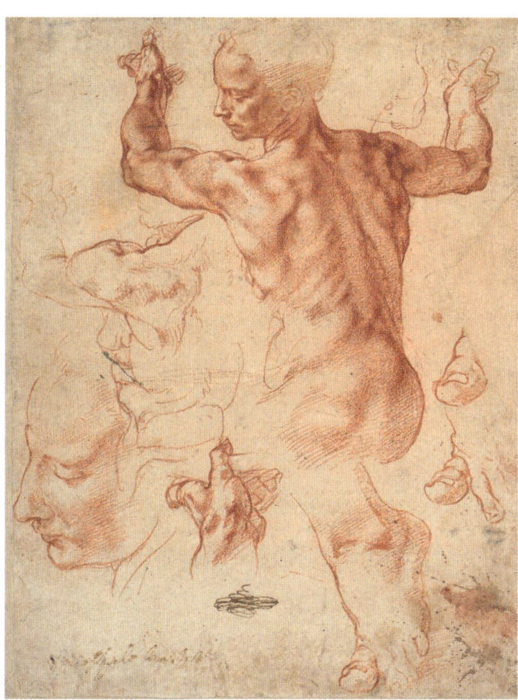

7. Michelangelo Buonarroti (1475–1564)
*Studies for the Libyan Sibyl*, c. 1510–11
Red chalk on paper, 11 × 8½ in.
(28.9 × 21.6 cm)
Metropolitan Museum of Art, New York; Purchase, Joseph Pulitzer Bequest, 1924, 24.197.2

inal drawing at the Metropolitan Museum of Art. As I studied the delicate yet powerful rendering and line work, I saw Michelangelo's dedication to the study of anatomy—how the bones and muscles were in perfect alignment with each other under the skin of the model. Even the gesture, though strong and muscular, is so graceful that it flows in the most natural way. It was also encouraging to see that as knowledgeable as Michelangelo was about anatomy, his sketches and additional studies and details surround the portrait of the model. A close-up of the profile, examinations of the left hand's position, the relationship of the scapula to the shoulder, and even several details of the right toe are evidence of this great master's need to keep studying and working toward the very best end result. Michelangelo's approach is mirrored by Rockwell, who also created detailed and elaborate studies for paintings long before even touching a brush. And so, above all, to this very day, I return to the greatest source of overall inspiration for me, Rockwell himself.

In almost every instance, the intimacy and life depicted in Rockwell's work is realized at the crucial drawing stage. Whether he is working through ideas using charcoal or a Wolff's carbon pencil or a simple graphite pencil, it is at once elevated to a supreme instrument in his hands, as it is in his drawings that his ideas all come together. Not intended to be seen by the public, Rockwell's drawings were studies and problem-solving exercises toward an

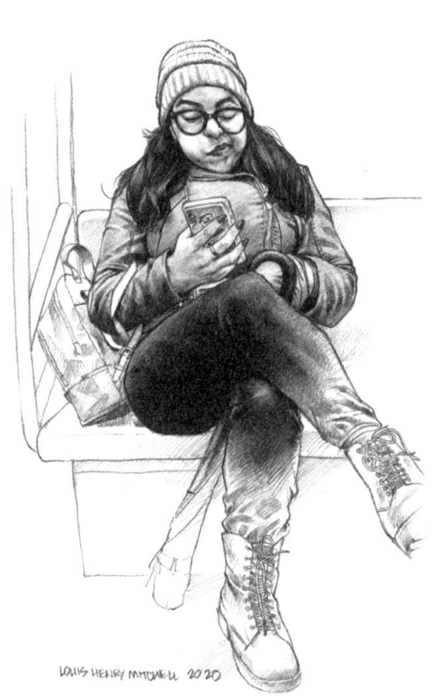


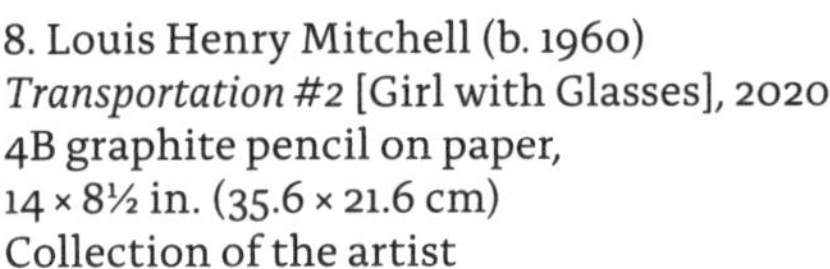
8. Louis Henry Mitchell (b. 1960)
*Transportation #2* [Girl with Glasses], 2020
4B graphite pencil on paper,
14 × 8½ in. (35.6 × 21.6 cm)
Collection of the artist

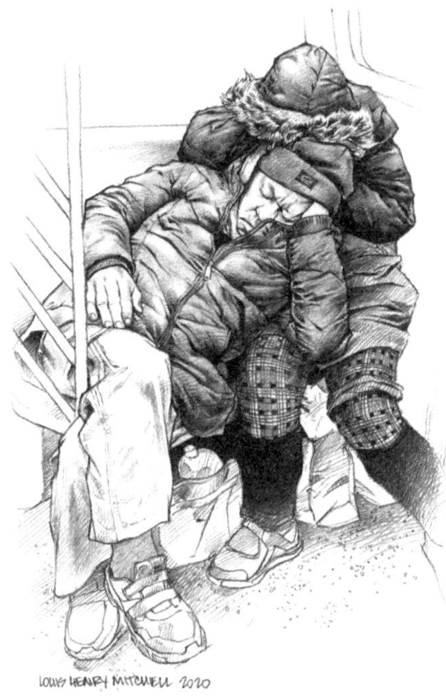


9. Louis Henry Mitchell (b. 1960)
*Transportation #4* [Sleeping Couple], 2020
4B graphite pencil on paper,
14 × 8½ in. (35.6 × 21.6 cm)
Collection of the artist

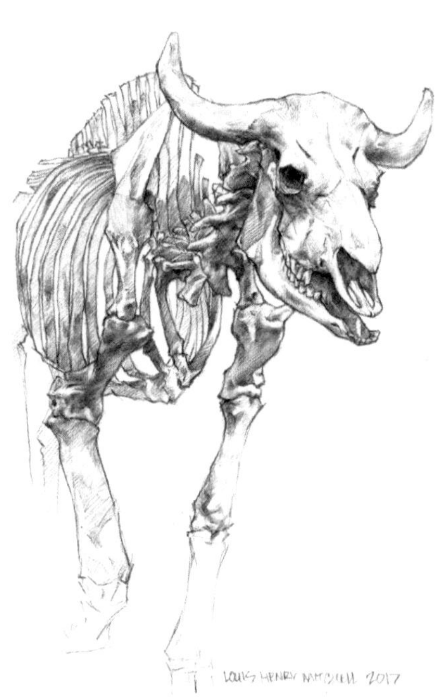


10. Louis Henry Mitchell (b. 1960)
Untitled [Bison], 2017
4B graphite pencil on paper,
14 × 8½ in. (35.6 × 21.6 cm)
Collection of the artist

expected end. But the love and attention that went into them is the reason this book is so necessary. If one is to truly understand what brought Rockwell's masterpieces to life, it is crucial to observe his steps in their creation from beginning to end. The beautiful posture of the old woman in *Saying Grace* (1951) was fully imagined and rendered in charcoal before one brushstroke of paint was applied to canvas. The eager anticipation of the young man in *Breaking Home Ties* (1954), contrasted by the forlorn look of his father and dog preparing to say farewell, is tangible. Rockwell completed multiple charcoal finishes as he explored just the right setting for this powerful and emotional moment, and each and every one was as tender and moving as the previous. This is also true of *Girl with Black Eye*, his 1953 *Saturday Evening Post* cover illustration featuring a little girl proudly displaying her black eye after a scuffle—the bold yet subtle nuances of her wounded eye made real. The charcoal study for this work, like so many of Rockwell's complex preliminary studies, could have been published as the finished piece, but as always, spectacular technique, accuracy, and the richness of detail are ultimately placed in the service of storytelling.

Providing an ever-increasing motivation for me in my Sesame Street work as well as my own artwork, Rockwell's drawings inspire me to draw each morning before I begin the day's assignments. The practice of drawing regularly helps to enhance my skills and sharpen my hand-eye coordination (plates 8 and 9). I still go to New York's American Museum of Natural History to practice drawing from the displays and specimens there, always keeping in mind Rockwell's high standard of rendering his discipline and the emphasis he placed on study and planning (plate 10). How excited I was when I discovered that Rockwell had studied anatomy under the famed artist and teacher George Bridgman, in the very same drawing studio where I took classes at the Art Students League many years later.

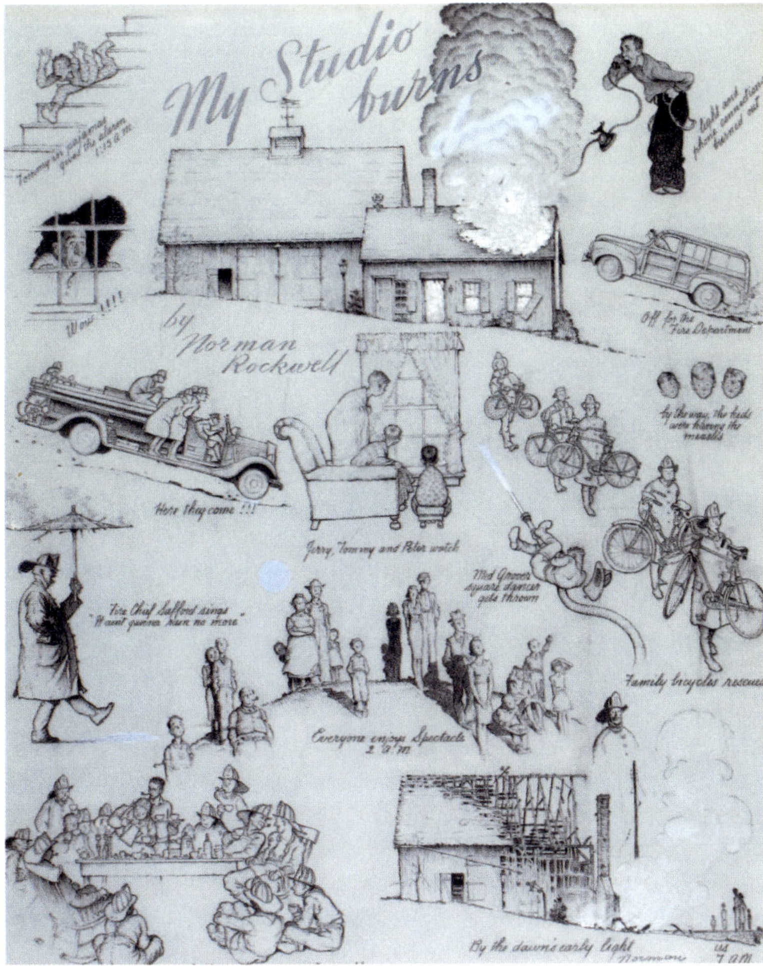


11. *My Studio Burns*, 1943
Pencil on illustration board, 21½ × 17 in. (54.6 × 43.2 cm)
Illustration for the *Saturday Evening Post*, July 17, 1943
Private collection

As I delved more deeply into Rockwell's artwork and teaching, my own work began to show promise. In my youth, I knew my work was nowhere near the level of his, but the progress I was making through the study of his artistic process began to cultivate a confidence within me, making it possible to envision actual goals in the fields of art that I was interested in. Comic book illustration was a focus for me once I discovered the work of an artist named Neal Adams. Back in the 1970s, he envisioned Batman as the dark and mysterious figure that we see to this day, and he is a huge Rockwell fan. I discovered Adams when I was eleven years old, and the high standards that he presented in the comics medium prepared me for my eventual encounter with Rockwell's illustrations. Adams's artwork helped me to appreciate the importance of putting my best effort forward, and I marveled at his accomplishments. Eventually, I was able to show Adams my drawing books, and he hired me to draw for him on the spot when I was just seventeen years old. Though not as highly regarded as other art forms, sequential art has its roots in humankind's earliest form of pictorial communication, as revealed in drawings on cave walls in Sulawesi, Indonesia, probably the most ancient in the world, and Chauvet, France. Soon after my discovery of Adams's work, I found that Rockwell had also created sequential art in works that invited Americans to meet the president, trace and find the source of community gossip, and serve as eyewitnesses to the events of his Arlington, Vermont, studio fire (plate 11). These sequential compositions demonstrate Rockwell's ability to transport us through time, space, and a variety of narratives that capture our interest and inspire anticipation.

Rockwell's superb compositional prowess can also be seen in his beautiful charcoal drawings for the Massachusetts Mutual Life Insurance Company. The powerful organization of every element and detail in these vignettes is striking—entire stories are contained in single-panel visual statements that are deceptively simple. In eighty-one drawings created for Mass Mutual in the 1950s and 1960s, Rockwell masterfully reveals the love, hope, and security that the company was offering to its customers. The warmth of family gatherings, a dog who has become a new mother, a father inspecting his anxious-looking son's report card (plate 12), and even a drawing of Rockwell himself, contemplating who will get his vote, are scenes that serve as mirrors of humanity, seen at its very best, engaged in the simple moments that make up a full life.

The challenges of openly celebrating Norman Rockwell came as criticism from many of my friends and fellow art students who were also African American. "He only shows white people in his art," they said. They felt that I was betraying the movement that, only a decade before I discovered Rockwell, had been at the height of its activity—1968, the year Dr. Martin Luther King Jr. was assassinated, was only eight years before I walked into that bookstore and found my creative hero. It never dawned on me that

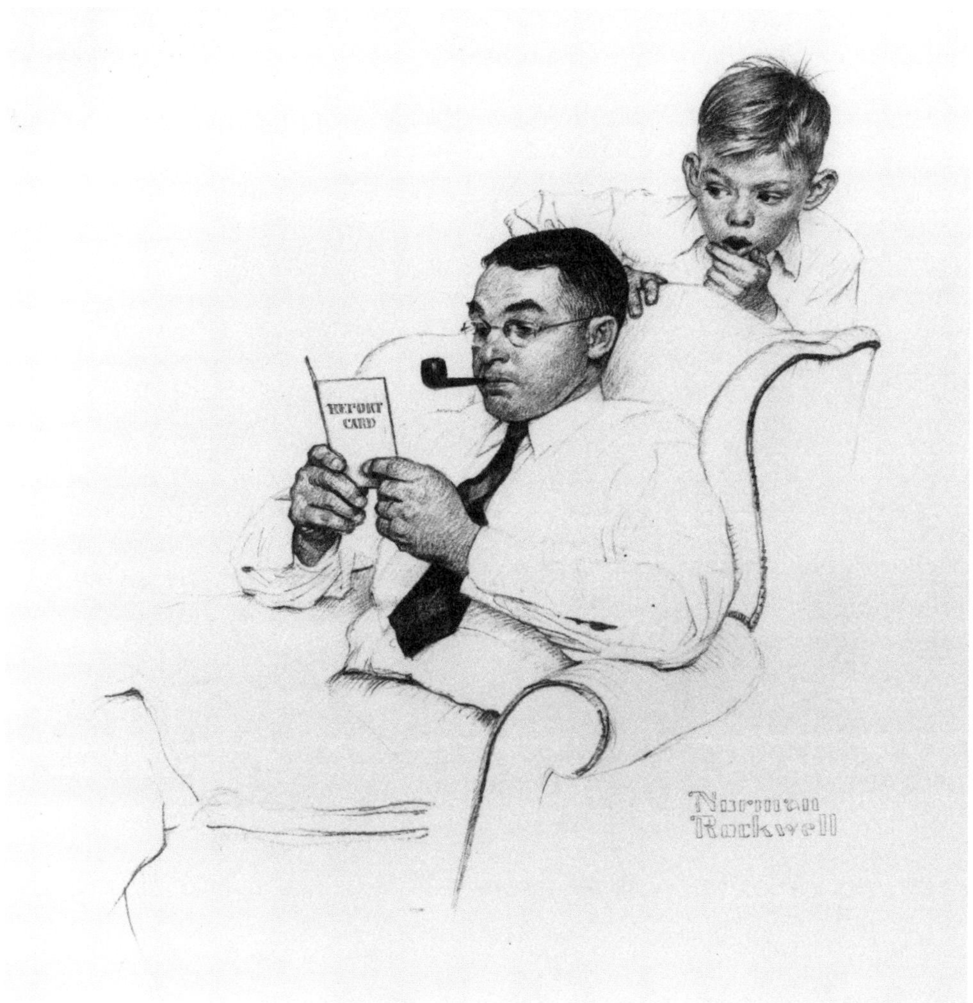


12. *Report Card*, 1953
Pencil on paper, 15 × 13 in. (38.1 × 33 cm)
Advertising illustration for Massachusetts
Mutual Life Insurance Company
NRM.1983.44, 1953 (Gift of Massachusetts
Mutual Life Insurance Company)

I was not seeing any people of color, as I admired those *Saturday Evening Post* covers and many of Rockwell's other works. Furthermore, my precious and feisty mother raised my sisters and me to be aware of racism but not distracted by it. Although I shrugged off the criticism of my love for Rockwell's work, I was intrigued by the fact that I did not see people like me in

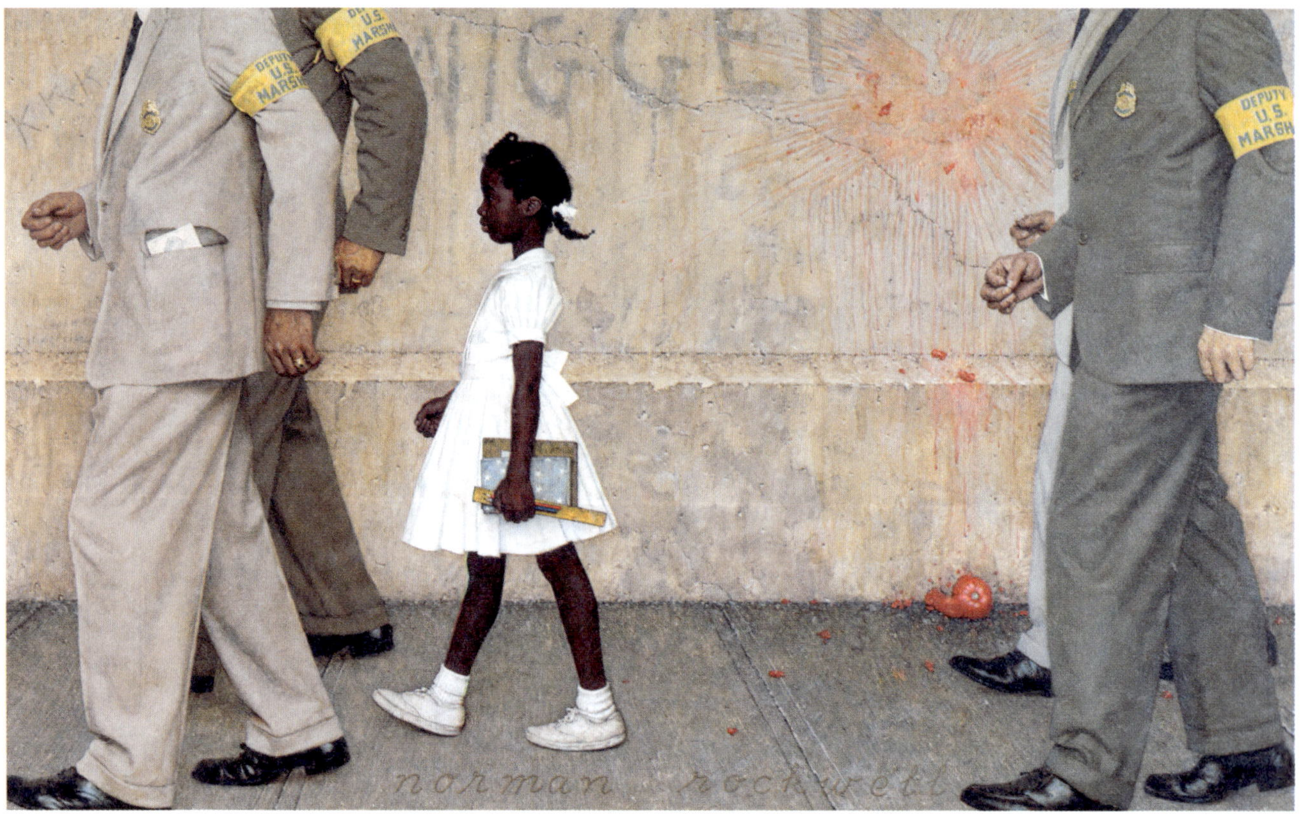


13. *The Problem We All Live With*, 1963
Oil on canvas, 36 × 58 in. (91.4 × 147.3 cm)
Illustration for *Look*, January 14, 1954
NRM.1975.01 (museum purchase)

his art. It wasn't until much later, when I broadened my knowledge of his career, that I learned the truth. Editorial policy prevented Rockwell from depicting people of color on the covers of the *Post* in anything but subservient roles, reflecting discriminatory attitudes toward race at the time. Determined to portray people of color with dignity, Rockwell did manage to place African Americans on the occasional cover without compromising his standards. On the March 17, 1934, cover of the *Post*, Rockwell shows a little African American boy pointing the way to a runaway horse belonging to a white woman sprawled before him. She has obviously taken a spill, and the child is helping her find her mount. The little boy, dressed in tattered clothing, stands in contrast to the woman, who is clad in a fancy equestrian attire, her riding crop off to the side. My recognition of that child's dignity, in comparison to the woman's lack thereof, was a miraculous moment for me. It launched a quest to find more Rockwell art in which people of color were shown. The wealth of imagery I began to discover blotted out all the criticism from those who simply did not perceive the breadth of Rockwell's work and career.

Committed to equality for African Americans and for all people, Rockwell was a life member of the NAACP at the time when Dr. King was also affiliated with the organization. In later years, as an illustrator and visual journalist for *Look*, his hands were no longer tied, and he felt free to create artworks that underscored his personal beliefs and called attention to the civil rights issues of the day. Among his most famous published works are *Golden Rule* (1961), a beautiful kaleidoscope of hope for humanity that was one of his final illustrations for the *Post*, and *The Problem We All Live With* (1963), his first *Look* illustration, which took inspiration from Ruby Bridges's own school desegregation story (plate 13).

So as I study those who are considered the great masters, I always include Norman Rockwell among them all. There will undoubtedly be those who would attempt to argue with me on this point. However, their voices would fall upon deliberately deaf ears. At sixteen years old, I read the words of the man who would become the most influential artist of all to me. Those words not only enhanced my dreams of becoming the best artist I could be; they elevated my desire to become the best person I could be. For me, personally, I return to those words I learned from Rockwell all those years ago in that bookstore . . .

". . . it is almost criminal not to do it that way."

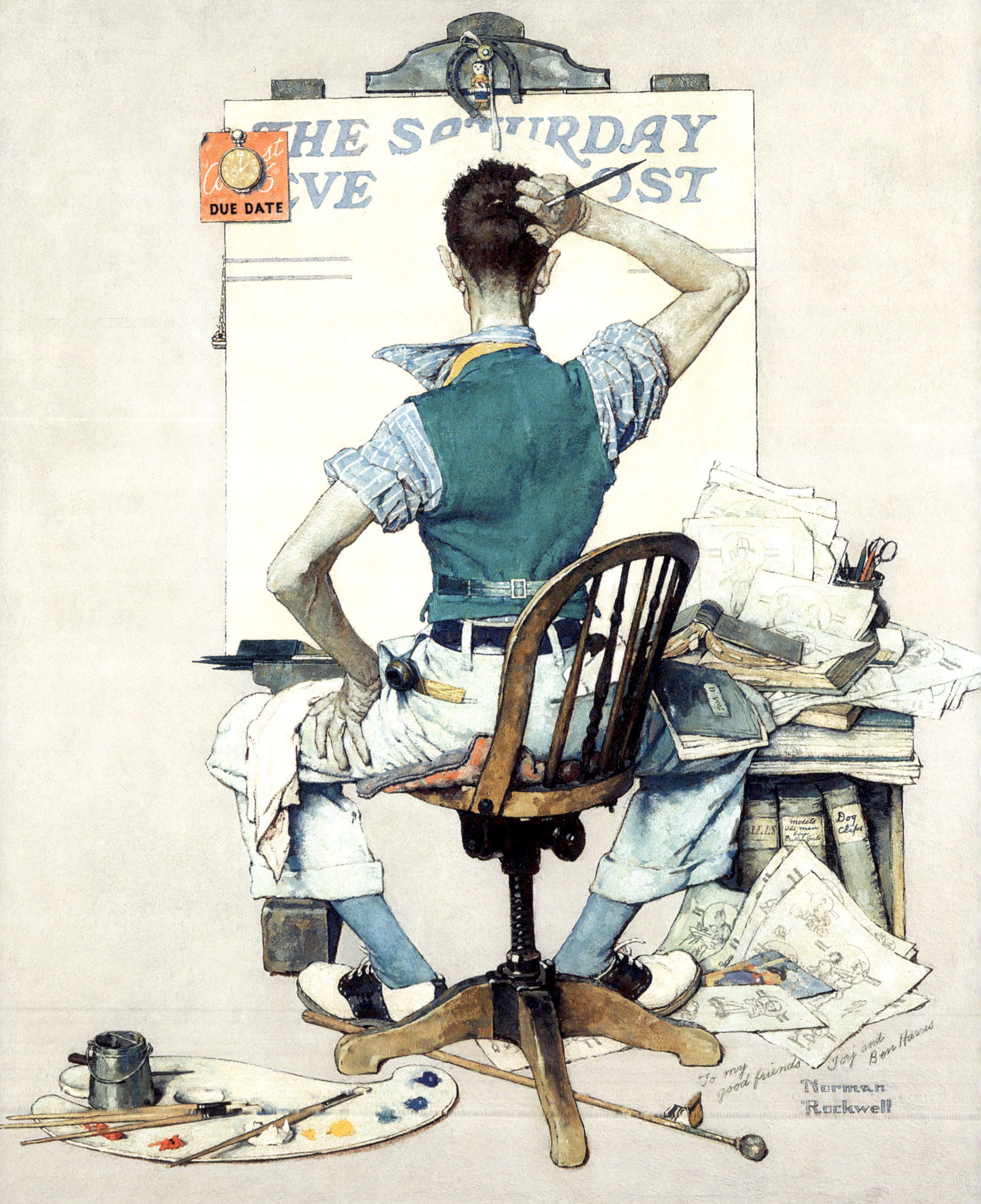
DUE DATE
Dog Clips
To my good friends Tory and Ben Harris
Norman Rockwell

# INTRODUCTION

# Norman Rockwell: Drawings, 1911–1976

STEPHANIE HABOUSH PLUNKETT
DEPUTY DIRECTOR/CHIEF CURATOR,
NORMAN ROCKWELL MUSEUM

> [Drawing] is a complete expression of my idea in line and tone—in fact, everything but color. Sometimes I feel that making this sketch is the most creative part of the whole process of making a picture.
>
> —Norman Rockwell, *How I Make a Picture*, 1948[1]

Detail of *Artist Facing Blank Canvas (Deadline)*, 1938
See plate 8.12.

Though best known for his painted magazine covers and illustrations for stories, books, and advertisements, Norman Rockwell was also a prolific and masterful draftsman who utilized drawing as an essential underpinning of his art. *Artist Facing Blank Canvas (Deadline)*, painted in 1938 for the cover of the *Saturday Evening Post*, represents Rockwell's traditional rather than experimental approach to drawing. Whether the finish was rough or highly refined, Rockwell's drawing process made it possible for him to envision every aspect of a final work before it was begun. In the painting and related "doodle" titled ***Norman Rockwell from the Cradle to the***

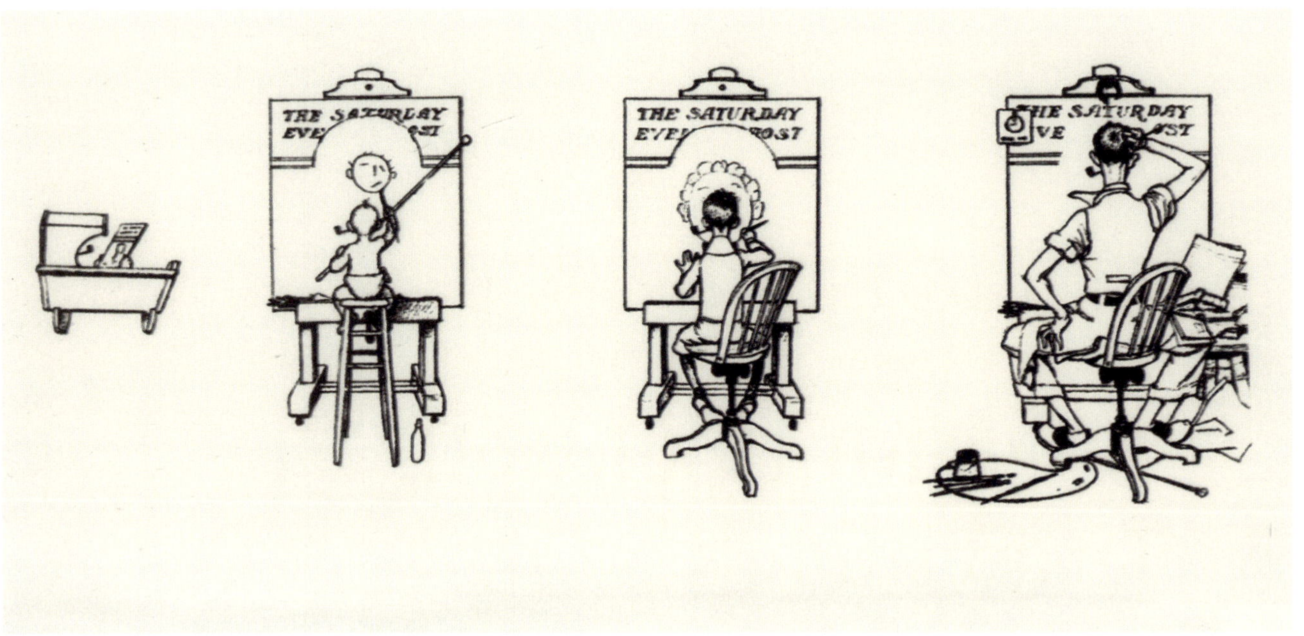


Detail of *Norman Rockwell from the Cradle to the Grave*, 1946
See plate 8.13.

***Grave***, the artist is surrounded by studies and a range of visual references—but this lively, empathetic self-portrait is misleading. Rockwell rarely began a painting at the oil-on-canvas stage. By the time a canvas was on his easel, he would have completed several stages of preparation, including the creation of sketches, photographic references, and at least one highly detailed tonal drawing to be traced onto canvas.

Their utilitarian purpose belies the strength and aesthetic beauty of Rockwell's drawings, which traverse all phases of his six-decade career—from his earliest art school explorations to the exceptionally accomplished tonal charcoals that preceded his most popular midcentury *Post* covers. Guided by Rockwell's imagination and astute observational skills, character, plot, and setting are brought together in the carefully considered elements of the artist's visual narratives, in drawings that are increasingly refined through his painstaking perfectionism.

Despite urgent deadlines, which Rockwell called the scourges of an illustrator's life, each illustration involved from five to as many as fifteen steps. Cementing his story concepts in rough thumbnail sketches, he gathered models and props and directed a series of photo shoots to capture visual information. Using his photographs as a reference, he worked with the details of composition and value in richly detailed black-and-white Wolff pencil and charcoal drawings.

"I take the making of the charcoal layouts very seriously," he said. "Too many novices, I believe, wait until they are on the canvas before trying to solve many of their problems. It is much better to wrestle with them ahead through studies."[2] Rockwell applied charcoal freely, blending it with his thumb to achieve a range of textures and tones. This was the reason his right-hand thumb was so large, observed his son Tom. If an image needed reworking, and many erasures had thinned the paper, that portion was cut away, fresh paper added, and the area redrawn. Pinholes in the paper appear where photos had been attached for reference. The size of the final drawing indicated the size of the final painting, as the drawing's basic outlines were transferred to a canvas of the same scale and dimensions. Since Rockwell was so thorough in working out composition, tonal values, and pictorial details in his final charcoal drawings, they are as complete as the final paintings, transcending their status as a stage in his journey to the completion of a final illustration.

This richly illustrated book presents the first in-depth survey of Rockwell's drawings—artworks that he would not likely have expected to appear in publication in any other form than an instructional capacity. Ephemeral by nature, Rockwell's studies and final drawings were rolled and stored away in his studio once their practical purpose had been satisfied—remnants of an extensive and often laborious editorial process. Many of the drawings presented here are among the collections of the Norman Rockwell Museum and, over the course of two decades, have undergone extensive conservation to preserve them for future generations. This important body of work, which could easily have been lost if not for the museum's ongoing commitment to their care, comprises hundreds of thumbnails and detailed sketches as well as highly finished drawings that have in some cases been reassembled from their parts for public study and enjoyment. We are honored to shine a light on Rockwell's mastery as a draftsman and graphic composer, and to explore the place that the act of drawing as a tool for seeing held in his life and artistic practice.

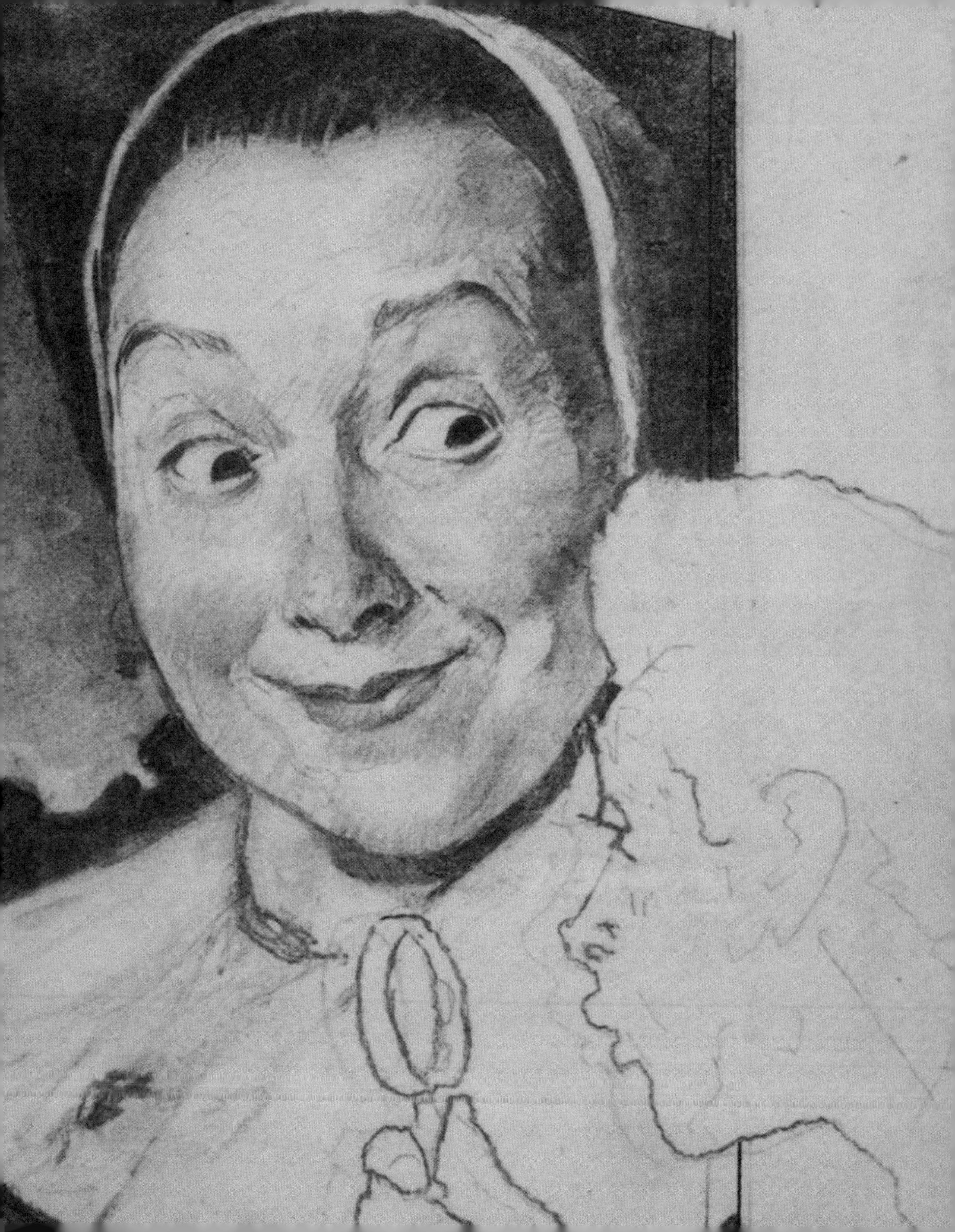

# 1 Norman Rockwell and the Continuum of Drawing

STEPHANIE HABOUSH PLUNKETT

> There was a time when the idea of a visual artist who did not know how to draw would have been unimaginable. It was through drawing . . . that artists learned how to fine-tune their visual perceptions and mirror truthfully with handmade marks the mercurial vagaries of psychological experience. It was the foundation that no career in painting or sculpture could be securely built without.
>
> —Ken Johnson[1]

The act of drawing as an artistic endeavor is almost as old as humankind. For many centuries, drawing played an instrumental but subordinate preliminary role for artists in their creation of paintings, illustrations, sculptures, mosaics, murals, and architecture. It was not until the twentieth century that drawing attained an autonomy independent of other forms, taking its place as a powerful and expressive graphic art in and of itself.

Detail of a study for *Art Critic*, 1955
See plate 1.12.

Over time, drawings have been an essential vehicle for communication and interpretation, employed by artists for research and documentation as well as storytelling, experimental practice, and even performance art. As exemplified by Rockwell, many of the world's most accomplished drafts-people have also pursued primary careers as distinguished illustrators, painters, sculptors, printmakers, and architects. The notion of the artist's hand as a personal, stylistic reflection of a maker's identity and point of view is as evident in drawing as in any other art form, as are the characteristics of period and regional style. However, drawing differs in its unique mediums, from the graphite and charcoal that Rockwell preferred to the plethora of available materials that have been employed across the centuries—from traditional ink, pencil, and chalk to today's digital platforms.

Throughout his career, Rockwell readily acknowledged that great art is not created in a vacuum. Like solving a mystery, discovering the inspirations for an artist's work is an adventure back in time. A student of art history, Rockwell scrutinized the work of artists and illustrators by referencing his extensive and well-worn collection of books, journals, and prints. An avid museum- and gallery-goer, he studied original paintings and drawings throughout the world and sought out opportunities to visit other artists in their studios to compare notes about ideas, projects, and techniques. These experiences imprinted Rockwell with visual memories and impressions that proved inspirational. "I guess an artist just stores up in his mind what he learns from looking at the work of other artists. And after a while all the different things he has learned become mixed with each other and with his own ideas and abilities to form his technique, his way of painting," said Rockwell in his 1960 autobiography, *My Adventures as an Illustrator*.[2]

Historically, drawing developed as a significant art form in fifteenth-century northern Italy, when studio emphasis on producing faithful copies of antique sculptures and casts and exacting studies from nature gave way to more exploratory, creative approaches.[3] In the early fifteenth century the International Gothic or Soft style of drawing, which smoothed the irregularities of natural form in favor of the elegant realism favored by the royal courts, still largely predominated over the draftsperson's personal hand. At midcentury, however, distinct variations in drawing style according to region and the artist's taste and temperament began to emerge. This striking shift in philosophy and approach was destined to remain an essential aesthetic criterion for generations of artists to come.

During the Italian Renaissance, individual artists' studios became lively centers of drawing. In these active spaces, drawing was put into service for a variety of purposes—as a teaching aid for apprentices, for the preparation of engravings, and for the realization of creative ideas that would eventually establish the direction of a master's final work in whatever form it would ultimately take.

The drawings of several artists from this period are strongly represented in Rockwell's books, prints, and clippings files, including Leonardo da Vinci (1452–1519), whose scientific interests and ideal conception of the human form are represented in his many drawings, as well as Michelangelo di Lodovico Buonarroti Simoni (Michelangelo, 1475–1564) and Raffaello Sanzio da Urbino (Raphael, 1483–1520), both exceptional draftsmen. In their own way, each employed the drawing process to allow concepts for final works to develop and mature, as Rockwell would do centuries later. Michelangelo is known to have created the first so-called connoisseur drawings, produced as personal documents, which were precursors of the autonomous drawings intended for collectors in the later sixteenth century.[4]

One such image in Rockwell's collection was Michelangelo's *Madonna and Child (Madonna col Bambino*, c. 1525; plate 1.1), a reproduction of the pencil and chalk drawing that was found in the Florentine's studio when its contents were catalogued. Michelangelo created at least twenty drawings on this theme as preparatory works for paintings and sculptures during his long life—some, as in this work, in which the baby Jesus suckles at Mary's breast. Here, the Madonna is loosely sketched and emphasis is placed on the child, who is carefully articulated through the torso and right arm. As Rockwell would learn centuries later, convincing emotional and anatomical portrayals require careful observation and exceptional technical ability. Like Michelangelo, he was willing to put in the time to learn his craft and to draw and redraw similar subjects over and over, in order to advance his skills. Mothers and children appear frequently in Rockwell's art in a secular context, but the classical arrangement of the *Madonna and Child* is a clear influence. The artist's 1961 *Golden Rule* (plate 1.2) and its 1953 antecedent drawing (plate 1.3), inspired by the work of the United Nations, are poignant examples, emphasizing the maternal bond and constancy of generational turning. As a personal remembrance, Rockwell painted his late wife, Mary Barstow Rockwell, into the upper right corner of *Golden Rule*, behind the man with gray hair—she had died in 1959 but is seen holding her first grandson, Geoffrey, whom she never had the opportunity to meet.

Rockwell's reference files also contained reproductions of works by other artists of the Renaissance period who were noted for their drawing abilities, including Albrecht Dürer (1471–1528), whose mastery the illustrator acknowledged in his February 13, 1960, *Saturday Evening Post* cover, *Triple Self-Portrait*. A draftsman, painter, printmaker, mathematician, and theorist of the German Renaissance, Dürer created a vast body of work characterized by a sense of pictorial compactness, featuring fine, precisely executed detail—an interest that Rockwell shared. Dürer's *Head of the Twelve-Year-Old Christ* (plate 1.4), an expressive brush drawing, reflects the clarity and specificity combined with a depth of feeling that Rockwell sought in his

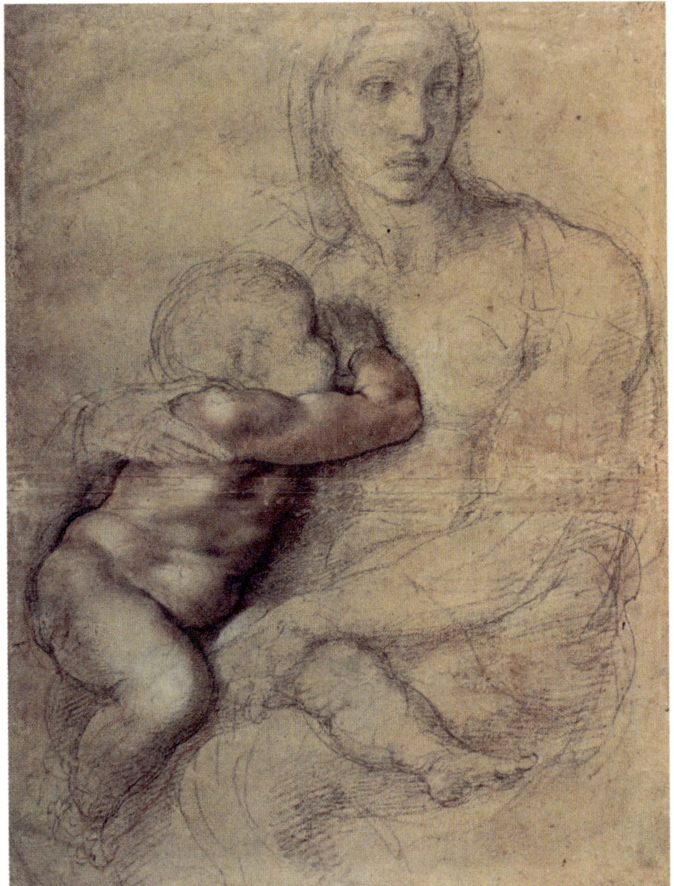

1.1. Michelangelo Buonarroti (1475–1564)
*Madonna and Child*, c. 1525
Print
ST1976.1431

work. The drawing—a study for the Christ Child in *Jesus Among the Doctors*, painted in 1506—is created in full tonal range. Jesus's eyes are cast down, and his hair is tousled, as if to express the weight of his circumstances.

From his studio collections of clippings and prints, books, interviews, and writings, we know that Rockwell gave much thought to the artists who preceded him and sometimes emulated aspects of their work. "Most of the time," he said, "no one but myself can tell that I had another artist's work in mind. Not with the intentions of copying . . . but of capturing a similar effect—the way the light falls on a face, the movement of the picture. I can't say who has influenced me, really. Or at least I can't say *how* the artists I have admired have influenced me," and, "Ever since I can remember, Rembrandt has been my favorite artist. Vermeer, Breughel, Velásquez, Canaletto, Dürer, Holbein, Ingres as draftsmen. Matisse, Klee—these are a few of the others I admire now. During my student days I studied closely the works of Edwin

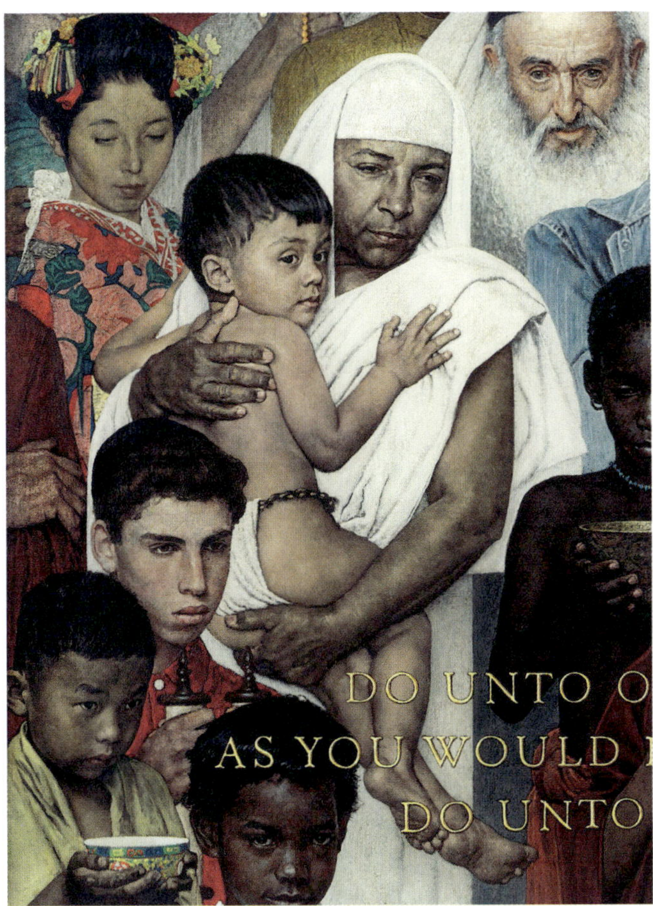


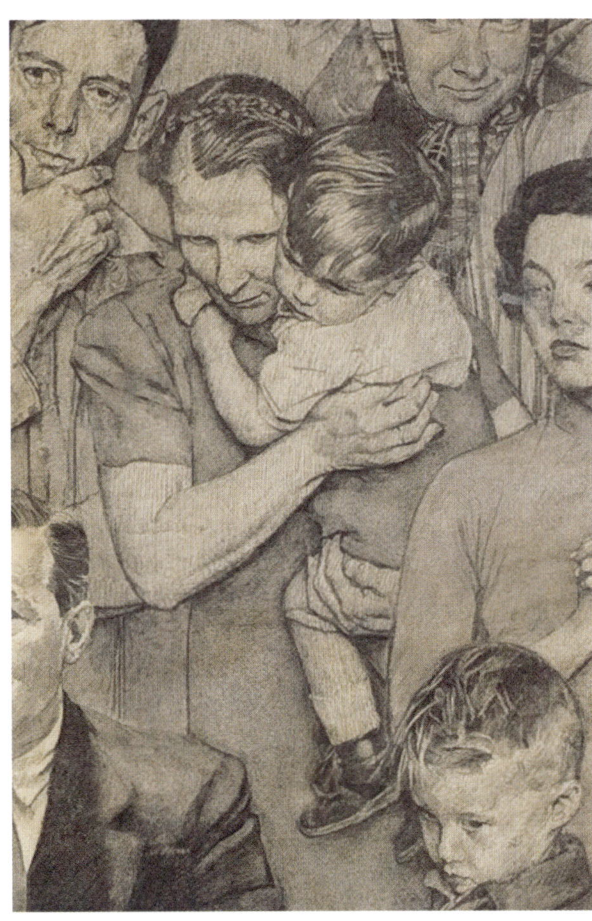

LEFT
1.2. Detail of *Golden Rule*, 1961
Oil on canvas, 44½ × 39½ in. (113 × 100.3 cm)
Cover illustration for the *Saturday Evening Post*, April 1, 1961
NRACT.1973.010
See plate 4.44.

RIGHT
1.3. Detail of *United Nations*, 1953
Graphite and charcoal on paper, 27¼ × 73½ in. (69.2 × 186.7 cm)
Unpublished study
NRACT.1973.113
See plate 4.26.

Austin Abbey, J. C. and Frank Leyendecker, Howard Pyle, Sargent, Whistler."[5] In drawing upon other artists' work and incorporating inspirational aspects into his own, Rockwell found an effective means of telling visual stories by making use of a familiar, or common, visual language.

One of the greatest draftsmen and masters of light in the history of art, Rembrandt Harmenszoon van Rijn (1606–1669) is recognized for the unique qualities of his drawings, created with spontaneity and an economy of line as a record of his observations and impressions—whether genre or biblical scenes, figure and animal studies, or landscapes and portraits. Skillfully balancing linear and tonal elements, he worked in red and black chalk, ink and quill or reed pen, and brush washes. Unlike Rockwell, Rembrandt made relatively few preparatory studies for his paintings, and even fewer finished drawings, which would have been presented to clients as proposals for commissioned work.

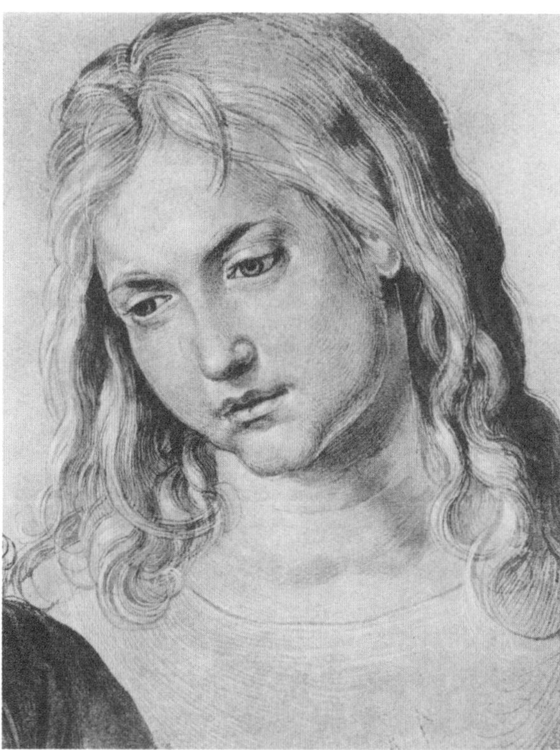

1.4. Albrecht Dürer (1471–1528)
*Head of the Twelve-Year-Old Christ*, c. 1506
Book plate
ST1976.1182

Rembrandt's work as a printmaker ran parallel with his career as a painter, and the reasons for Rockwell's interest in a small but spellbinding etching featuring Christ speaking to a group of townspeople in Jerusalem are not difficult to deduce. Found among Rockwell's print files, *Christ Preaching* (plate 1.5) presents Jesus as the central figure in his composition, surrounded by people exhibiting a realistic range of reactions, from interest and attentiveness to boredom and distraction. Rembrandt's use of chiaroscuro and strong lights and darks, and the invisible glances directing viewers to the most significant figure in the piece, are approaches that Rockwell too would employ, in works such as his 1943 *Freedom of Speech* (plate 1.6).

Not surprisingly, many of Rockwell's narratives focus on something he knew a great deal about—the close examination of artworks and the process of their creation. In *Art Critic*, he cleverly incorporates the characters of Dutch Golden Age painter Frans Hals (1581–1666) and Flemish artist and diplomat Peter Paul Rubens (1577–1640), to whom he pays a debt of artistic homage. Rembrandt's gifted contemporary in neighboring Flanders was Rubens, whose unparalleled drawings seemed to flow from his hand with ease. Rubens drew copiously, working on preparatory renderings of children, elegant portraits of noblemen and women, lively animal studies, bucolic landscapes, and more intimate personal works.

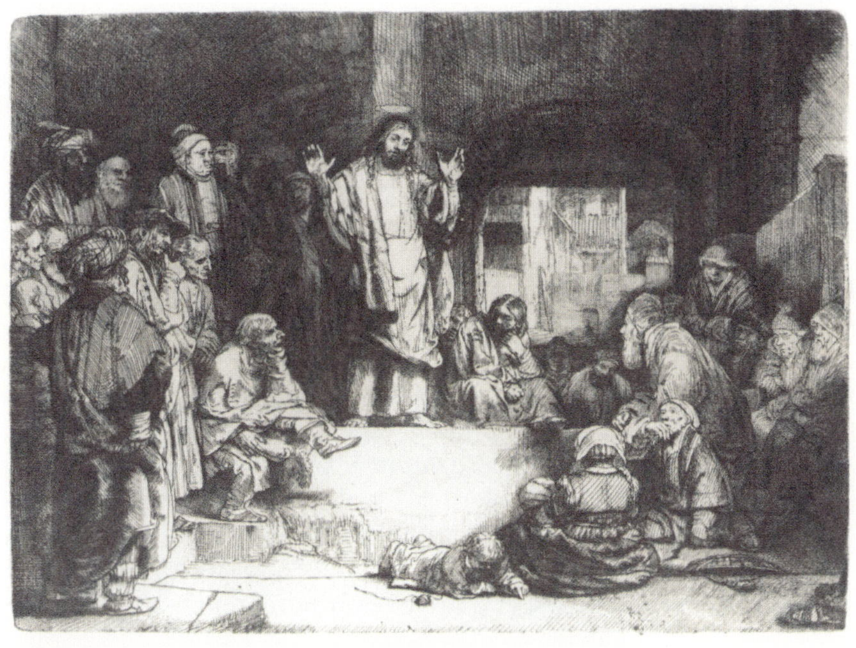

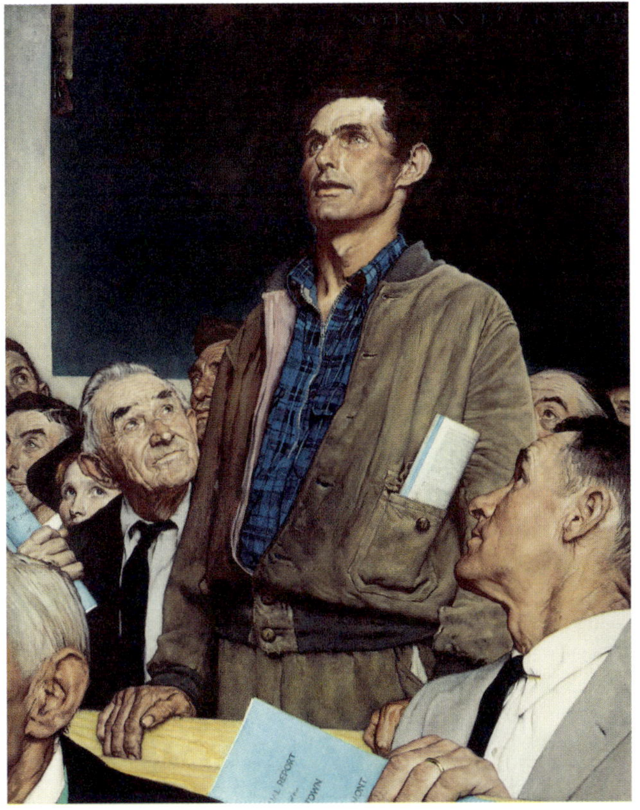

ABOVE
1.5. Rembrandt (Rembrandt van Rijn) (1606–1669)
*Christ Preaching (La Petite Tombe)*, c. 1657
Print
ST1976.1409

LEFT
1.6. *Freedom of Speech*, 1943
Oil on canvas, 45¾ × 35½ in. (116.2 × 90.2 cm)
Illustration for the *Saturday Evening Post*, February 20, 1943
NRACT.1973.021

*Art Critic* is one of Rockwell's most popular and extensively analyzed works. His photographer, Bill Scovill, who worked with the artist to capture references for the piece, believed that it "gave him the most trouble and . . . agony of any. He had a terrible time finishing it." At least thirteen different drawn and painted studies preceded the finished painting. The modestly risqué nature of the composition might account for Rockwell's struggles, or it may have been the delicacy he felt about using, as his final models, his wife, Mary, who ultimately posed for the Rubens-inspired portrait, and their oldest son, Jarvis, an art student at the time, who modeled as the inquisitive young man. Rockwell once said he envied students who swooned when viewing the *Mona Lisa* because he never felt such passion. He may have viewed himself as a more analytical artist, like the one examining the seventeenth-century Dutch–style painting, which closely resembles Frans Hals's 1664 canvas *Regents of the Old Men's Alms House*.

Rockwell was the consummate doodler and he often began his artistic process by making small rough sketches, or thumbnails, that expressed the germ of an idea purely from his imagination. His first conception of *Art Critic* (plate 1.7) portrays an older, bohemian protagonist, later replaced by

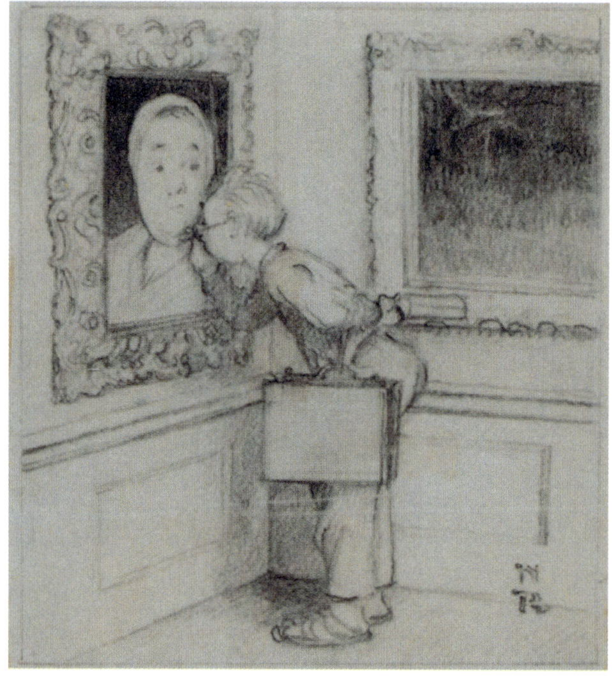

1.7. *Art Critic*, 1955
Pencil and charcoal on paper, 4¾ × 4 in. (12.1 × 11.1 cm)
Cover study for the *Saturday Evening Post*, April 16, 1955
NRACT.1973.003d

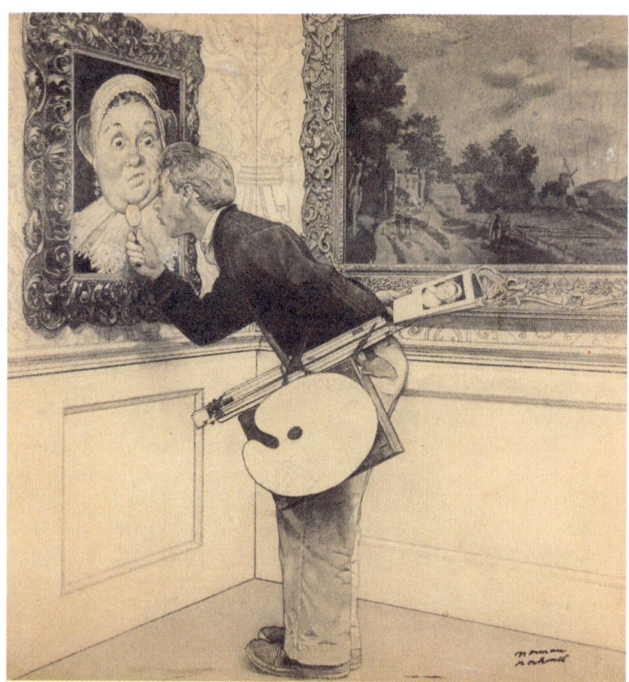

1.8. *Art Critic*, 1955
Pencil and charcoal on paper, 38 × 36 in. (96.5 × 91.4 cm)
Cover study for the *Saturday Evening Post*, April 16, 1955
NRACT.1973.003e

a young art student. At this stage, the specific nature of the artworks to appear in each picture frame on the wall is unclear.

In a later study for *Art Critic* (plate 1.8), an inquisitive student examines a Frans Hals–style portrait in what appears to be a gallery of Dutch art. But Rockwell's recurring theme of fantasy and reality exchanging places seems to have taken over, and the illustration changed course. In the final painting (plate 1.9), with typical humor, he replaced the indignant woman with one more alluring, inspired by a Peter Paul Rubens portrait of his wife, Isabella Brandt (plate 1.13), and photography of Rockwell's own wife, Mary (plates 1.14 and 1.15). Replacing the quiet landscape is an animated group of Dutch cavaliers, enlivening the picture with expressions of shock and

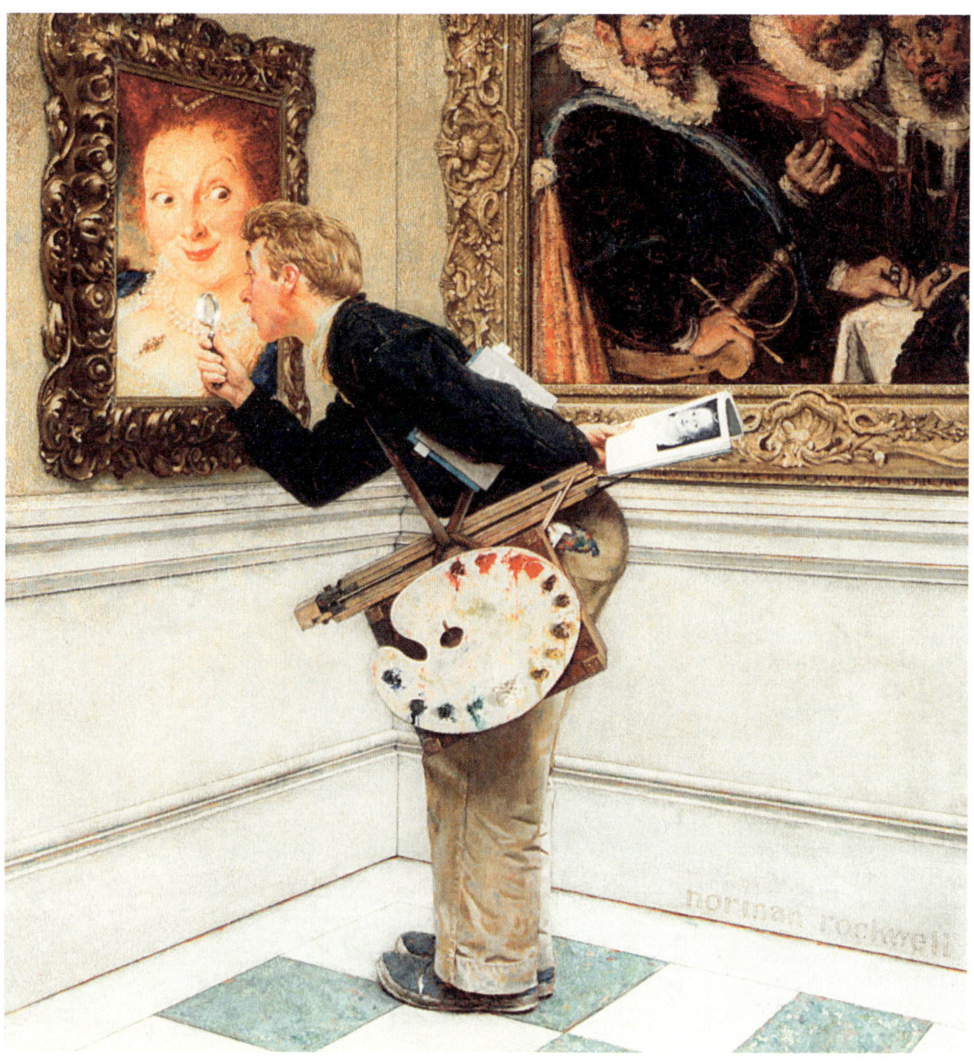


1.9. *Art Critic*, 1955
Oil on canvas, 39½ × 36¼ in. (100.3 × 92.1 cm)
Cover illustration for the *Saturday Evening Post*, April 16, 1955
NRM.1998.04 (museum purchase)

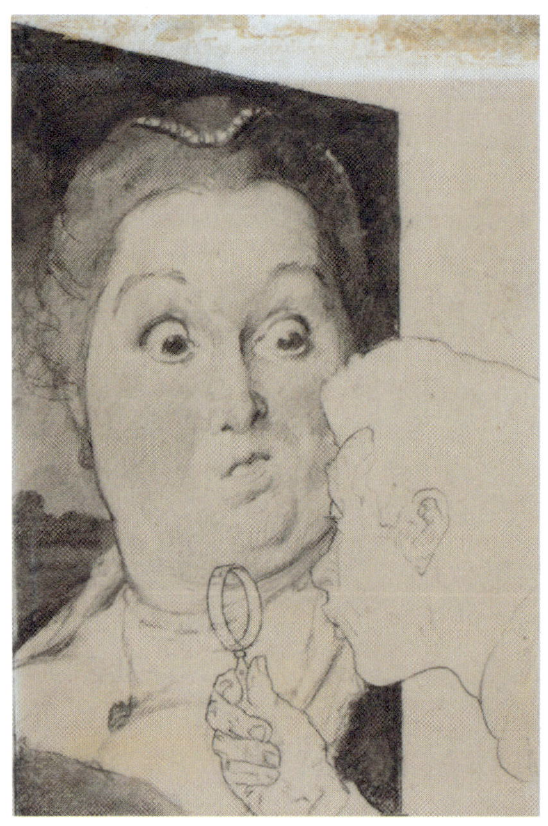

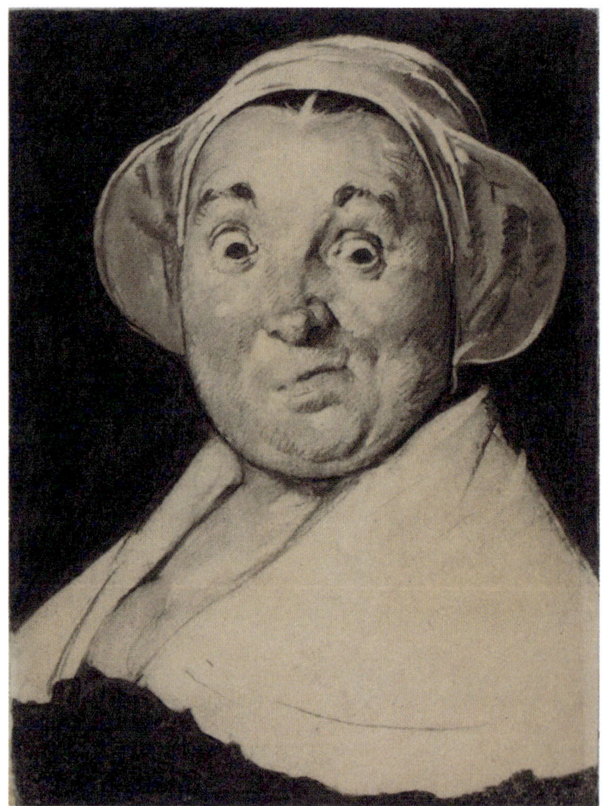

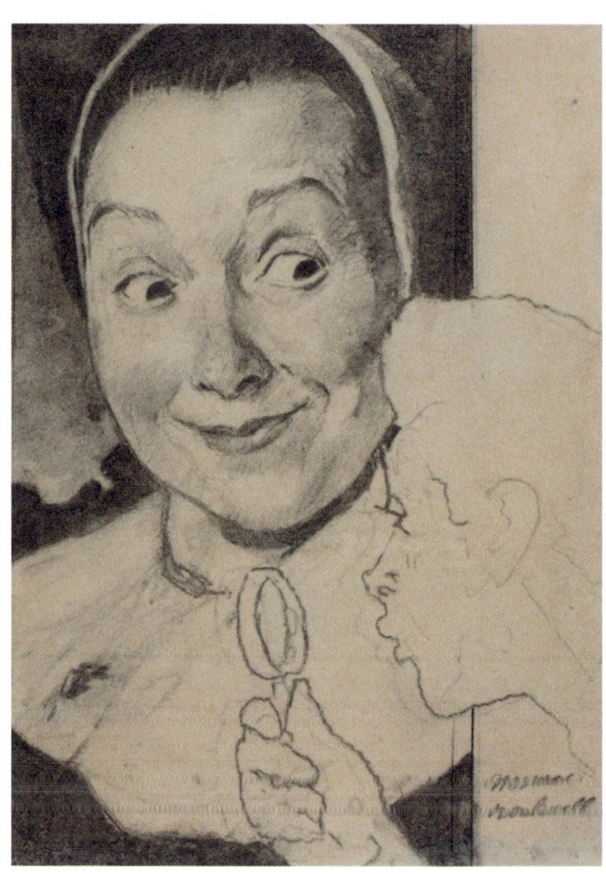

TOP LEFT
1.10. *Art Critic*, 1955
Pencil and charcoal on paper,
11 × 8 in. (28.9 × 20.3 cm)
Cover study for the *Saturday Evening Post*, April 16, 1955
NRACT.1973.003b

TOP RIGHT
1.11. *Art Critic*, 1955
Pencil and charcoal on paper,
11½ × 8¼ in. (29.2 × 21 cm)
Cover study for the *Saturday Evening Post*, April 16, 1955
NRM.1994.02

RIGHT
1.12. *Art Critic*, 1955
Pencil and charcoal on paper,
11 × 7½ in. (27.9 × 19.1 cm)
Cover study for the *Saturday Evening Post*, April 16, 1955
NRACT.1973.003a

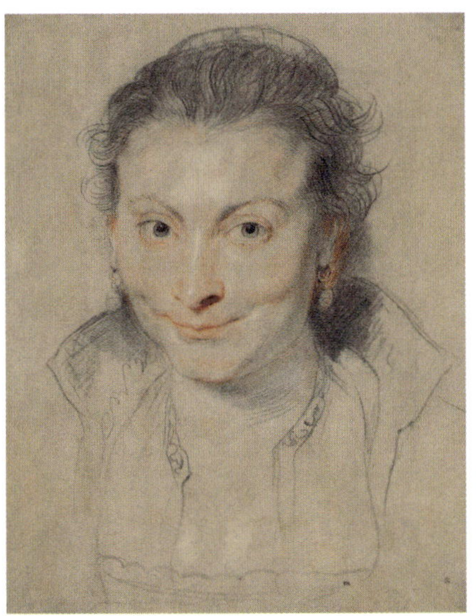

1.13. Peter Paul Rubens (1577–1640)
*Portrait of Isabella Brandt*, 1621–22
Black and red chalk, with some brown wash, heightened with white, on light gray-brown paper, 15 × 11½ in. (38.1 × 29.2 cm)
British Museum, London

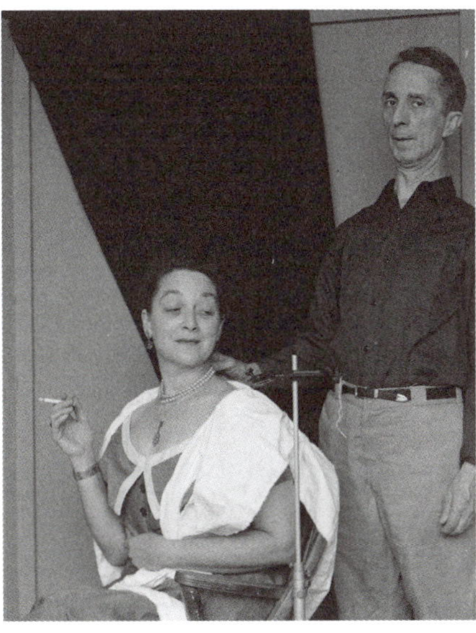

1.14. Mary Barstow Rockwell poses for *Art Critic*, 1955
Reference photograph (film negative) for cover illustration for the *Saturday Evening Post*, April 16, 1955
ST1976.3361

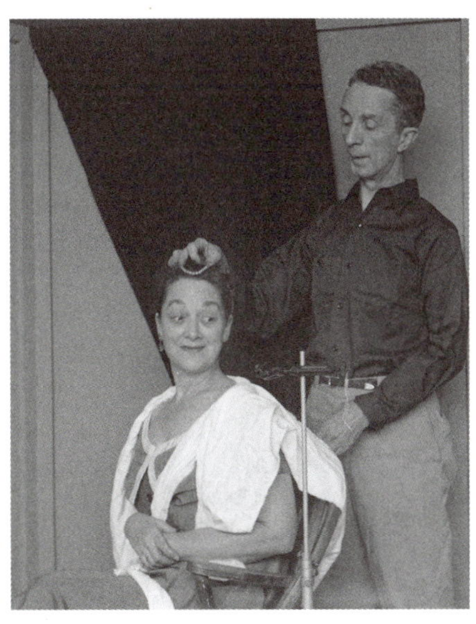

1.15. Mary Barstow Rockwell poses for *Art Critic*, 1955
Reference photograph (film negative) for cover illustration for the *Saturday Evening Post*, April 16, 1955
ST1976.3349

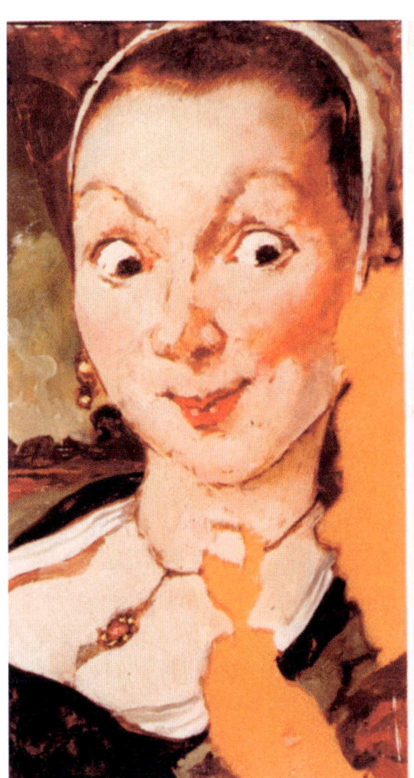

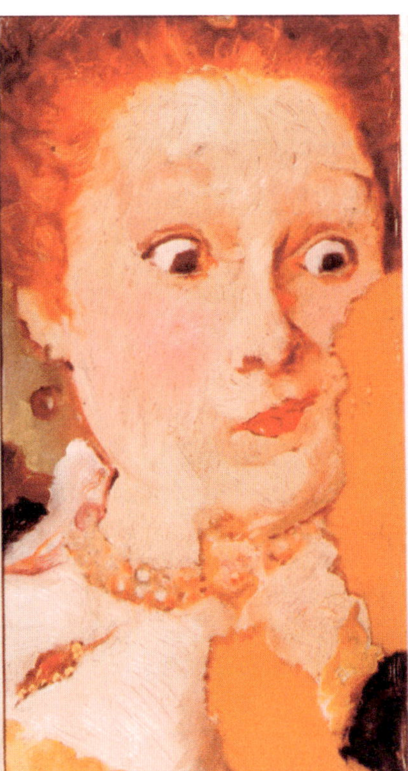

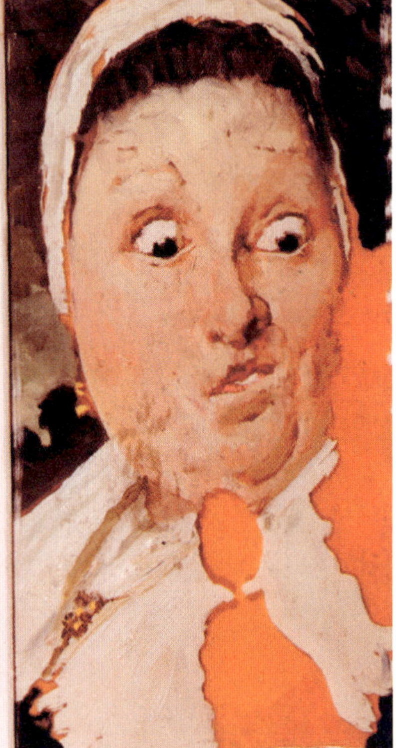

1.16. *Art Critic*, 1955
Oil on acetate mounted on board, 17 × 27 in. (43.2 × 68.6 cm)
Cover studies for the *Saturday Evening Post*, April 16, 1955
NRM.1973.003c

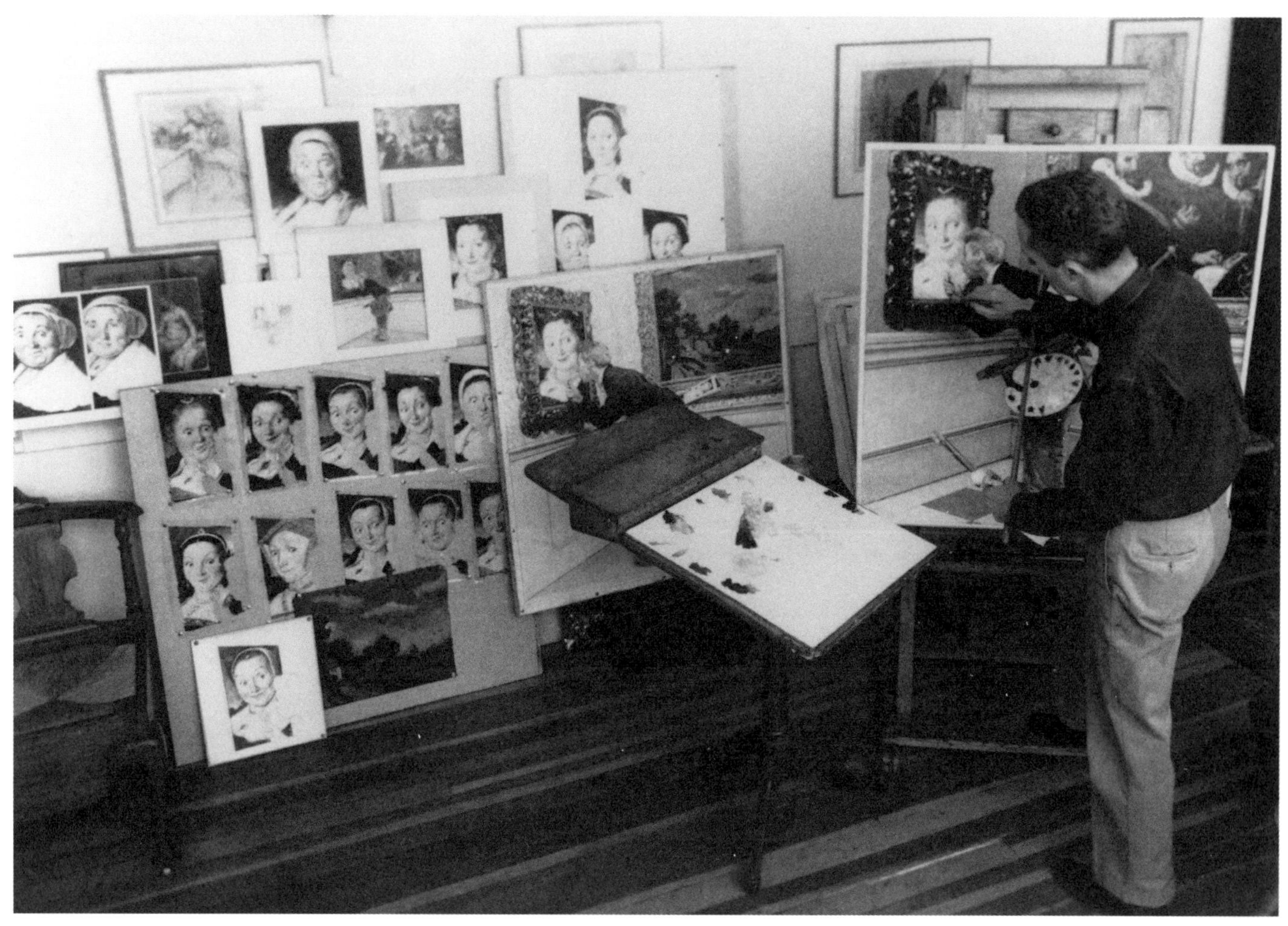

1.17. Henry (Bill) W. Scovill II (1913–1996)
Norman Rockwell with *Art Critic* studies in his Main Street, Stockbridge, Massachusetts, studio, 1955
Photograph, 8 × 10 in. (20.3 × 25.4 cm)
Norman Rockwell Museum collection

concern. Is the student getting too close to the painting, or is he becoming too familiar with their gallery acquaintance?

Rockwell's preference for mars violet or yellow ochre as an imprimatura for portraiture demonstrates his kinship with—and reliance upon the techniques of—the Old Masters. Several stylistic and expressive alternatives for the portrait in the frame (plate 1.16) were painted on clear acetate and laid over his charcoal drawing to determine which would work best.

*Rosie the Riveter* (plate 1.19), painted in 1943 for a *Saturday Evening Post* cover, may be the most direct of Rockwell's appropriations and the most fa-

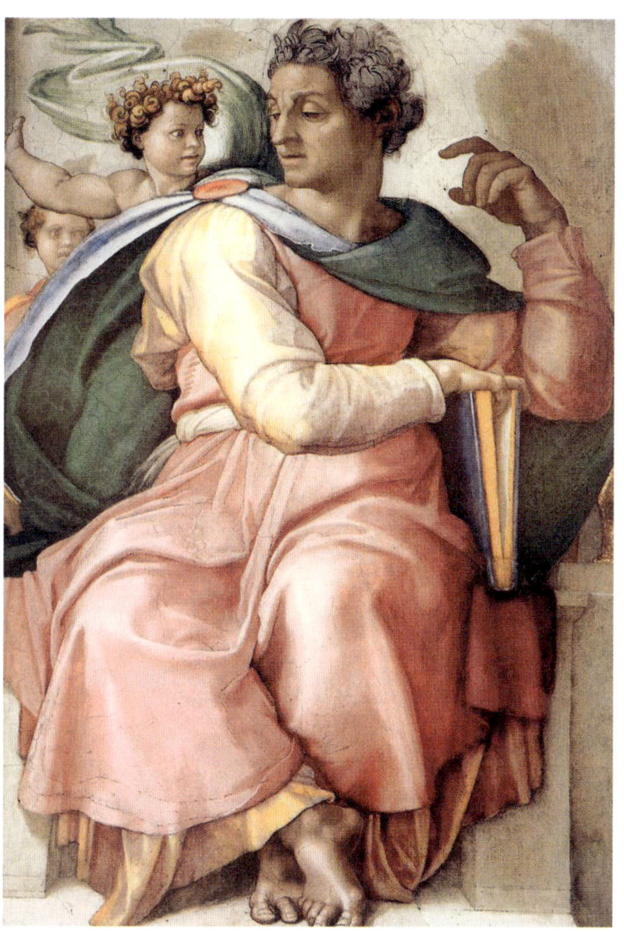

1.18. Michelangelo Buonarroti (1475–1564)
*Prophet Isaiah*, c. 1511
Fresco
Sistine Chapel ceiling, Vatican Palace, Vatican City

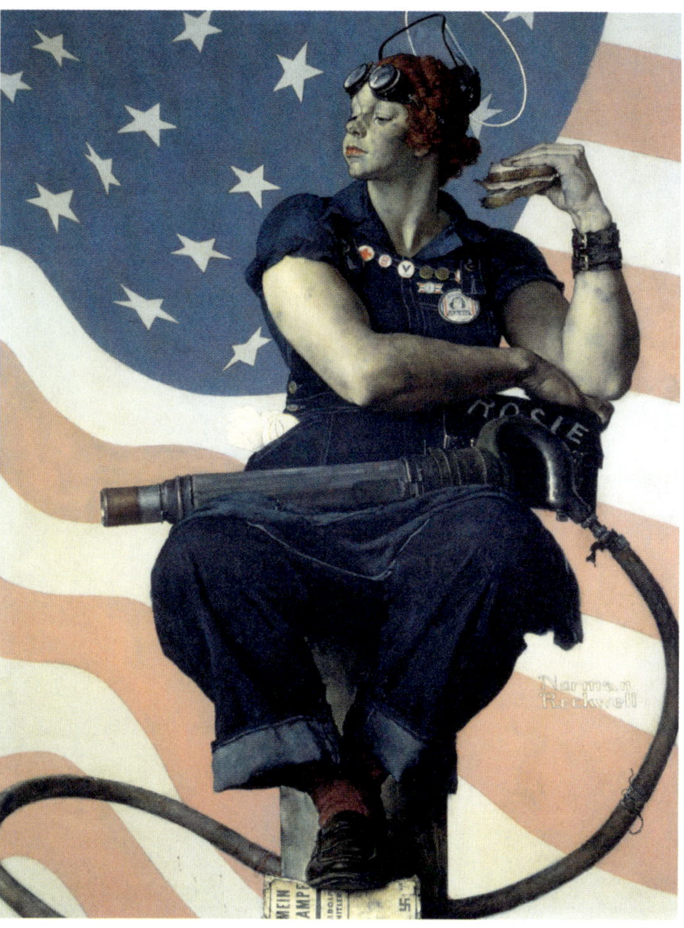


1.19. *Rosie the Riveter*, 1943
Oil on canvas, 52 × 40 in. (132.1 × 101.6 cm)
Cover illustration for the *Saturday Evening Post*, May 29, 1943
Crystal Bridges Museum of American Art, Bentonville, Arkansas

mous example of the synergy that Rockwell felt with the Old Masters—his female World War II factory worker is boldly portrayed in the same pose as Michelangelo's *Prophet Isaiah*, painted c. 1511 for the Vatican's Sistine Chapel (plate 1.18). Since Rockwell thought of himself as an illustrator rather than a fine artist, being purely original in everything he produced was not an obligation. The combined need to produce images often and quickly impelled him to find inspiration in a variety of visual resources and, occasionally, to recycle the best of his own ideas.

The universality of Rockwell's work and its ability to communicate across

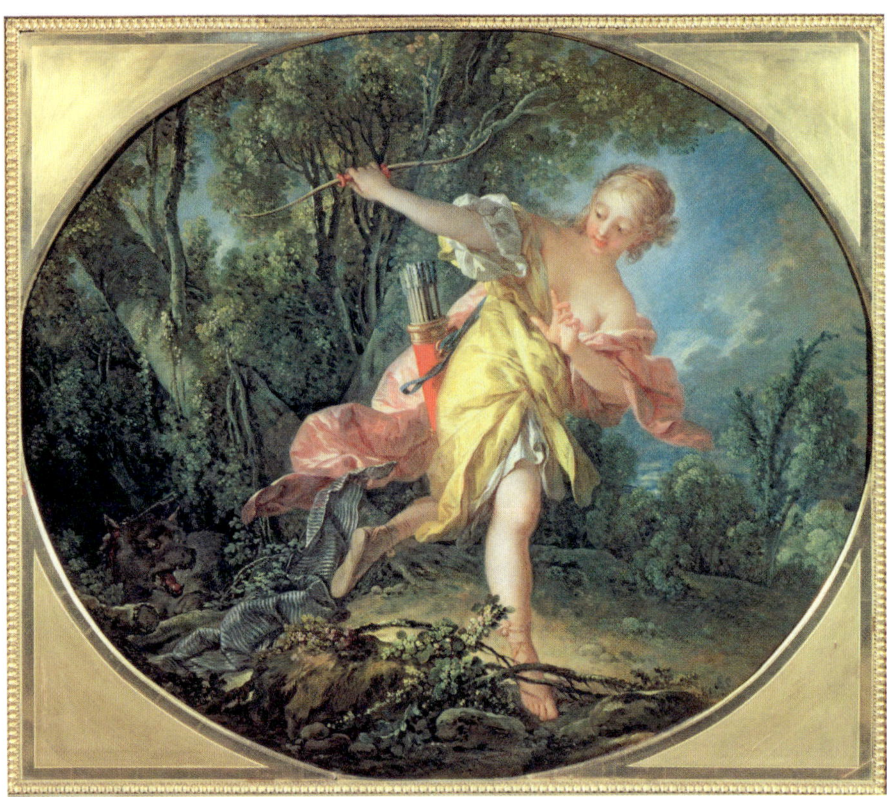

cultures and time has long been cited. The artistic connections that viewers may have sensed but not fully recognized demonstrate that his artistic contributions are part of a long chain linking generations of artistic vision and experience. In turn, Rockwell's art and vision were influential as a constant presence in more than thirty weekly and monthly magazines, in books, and in advertisements over the course of six decades.

In choosing to adapt an artist's work for his own purpose, Rockwell aspired to do it justice. In his pen and ink drawing *Chasing the Muse* (plate 1.21), he pays homage to François Boucher (1703–1770), never presuming to artistically master or better Boucher's beautiful scene of Rhea Silvia chased by a wolf (plate 1.20), and probably hoping not to diminish the seventeenth-century French master. Of the nine muses of Greek mythology, none were inspirers of the visual arts, but Rockwell corrected this omission with the stroke of his pen. True to his nature, he saw and depicted his muse as somehow just beyond his reach, and the victory she could bestow or reward as something for which he was always striving.

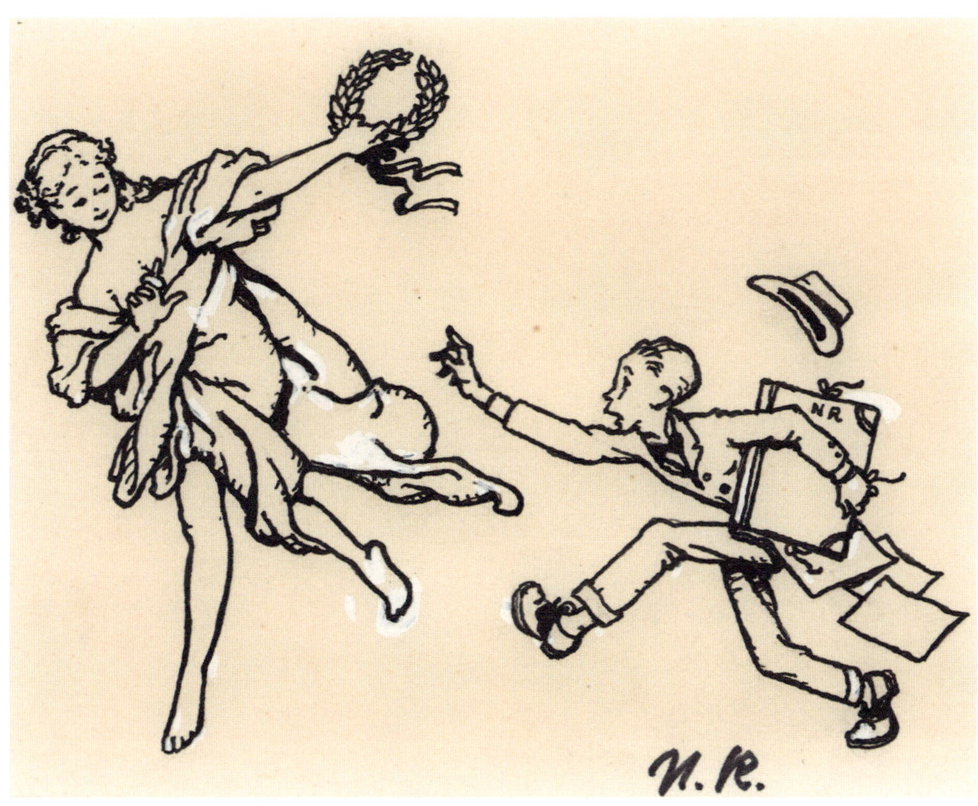


OPPOSITE
1.20. François Boucher (1703–1770)
*Rhea Silvia Fleeing from the Wolf*, 1756
Oil on canvas
Musée des Beaux-Arts, Tours, France

ABOVE
1.21. *Chasing the Muse*, 1959
Ink on paper, 4¾ × 6 in. (12.1 × 15.6 cm)
Chapter heading illustration for Norman Rockwell with Thomas Rockwell, *My Adventures as an Illustrator* (Garden City, NY: Doubleday, 1960)
Private collection

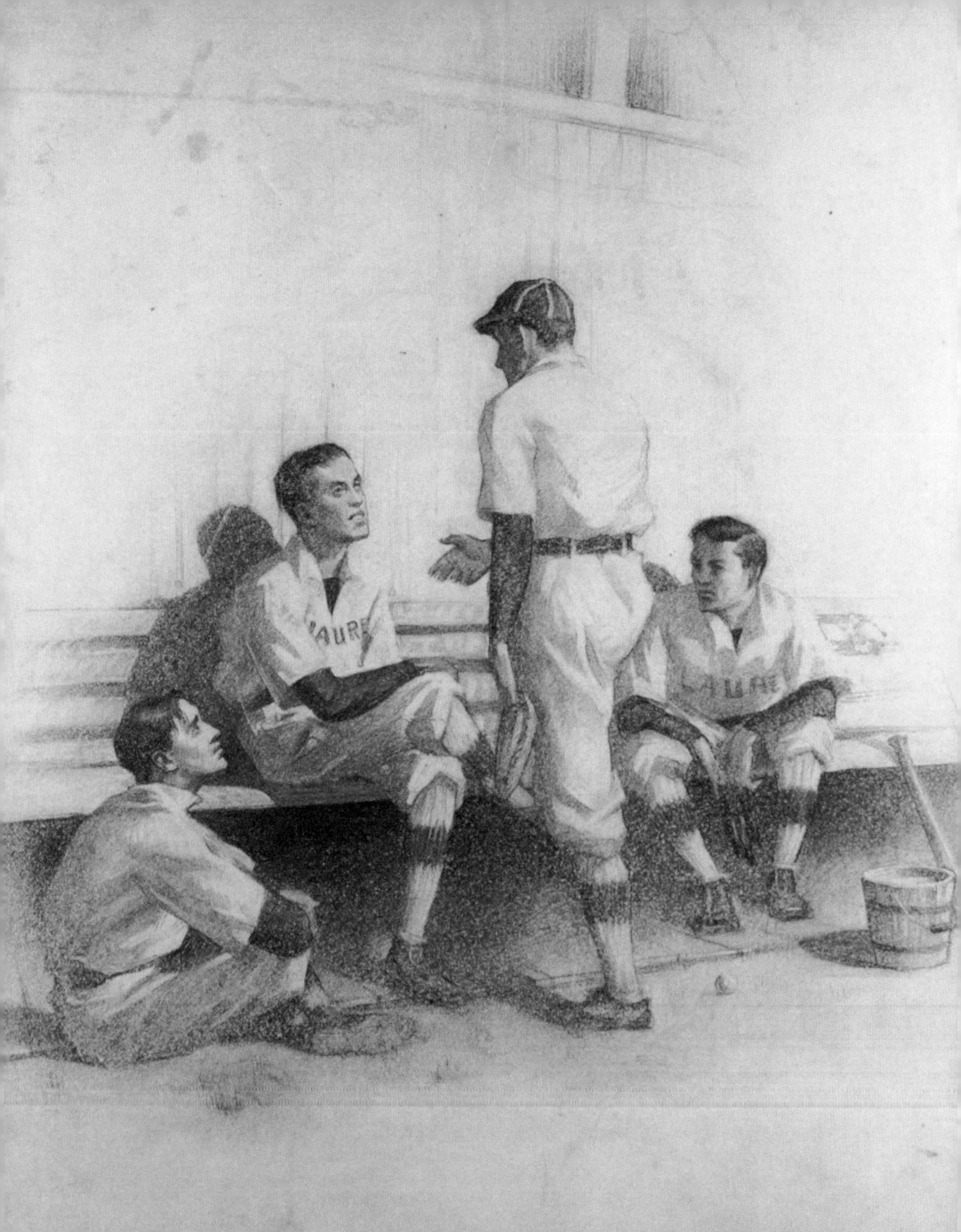

# 2 Learning to Draw: Training, Teachers, and Early Assignments

STEPHANIE HABOUSH PLUNKETT

Detail of *I'm Going to Put You in the Box,* 1913
See plate 2.19.

Norman Rockwell's choice to pursue art as a career had influences from both sides of his family. Rockwell was born in New York City on February 3, 1894. His father, Jarvis Waring Rockwell, worked in the office of George Wood and Company, a New York City textile firm, but in his spare time at home, he made copies of famous artists' drawings. The earliest evidence of Rockwell's interest in art appears in his remembrance of his father copying illustrations from magazines in the evening after dinner, such as *Woman in Snow* (plate 2.1). Rockwell said he joined him, sketching dogs, houses, and vegetables, and from his imagination, pirates and adventurers.

His mother's father, Howard Hill (1822–1888), immigrated to America from England sometime after the Civil War, and earned his living paint-

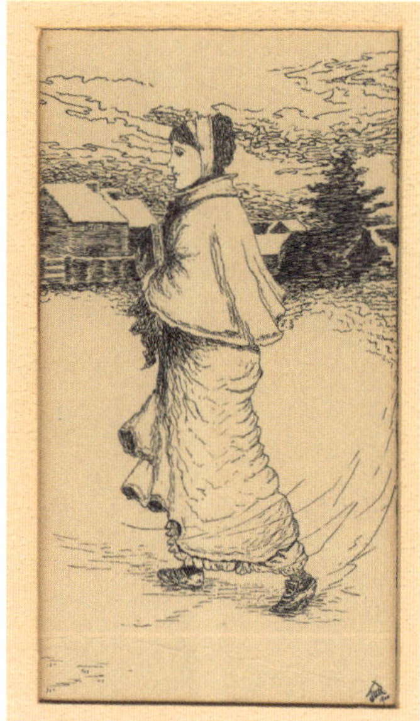

2.1. Jarvis Waring Rockwell (1867–1931)
*Woman in Snow*, 1900
Ink on paper, 7 × 3½ in. (17.8 × 8.9 cm)
NRACT.1976.133

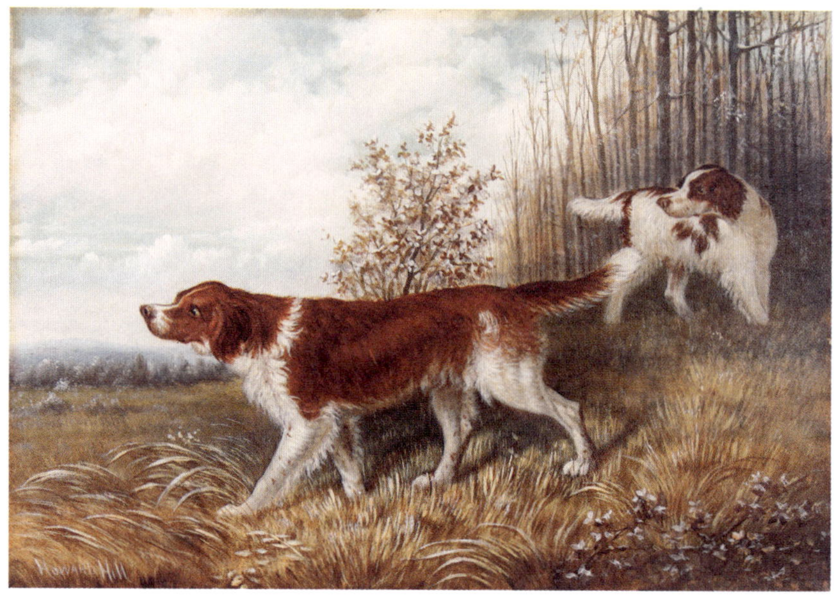

2.2. Howard Hill (1822–1888)
*Two Hunting Dogs*, c. 1870
Oil on canvas, 20 × 24¾ in. (53 × 62.9 cm)
NRM.1997.13 (museum purchase)

ing meticulous portraits of hunting dogs (plate 2.2), family pets, people's homes, and wild game in lush landscapes—sometimes with the assistance of his children, assembly style. He exhibited at the National Academy of Design in 1865 and 1866, and hoped to open a studio as a portrait and landscape painter. But with commissions scarce and twelve offspring to support, he subordinated his artistic aspirations to take up work as a housepainter. Despite this, Hill's art had an impact on young Rockwell, who reflected that his grandfather "painted in great detail—every hair on the dog was carefully drawn; the tiny highlights in the pig's eyes—great watery human eyes—could be clearly seen. I sometimes think that's one of the reasons I paint in such great detail."[1] Unlike his older brother, Jarvis, who excelled in athletics and eventually in business, Rockwell would grow up to be an artist, moving not along his grandfather's path, but toward the deadline-driven, financially rewarding career of illustration.

Though Rockwell claimed to have few specific early memories of his parents, he recalled fondly "those nights when my father would read Dickens to us in his even, colorless voice, the book laid flat before him to catch the light of the lamp, the muffled voices of the city . . . becoming the sounds of London streets."[2] Even as a boy, Rockwell was inspired to draw such characters as Mr. Pickwick, Oliver Twist, and Uriah Heep as he listened. Rockwell read Dickens throughout his life and adopted the author's literary view, observing the world around him and everyday life for its rich and varied narratives.

In 1907, when Rockwell was thirteen years old, he and his family moved into a deceased uncle's home in Mamaroneck, a suburban village ten miles north of New York City. With the realization that his youthful drawings impressed people, Rockwell became determined to attend art school. Rockwell's Mamaroneck High School report card notably includes his grade in art, for which he received a seventy—he also received a seventy in advanced drawing, and English seems to have been his best subject. However, he did not let this dissuade him. "During my first year in high school I went every Saturday to study art at the Chase School in New York City," Rockwell wrote.[3] After Thanksgiving, his high school principal excused him on Wednesdays so that he could attend art classes twice a week. "In the middle of my sophomore year . . . when I was sixteen years old, I quit and began to go to art school full time."[4]

Rockwell began full-time art studies at the National Academy School in New York City in 1910. There, students began in the antique class, and after learning the fundamentals of drawing, were promoted to the life class. As he toiled away at depictions of Mercury or Venus, Rockwell recalled the teacher walking about the room, stopping to correct student drawings created after classical sculptures and prints, while he longed to work from life. After "tedious and dull"[5] drawing from plaster casts eight hours a day for several months, he was finally given the chance. In life drawing class, students worked directly from the model, who took the same pose every day for two weeks. Though classes there were free, Rockwell found them to be "stiff and scholarly."[6] In October 1911, at the age of seventeen, he made the decision to enroll instead at the Art Students League on West 57th Street, where he found relationships between students and teachers to be more vital and inspiring.

The League was unique in that it offered classes in both the fine and applied arts, and students could sign up monthly with teachers of their choice. Rockwell initially signed up for two courses in Illustration and Composition with painting and illustration instructor Ernest L. Blumenschein (1874–1960),[7] but found the step-by-step approach to process less appealing than he had thought. He then registered for Life Drawing for Men taught by the League's most prestigious teacher, George Bridgman (1864–1943), which met every afternoon for three and a half hours, and the course was exactly what he was looking for. He tackled his drawing assignments with a dedication that earned him the nickname "the Deacon," and became one of Bridgman's most promising draftsmen. Each Friday afternoon, student drawings were ranked and Rockwell was frequently at the top of the class.

A taskmaster, Bridgman corrected student work on top of their own by redrawing a figure's central axis, action lines, and proportions to emphasize and clarify his points. "Occasionally," Rockwell wrote, "Mr. Bridgman would sketch the head, a muscle, the pelvis, on the side of my drawing to show me what he meant. I treasured those little sketches. . . . Professional artists, muralists mostly, often commissioned him to draw in the figures in their pictures." Bridgman once asked Rockwell why he looked deflated after a grading session. Rockwell said, "I'm just no good, that's all," to which Bridgman replied, "Look, don't worry about being number 1. Be an individual."[8]

In a humorous drawing, Rockwell depicts himself as an art student being observed by a life drawing model smoking a cigar (plate 2.3). This scene would have been accurate—Rockwell studied life drawing and anatomy with George Bridgman, who believed that working from the nude model was an important aspect of study. Models were asked to hold both short and long poses, and during breaks, it would not have been unusual for them to scrutinize student work.

Bridgman's illustrated book, *Constructive Anatomy*, was first published in 1920, and this and others by the artist remain seminal instructional refer-

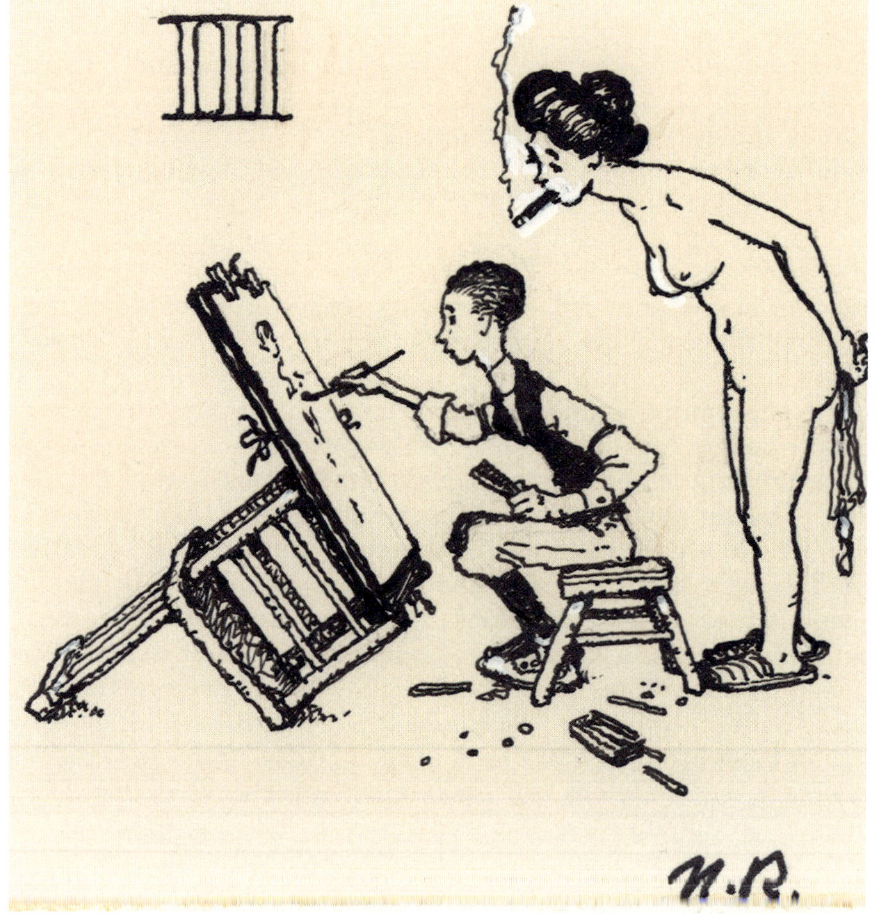


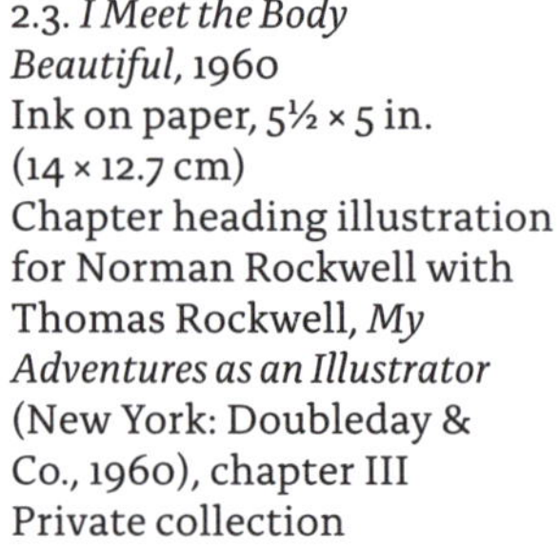

2.3. *I Meet the Body Beautiful*, 1960
Ink on paper, 5½ × 5 in. (14 × 12.7 cm)
Chapter heading illustration for Norman Rockwell with Thomas Rockwell, *My Adventures as an Illustrator* (New York: Doubleday & Co., 1960), chapter III
Private collection

ences on drawing the human form today. In his introduction, Bridgman offers observations based upon his vast experience:

> The drawings that are presented here show the conceptions that have proved simplest and most effective in constructing the human figure. The eye in drawing must follow a line or a plane or a mass. In the process of drawing, this may become a moving line, or a moving plane, or a moving mass. The line, in actual construction, must come first; but as a mental construction must precede physical, so the concept of mass must come first, that of plane second, that of line last.

Bridgman advised students to "think in masses, define them in line,"[9] a lesson that Rockwell took to heart.

As most figurative artists can attest, drawing the human hand accurately and convincingly can be particularly challenging. Bridgman's books examine this subject in articulated detail, providing delineated anatomical studies of the wrist, hand, fingers, and thumb (plates 2.4 and 2.5). Given his facility in drawing the human figure, Rockwell must have absorbed Bridgman's lessons through carefully observed class demonstrations focusing on the hand, and on each segment of the human form.

BELOW LEFT
2.4. George B. Bridgman (1864–1943)
*The Hand, Thumb Side*, c. 1920
Pencil on paper, 10½ × 7 in. (26.7 × 17.8 cm)
Illustration for George B. Bridgman, *The Book of a Hundred Hands* (New York: Dover Publications, Inc., 1971), 75
NRM.2010.58.87 (Gift of the Blakeman Family)

BELOW RIGHT
2.5. George B. Bridgman (1864–1943)
*Veins*, c. 1920
Pencil on paper, 10½ × 7 in. (26.7 × 17.8 cm)
Illustration for George B. Bridgman, *The Book of a Hundred Hands* (New York: Dover Publications, Inc., 1971), 75
NRM.2010.58.15 (Gift of the Blakeman Family)

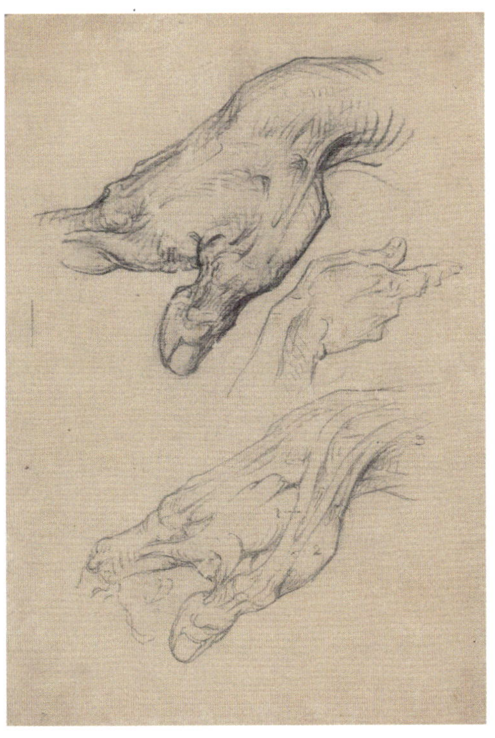

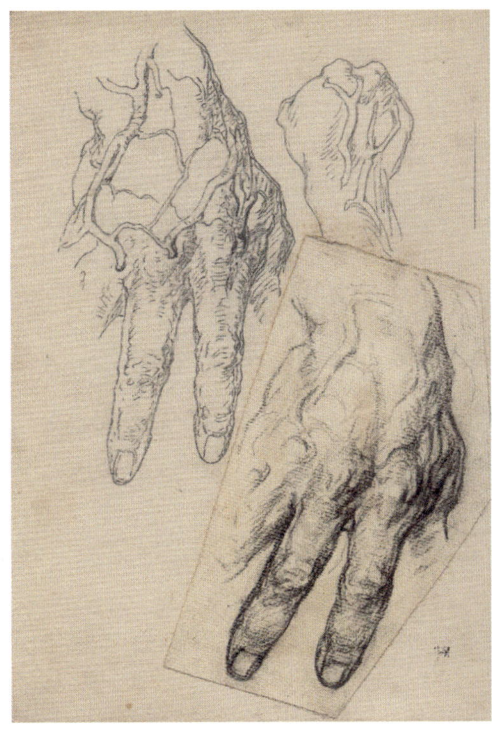

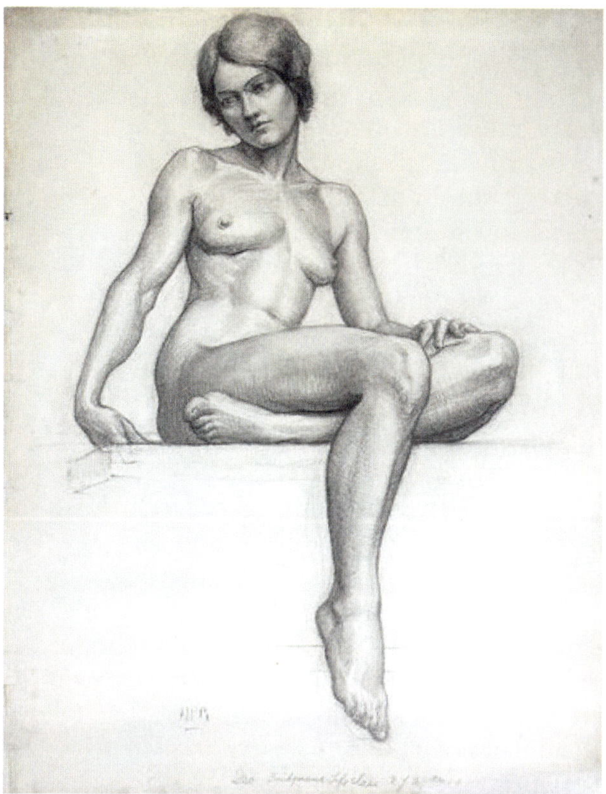

2.6. *Figure Drawing*, 1912
Charcoal on paper, 18 × 24½ in. (45.7 × 62.2 cm)
The Robinson Family Collection, Austin, Texas

A rare example of a Rockwell student figure drawing reveals the artist's precocious skill as a teen (plate 2.6). Created at the Art Students League, it emphasizes anatomical structure and form, but also uses line, tone, and directional light to establish the illusion of mass and volume. A notation at the bottom of the piece places its creation in Bridgman's class. As a constant reference and reminder, a full human skeleton was a permanent fixture in Bridgman's classroom. "'How many muscles d'you think it takes to move your little finger? Eleven . . . Eleven,' Bridgman would say. Then, falling silent, he'd rotate the chest of the skeleton and move the arms about, shaking his head. 'It's a damned wonderful thing,' he'd say."[10]

As a student, Rockwell became friends with the gifted young draftsman, Edmund F. Ward (1892–1990), with whom he shared classes and studio space, and the two spurred each other on. Their first studio together in Manhattan, off Broadway in the west 40s, was discovered to be a brothel, so it was quickly vacated for a space under the Brooklyn Bridge. Drawing from the costumed model, as in Ward's drawing (plate 2.7), was an essential part of an illustrator's education at the time. Many publications featured illustrations in which the clothed figure played a central role. Ward was also an accomplished painter and visual storyteller who went on to be a prominent illustrator. Born in White Plains, New York, he began his career before turning twenty years old with the *Saturday Evening Post* and continued to work for the publication for many years. Ward's rich tonal illustrations would also appear in *Youth's Companion*, *Liberty*, *Ladies' Home Journal*, *Redbook*, *Pictorial Review*, *McCall's*, *Country Home*, *Country Gentleman*, *Woman's Home Companion*, and *Collier's*.

At the Art Students League, Rockwell also registered for illustration classes with Thomas Fogarty (1873–1938), which met from 8:30 a.m. to 12:30 p.m. daily. Fogarty's fine narrative pen and ink drawings were published regularly in books and magazines (plate 2.8), and he became an influential in-

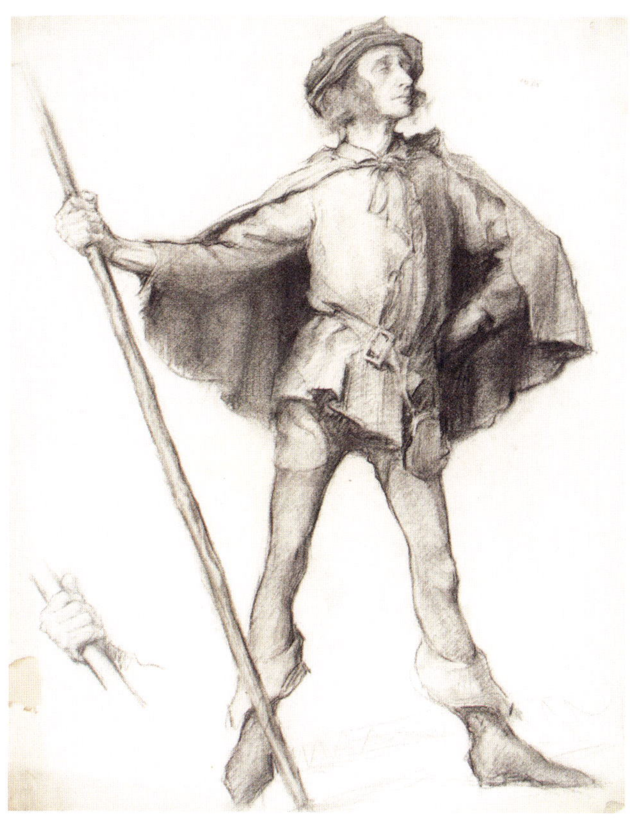

2.7. Edmund F. Ward (1892–1990)
*Costumed Figure Study*, c. 1912
Charcoal on paper, 24½ × 18½ in. (62.2 × 47 cm)
NRM.2010.61.183 (Gift of the Kelly Collection of American Illustration)

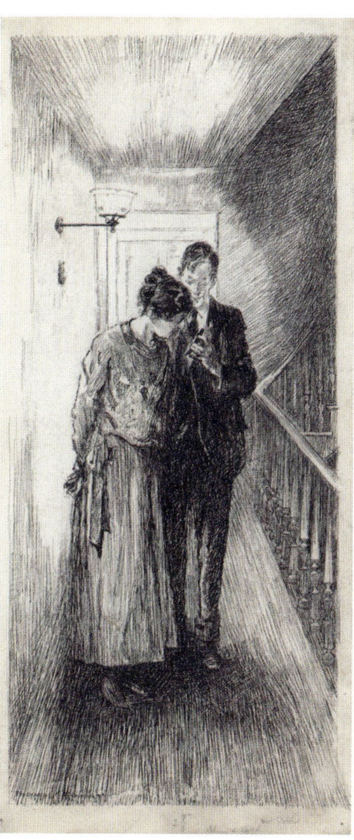

2.8. Thomas Fogarty (1873–1938)
*A Horseshoe over His Door*
Ink on paper, 10 × 7½ in. (25.4 × 19.1 cm)
NRM.2009.05 (Gift of Robert T. Horvath)

structor for Rockwell and a generation of American illustrators. A practical teacher, Fogarty wished to get his students to the illustration marketplace as quickly as possible. His assignments mimicked those that artists might receive from a contemporary magazine at the time, and required them to design an original composition using authentic costumes and props. Fogarty would "sketch the outlines of a story and discuss how to illustrate it with us—what scene in the story we should select, the characters, how they dressed, etc. He'd show us illustrations of which Pyle or Abbey or Remington had made for the story, pointing out how they'd managed to catch the tone of the story, why they'd used a dark instead of a light background, why they'd done a line drawing instead of a wash drawing."[11] Insistent upon authenticity, Fogarty emphasized the importance of research and reliable visual reference. "If the author sat a character in a Windsor chair, the chair in the illustration had to be just that, even if it meant that we all had to go up to the Metropolitan Museum to find out what a Windsor chair looked like," Rockwell recalled.[12]

In order to obtain assignments for his students and help them build a portfolio, Bridgman connected with lesser magazines willing to publish the work of fledgling illustrators if it was sufficiently accomplished. That was very important in launching his career, Rockwell said, because then students had published work to show. "When you're breaking into illustration your first concern is to convince the art directors that you can be trusted to do an acceptable job and deliver it on time. If your work has been published, even in a shoddy little magazine, the art director will . . . try you out with some unimportant bit of illustration. After that, if you're good, you'll get more jobs."[13]

At the end of his first year in illustration class, Rockwell was awarded the Thomas Fogarty Award and scholarship for *The Deserted Village*, a poem by Oliver Goldsmith first published in 1770. Popular during the eighteenth and nineteenth century, the piece describes the decline of a rural village and the immigration of many of its residents to America. It criticizes the moral corruption, consumerism, and pursuit of wealth that has driven people to leave, but it does not specifically describe the scene in Rockwell's drawing (plate 2.9). His moody charcoal drawing sets an emotional tone, revealing Rockwell's ability to think for himself and find nuanced narratives without adhering to literal interpretation. Inscribed at the bottom of the drawing are the words: "But in his duty prompt at every call / He watched, he wept, he prayed and felt for all."

During Rockwell's second year at the Art Students League, he was a monitor in Bridgman's class, a prestigious opportunity for the artist. In addition to classroom maintenance, administrative tasks, and assisting the model, monitors gave teaching demonstrations and received free tuition in exchange. But much of Rockwell's time that year was spent seeking profes-

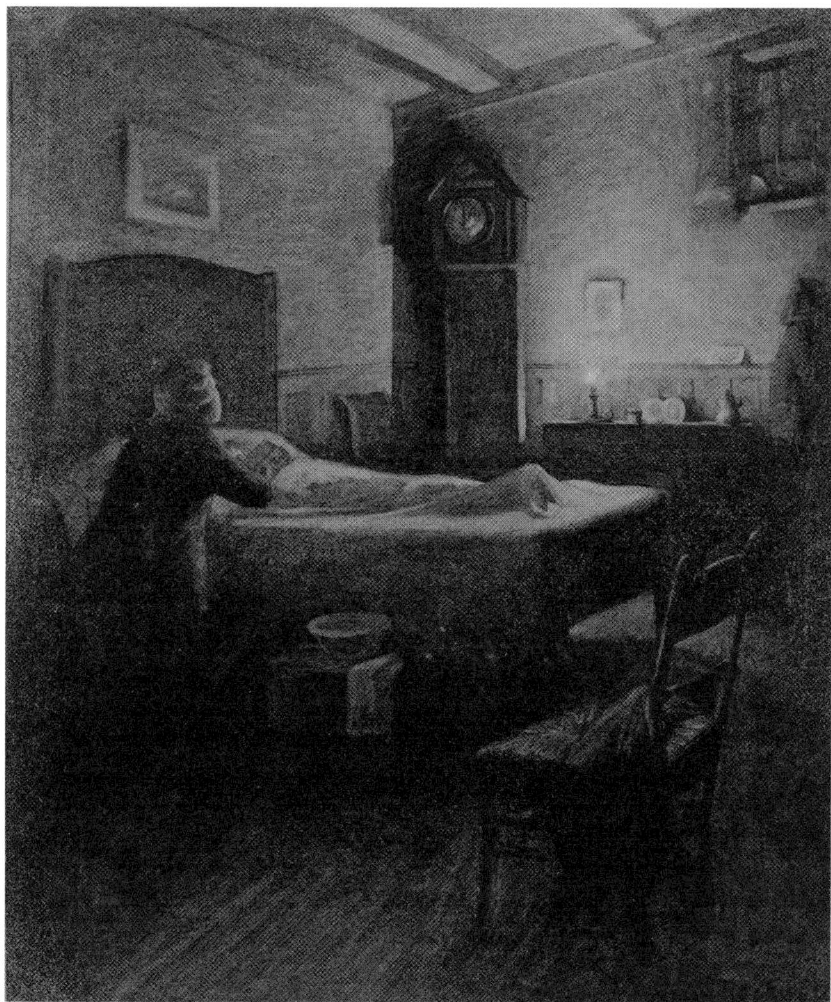

2.9. *But in His Duty Prompt at Every Call, He Watched, He Wept, He Prayed and Felt for All*, c. 1911
Graphite and charcoal on paper, 20 × 16 in. (50.8 × 40.6 cm)
Illustration for Oliver Goldsmith, *The Deserted Village* (1770)
The Art Students League of New York

sional illustration assignments—he was anxious to launch his career as his finances depended on it. He visited New York publishers with little success until an art director at the American Book Company, a national educational publisher whom Rockwell had visited many times, finally conceded to give him some work. The artist's first published illustrations were a series of drawings for *Founders of Our Country*, a 1912 history book by author Fanny Eliza Coe. Rockwell was assigned five scenes illustrating Samuel de Champlain's expeditions to the new world, and two were ultimately chosen to be reproduced in the textbook. The art director's initial review was critical, and Rockwell was asked to redraw the scene featuring Champlain in Quebec pointing at the boats on the river below to adjust the level of the watery horizon (plate 2.10). In 2017, the drawings were a treasured and unexpected find among the American Book Company's papers at Syracuse University

Libraries' Special Collections Research Center. Curator Andrew Saluti observed: "This job had a formidable impact on Rockwell. The consequence of this experience was a resolution to never let any work leave his studio without vigorous review. Rockwell became renowned for his meticulous and painstaking approach to crafting his scenes."[14]

With Fogarty's recommendation, Rockwell gained entry to the New York publisher McBride, Nast & Company, which hired him to do eight illustrations for an edition of C. H. Claudy's *Tell-Me-Why: Stories about Mother Nature* (plate 2.11). Rockwell considered this to be his first substantial assignment, and many assignments for children's magazines followed.

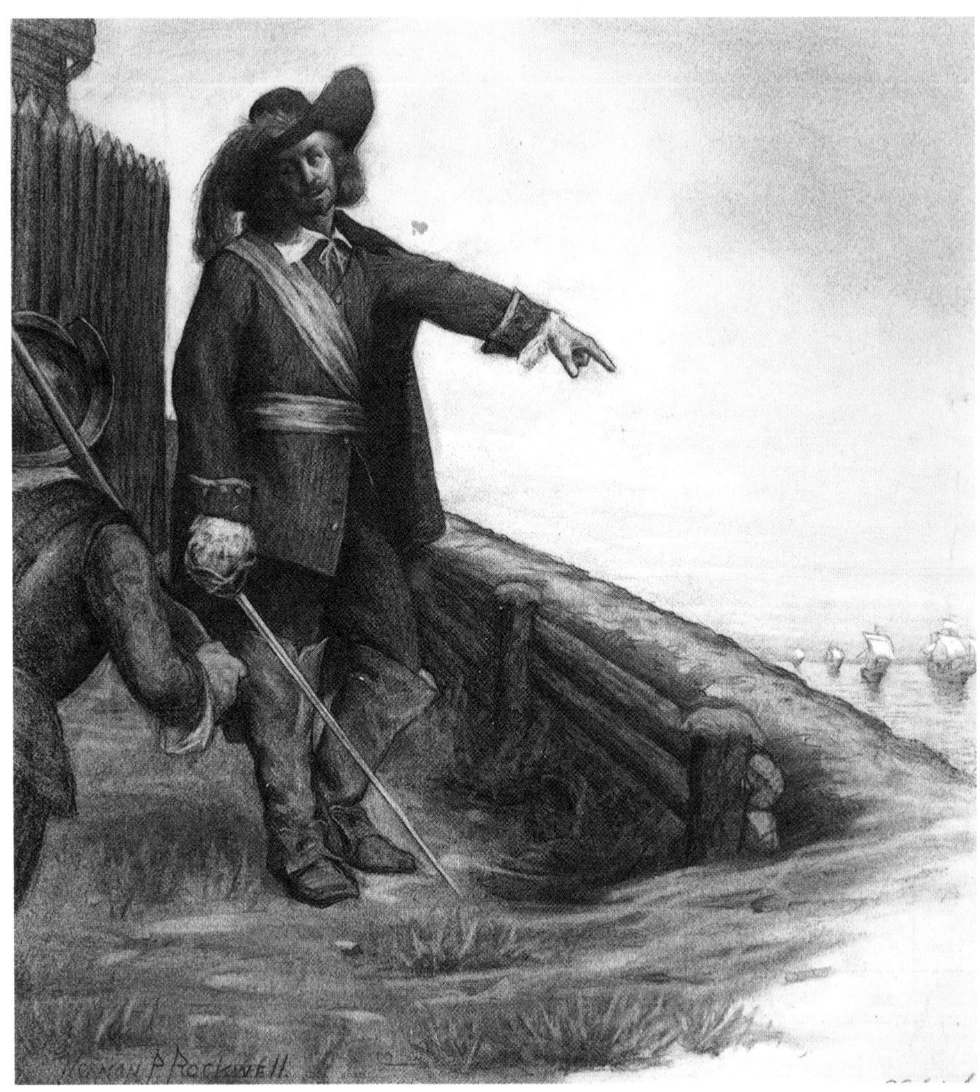


2.10. *An English Fleet Came Sailing up the St. Laurence*, 1911
Illustration for Fanny Eliza Coe, *Founders of Our Country* (New York: The American Book Company, 1912), 124–25
Syracuse University Libraries, Special Collections Research Center, New York; The American Book Company Records

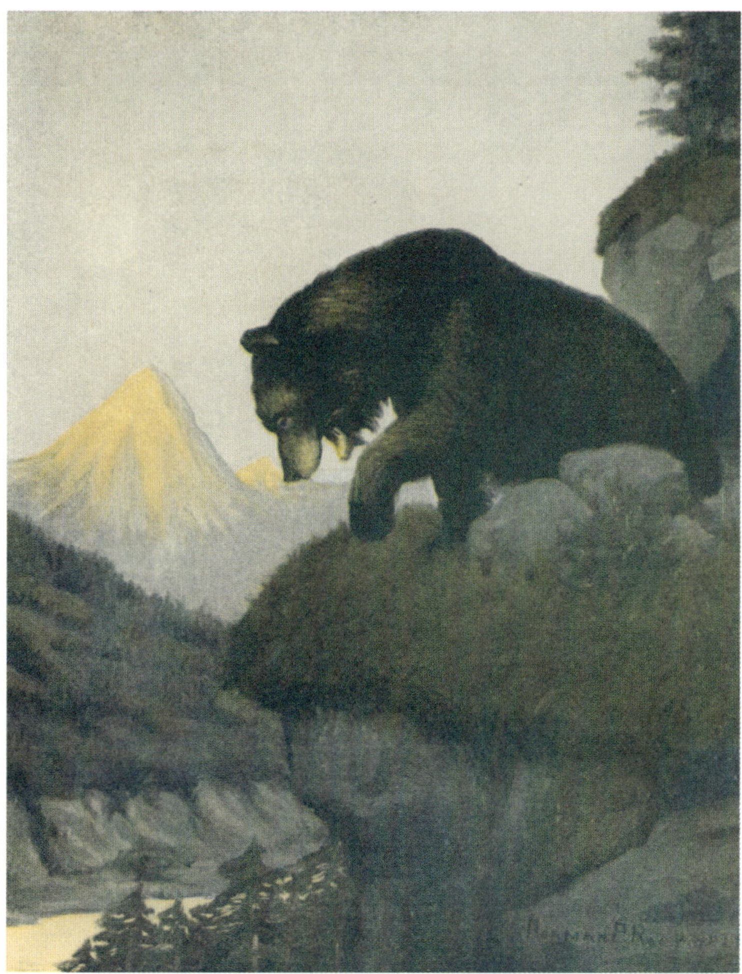

2.11. *Then Mother Nature Woke the Bear, and the Bear Woke Up What Other Animals He Could Find . . .*, 1911
Book plate
Illustration for C. H. Claudy, *Tell-Me-Why: Stories about Mother Nature* (New York: McBride, Nast & Company, 1912), facing page 124
Norman Rockwell Museum collection (Gift of John F. Butler Jr. in memory of John F. Butler Sr.)

It was not long before Edward Cave, editor of the Boy Scouts' monthly magazine *Boys' Life*, asked Rockwell to illustrate a Boy Scout handbook that he had just written. As a youth of just nineteen, Rockwell was retained as art director of *Boys' Life*, which was expanding to national circulation. Even in these early works, Rockwell's insistence on making each character a unique individual is clear. He did not yet have the ability to capture the nuances of gesture and expression, but his choice to individualize his characters rather than to create "types" was an element of his work that would set him apart from many of his peers. In a 1972 interview, Rockwell's son Peter recalled his father saying, "Do you know why Brueghel was able to paint such beautiful trees? Because Brueghel painted each tree as an individual." From the earliest days in his career and across more than six decades, drawing was the essential underpinning of the artist's extensive body of work.

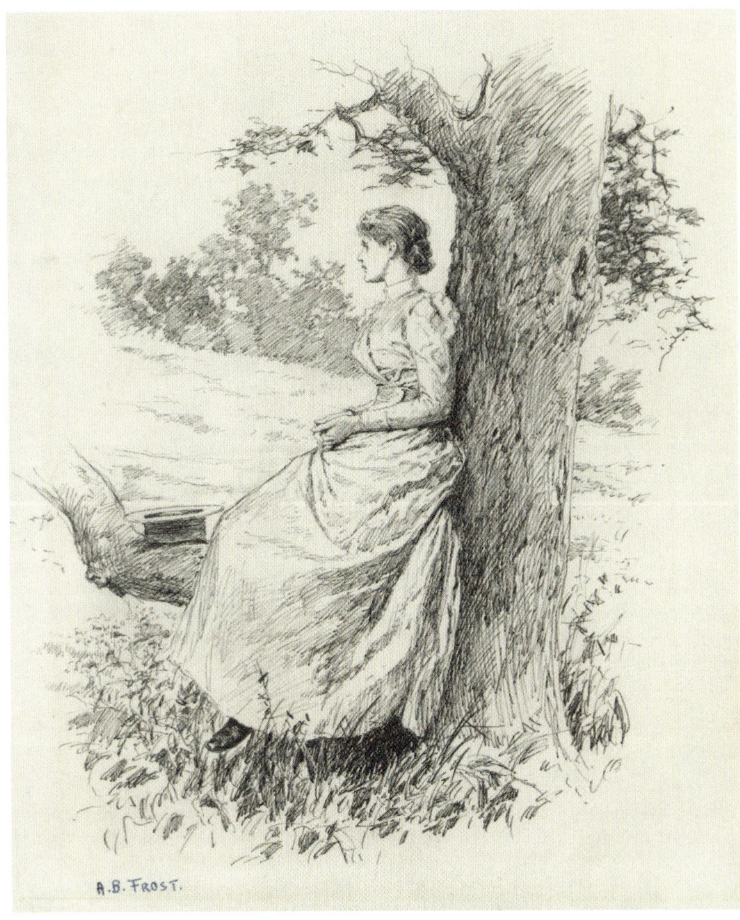


Rockwell greatly admired the work of American illustrator, graphic artist, and comics writer A. B. Frost (1851–1928), who was known for his dynamic representation of motion and sequence. Frost illustrated more than ninety books, including *The Squirrel Inn* by Frank R. Stockton, which featured thirty-three of his drawings. The one reproduced here was in Rockwell's personal collection.

ABOVE
2.12. A. B. Frost (1851–1928)
*Ida Makes Herself Comfortable*, 1891
Ink on paper
Illustration for Frank R. Stockton, *The Squirrel Inn* (New York: The Century Co., 1891)
Private collection

OPPOSITE
2.13. Howard Pyle (1853–1911)
*Peter Stuyvesant Leaving Fort Amsterdam after Surrendering to the English on September 8, 1664*, 1893
Ink on paper, 9½ × 7¼ in. (24.1 × 18.4 cm)
Illustration for Thomas A. Janvier, "The Evolution of New York, I," *Harper's New Monthly Magazine*, May 1893, 829
NRM.2006.21 (Gift of Robert T. Horvath)

Rockwell began his studies at the Art Students League in 1911, when legends of illustrator Howard Pyle's time there as a drawing and composition student, from 1876 to 1878, were still shared among the school's faculty. Even the League's longtime models, who were said to have posed for Pyle, were questioned by art students: "How did he begin a painting?" "What kind of paints did he use?" "Did he make preliminary sketches?"[15] Pyle's association with historical subjects and "fine writing" rather than advertising was valued, as ads were considered too commercial by an idealistic Rockwell and his fellow students. "Had Pyle or Abbey done advertisements? we asked each other. No. And we wouldn't either." Rockwell's prediction did not ultimately stand—at least one quarter of his four thousand works was created for prominent corporations.

A Pyle ink drawing for a story by Thomas A. Janvier was in Rockwell's own collection. Pyle and Janvier were regular contributors to *Harper's*—the author published several historical essays illustrated by Pyle in the magazine, and his book, *In Old New York*, had been released under the Harper and Brothers imprint in 1894.[16] Deft as a draftsman and painter, Pyle was noted for his luxurious pen and ink drawings. Stylistically precise yet expressive, they reproduced well and were sought after by the publications of the day.

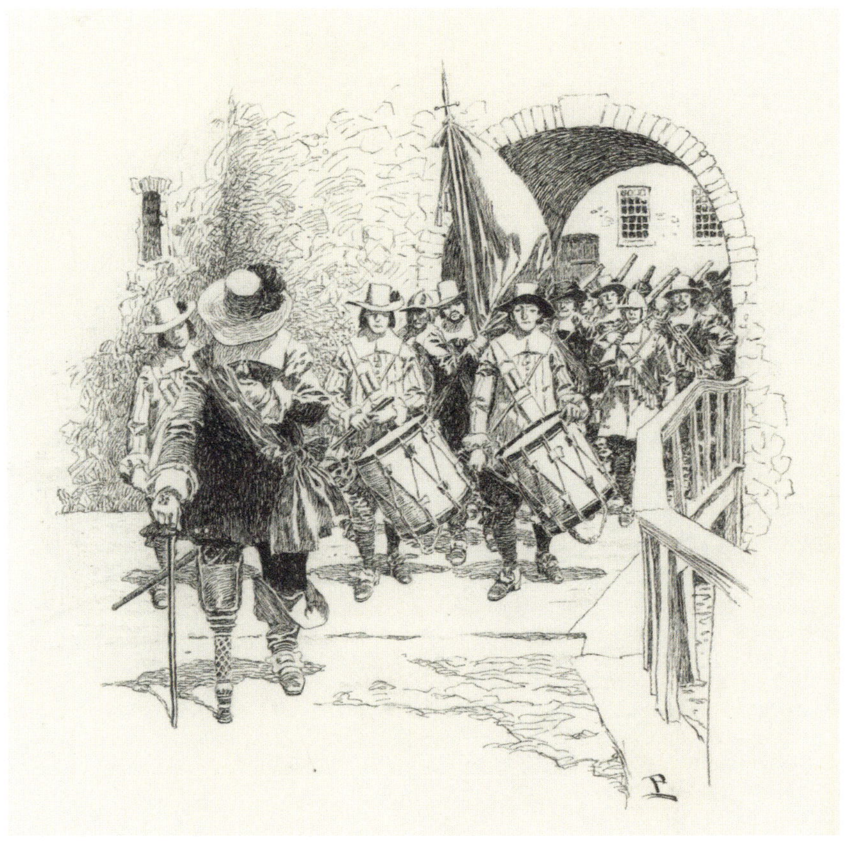

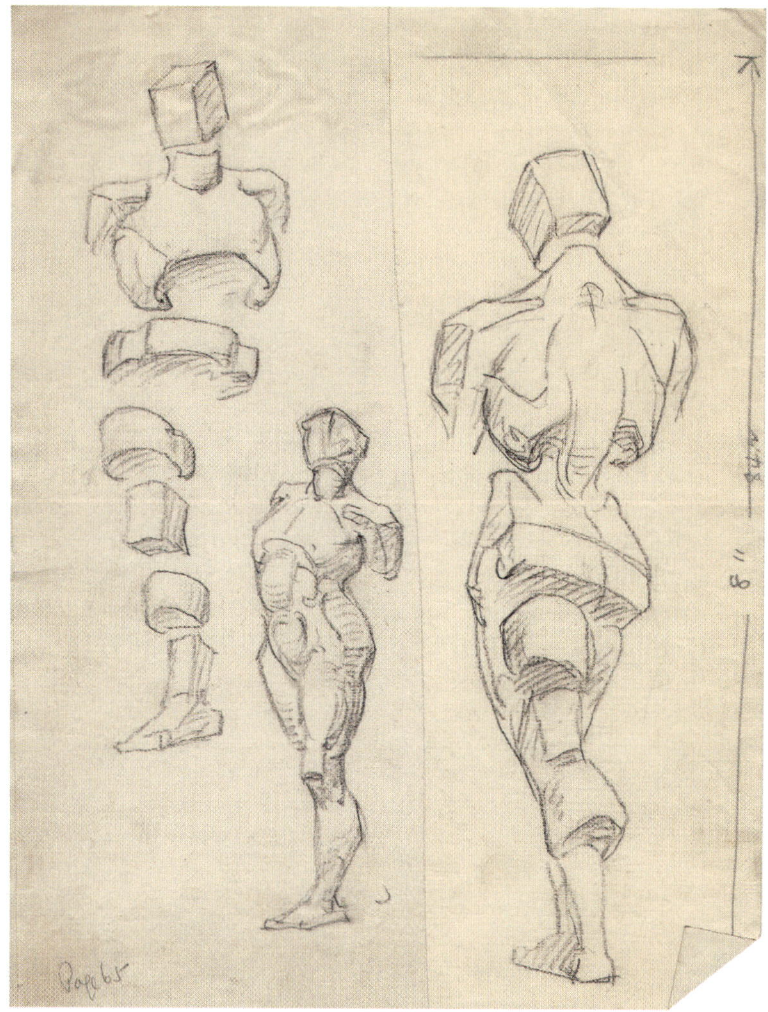

Bridgman, whose tenure at the League lasted for almost half a century, used box forms to represent the major masses of the figure (head, thorax, and pelvis), which he would tie together with gestural lines to create "wedges," or simplified interconnecting body forms in motion. Countless art students since the 1920s have used Bridgman's anatomy books to establish a solid foundation on the subject.

2.14. George B. Bridgman (1864–1943)
*Distribution of the Masses*, c. 1924
Pencil on paper, 10 × 7¾ in. (26.4 × 19.7 cm)
Illustration for George B. Bridgman,
*Bridgman's Life Drawings* (Pelham, New
York: Edward C. Bridgman, 1924), 70
NRM.2010.58.12 (Gift of the Blakeman Family)

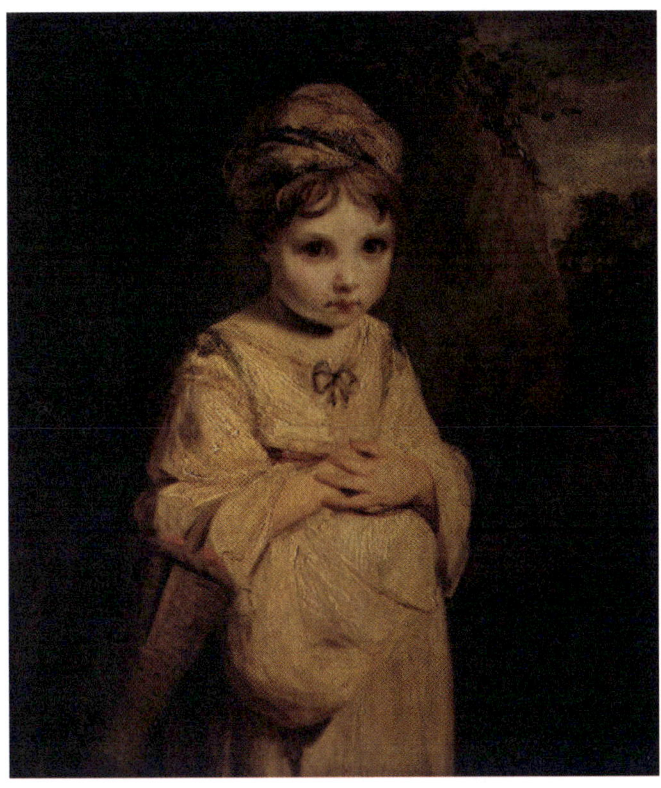

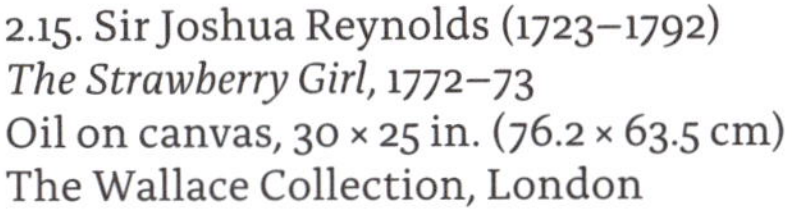

2.15. Sir Joshua Reynolds (1723–1792)
*The Strawberry Girl*, 1772–73
Oil on canvas, 30 × 25 in. (76.2 × 63.5 cm)
The Wallace Collection, London

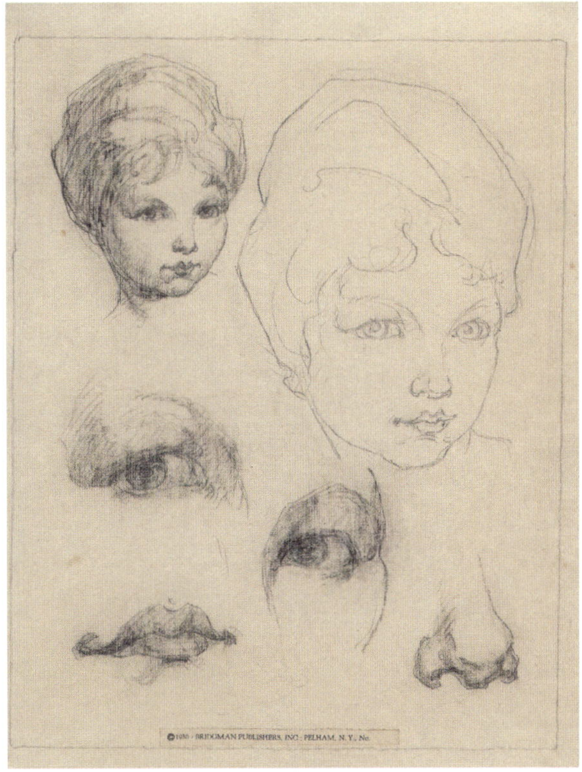

2.16. George B. Bridgman (1864–1943)
*After the Strawberry Girl by Sir Joshua Reynolds*, 1930
Pencil on paper, 14¼ × 9 in. (36.2 × 14.3 cm)
Illustration for George B. Bridgman, *Heads, Features and Faces* (Pelham, New York: Bridgman Publishers, 1942), 33
NRM.2010.58.21 (Gift of the Blakeman Family)

*The Strawberry Girl* is one of a series of English painter Sir Joshua Reynolds's portrayals of children in sentimental poses and dress. Though this work was inspired by a young strawberry seller, his painting removes her from her urban setting to present a more idealized and imagined perspective. The painting remained in Reynolds's collection until the end of his life and he believed it to be among his most original works.[17] Reynolds's painting became the inspiration for a Bridgman's drawing that takes a closer look at the construction of the girl's eyes, nose, and mouth.

Thomas Fogarty considered illustration to be "a meeting of the artist and author,"[18] and condemned all flights of fantasy. Fogarty was a practical-minded teacher, giving his students assignments akin to those they would receive from magazines, such as *Life of Coolidge*. After giving them a story to read, he asked students to develop an accompanying composition using carefully chosen costumes, props, and settings. He also urged students to imagine each character as a real person with a backstory rather than a stereotype, as exemplified in this pen and ink drawing for *Cosmopolitan* magazine. Fogarty's active line quality describes the appearance and character of his subjects, and also establishes a wide tonal range that is preferable for printing.

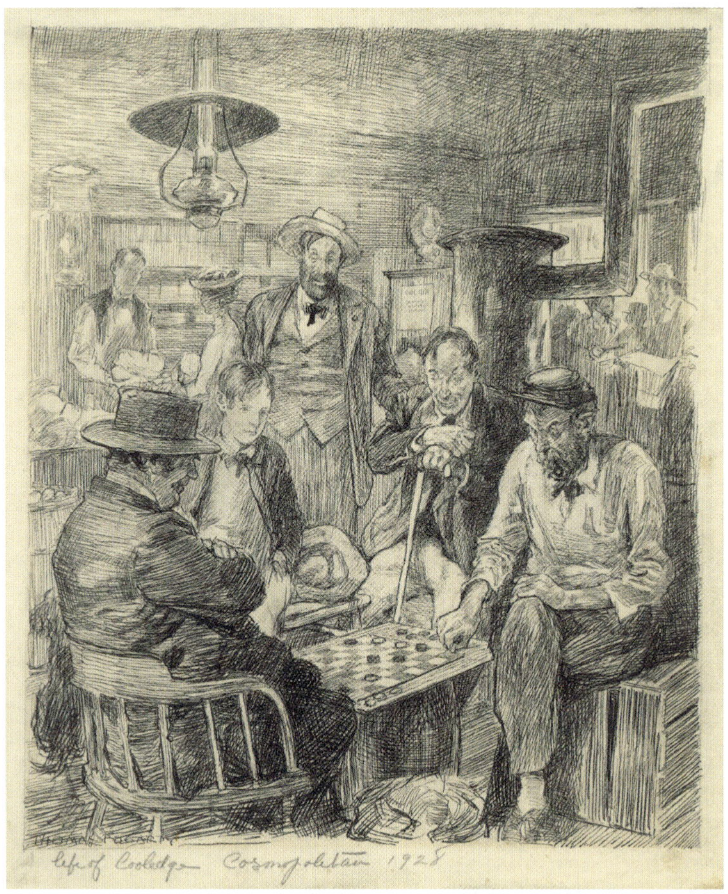


2.17. Thomas Fogarty (1873–1938)
*Life of Coolidge*, 1928
Ink on paper, 13½ × 11½ in. (34.3 × 29.2 cm)
Illustration for *Cosmopolitan*, 1928
NRM.2012.22.07 (Gift of Thomas A. Fogarty)

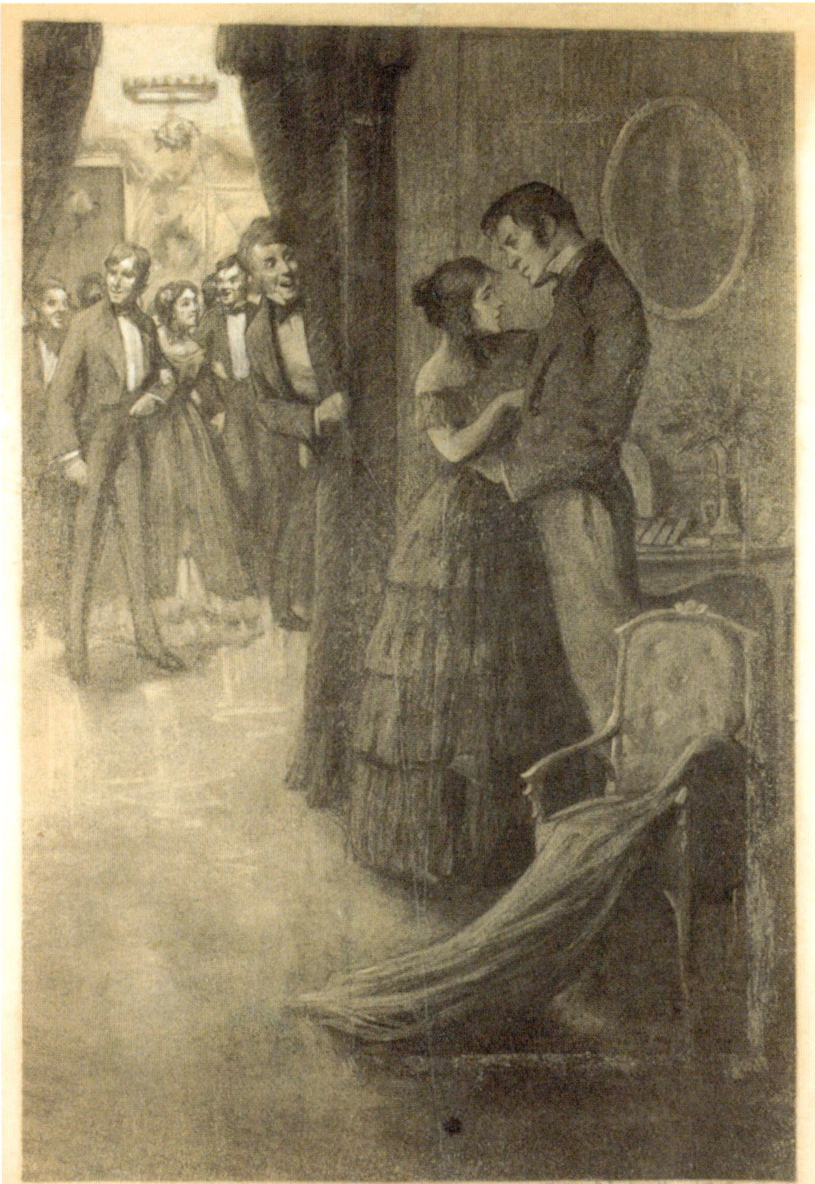

2.18. *No Doubt She Told Him Her Opinion of It, When They Were So Very Confidential Together, Behind the Curtains*, 1912
Charcoal on board,
22 × 17 in. (55.9 × 43.2 cm)
Student illustration for Charles Dickens, *A Christmas Carol*
NRM.1985.01 (museum purchase)

Of Dickens's stories, Rockwell said, "I began to look at things the way I imagined Dickens would have looked at them."[19] In this student illustration (plate 2.18) inspired by a scene from *A Christmas Carol*, Rockwell portrays a Christmas party at the home of Scrooge's nephew, who is seen here courting a young woman during a game of blind man's bluff. In the story, Scrooge and the Ghost of Christmas Present observe the scene unnoticed.

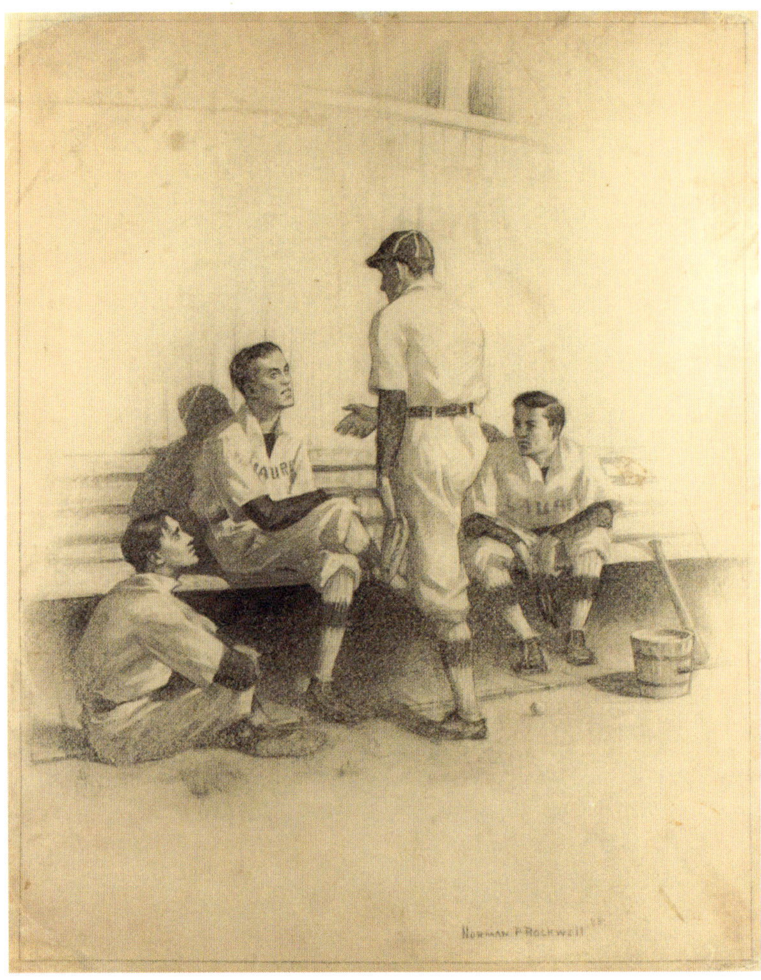

As art director of *Boys' Life*, Rockwell received a salary of $50 per month, and was responsible for producing cover art, illustrating one story per issue, such as *I'm Going to Put You in the Box*, and hiring and editing all additional artwork for the magazine. Though Rockwell did not consider himself an athlete, the subject of sports was a popular one for illustrations in the magazine. In this early drawing, Rockwell focuses on the connectivity of the team players as he works to refine his skills as a draftsman.

2.19. *I'm Going to Put You in the Box*, 1913
Charcoal on board, 21¾ × 17 in. (55.2 × 43.5 cm)
Illustration for Leslie W. Quirk, "Crossed Signals," *Boys' Life*, May 1913, 3
NRM.1985.02

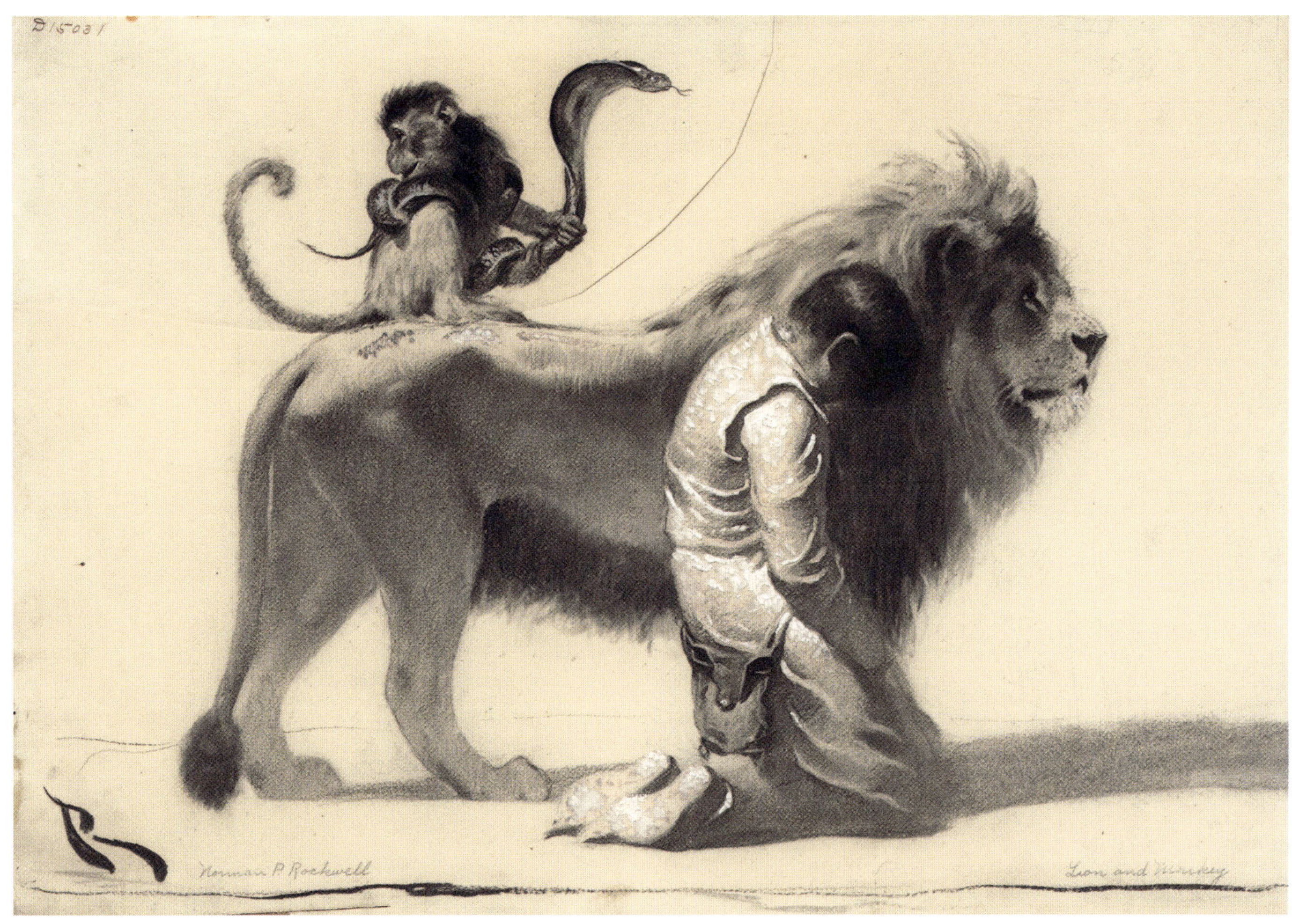


Rockwell's work for *Boys' Life* magazine led to commissions for other children's publications, including *St. Nicholas* and *The Youth's Companion*. *St. Nicholas* was a New York–based monthly filled with literature and illustrations by such noted artists as Howard Pyle and Maxfield Parrish. In this fantastical early work, the upper right portion of the drawing was cut away and replaced, a technique that Rockwell used to refine images throughout his life. At the age of twenty-three, the artist had begun to master both human and animal physiognomy and the ability to convey emotion in his art.

2.20. *The Whole Court Was Filled with Confusion, Though the Animals, with No Attempt to Injure Anybody, Made Their Way Close to the Side of the Peasant*, 1917
Charcoal and gouache on board, 21¾ × 17 in. (55.2 × 43.5 cm)
Illustration for Grace Dietrich McCarthy, "The Ungrateful Man," *St. Nicholas*, January 1917, 218
NRM.1981.03 (museum purchase)

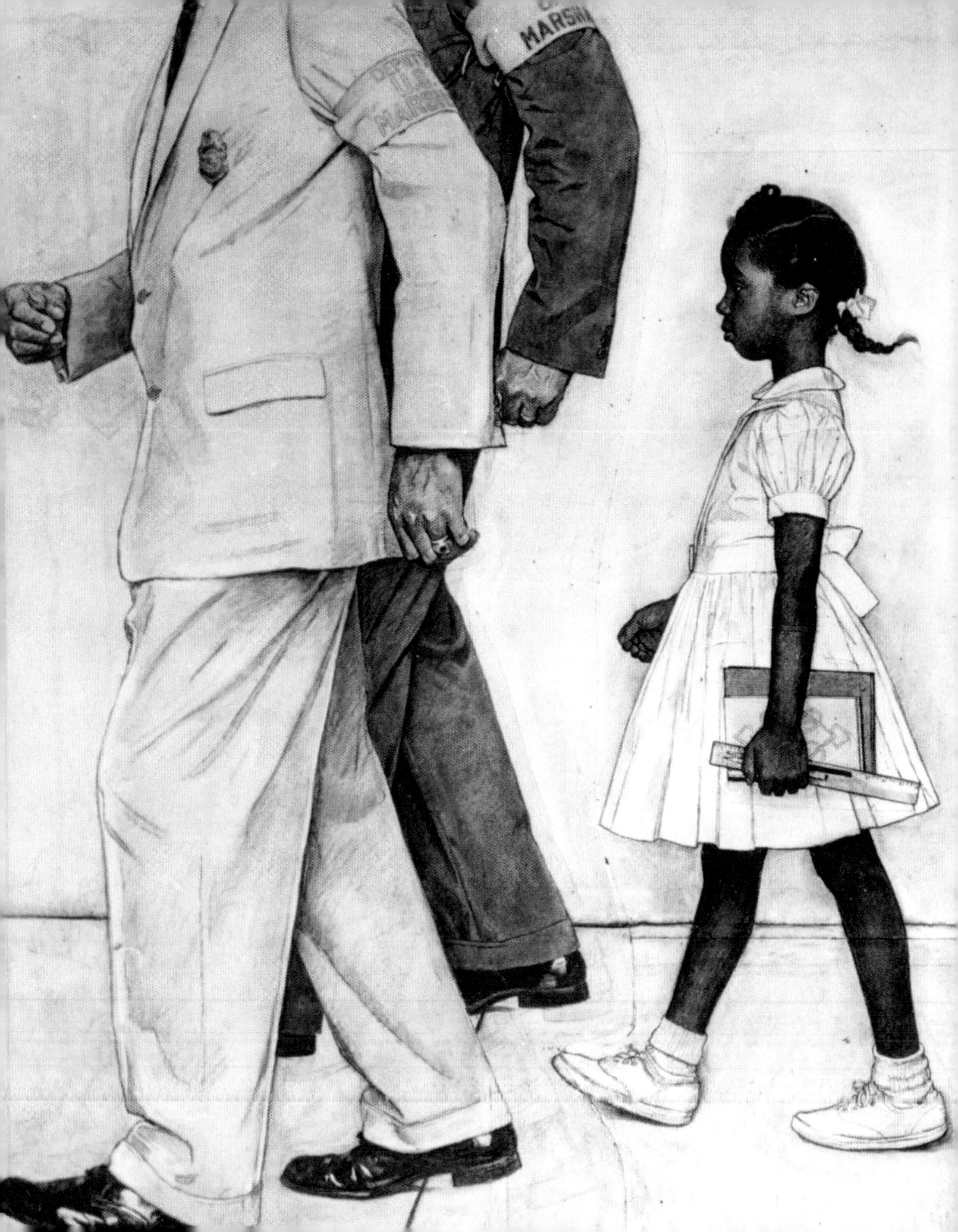
DEPUTY
U.S.
MARSH
MARSHA

# 3 Thumbnails to Finished Art: Rockwell's Artistic Process

JESSE KOWALSKI
CURATOR OF EXHIBITIONS,
NORMAN ROCKWELL MUSEUM

Detail of study for *The Problem We All Live With*, 1963
See plate 3.12.

Despite urgent deadlines, each of Rockwell's illustrations involved five to as many as fifteen steps. Knowing that the success of his storytelling covers and advertisements depended on the strength of his ideas, Rockwell would first make numerous small sketches to establish the concept of a work. Once he had a direction firmly in mind, he would begin to select models, costumes, and props. In his first decades as an illustrator, he could not paint without studio models in continual view as he worked, explaining that it had "never been natural" for him to "deviate from the facts" of the subject before him.[1] Acting as a director might, he posed his subjects just as he envisioned. Later in his career, however, Rockwell used a photographer to record the elements of the scene.

Rockwell first began incorporating photography into his process during research for a 1935 commission to illustrate a new edition of Mark Twain's classic novel *The Adventures of Tom Sawyer*. Rockwell "turned to the camera as a logical aid" to document the scenery and neighborhoods of Hannibal, Missouri, and to capture images of models, rather than have them spend hours posing for Rockwell when he could simply refer to a still image.[2]

Rockwell used photography as an efficient, accurate, and liberating means to satisfy his literalism. By photographing his props wherever he found them, he no longer had to assemble together the disparate objects his narratives required; by photographing far-flung settings, he was able to introduce true-to-life backgrounds; and by freeing him from the drawbacks of live models, photography dramatically expanded his vocabulary of available postures and possible expressions. "I no longer had to depend on the professional models. Now anybody could pose for me," Rockwell said, and he took full advantage of the opportunity.[3] Rockwell's trademark animated faces became possible because they could first be captured on film.

Norman Rockwell adeptly coaxed his characteristic expressions from a cast of amateur performers with the skill of a seasoned filmmaker. Before posing, the model would review Rockwell's rough sketches, and he would explain the themes he wanted to represent within the painting. He would sometimes strike the poses to demonstrate the proper stance to the model. He wrote, "I work with the model . . . and when the smile has widened and the eyebrows are way up and the eyes are sparkling, the photographer snaps the picture and I have it." With professional models, "I'd had to settle right away for a fairly static pose. There was a limit to the number of sketches I could make; nor could I keep changing the pose. But now, with photographs, I can try endless variations."[4]

The total number of reference photos that Rockwell generated over the course of his career was staggering: he typically had individual photos taken of each prop, model, and background (plates 3.1, 3.2, and 3.3). This process sometimes required over one hundred photographs for each painting, and many more on occasion. He would sometimes use close-ups of models' body parts and select the best image to make the perfect representation, as one might put together puzzle pieces. Unfortunately, when his studio in Arlington, Vermont, burned down in 1943, nearly all the reference photos he had taken up to that point were lost, in addition to scores of props, artworks, and source materials.

Because of this loss, it is easier to trace Rockwell's creative process from start to finish using a later work for which more complete reference photos

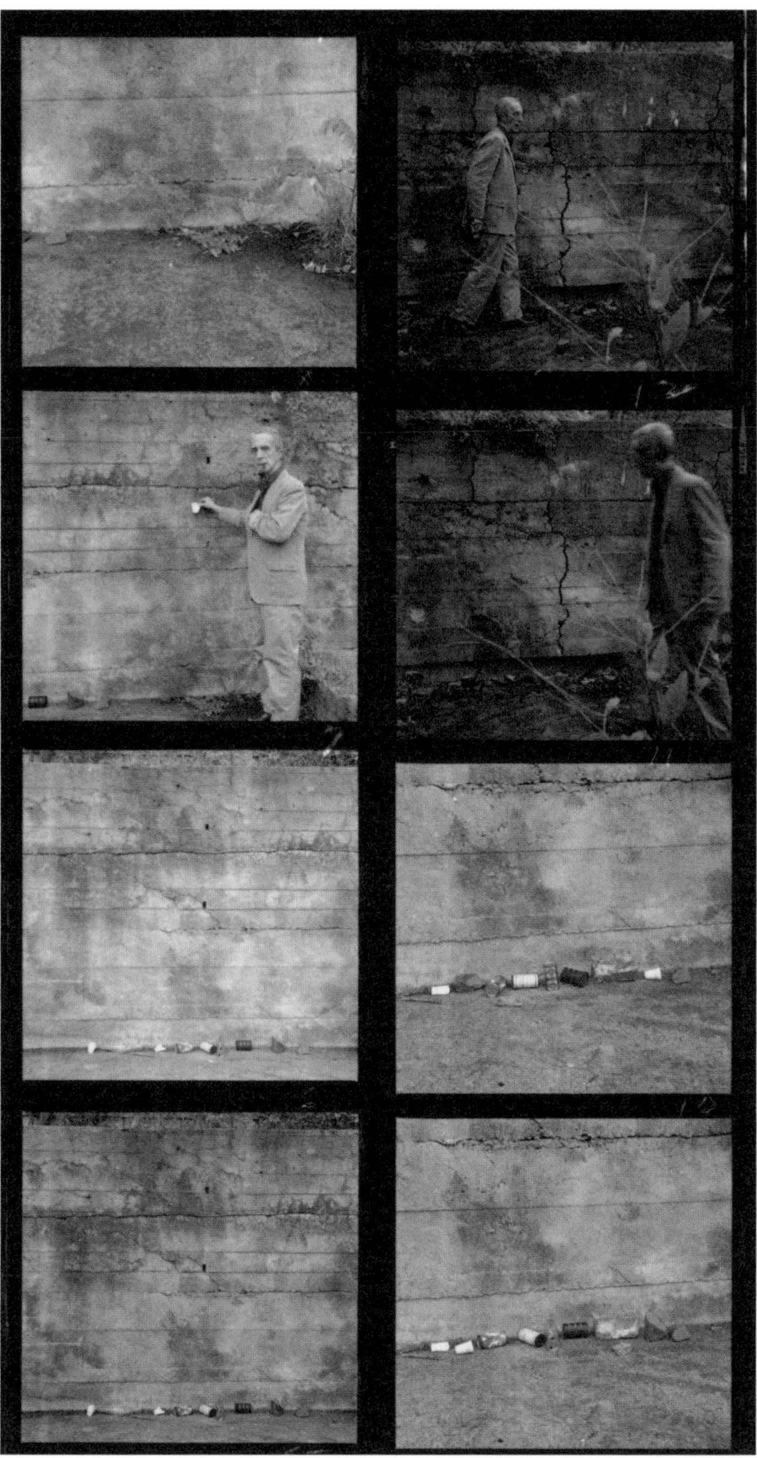

3.1. Louis Lamone (1918–2007)
Reference photograph for *The Problem We All Live With*, 1963
Photograph (from negative), 10 × 8 in. (25.4 × 20.3 cm)
Contact sheet of Norman Rockwell piling cans against a wall
ST.1976.20032.81.28

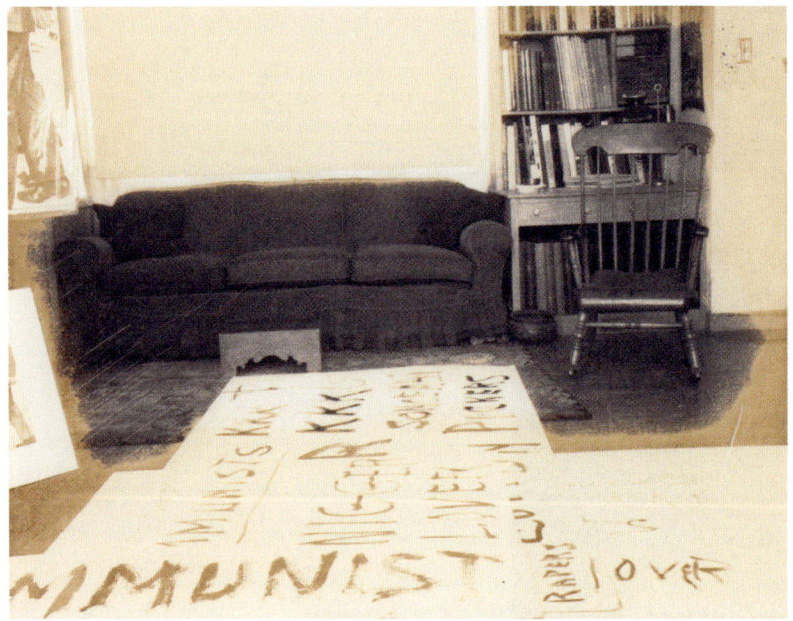


3.2. Louis Lamone (1918–2007)
Reference photograph for *The Problem We All Live With*, 1963
Gelatin silver print, 3½ × 4½ in. (8.9 × 11.4 cm)
Hand-painted signs with racial epithets
ST.1976.20032.81.30

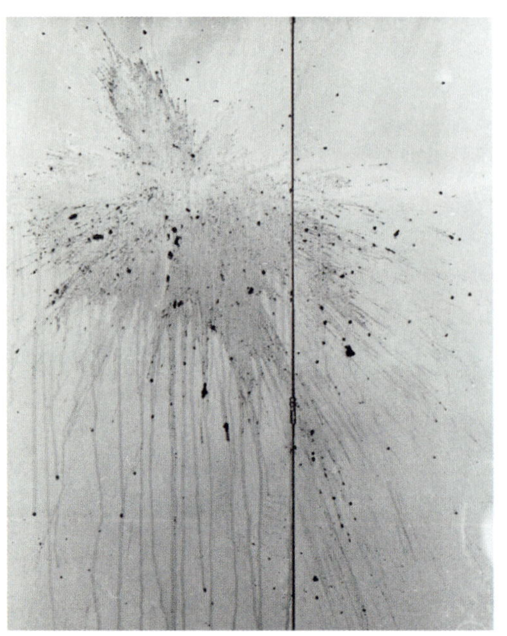

3.3. Louis Lamone (1918–2007)
Reference photograph for *The Problem We All Live With*, 1963
Gelatin silver print, 10 × 8 in. (25.4 × 20.3 cm)
Tomato thrown by Rockwell at a wall
ST.1976.20032.81.27

and drawings survive. We will take as our example a painting that represented a turning point in the artist's career.

After resigning his forty-seven-year tenure with the *Saturday Evening Post* in 1963, Rockwell was free to embrace the challenge of creating imagery that addressed the nation's changing cultural landscape. One outlet that welcomed such socially conscious imagery was *Look* magazine. Rockwell's first assignment for *Look* was an illustration of Ruby Bridges, a six-year-old Black schoolgirl being escorted by four U.S. marshals to her first day at an all-white school in New Orleans on November 14, 1960.

Ordered to proceed with school desegregation after the 1954 U.S. Supreme Court ruling *Brown v. Board of Education*, Louisiana lagged behind until May 16, 1960, when Federal Judge Skelly Wright forced the school board to begin desegregation. On Bridges's first day, all the teachers at Frantz Elementary School stayed home out of protest except for one: Barbara Henry. For the remainder of the school year, U.S. marshals accompanied Bridges

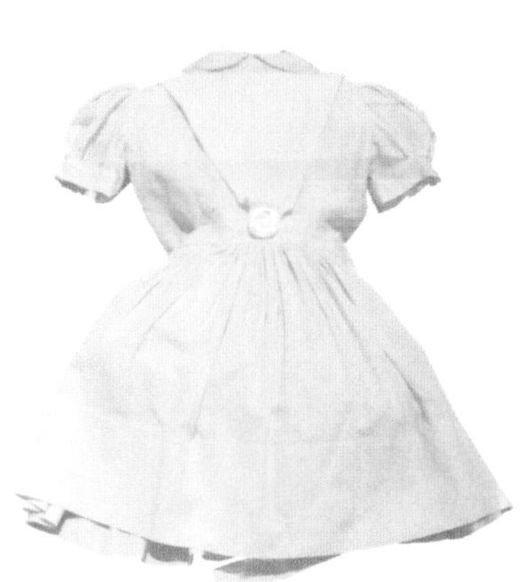

3.4. Dress worn by the models for *The Problem We All Live With*, 1963
Cotton, 23 × 18 in. (58.4 × 45.7 cm)
NRM.2016.03.2 (from Lynda Gunn, Norman Rockwell model for *The Problem We All Live With*)

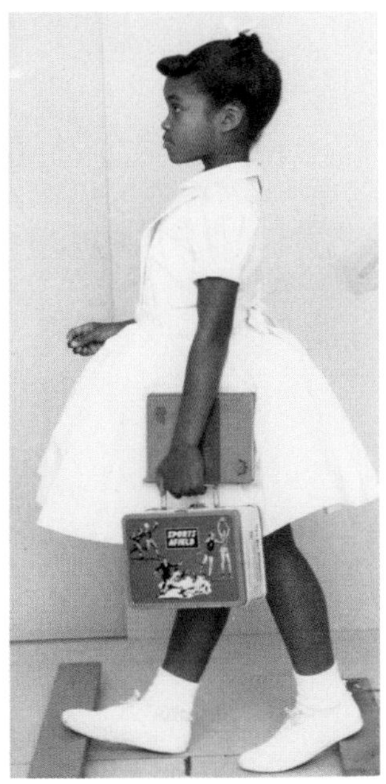

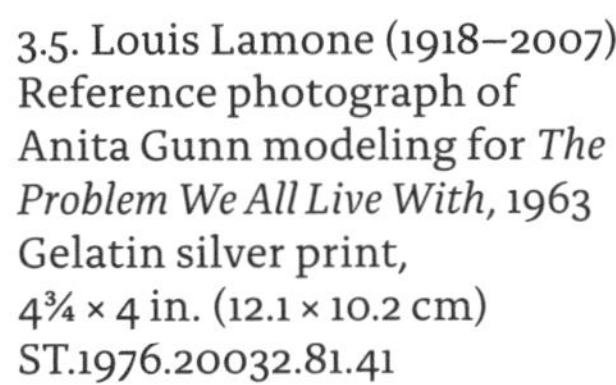

3.5. Louis Lamone (1918–2007)
Reference photograph of Anita Gunn modeling for *The Problem We All Live With*, 1963
Gelatin silver print, 4¾ × 4 in. (12.1 × 10.2 cm)
ST.1976.20032.81.41

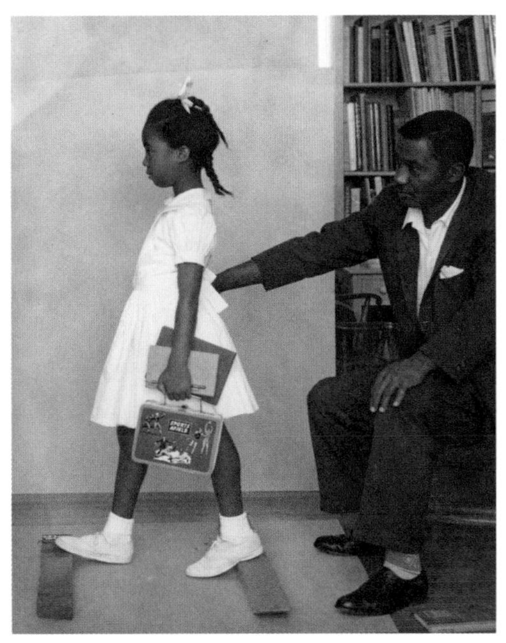

3.6. Louis Lamone (1918–2007)
Reference photograph of Lynda Gunn modeling for *The Problem We All Live With*, 1963
Gelatin silver print, 10 × 8 in. (25.4 × 20.3 cm)
ST.1976.20032.81.3

to school daily, where she was Barbara Henry's only student. Bridges later noted Henry was "the nicest teacher I ever had."[5]

As he did with other paintings, Rockwell did not paint the scene true to life, but imagined an emotional representation of the event. As biographer Deborah Solomon notes, "Even when he was depicting an event out of the headlines, he was not transcribing a scene but inventing one—he added the tomato and the defaced wall and changed various details."[6] This included the color of Bridges's dress, which was pink in the photographs. Rockwell altered the color to white to create a better composition, but also to emphasize the innocence of the vulnerable child (plate 3.4).

To help him find a model for Ruby Bridges, Rockwell contacted David Gunn, who had modeled along with his son for Rockwell's *Golden Rule* painting years before and was chairman of the Berkshire County chapter of the NAACP. He recommended two of his granddaughters, first cousins Lynda and Anita Gunn.[7] Anita was the first to pose for Rockwell, though he

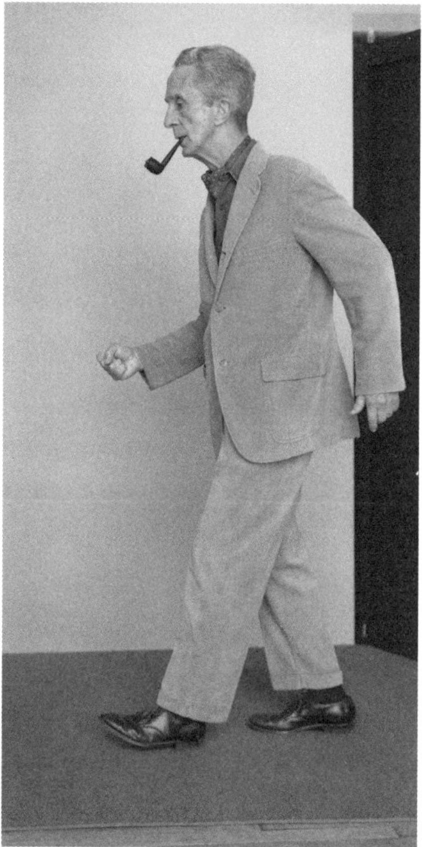

3.7. Louis Lamone (1918–2007)
Reference photograph of Rockwell posing as a U.S. marshal for *The Problem We All Live With*, 1963
Photograph (from negative), 5 × 4 in. (12.7 × 10.2 cm)
ST1976.3850

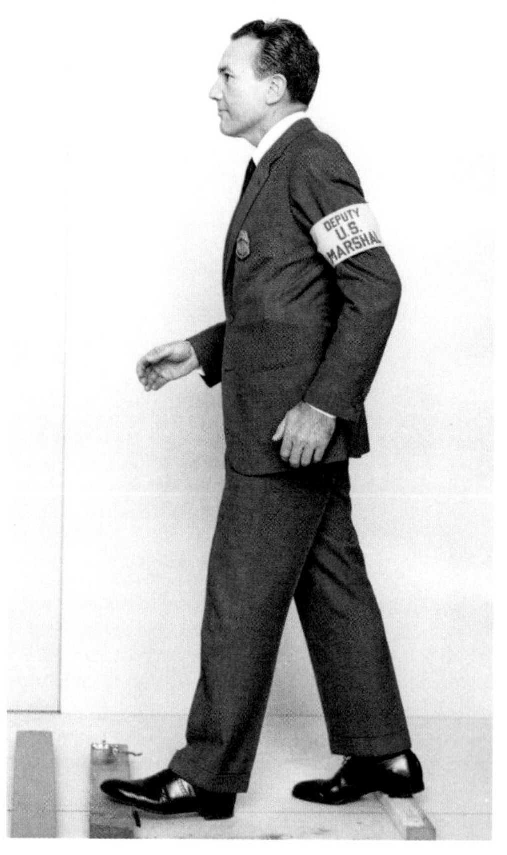


3.8. Louis Lamone (1918–2007)
Reference photograph of U.S. Marshal Robert Morey modeling for *The Problem We All Live With*, 1963
Gelatin silver print, 10 × 8 in. (25.4 × 20.3 cm)
ST.1976.20032.81.14

ultimately based the girl on Lynda Gunn's likeness. This was not unusual: Rockwell often photographed multiple models for each subject, making his selection only when the photographic prints were in his hands. To capture a feeling of action, Rockwell wedged books or boards under a heel or a toe to obtain the precise angle of a walking foot while relieving stress on the model. For *The Problem We All Live With*, Rockwell described the stance to the girls, posed them on the boards in the white dress with the book and lunchbox in hand, and had numerous black-and-white photographs taken of Anita and Lynda Gunn (plates 3.5 and 3.6).

At least two of the male models were actual U.S. marshals from Boston,

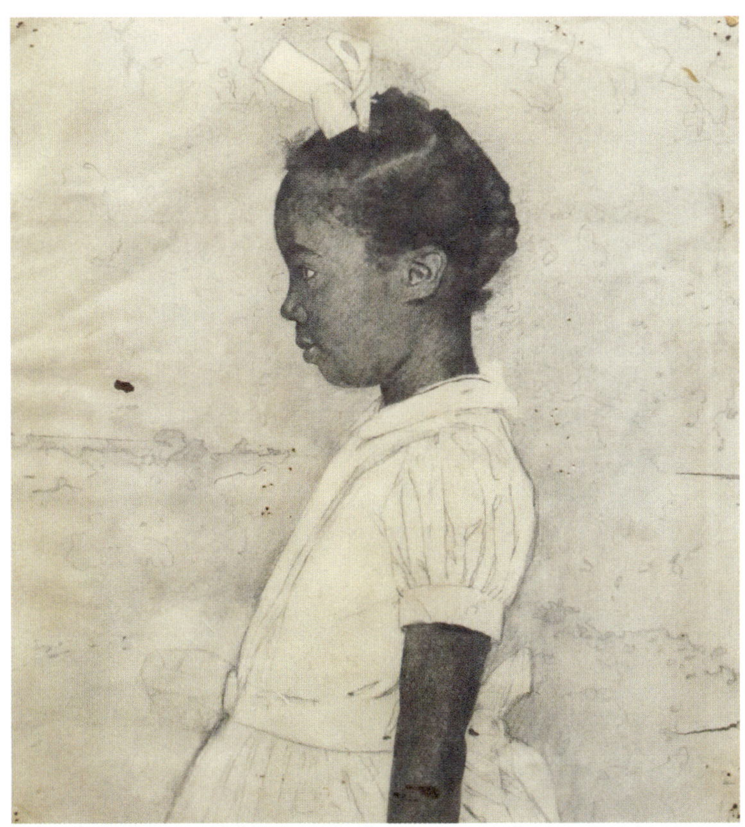

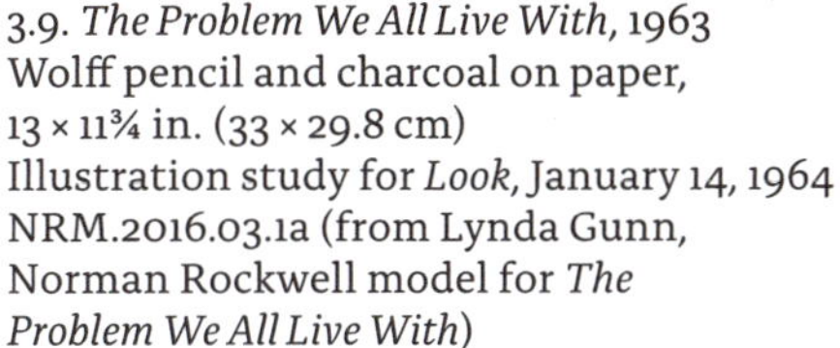

3.9. *The Problem We All Live With*, 1963
Wolff pencil and charcoal on paper,
13 × 11¾ in. (33 × 29.8 cm)
Illustration study for *Look*, January 14, 1964
NRM.2016.03.1a (from Lynda Gunn,
Norman Rockwell model for *The
Problem We All Live With*)

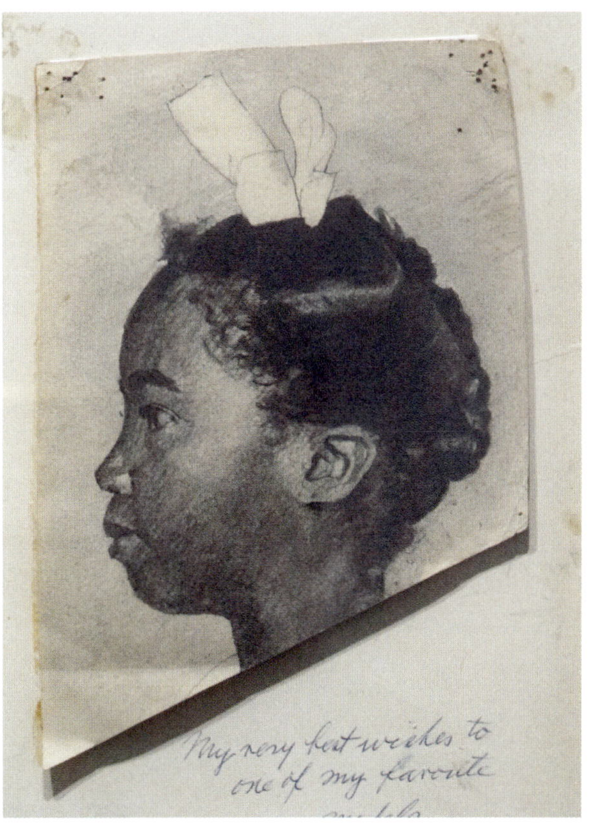


3.10. *The Problem We All Live With*, 1963
Wolff pencil and charcoal on paper,
7¼ × 5 in. (18.4 × 12.7 cm)
Illustration study for *Look*, January 14,
1964; autographed to Lynda Gunn
NRM.2016.03.1b (from Lynda Gunn, Norman
Rockwell model for *The Problem We All Live With*)

for whom Rockwell demonstrated the desired pose (plates 3.7 and 3.8). Another was Stockbridge Police Chief William J. Obanhein, who would later become famous when depicted as "Officer Obie" in Arlo Guthrie's 1967 hit song "Alice's Restaurant."

After choosing the best photographs to tell his story, Norman Rockwell began the process of translating these images into his finished painting. First, he created a detailed charcoal drawing (plate 3.12) from which he developed and refined his narrative and worked out compositional details. Rockwell began by placing his initial sketch in the Balopticon (plate 3.11), which projected onto roughened architect's paper on a vertical easel. Positioning it closer or farther away to achieve the desired size, he drew lightly to outline his design.

Beginning with the most important subjects, Rockwell placed his photographs one by one in the Balopticon. Maneuvering each element into position until it fit the outlined sketch, he lightly traced the projected photographs, erasing the first sketched figures as he worked. Rockwell sometimes cut out and used only the specific details that interested him, discarding the remainder of the photographic image as he fine-tuned his composition. If the result did not please him, he rubbed out or replaced the detail, rubber-cementing in a new paper section. With the complete composition roughed in, he started again at the beginning, tracing each photographic element in greater detail and making notations on lighting and tonality.

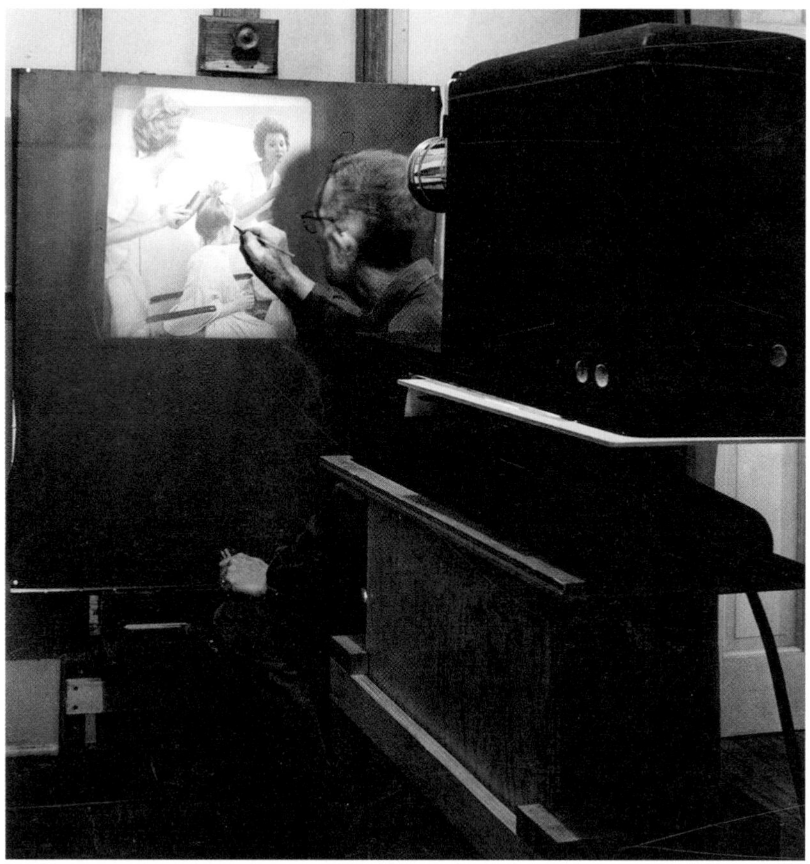

3.11. Bill Scovill (1915–1996)
Norman Rockwell using a Balopticon while working on *First Trip to the Beauty Shop*, 1972
Gelatin silver print, 10 × 8 in. (25.4 × 20.3 cm)
Norman Rockwell Museum collection

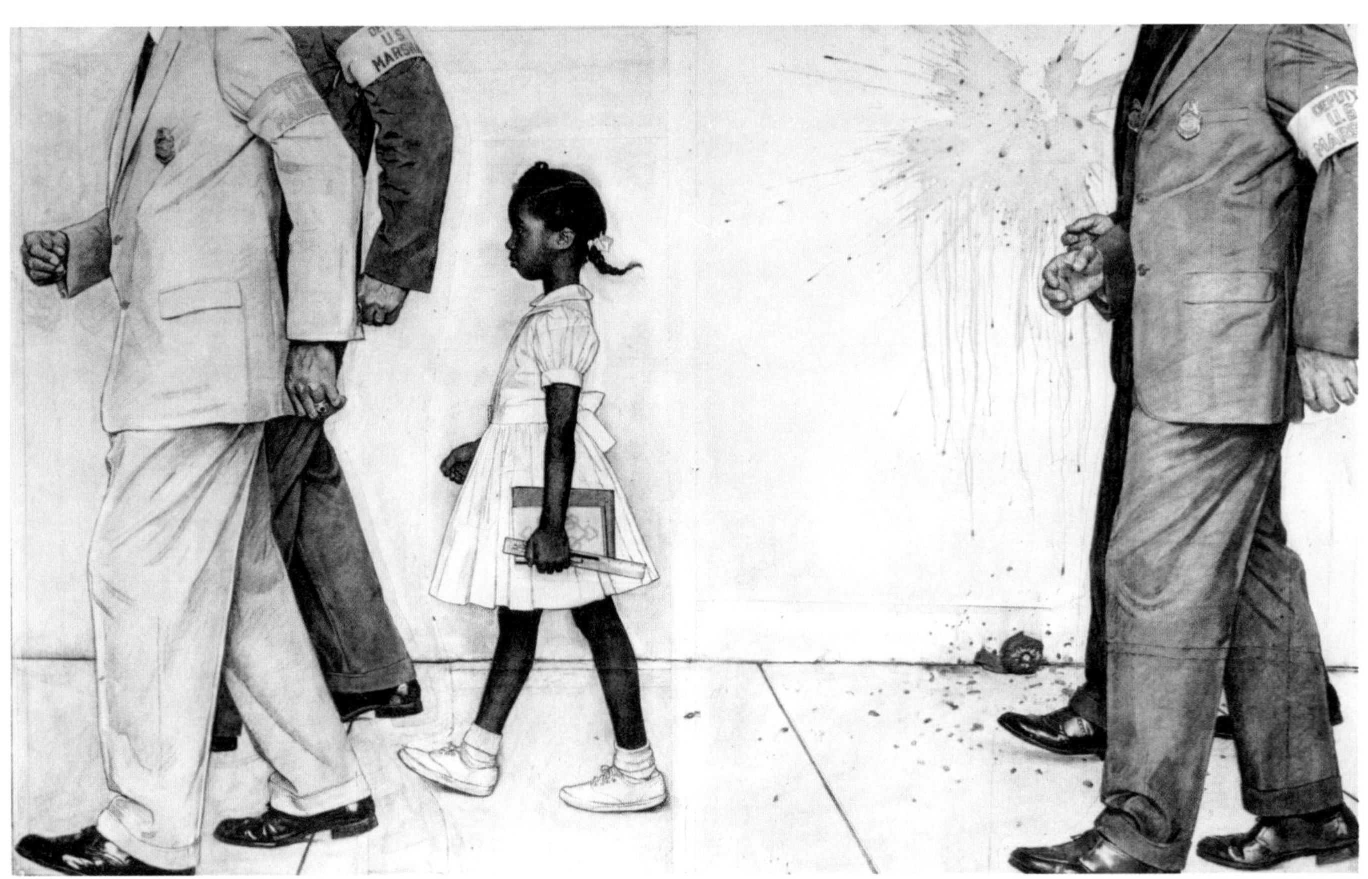

3.12. *The Problem We All Live With*, 1963
Charcoal on paper
Illustration study for *Look*, January 14, 1964
Private collection

3.13. *The Problem We All Live With*, 1963
Oil on board, 13 × 20½ in. (33 × 52.1 cm)
Illustration color study for *Look*, January 14, 1964
NRACT.1973.087a

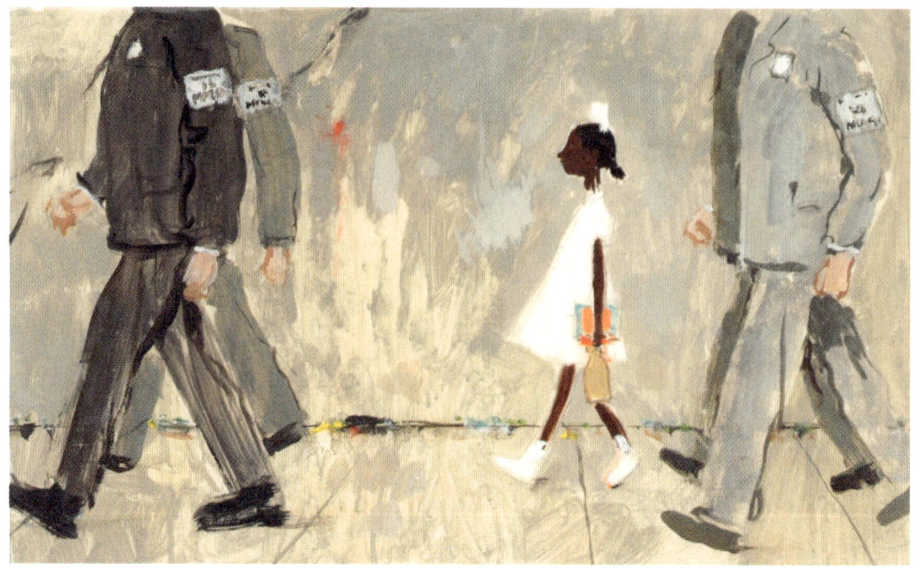

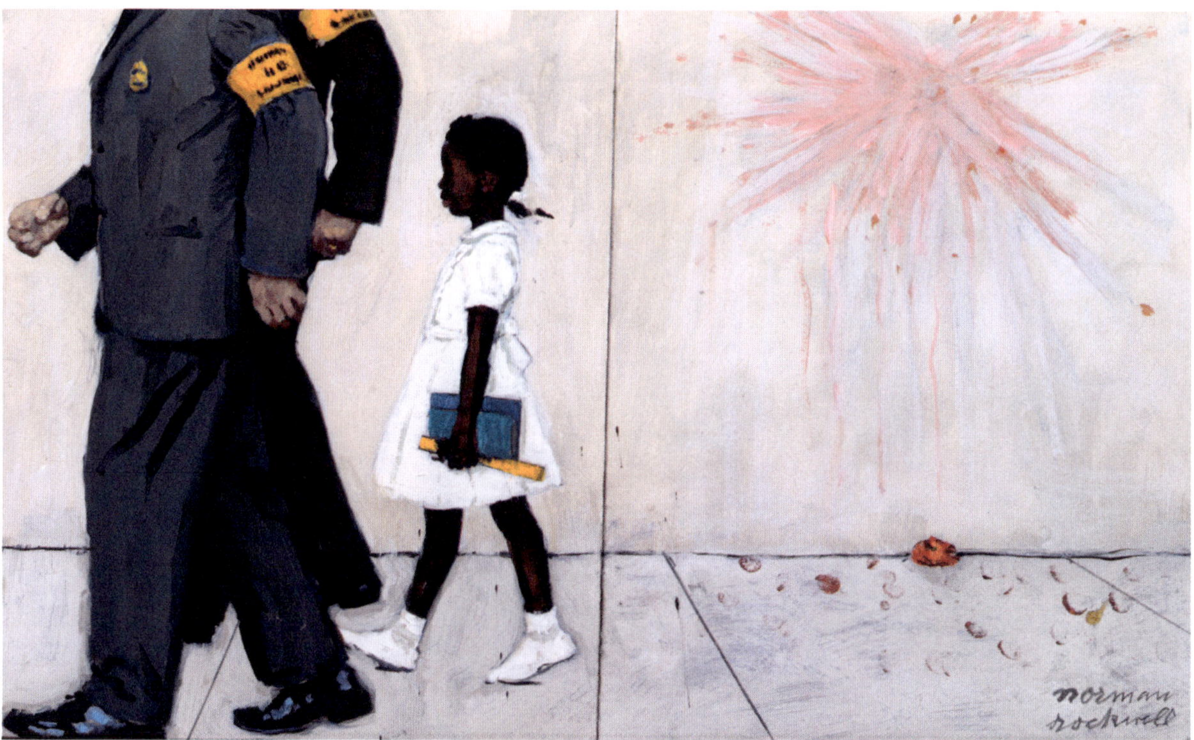



3.14. *The Problem We All Live With*, 1963
Gouache on paper, 13 × 21 in. (33 × 53.3 cm)
Illustration color study for *Look*, January 14, 1964
Private collection

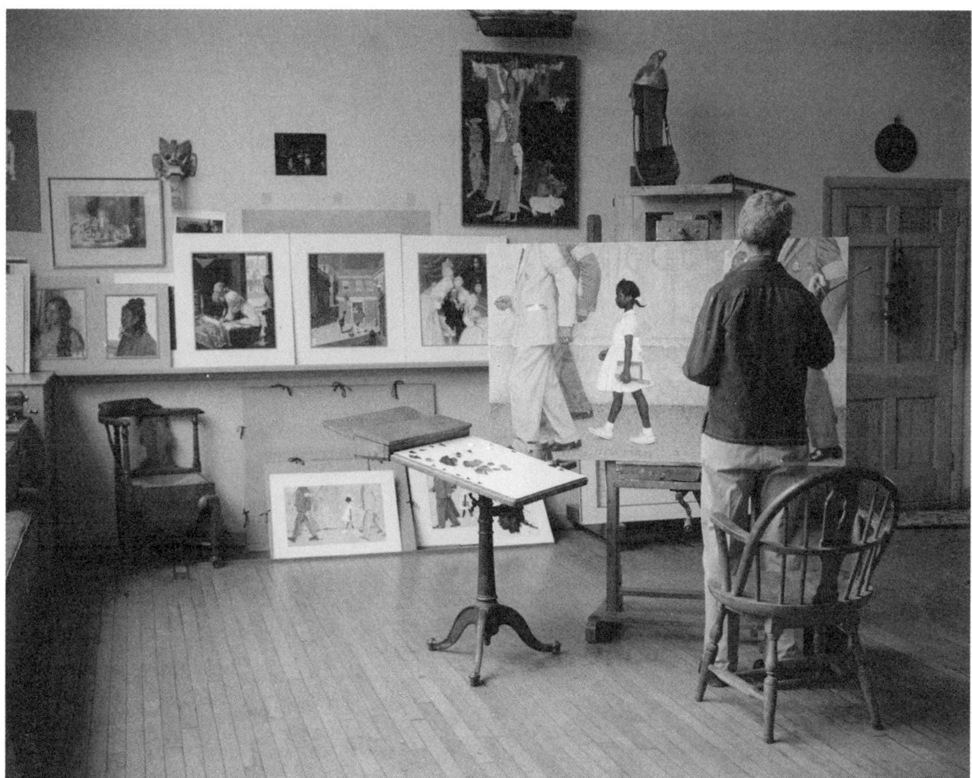

3.15. Louis Lamone (1918–2007)
Norman Rockwell painting *The Problem We All Live With*, 1963
Photograph (from negative), 4 × 5 in. (10.2 × 12.7 cm)
ST.1976.3849

To make the leap to canvas, Rockwell transferred the outlines of his charcoal drawing to primed canvas using transfer paper. Alternately, Rockwell had his charcoal drawing photographed, projected onto canvas, and traced.

In a separate step, Rockwell produced a new version—in color and to the size of the intended reproduction—with which he planned the palette of the final painting. Sometimes created early in his creative process, Rockwell's color studies often possess a loose, painterly vitality quite unlike the finished, more detailed illustration (plates 3.13 and 3.14).

After transferring his charcoal study to canvas and sealing it with thinned shellac, Rockwell began the demanding process of laying down paint. Surrounded by all the reference materials he had collected for the work at hand, his photographs played a final role as he tacked snippets cut from them to his easel as he worked.

Rockwell endured long, often stressful days at his easel as he completed his creative process (plate 3.15). Striving to get everything exactly right, he was known to repeatedly paint over entire sections of a composition, or scrape the paint down to the canvas and start over. Sometimes, even fin-

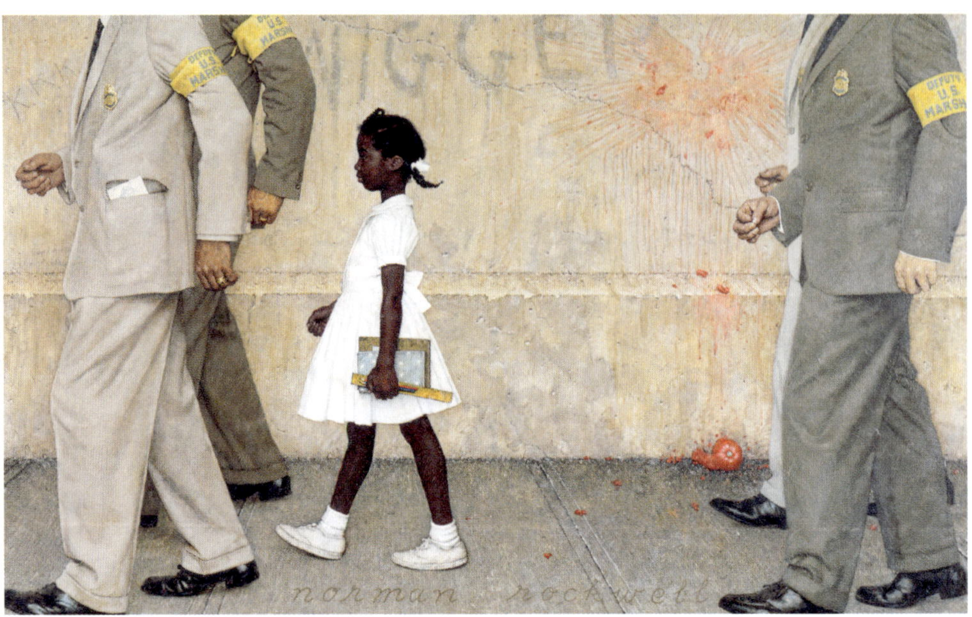

3.16. *The Problem We All Live With*, 1963
Oil on canvas, 36 × 58 in. (91.4 × 147.3 cm)
Illustration for *Look*, January 14, 1964
NRM.1975.01

ished works could be discarded. He routinely asked anyone who came into his studio to critique a work in progress as a way to test his artistic choices and gauge the clarity of his narrative.

Of course, the final test of an illustration was its reception by the public. Following the publication of *The Problem We All Live With* (plate 3.16), letters to the editor were a mix of praise and criticism. One reader from Tennessee wrote, "Allow me to say that I have never been so deeply moved by a picture as by [this painting]. . . . The truth is pretty hard to take until we get it from a Norman Rockwell."[8] A man from Chicago wrote, "Your picture illustrates . . . more forcibly than a whole library . . . what our constitution . . . [means] to each and every citizen. . . . It should take its place with the great historical paintings of our country."[9] Other readers objected to Rockwell's image. A man from New Orleans wrote, "It is nothing short of a heinous crime to mix little white and black children. . . . THERE CAN BE . . . NO COMPROMISE WITH THE VICIOUS CRIME OF RACE MIXING AND INTEGRATION."[10]

But irate opinions did not stop Rockwell from pursuing his course. In 1965, he illustrated the murder of civil rights workers in Philadelphia, Mississippi, and in 1967, he chose children, once again, to illustrate integration, this time in our nation's suburbs.

Although Rockwell's process was meticulous, it was, like any artistic endeavor, still one of trial and error, and the outcome was not guaranteed. One of Rockwell's most instructive (and well-documented) failures occurred in 1948, when he set out to create a murder-mystery-themed cover for the *Post*.

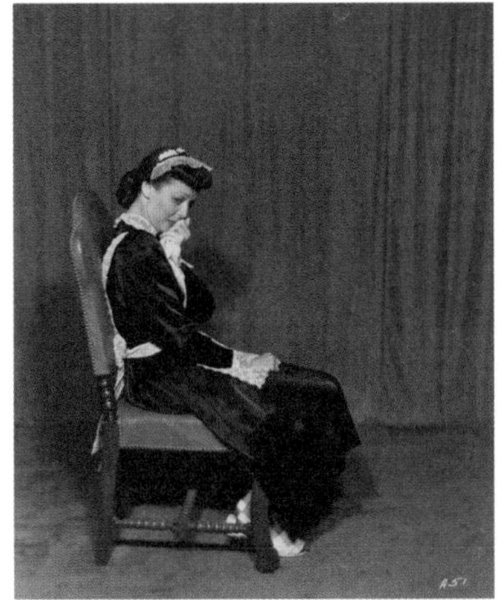
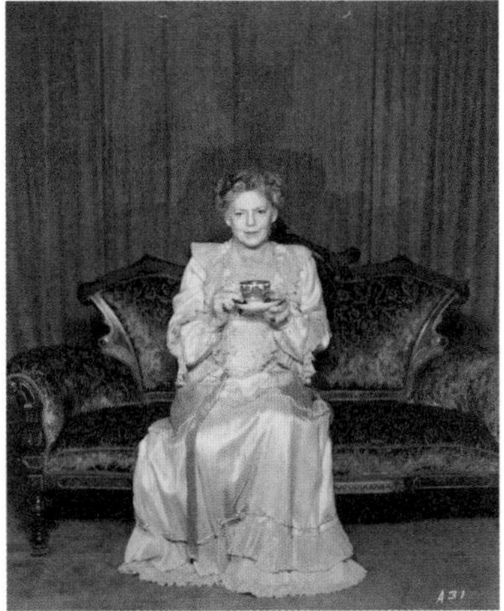
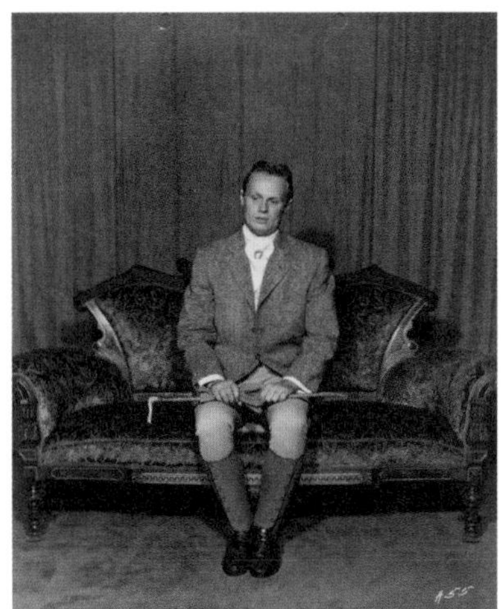
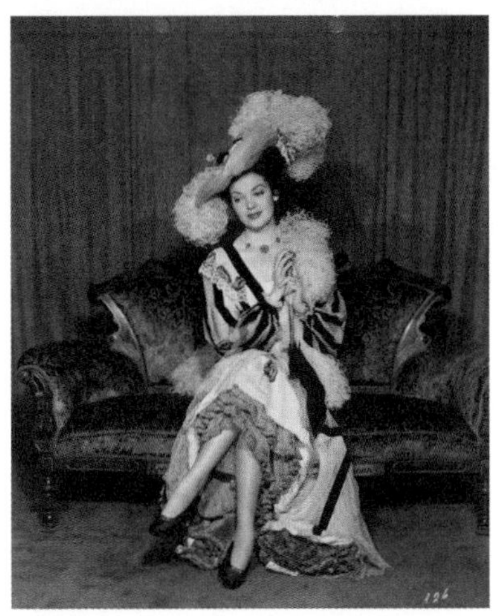
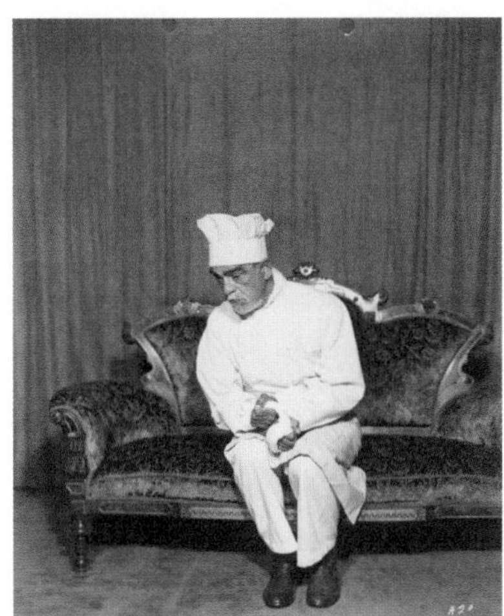
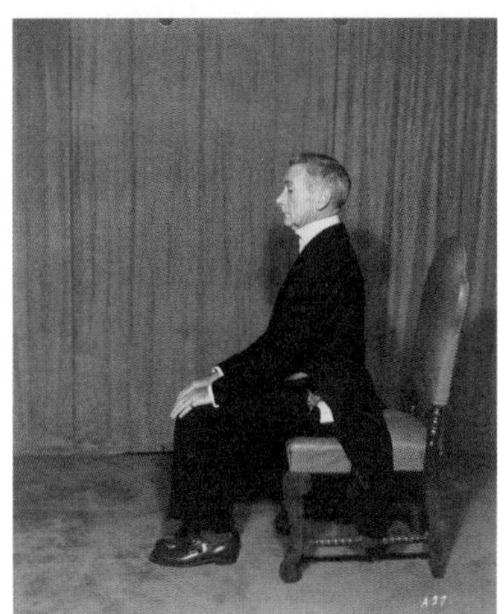
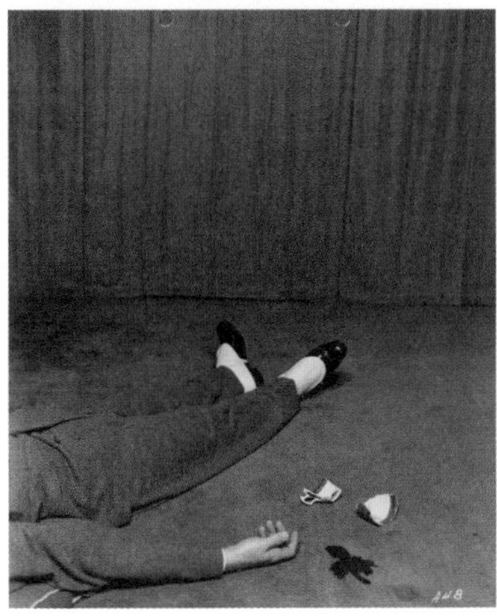
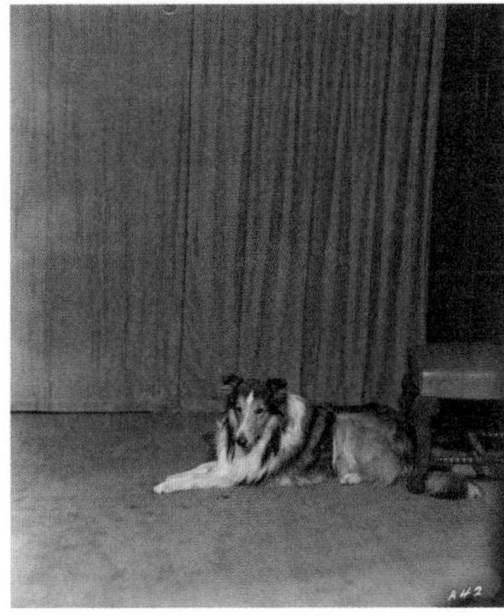

3.17a–h. Photographer unknown
Reference photographs for *Murder Mystery (Who-Dun-It)*, 1948
Gelatin silver prints, 10 × 8 in. (25.4 × 20.3 cm) each
*Top row*: Loretta Young (ST.1976.20032.91.18), Ethel Barrymore (ST.1976.20032.91.9), Richard Widmark (ST.1976.20032.91.21)
*Middle row*: Linda Darnell (ST.1976.20032.91.35), Boris Karloff (ST.1976.20032.91.28), Clifton Webb (ST.1976.20032.91.5)
*Bottom row*: Van Johnson (ST.1976.20032.91.16), Lassie the dog (ST.1976.20032.91.14)

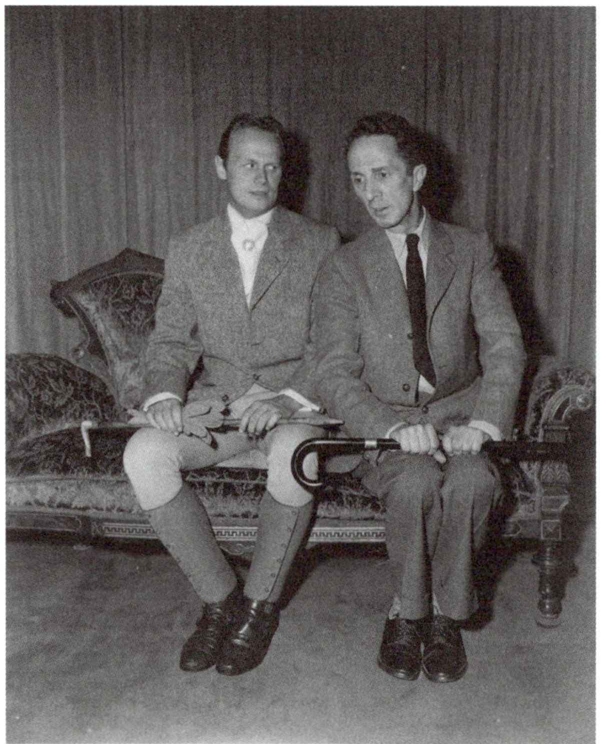

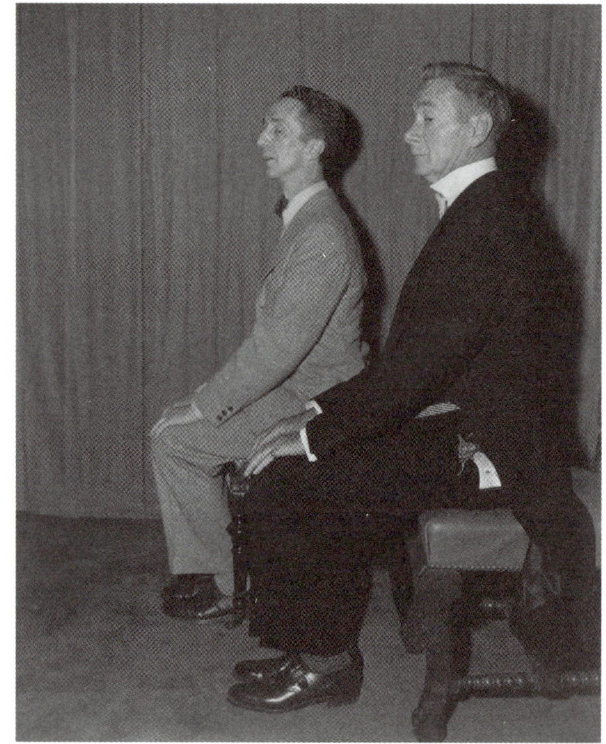

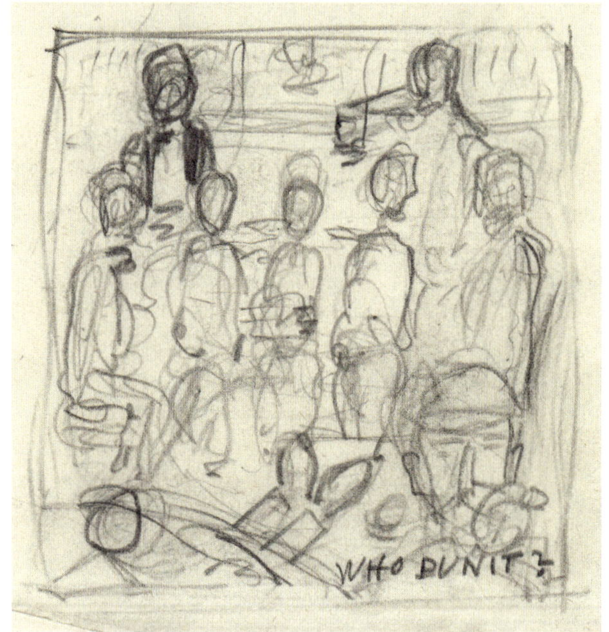


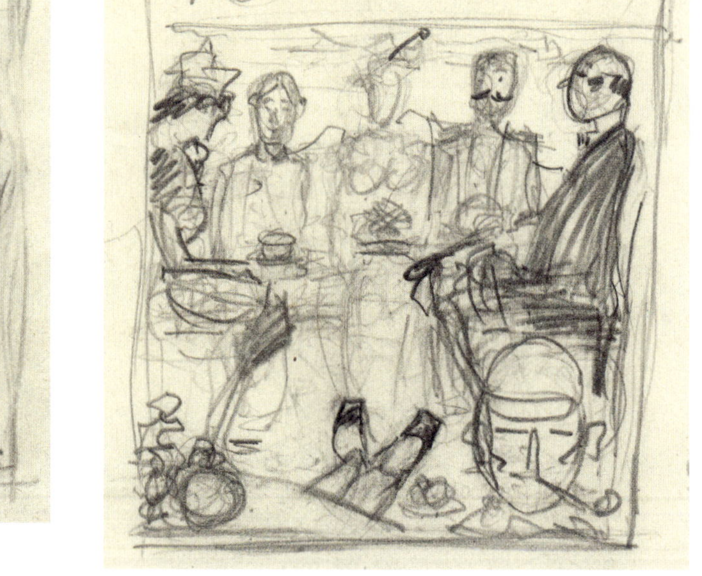


3.19a–b. Studies for *Murder Mystery (Who-Dun-It)*, 1948
Pencil on paper, 11 × 8½ in. (27.9 × 21.6 cm) total
NRACT.1976.68

He noted, "The clues to the solution would be present in the picture and *Post* readers would be asked to solve the crime."[11]

Rockwell hoped to heighten the interest of the murder mystery by using famous actors as his models (plates 3.17 and 3.18). An entire cast of stars posed for him on the Twentieth Century–Fox lot in Los Angeles, including Ethel Barrymore as the old lady, Boris Karloff as the sinister chef, Linda Darnell as the scandalous actress, Loretta Young as the demure maid, Richard Widmark as the wastrel holding the riding crop, Clifton Webb as the haughty butler, and Lassie as the dog. The victim's legs belong to Van Johnson.

Rockwell created several sketches for the work (plates 3.19 and 3.20), along with a color study (plate 3.21) and a final charcoal drawing (plate 3.22). Rockwell sent the charcoal drawing to the *Post*. The editors were honest in their dislike of Rockwell's proposed cover, telling him, "We don't think it's up to scratch. The movie stars kill it. The readers will be so busy recognizing the stars that the idea will be lost." After consideration, Rockwell agreed. He wrote in 1960, "I rolled the charcoal up and put it away in a drawer. It's still in a drawer."[12]

In its iterative nature, building up the final painting from sketches and studies, Rockwell's process was firmly rooted in the tradition of Western

OPPOSITE TOP
3.18a–b. Photographer unknown
Reference photographs for *Murder Mystery (Who-Dun-It)*, 1948
Gelatin silver prints, 10 × 8 in. (25.4 × 20.3 cm) and 5 × 4 in. (12.7 × 10.2 cm)
Rockwell showing the desired pose to Richard Widmark (ST.1976.20032.91.46),
Rockwell showing the desired pose to Clifton Webb (ST.1976.20032.91.45)

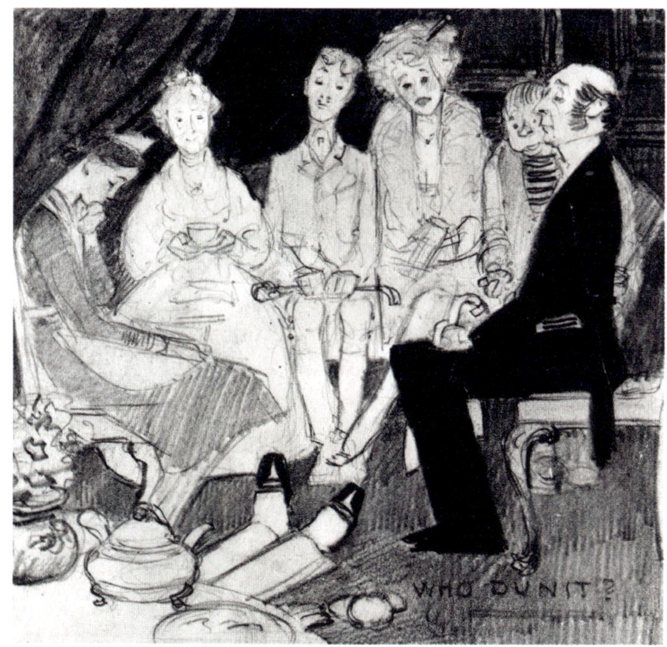


3.20. Study for *Murder Mystery (Who-Dun-It)*, 1948
Charcoal on paper
Private collection

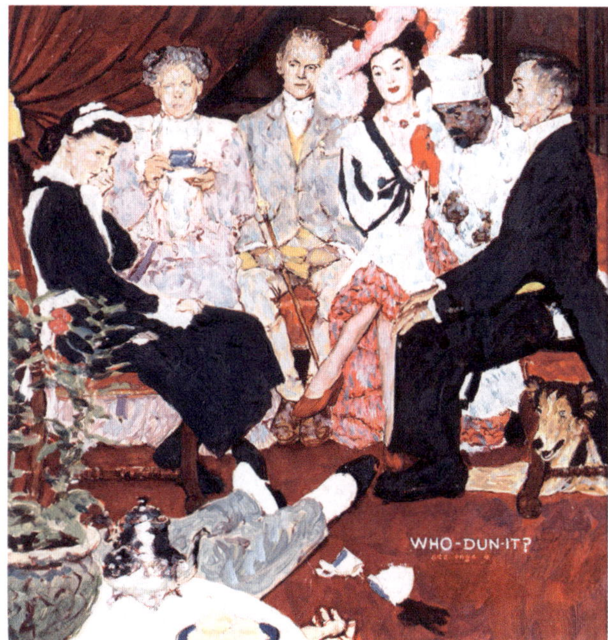


3.21. Color study for *Murder Mystery (Who-Dun-It)*, 1948
Oil on photograph on board,
11 × 10½ in. (27.9 × 26.7 cm)
NRM.1997.17

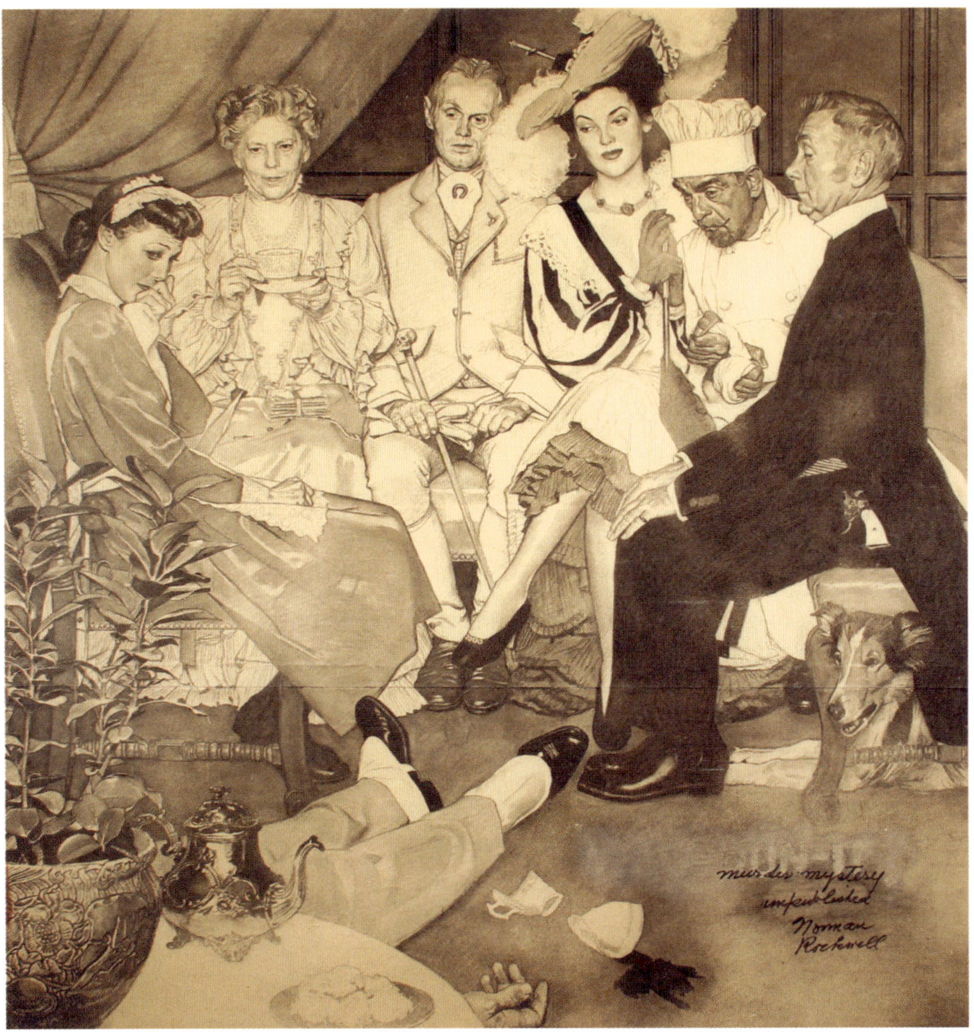


3.22. *Murder Mystery (Who-Dun-It)*, 1948
Charcoal and pencil on paper mounted on composition board, 44 × 41 in. (111.8 × 104.1 cm)
Private collection

art. Even his use of photography could be seen as a further evolution of that tradition, as the artist himself noted—emphasizing, somewhat defensively, that the camera was a *tool*, subordinate to the artist's creativity:

> Nowadays I use photographs for all my work. I still feel guilty about it. Whenever somebody comes into the studio I slip the photographs into a drawer. But I comfort myself with the thought that many of the great painters used aids to drawing: the camera obscura, the camera lucida, mirrors, et cetera. Holbein had a system for drawing on glass. Albrecht Dürer invented and presumably

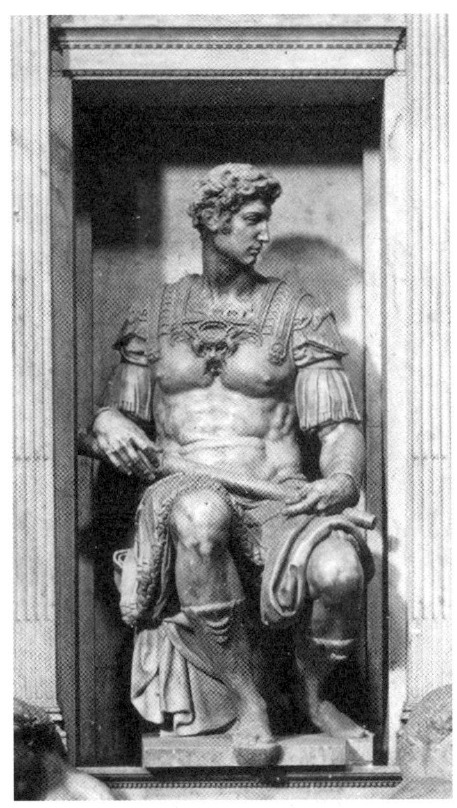

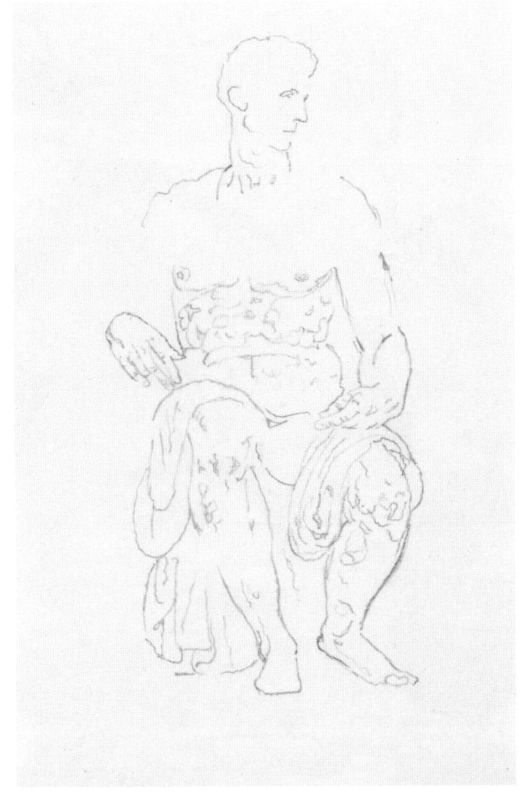

TOP LEFT
3.23. Michelangelo Buonarroti (1475–1564)
*Giuliano de' Medici*, 1526–34
Marble, height 66 in. (168 cm)
Medici Chapel, Basilica of
San Lorenzo, Florence

TOP RIGHT
3.24. *The Recruit*, 1959
Pencil on tracing paper,
11 × 8½ in. (27.9 × 21.6 cm)
Study for *The Recruit*, *Look*,
September 20, 1966
NRACT.1976.273

RIGHT
3.25. Louis Lamone (1918–2007)
Reference photograph for *The Recruit*, 1959
Photograph (from negative),
2¼ × 2¼ in. (5.7 × 5.7 cm)
ST1976.17528

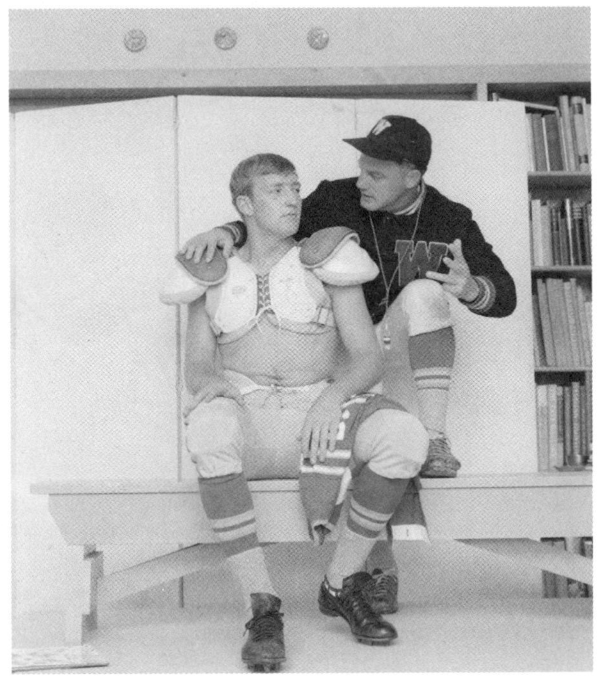

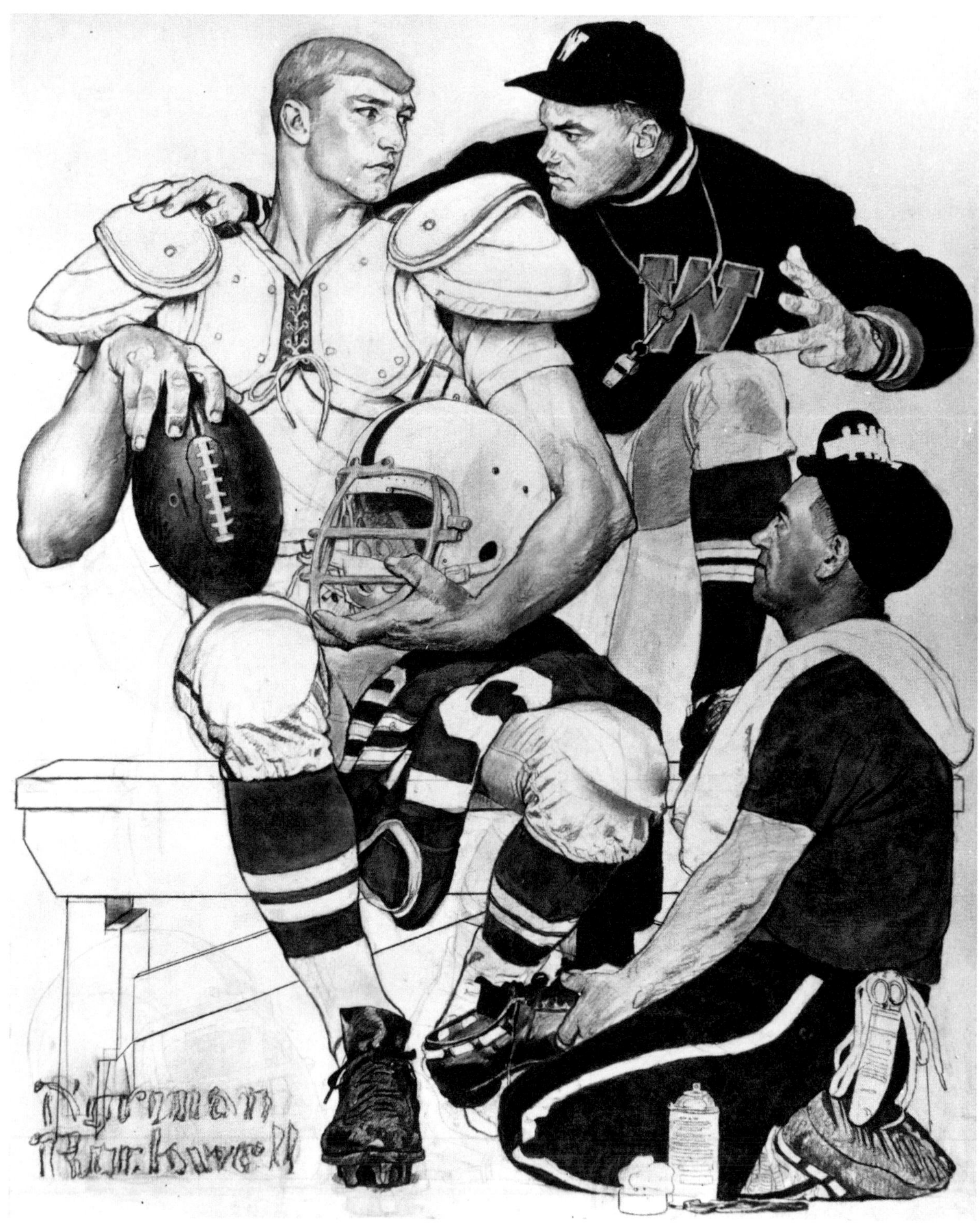


3.26. *The Recruit*, 1959
Charcoal on paper
Study for *The Recruit*, *Look*,
September 20, 1966
Whereabouts unknown

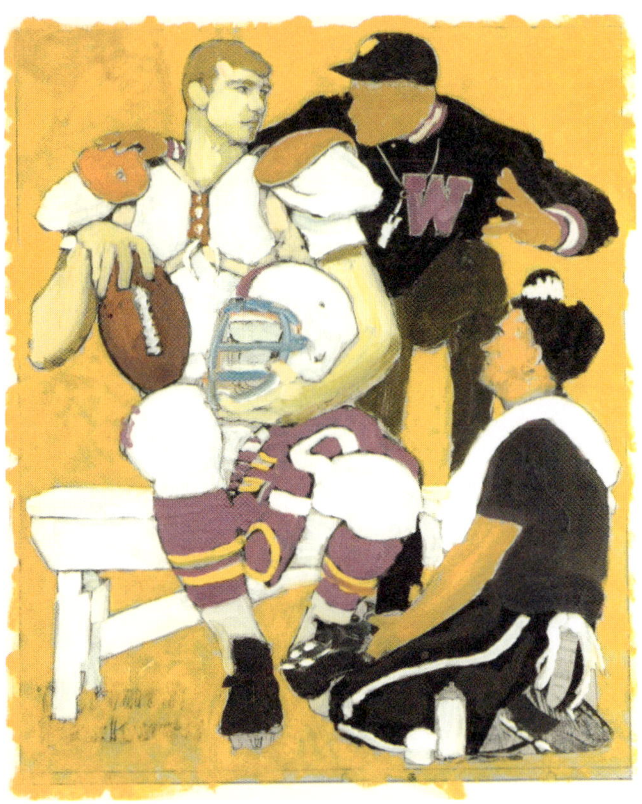

3.27. *The Recruit*, 1959
Oil on celluloid, 13 × 10½ in. (33 × 26.7 cm)
Study for *The Recruit*, *Look*, September 20, 1966
NRACT.1973.123

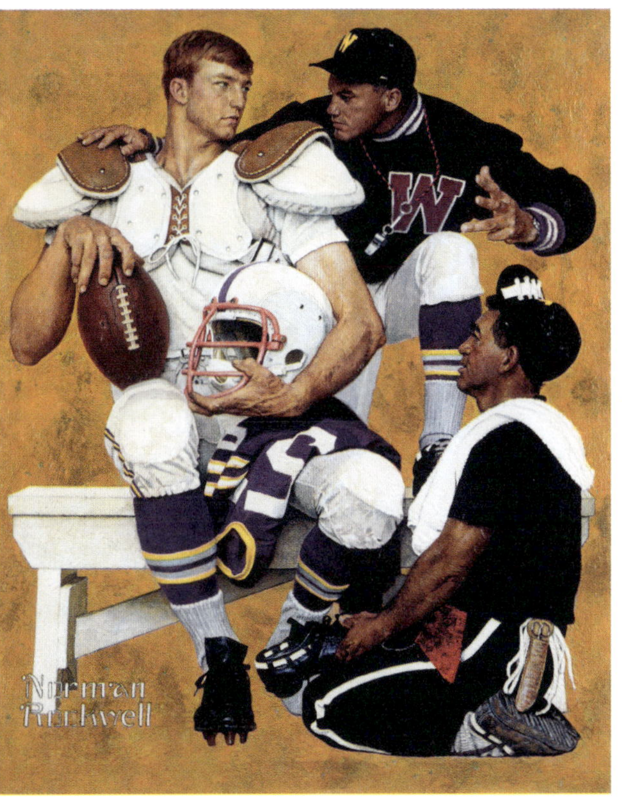


3.28. *The Recruit*, 1966
Oil on canvas, 34½ × 27½ in. (87.6 × 69.9 cm)
Illustration for Gerald Astor, "The Hunt for Strong Backs and Strong Minds," *Look*, September 20, 1966
NRACT.1973.128

> used a drawing aid. Toulouse-Lautrec and Degas worked from photographs sometimes. These men used the camera and the various other devices as *aids*, never slavishly. I think I do the same.[13]

Rockwell's deep ties to the old masters sometimes made themselves directly apparent, as in the case of *The Recruit*, which illustrated a 1966 story by *Look* sports editor Gerald Astor, about the intensifying competition among colleges to recruit student athletes (plate 3.28). To illustrate Astor's piece, Rockwell chose a football coach, trainer, and student from nearby Williams College to pose for his painting. Bridging four hundred years of art history, he based the football player on Michelangelo's sculpture of Giuliano de' Medici (plate 3.23), showing his model a photo of the sculpture to help him assume the pose (plate 3.25).

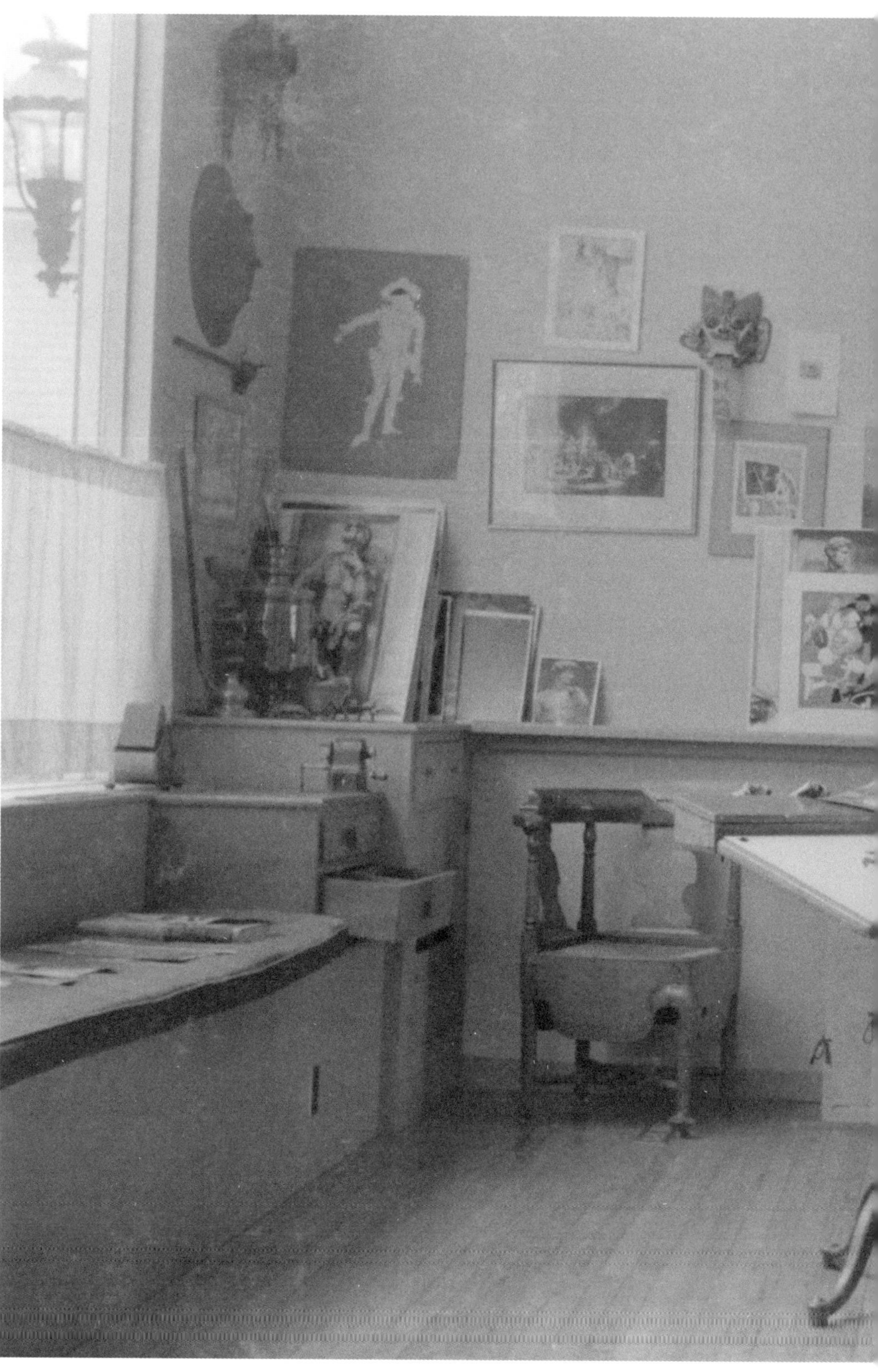

3.29. Louis Lamone (1918–2007)
Norman Rockwell painting *The Recruit*, 1959
Photograph (from negative), 1½ × 1 in. (3.8 × 2.5 cm)
ST1976.17526.c

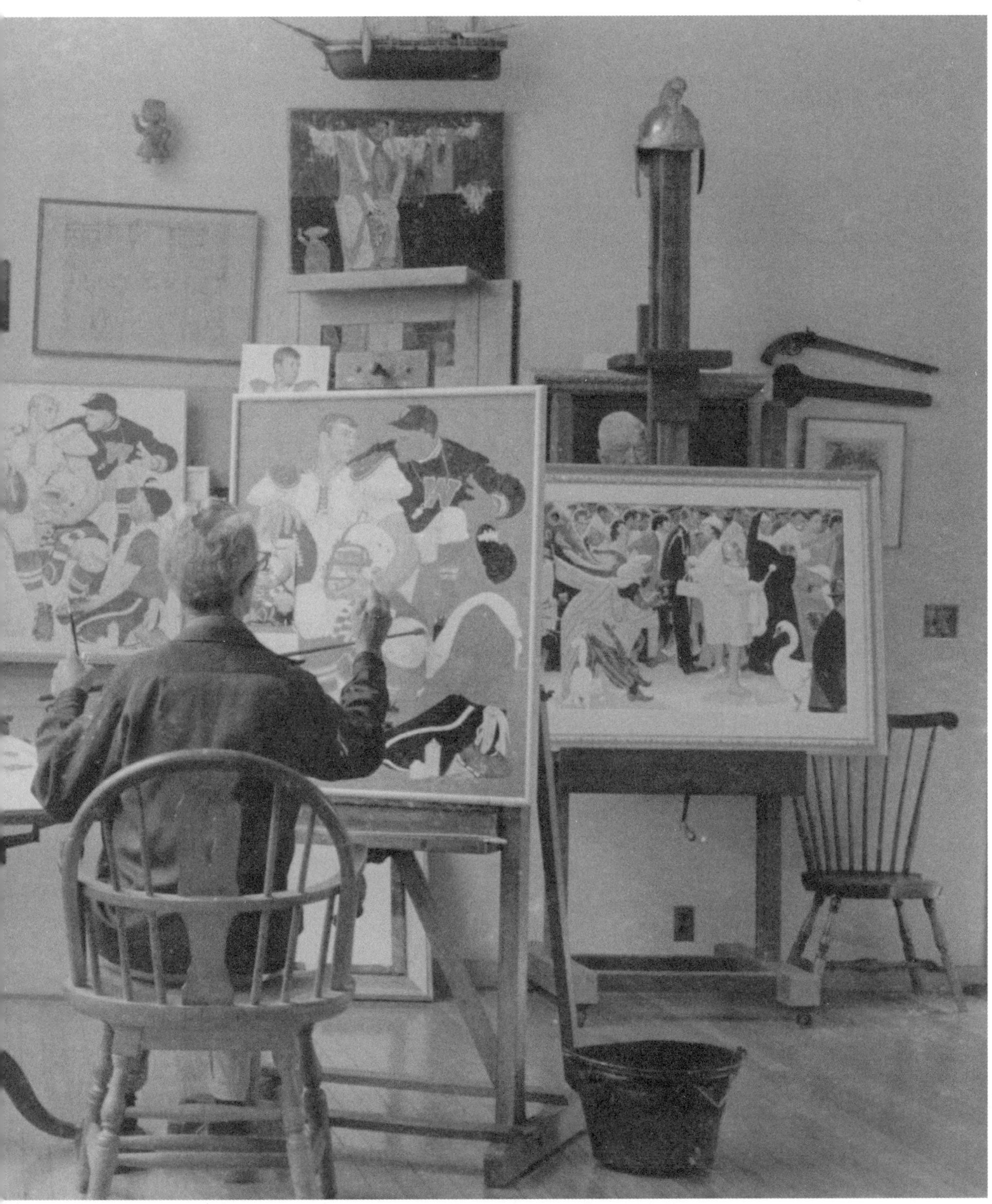

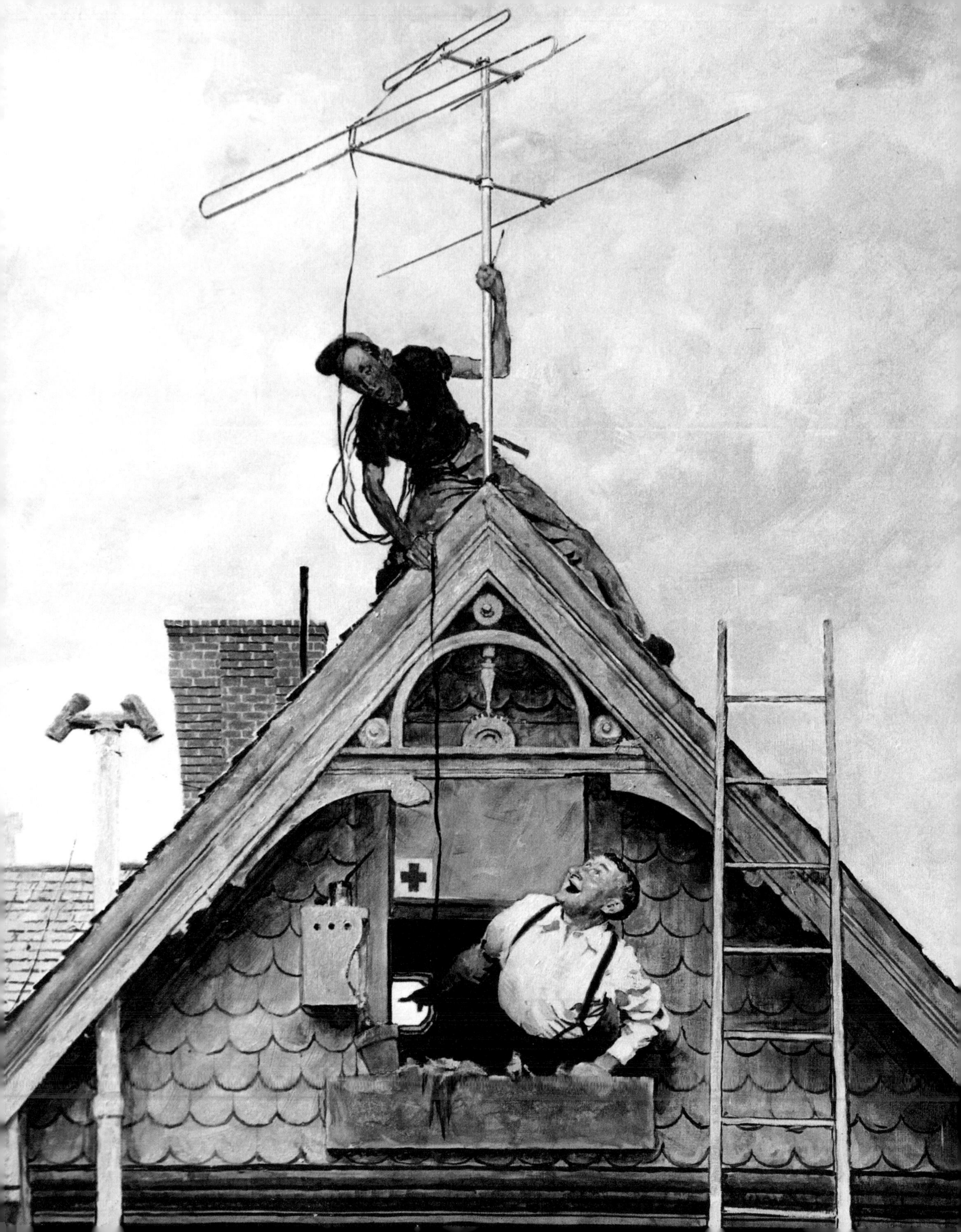

# 4 Imagining the Covers of the Post

JESSE KOWALSKI

Norman Rockwell was doing well for a young illustrator before he got his start at the *Saturday Evening Post*. His first cover illustration appeared on the September 1913 issue of *Boys' Life*, when he was just nineteen. In the next few years, Rockwell created numerous paintings and drawings that were published on the covers and interiors of periodicals such as *American Boy*, *Boys' Life*, *St. Nicholas*, and *Youth's Companion*. However, Rockwell declared, "I had a secret ambition: a cover on the *Saturday Evening Post*."[1]

Detail of study for *New Television Antenna*, 1949
See plate 4.24.

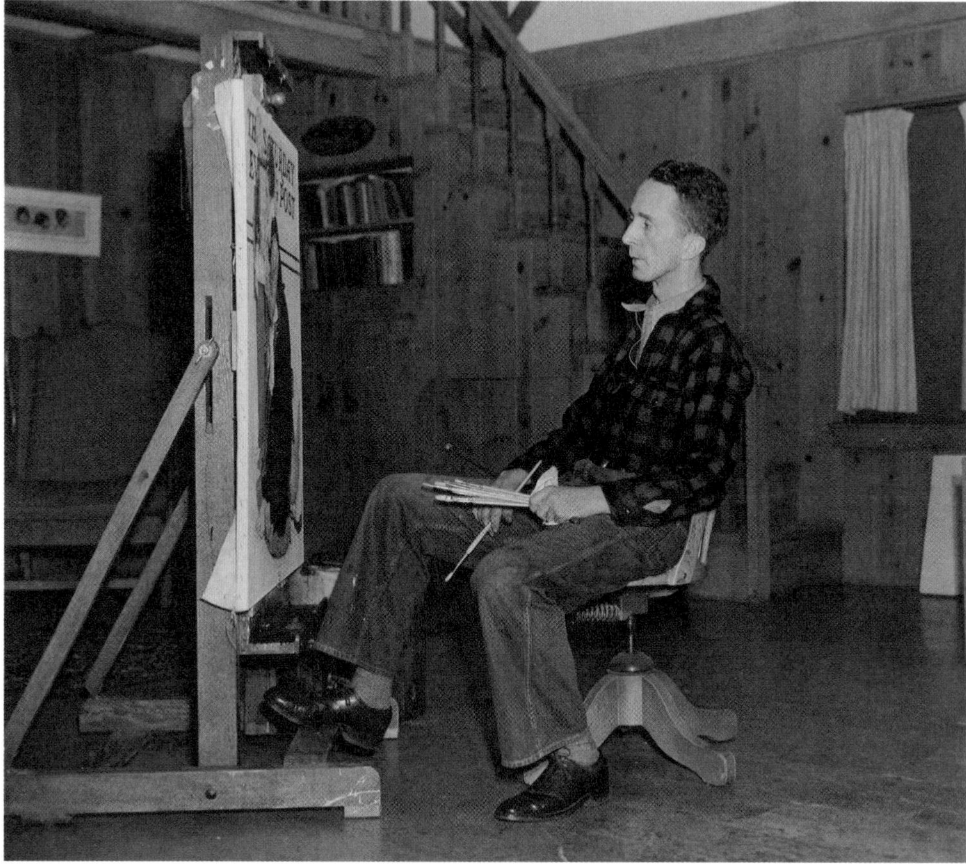

4.1. Culver Pictures, Inc.
Norman Rockwell in his Arlington, Vermont, studio painting *Summer Stock (Actress Putting on Make Up)* for the *Saturday Evening Post*, August 5, 1939 cover
Photograph (from negative), 8½ × 5½ (3.3 × 2.2 cm)
RC.2008.5

Rockwell's friend, cartoonist Clyde Forsythe (1885–1962), knew of this ambition, and encouraged him to submit his artwork to the *Post*. In March 1916, without scheduling an appointment, Rockwell entered the offices of Curtis Publishing in Philadelphia with a case packed with two finished paintings and three rough sketches for covers. He hoped to meet with editor George Lorimer, who had run the *Post* since 1899. The art editor, Walter Dower, took the artwork into Mr. Lorimer's office while Rockwell nervously sat in the waiting room. To his delight, Mr. Lorimer approved both paintings and the three sketches for covers. Rockwell was given a check for $150 (about $4,000 in today's money) for both cover paintings. Rockwell noted, "In those days the cover of the *Post* was the greatest show window in America for an illustrator. If you did a cover for the *Post* you had arrived. . . . Two million subscribers and then their wives, sons, daughters, aunts, uncles, friends. Wow! All looking at my cover."[2]

Dreaming up ideas for magazine covers and putting his idyllic visions to canvas for the world to see were Rockwell's true passions. Although he painted Boy Scout calendars for most of his life, in addition to countless advertisements and story illustrations, magazine covers gave Rockwell the freedom to create images that have come to symbolize American life in the early to mid-twentieth century. Other commissions often came with strict guidelines on the subject and composition, but at the *Saturday Evening Post*, with a few exceptions, Rockwell's creativity was largely unbound. In 1960, he noted, "The *Post* cover is my best and only opportunity to express myself fully. And [*Post* editor] Ken [Stuart] lets me do it. . . . He has created the atmosphere in which I can do my best work."[3]

Rockwell holds the record for the most *Post* covers—a total of 323—besting his idol, J. C. Leyendecker, who painted 322. Whether by a strange coincidence or out of respect for Leyendecker, Rockwell stopped at 321 paintings, though the *Post* reran previously published covers on two occasions. The public responded eagerly to Rockwell's mythologized view of American life, and the number of weekly *Post* readers grew from two million in 1916 to over six million by 1963, when he retired from the magazine.

## Early Career: 1916–29

Many of Rockwell's *Post* covers from the 1910s and 1920s feature children at play or other aspects of a lighthearted American family life. In depicting the ideal family, Rockwell often inserted his own wives and children into his paintings.

Until 1935, when he started using photographs of models and props as a way to simplify his creative process, Rockwell drew and painted from live models in his studio. Unfortunately for Rockwell, models wanted to look their best for their star turn on the cover of the *Saturday Evening Post*. Rockwell bemoaned,

> Women I've asked to pose because of the way they looked in a house dress without make-up will appear at the studio dressed to the teeth, rouged, manicured, and mascaraed. Once, on a bench in Central Park, I discovered a bum with a wonderful scraggly white beard down to his chest, smudged stained tattered patched clothes, and a hat of vast experience. I gave him ten dollars and told him to report to my studio the next day. He turned up all slicked out in a clean, well-tailored, new-secondhand suit—his beard shaved off, his hair plastered down with a sweet tonic.[4]

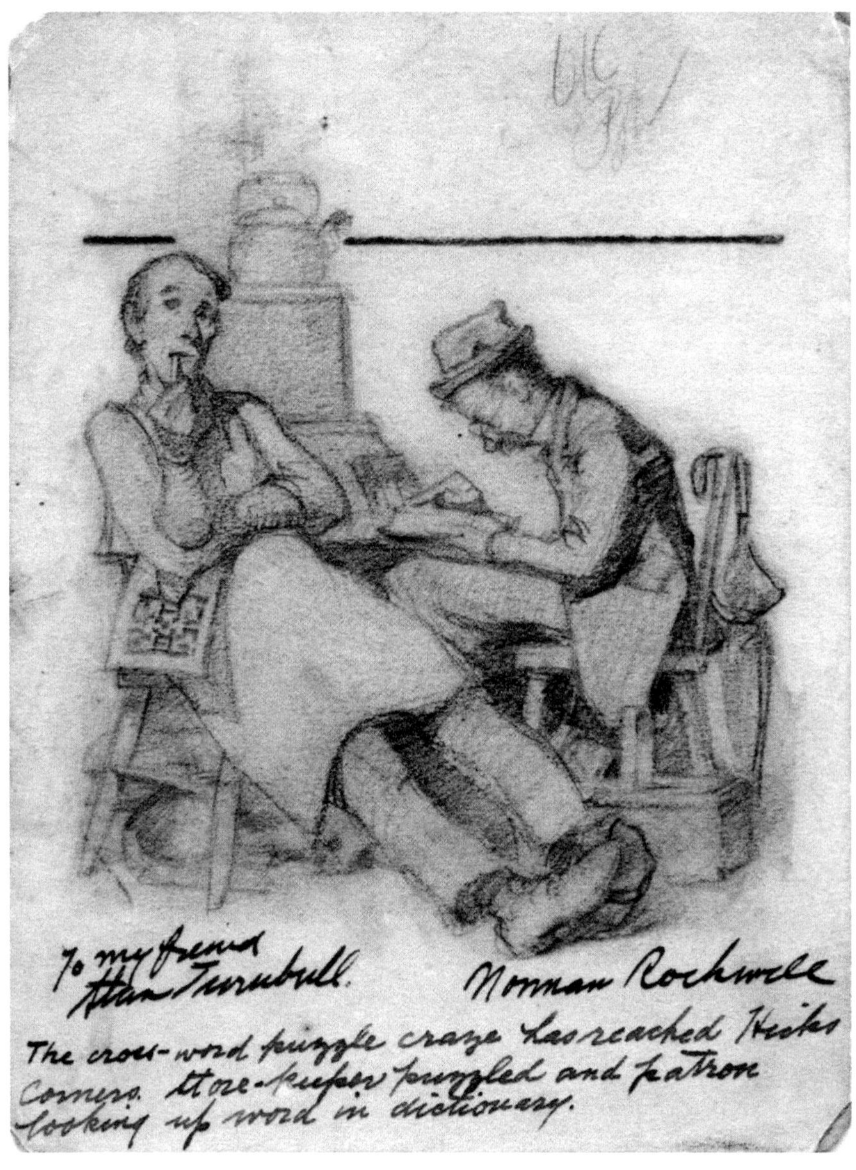


4.2. *The Crossword Puzzle*, 1925
Graphite on paper,
6 × 4 in. (15.2 × 10.2 cm)
Cover study for the *Saturday Evening Post*, January 31, 1925
Private collection

Rockwell often relied on familiar faces—friends and family members—to pose for him. However, in 1924, a stranger named James K. Van Brunt offered to model. At a scant five feet two inches tall and with exaggerated facial features, Van Brunt seemed to be a perfect model for Rockwell. Regarding his greatest asset, Van Brunt informed Rockwell, "This mustache, sir, is eight full inches wide from tip to tip. The ladies, sir, make much of it." Rockwell had to admit, "That certainly is the finest mustache I've ever seen." As he drew Van Brunt for the first time, Rockwell exclaimed to himself, "What a face!"[5] Van Brunt appeared in numerous *Post* covers in the 1920s, including *The Crossword Puzzle*, in which he is the figure at right.

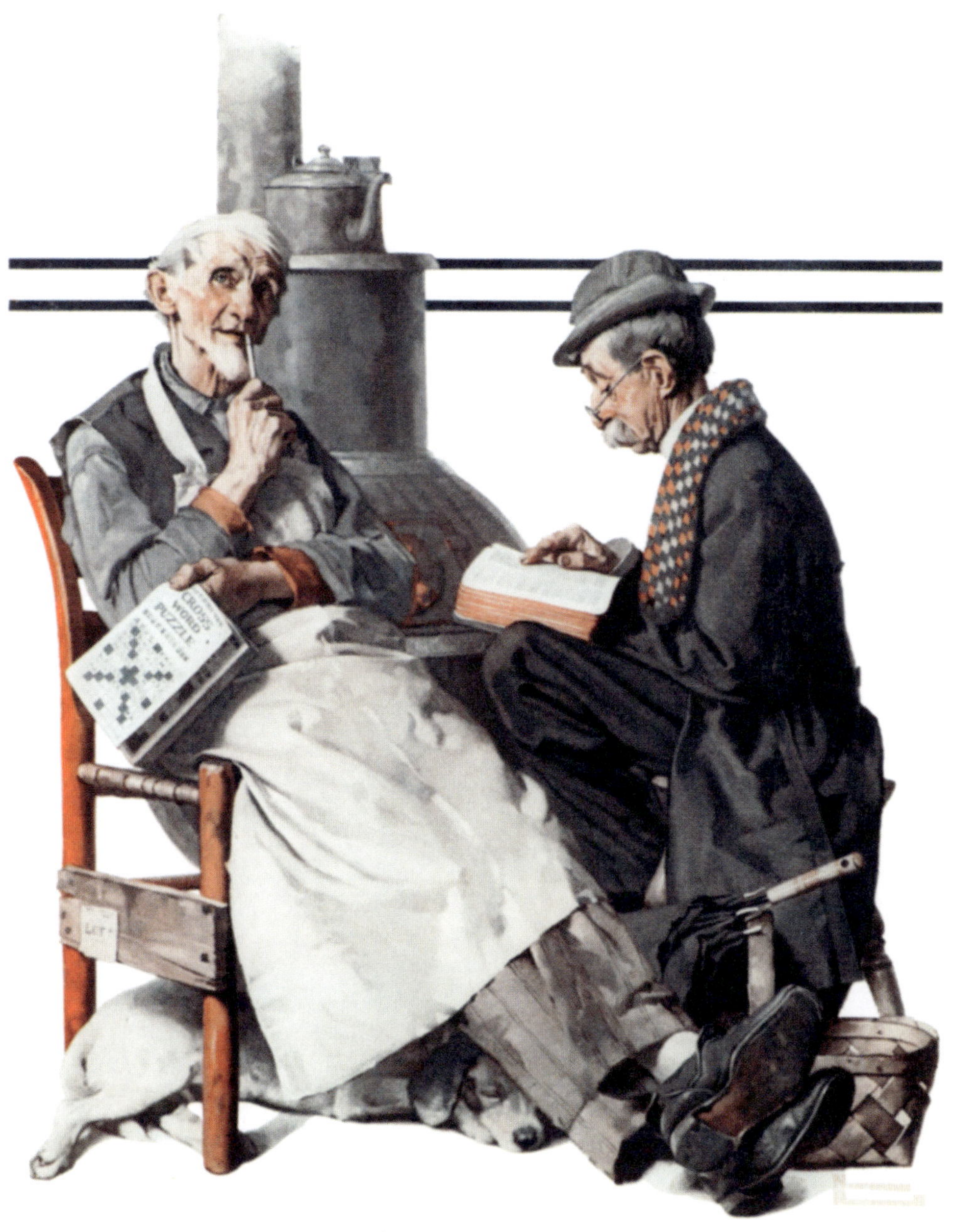


4.3. *The Crossword Puzzle*, 1925
Tear sheet, 14¼ × 11¼ in. (36.2 × 28.6 cm)
Cover illustration for the *Saturday Evening Post*, January 31, 1925
RC.2007.1.72 (Gift of John A. and Laura C. Savio)

Many of Rockwell's depictions of Christmas are inspired by the work of Charles Dickens, particularly *A Christmas Carol*. As he wrote in his autobiography, "On weekday evenings, after Jarvis [Rockwell's brother] and I had finished our homework, we would sit around the dining room table and my father would read Dickens out loud to us. . . . I was very deeply impressed and moved by Dickens."[6] Dickens's influence is clearly evident in this cover from 1921. Rockwell first sketched the holiday reveler from a live model. He then created a small color study, using pencil and red watercolor to mimic the magazine's two-color printing. The color study guided his treatment of the highlights and tones in the final painting.

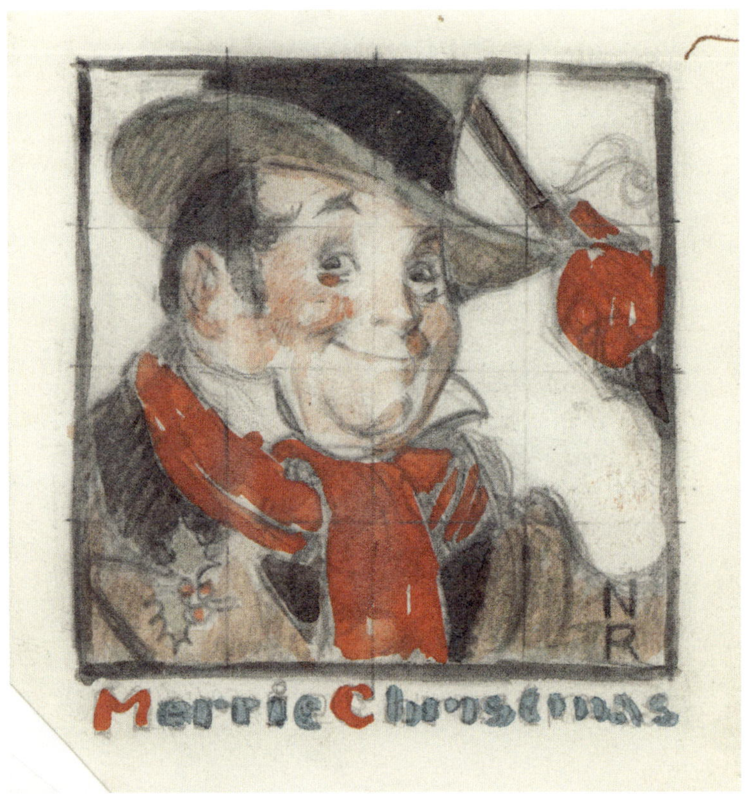


4.4. *Merrie Christmas (Jolly Man in Top Hat)*, 1921
Pencil and watercolor on paper,
3¾ × 3½ in. (9.2 × 8.6 cm)
Cover study for the *Saturday Evening Post*, December 3, 1921
NRM.1982.05

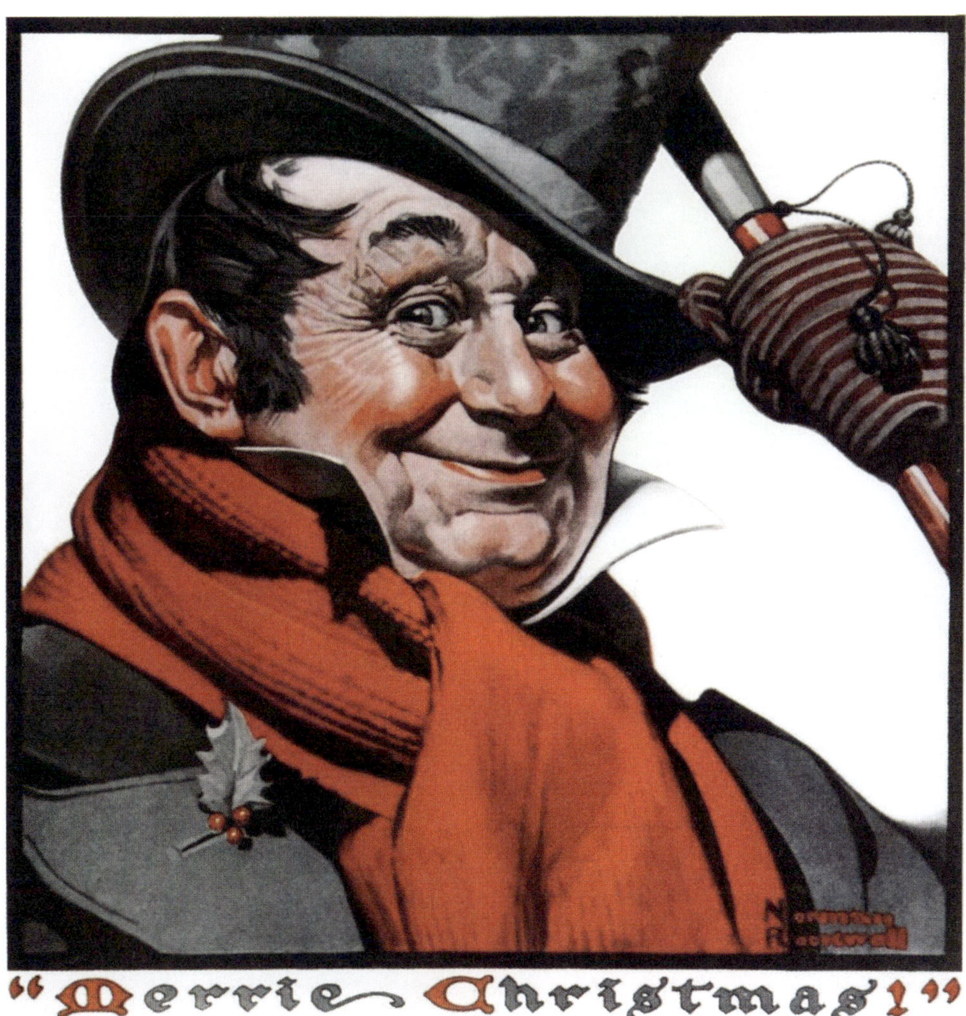


4.5. *Merrie Christmas (Jolly Man in Top Hat)* (detail), 1921
Tear sheet, 14¼ × 11¼ in. (36.2 × 28.6 cm)
Cover illustration for the *Saturday Evening Post*, December 3, 1921
RC.2007.1.42 (Gift of John A. and Laura C. Savio)

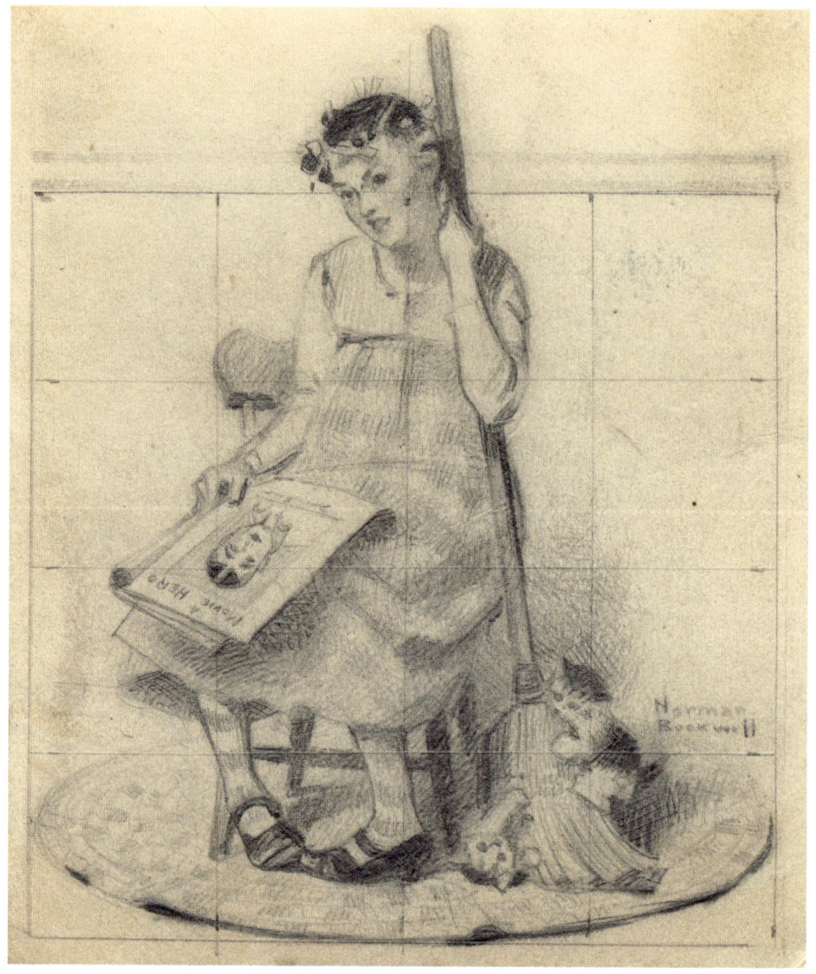


4.6. *Maid with Movie Magazine*, 1922
Pencil on paper, 5 × 4 in.
(12.7 × 10.5 cm)
Cover study for the *Saturday Evening Post*, November 4, 1922
NRM.1982.04

During the prosperous 1920s, the movie industry rapidly expanded, and magazines devoted to celebrities became popular. In the drawing, the man pictured in the magazine appears quite young, but the name seems to read "Douglas Fairbanks," who would have been thirty-nine in 1922. However, the final painting suggests that the screen idol who has caused the maid to swoon is another star, Rudolph Valentino.

The grid superimposed on the sketch was a common device for scaling up small drawings to a larger canvas, also employed by Leyendecker. Seeing the image on paper helped Rockwell decide what worked and what he should adjust when painting on canvas. The two major changes from the sketch to the painting are making the maid older and replacing her Mary Janes with slippers.

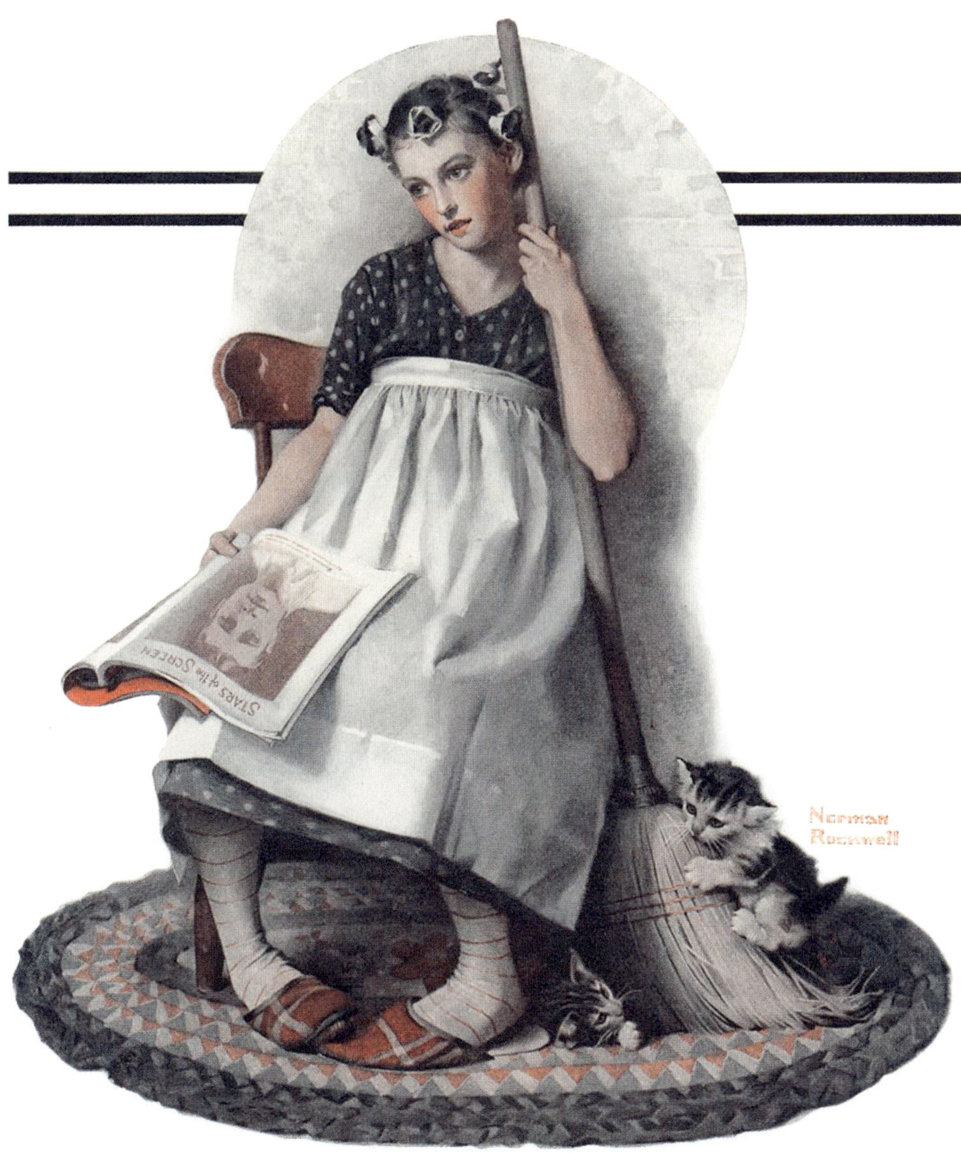


4.7. *Maid with Movie Magazine* (detail), 1922
Tear sheet, 14¼ × 11¼ in. (36.2 × 28.6 cm)
Cover illustration for the *Saturday Evening Post*, November 4, 1922
RC.2007.1.51 (Gift of John A. and Laura C. Savio)

When Rockwell began working for the *Saturday Evening Post* in 1916, they were printing their covers in duotone—black and one other color, which was usually red. When the *Post* changed to full color in 1926, Rockwell was given the honor of painting the cover. His *Pipe and Bowl Sign Painter* featured an artist painting a tavern sign dated 1785 with what appears to be a portrait of George Washington. Rockwell would later paint an actual tavern sign of Washington (plate 4.9) as a reference for his 1936 painting *The New Tavern Sign (Colonial Sign Painter)* (plate 5.2).

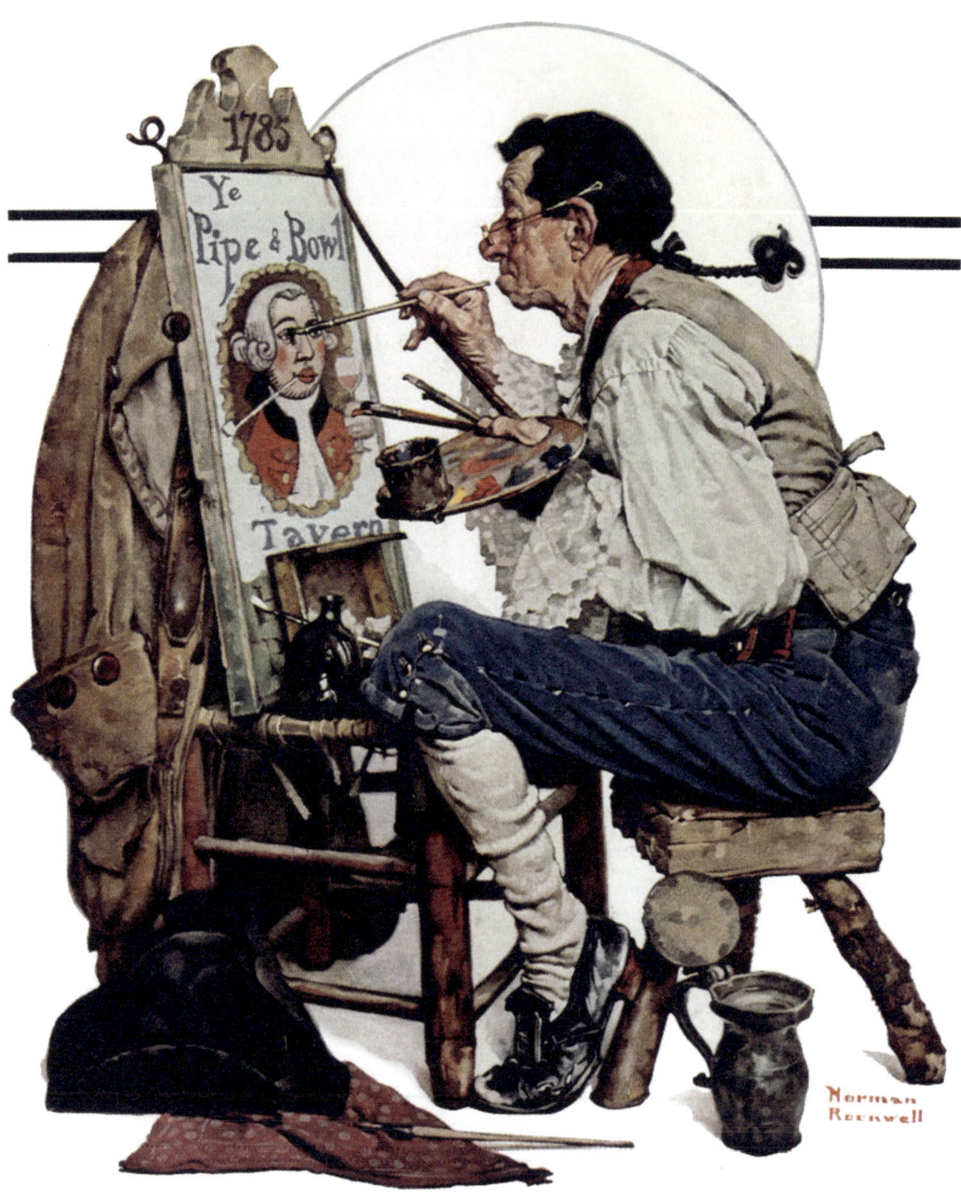

OPPOSITE
4.8. *Pipe and Bowl Sign Painter*, 1926
Tear sheet
Cover illustration for the *Saturday Evening Post*, February 6, 1926
RC.2007.1.82 (Gift of John A. and Laura C. Savio)

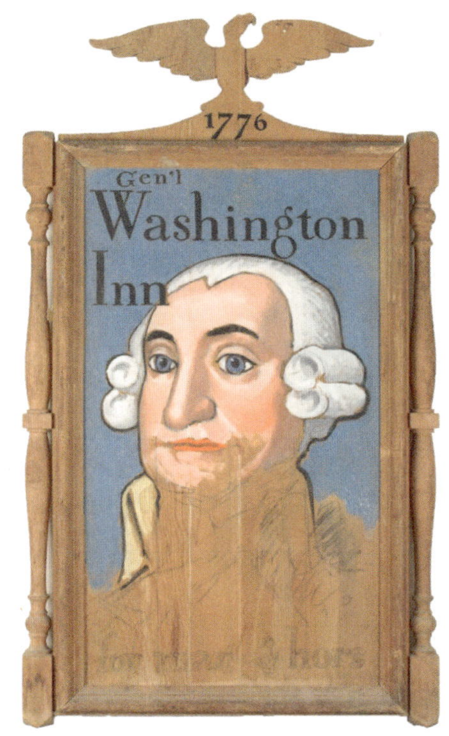


RIGHT
*New Tavern Sign (Washington)*, 1936
Tempera on board
35½ × 20 in. (90.2 × 50.8 cm.)
NRM.1988.09 (by purchase; Thomas Stapleton, Jr.)

## Mid-Career: 1930–49

In the 1930s, as the nation faced the challenges of the Great Depression, Rockwell underwent significant transitions in his own life, beginning with the divorce from his first wife, Irene, in 1930. Later that year, he married Mary Barstow, a schoolteacher. Their first son, Jarvis, was born in 1931, followed by Thomas in 1933 and Peter in 1936. In 1939, the family moved from their home in New Rochelle, New York, to Arlington, Vermont, where they would spend the next fourteen years.

Against this backdrop of change, the *Post* covers that Rockwell painted in the 1930s continued to convey overt messages of optimism, hope, and humor. However, the advent of the Second World War brought a different tone to Rockwell's covers, and led him to paint some of his most iconic works for the *Post*, including *Rosie the Riveter* and the Four Freedoms series, the latter of which bolstered U.S. support for World War II by raising $133 million for war bonds ($2 billion when adjusted for inflation). With the publication of J. C. Leyendecker's last *Post* cover in 1943, Rockwell became the magazine's indisputable master painter. By this time, the artist was in his prime, and his best work was yet to come.

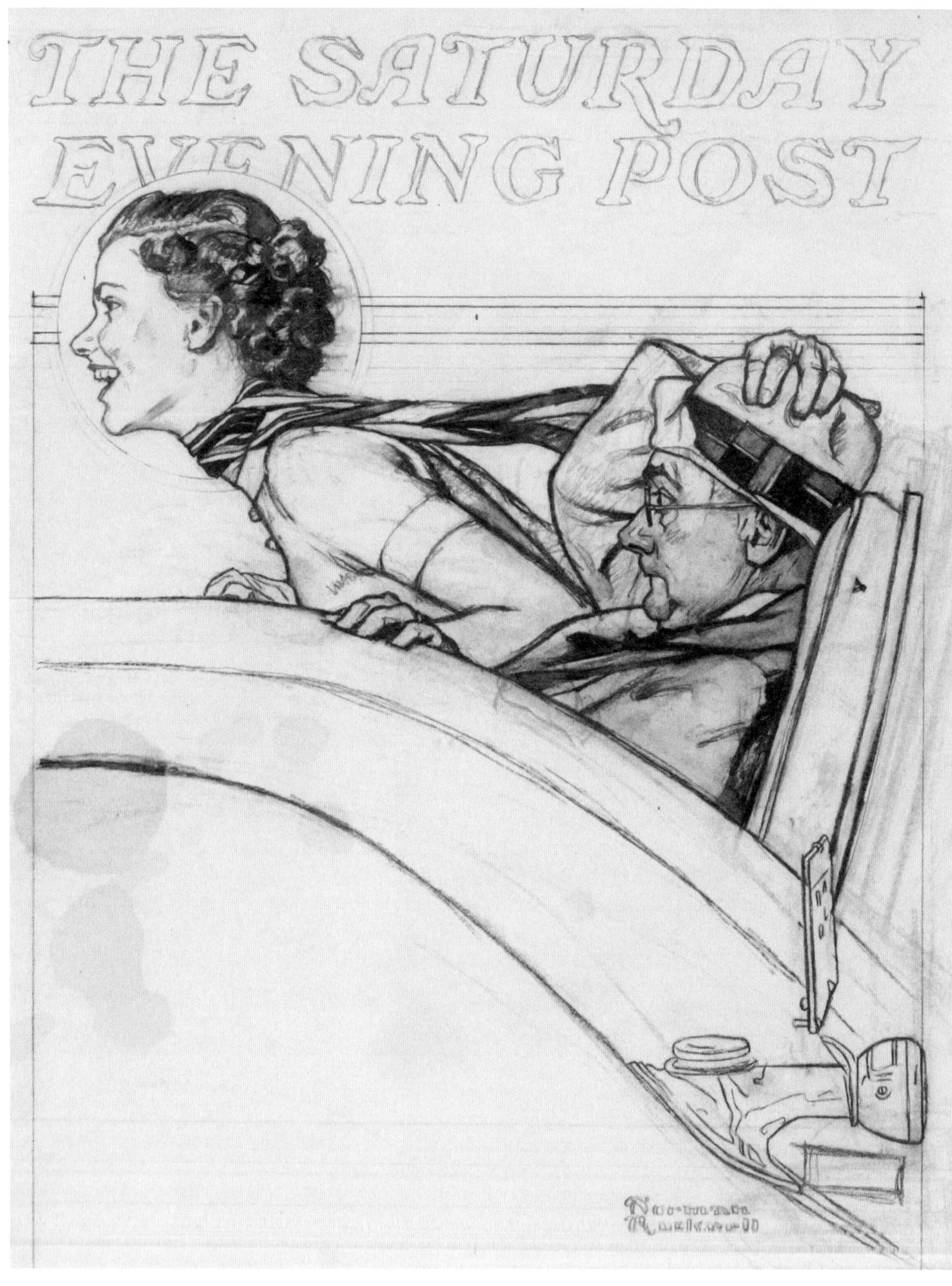
THE SATURDAY
EVENING POST

This cover from 1935 represents Rockwell's approach to depicting relations between the sexes, in which the viewer's expectations are sometimes humorously upended. By this time, Rockwell had developed his own distinct style. The pencil study for this work is characteristic of those he would execute for the rest of his career. The work is exquisitely drafted, from the tight curls in the woman's hair to the fine lines on the taillight—this attention to detail in his studies would aid Rockwell in creating the masterpieces to come. The drawing also features the thick lines of the *Post* masthead that Rockwell incorporated in many works. It does not, however, include the dog that improves the composition of the final painting. Rockwell loved dogs and frequently depicted them in his work.

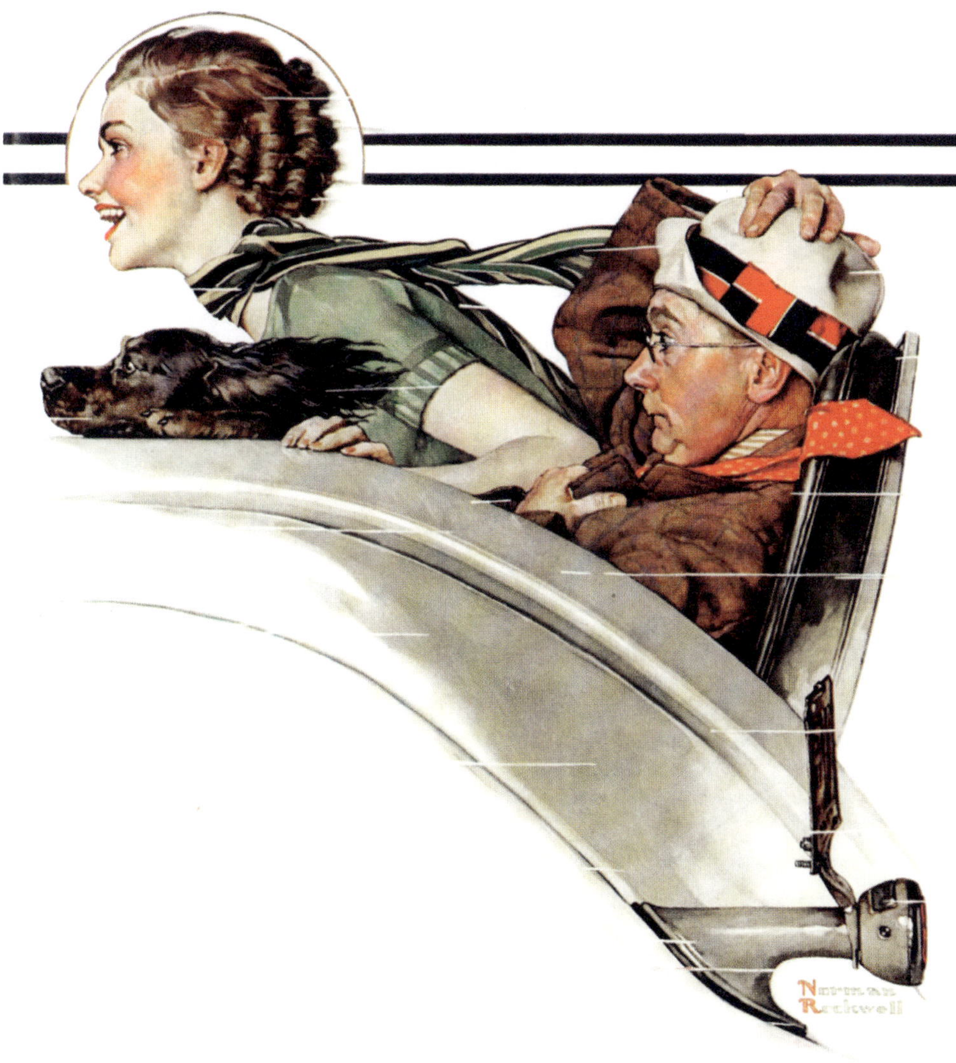


OPPOSITE
4.10. *Couple in Rumble Seat*, 1935
Pencil on paper, 23¼ × 17½ in. (59.1 × 44.4 cm)
Cover study for the *Saturday Evening Post*, July 13, 1935
Private collection

LEFT
4.11. *Couple in Rumble Seat* (detail), 1935
Tear sheet, 14¼ × 11¼ in. (36.2 × 28.6 cm)
Cover illustration for the *Saturday Evening Post*, July 13, 1935
RC.2007.1.156 (Gift of John A. and Laura C. Savio)

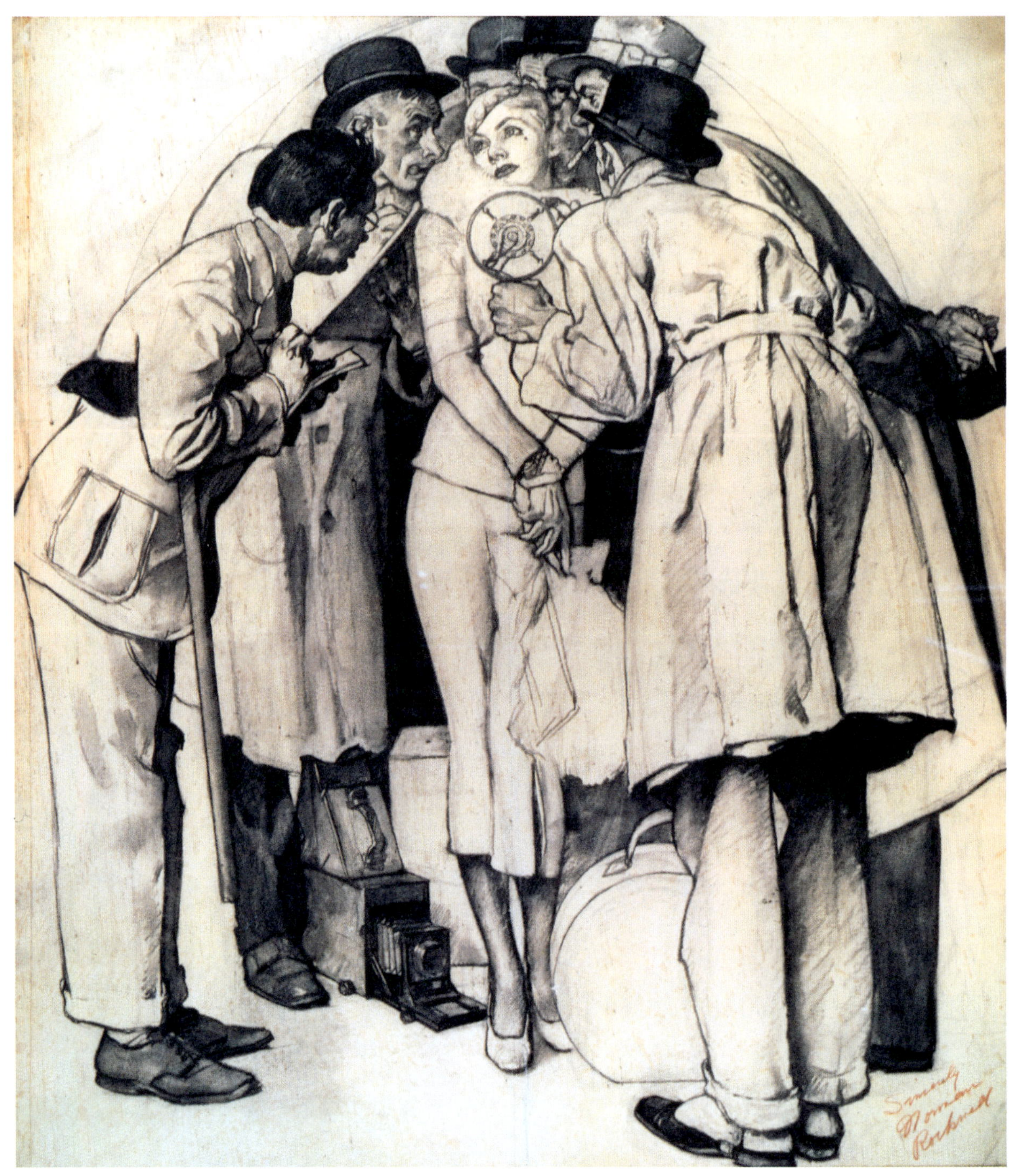

4.12. *Movie Starlet and Reporters*, 1936
Cover study for the *Saturday Evening Post*, March 7, 1936
Private collection

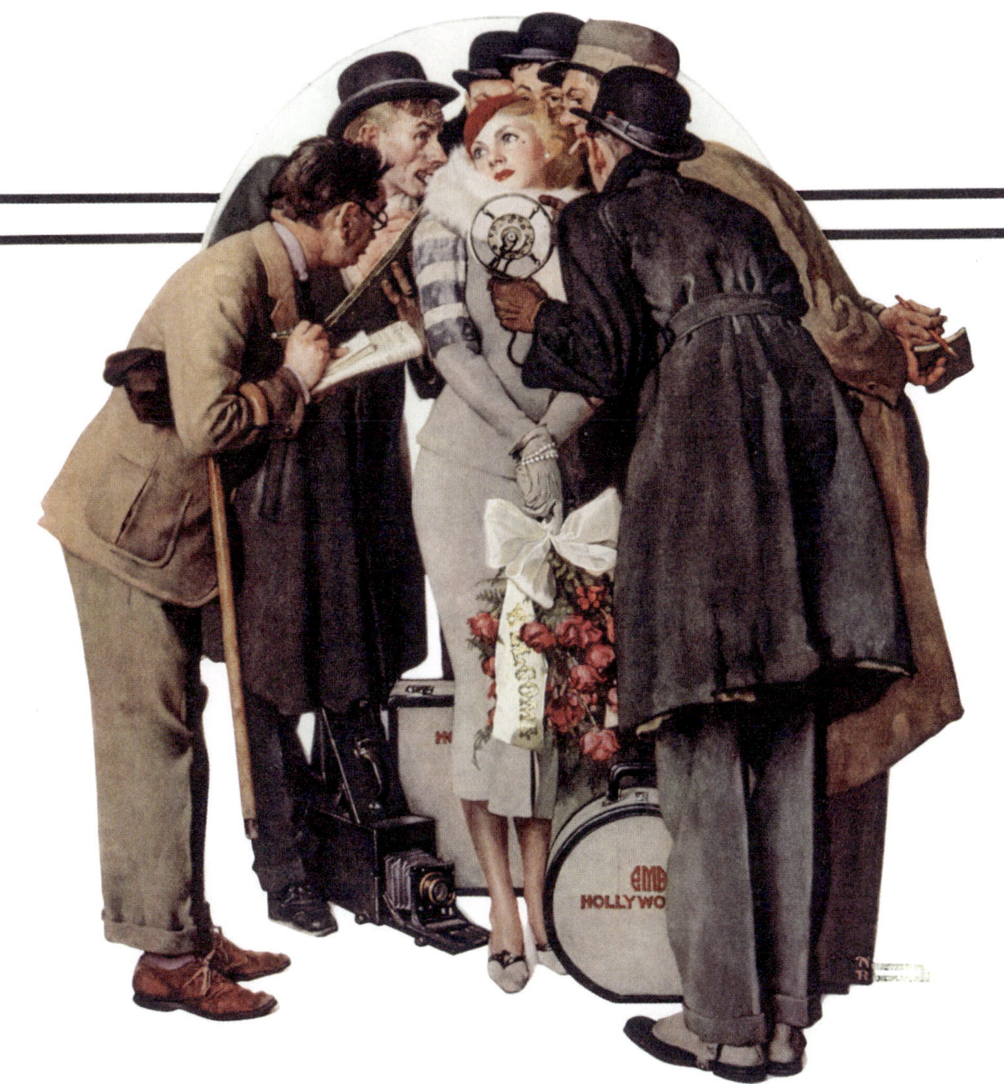


4.13. *Movie Starlet and Reporters* (detail), 1936
Tear sheet, 14¼ × 11¼ in. (36.2 × 28.6 cm)
Cover illustration for the *Saturday Evening Post*, March 7, 1936
RC.2007.1.161
(Gift of John A. and Laura C. Savio)

Despite his homespun image, Rockwell was fascinated by celebrity and welcomed many movie stars and pop culture icons into his studio, including Frank Sinatra, John Wayne (in full cowboy attire), and Kentucky Fried Chicken founder Colonel Sanders. Rockwell's *Movie Starlet and Reporters* reflects his interest in pop culture, although he does not depict a specific actress. The final cover is nearly an exact replica of his detailed drawing, with the exception of the flowers held by the starlet. Both versions feature an unusual circular outline in the back, which Rockwell must have anticipated would prevent the masthead from intruding on his work.

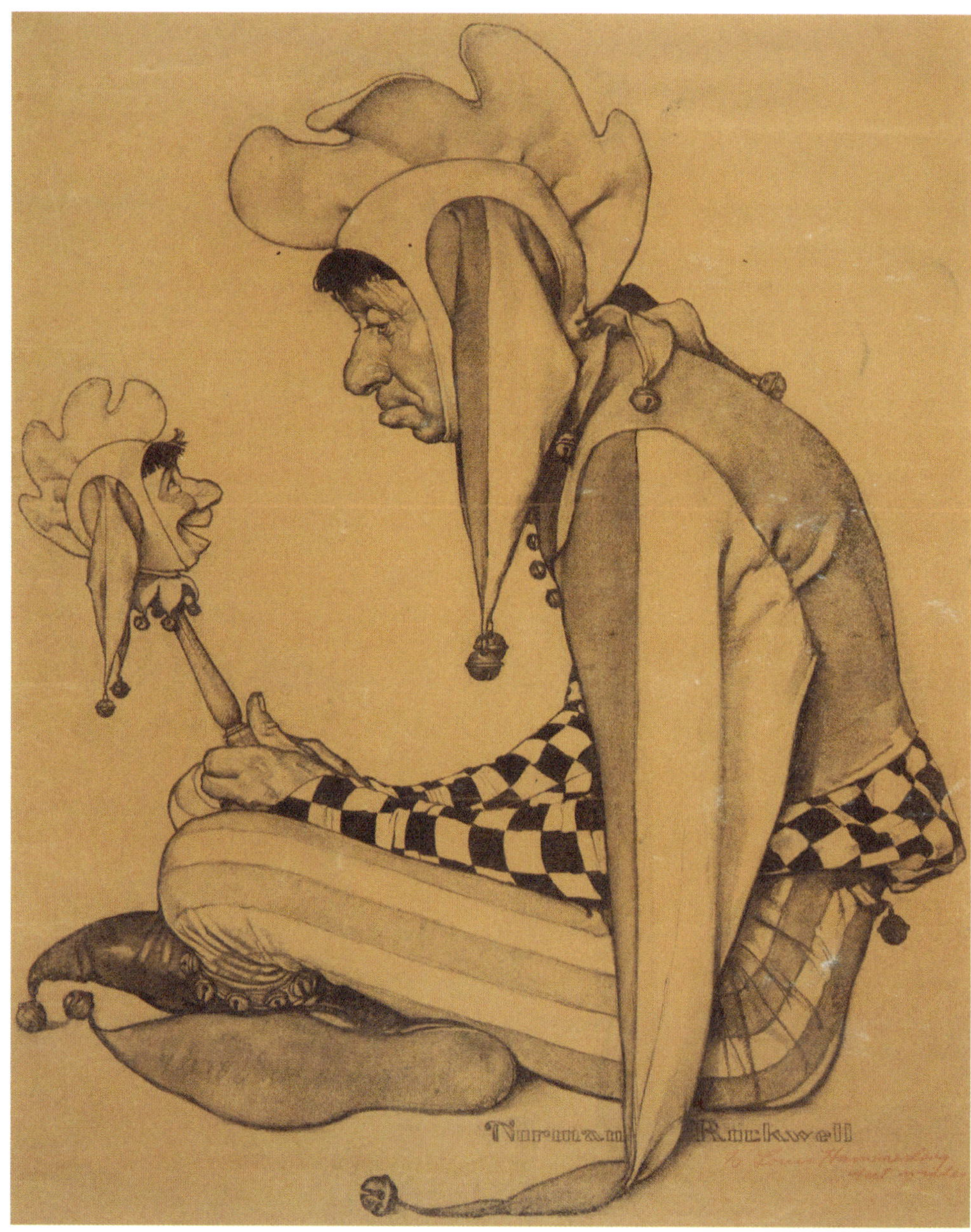


4.14. *Jester*, 1938
Charcoal on paper,
36 × 30 in. (91.4 × 76.2 cm)
Cover illustration for
the *Saturday Evening Post*, February 11, 1939
Private collection

The glum-looking jester is a departure from Rockwell's lighthearted covers. During the 1930s, Rockwell began to turn away from the "country bumpkins and barefoot boys of his early paintings"[7] to more sophisticated subjects. Rockwell drew the *Jester* study on a heavy brown paper, as he did on occasion—perhaps he wanted to see how gold paint would look on the final painting. Although the editors at the *Post* described *Jester* as "perfect," its

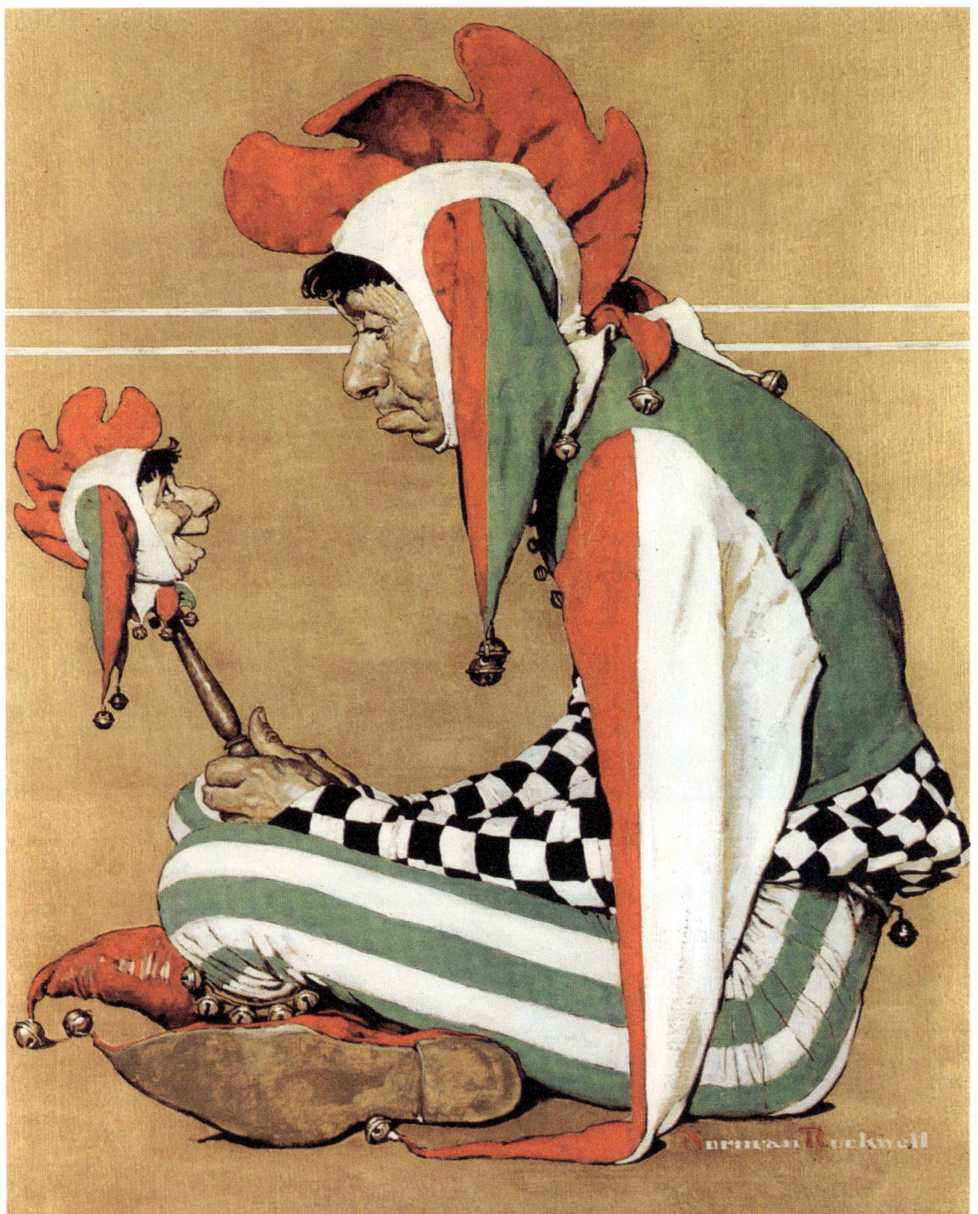


4.15. *Jester*, 1938
Oil on canvas, 31 × 25 in.
(78.7 × 63.5 cm)
Cover illustration for the *Saturday Evening Post*, February 11, 1939
Private collection

publication was delayed by its layer of gold paint. In November 1938, the magazine's printers and engravers held a meeting to discuss the image and figure out a way to print it. The *Post* did not have the technical capability of printing gold ink over or under other colors, so as a result, the editors sent the painting back to Rockwell to have him paint in areas where the gold was too clearly visible under the figure.

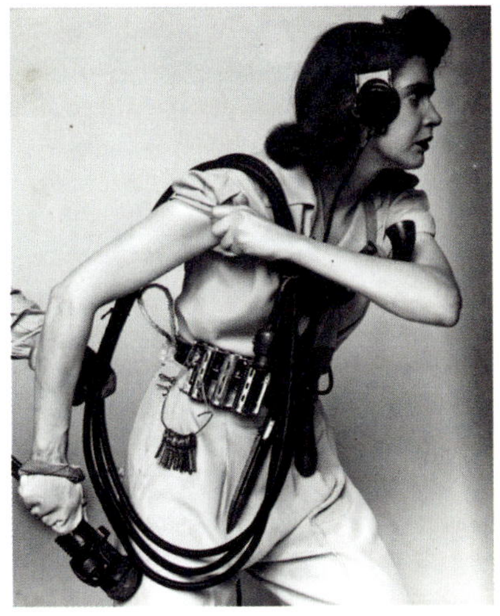

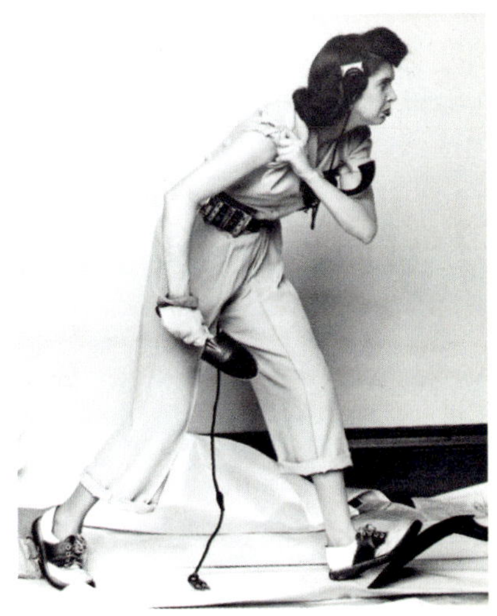

4.16a–b. Reference photos for *Liberty Girl*, 1943
Photographs (from negative)
ST.1976.20032.39.38;
ST.1976.20032.39.39

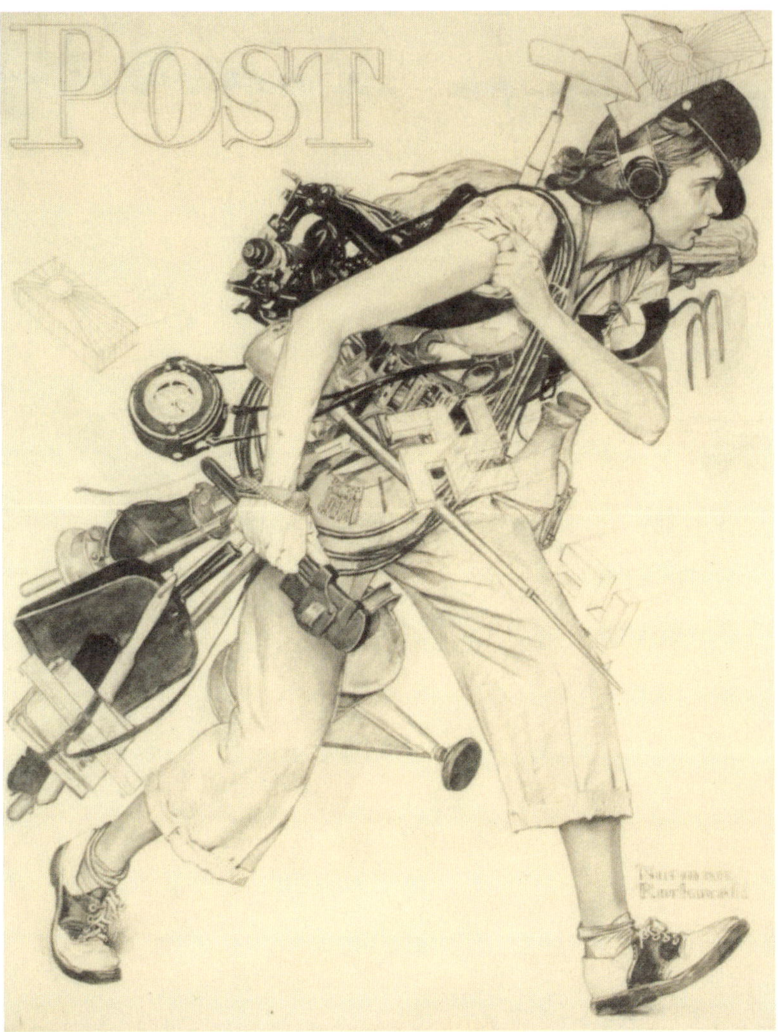


4.17. *Liberty Girl*, 1943
Charcoal on paper, 41 × 31 in. (104.1 × 78.7 cm)
Cover study for the *Saturday Evening Post*, September 4, 1943
NRM.1978.09 (Collection by purchase, Shutters Family)

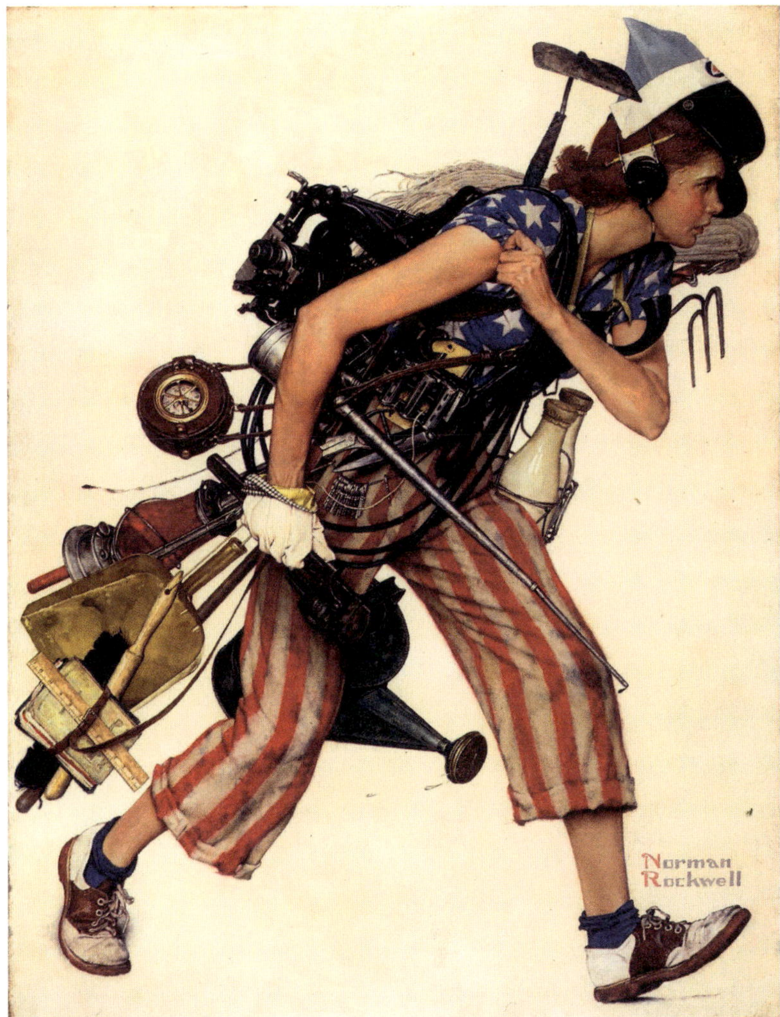


4.18. *Liberty Girl*, 1943
Oil on canvas
Cover illustration for the *Saturday Evening Post*, September 4, 1943
Location unknown

This cover was prompted by the Magazine Bureau of the Office of War Information, which asked magazine editors to promote the subject "Women at Work" in their Labor Day issues. Rockwell hired a professional model from New York to come to his Vermont studio to pose for this cover, which symbolized all the new roles that American women assumed during World War II. As a symbol of the ability of Americans to mobilize and transform themselves in the interest of society, Rockwell might have chosen a more idealized or classic portrayal—just as he based *Rosie the Riveter* on a classic Michelangelo painting—but he painted his *Liberty Girl* as a motivated girl next door, underscoring her authenticity. For the final painting, Rockwell eliminated the Nazi swastika (center and on left leg) and Japanese rising sun (at left and at top) present in his charcoal study.

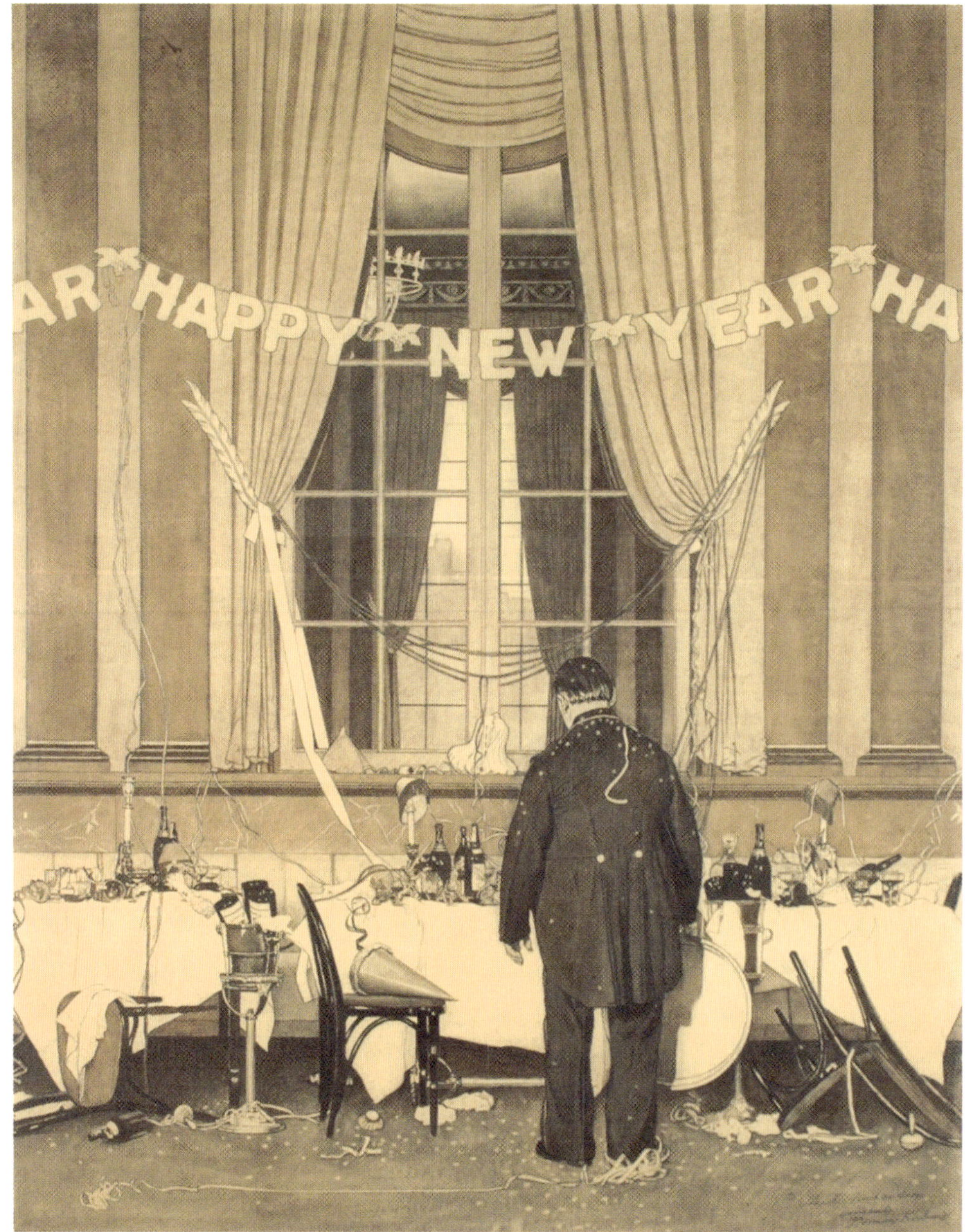


4.19. *Happy New Year*, 1945
Pencil, charcoal, and inkwash on paper,
47 × 36 in. (119.4 × 91.4 cm)
Cover study for the *Saturday Evening Post*,
December 29, 1945
NRM.1978.04

The charcoal study for *Happy New Year* is a stunning four feet tall. Though the artwork would be printed at less than fourteen inches high on the magazine cover, the larger scale allowed Rockwell to focus on fine details and experiment with tone and composition in a way that would be difficult at a smaller size. Set in the Waldorf Astoria's Wedgwood Room, the drawing includes empty champagne bottles and silver buckets left over from the previous night's celebration. The conservative editors of the *Saturday Evening Post* had these details removed from the final painting, because they disapproved of covers that alluded to the consumption of alcohol.

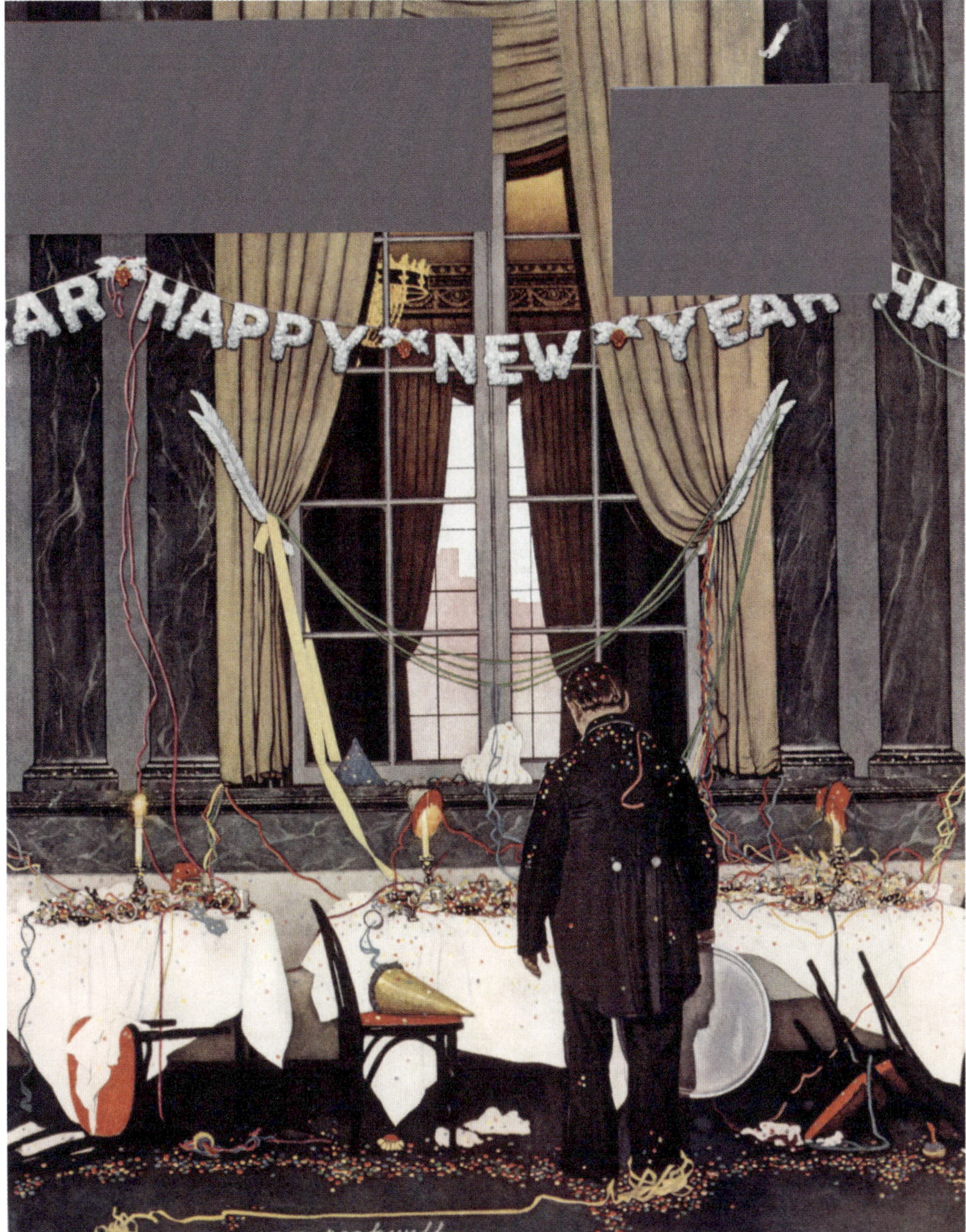


4.20. *Happy New Year* (detail), 1945
Tear sheet, 14¼ × 11¼ in. (36.2 × 28.6 cm)
Cover illustration for the *Saturday Evening Post*, December 29, 1945
RC.2007.1.232
(Gift of John A. and Laura C. Savio)

It was not uncommon for the *Post* to alter an illustrator's work, though they were careful to not upset their star artist unless they felt changes were necessary. In-house artists were assigned to carry out modifications to cover illustrations, such as the removal of brand names on products or shifting an artist's signature. Substantive changes were made to at least five of Rockwell's covers, in three instances without his prior consent. However, the most typical edits were to enlarge Rockwell's signature.[8]

Rockwell hired photographer Sam Calder to capture models and props for *New Television Antenna*. Calder took nearly one hundred photographs of potential material for the painting: birds in flight, a church steeple, a television set, houses, a man in studio pretending to look out of a window, and a man on a five-foot-tall makeshift roof peak photographed in the studio and outdoors.

The composition of Rockwell's first idea sketch was actually quite close to the final product. Another rough sketch included a bigger scene with a crowd gathered around to observe the installation of the antenna. The final painting shows a homeowner leaning out of an upstairs window with a childlike gleam on his face while he examines the work on his roof. Inside the window, a television set displays an image barely coming through. The sky is a cloudy gray with a possible storm brewing, and one wonders if sitting on a roof with a large metal antenna in hand is wise. Meanwhile, in the background is a church steeple, colored gray to match the sky. The steeple is topped with a lightning rod or weather vane that resembles the television antenna. No one is looking out of the steeple's open window as birds circle the church like vultures around a dying animal. The new is in contrast with the old, and readers of the *Post* in 1949 knew at which location the homeowner planned to be the rest of the day.

This sequence of images shows how Rockwell could turn a simple four-inch-square doodle of a house into a finely detailed and deeply expressive *Post* cover to be viewed by millions. And he did this an average of seven times a year.

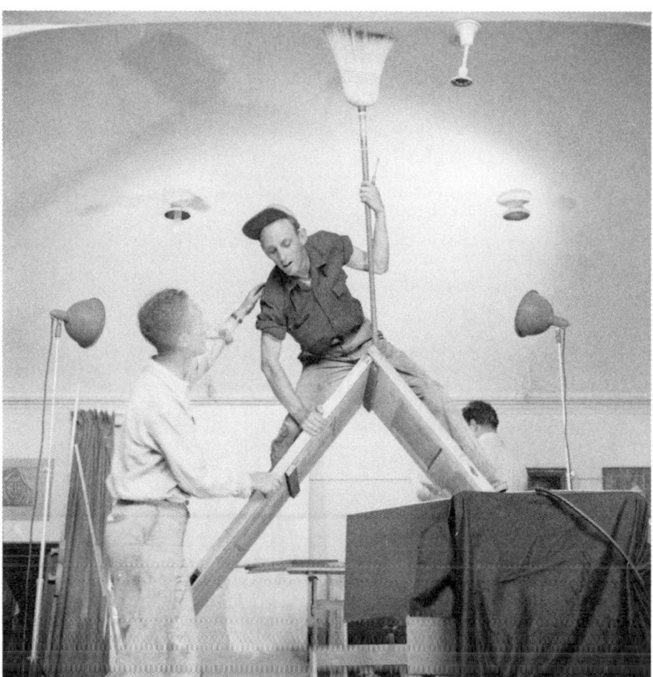

4.21. Sam Calder (1916–1991)
Norman Rockwell posing model for *New Television Antenna*, 1949
Photograph (from negative)
RC.1994.25.014

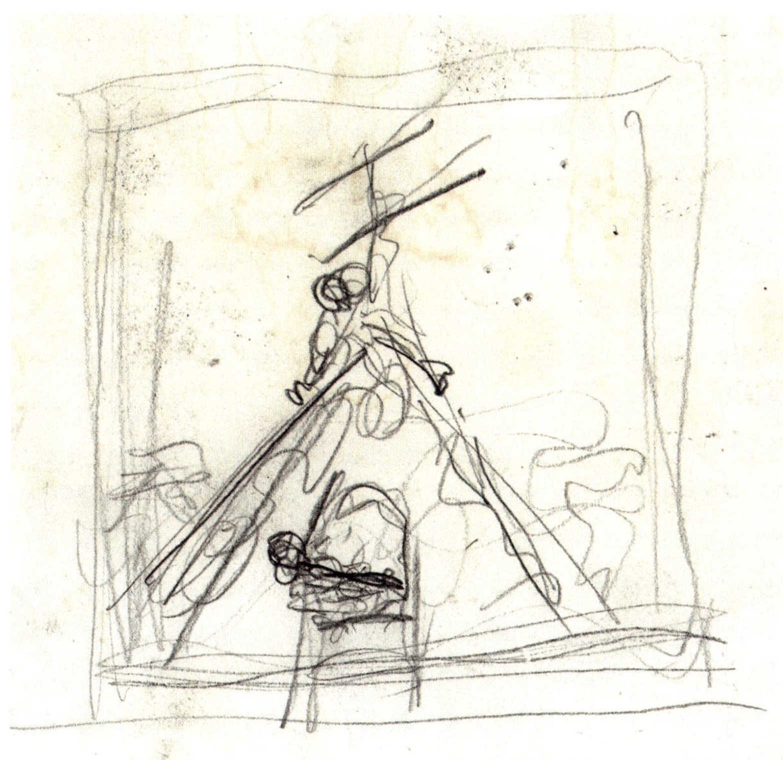

4.22. *New Television Antenna*, 1949
Pencil on paper, 4½ × 4 in. (11.4 × 10.2 cm)
Cover study for the *Saturday Evening Post*, November 5, 1949
NRACT.1976.94

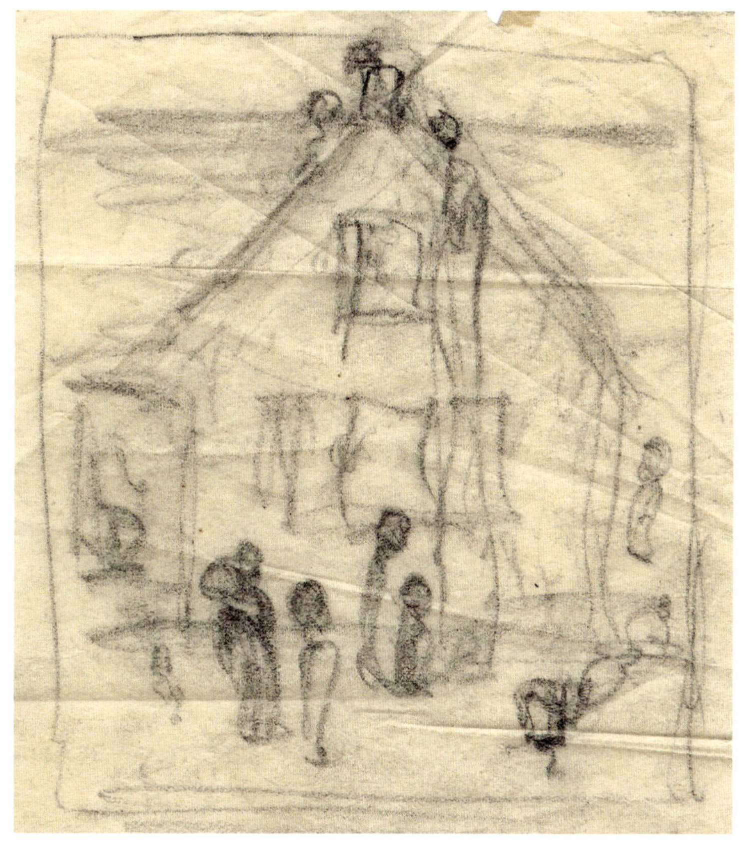

4.23. *New Television Antenna*, 1949
Pencil on paper, 4½ × 4 in. (11.4 × 10.2 cm)
Cover study for the *Saturday Evening Post*, November 5, 1949
NRACT.1976.368

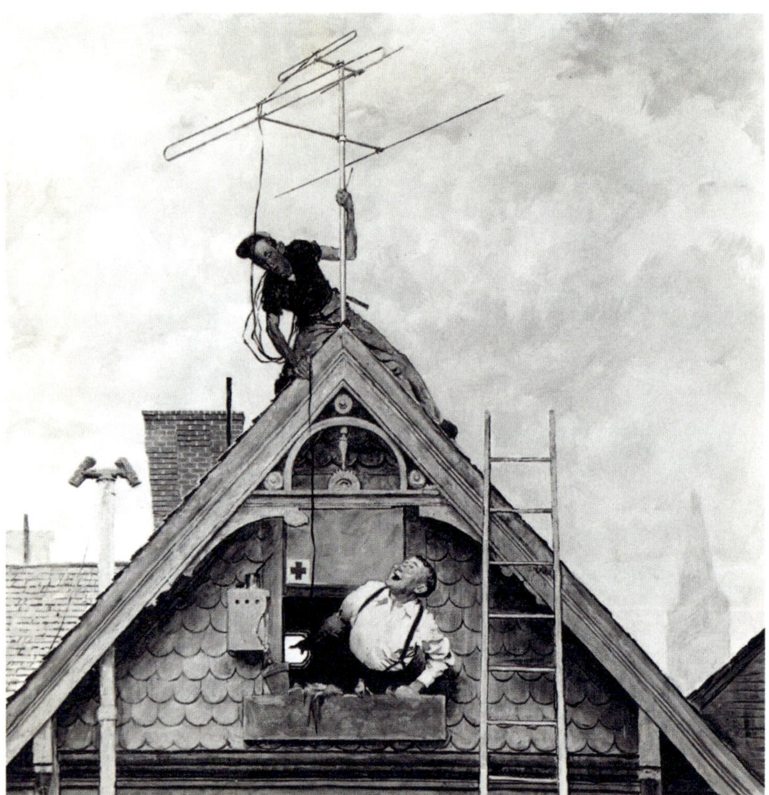

4.24. *New Television Antenna*, 1949
Wolff pencil on paper
Cover study for the *Saturday Evening Post*, November 5, 1949
Private collection

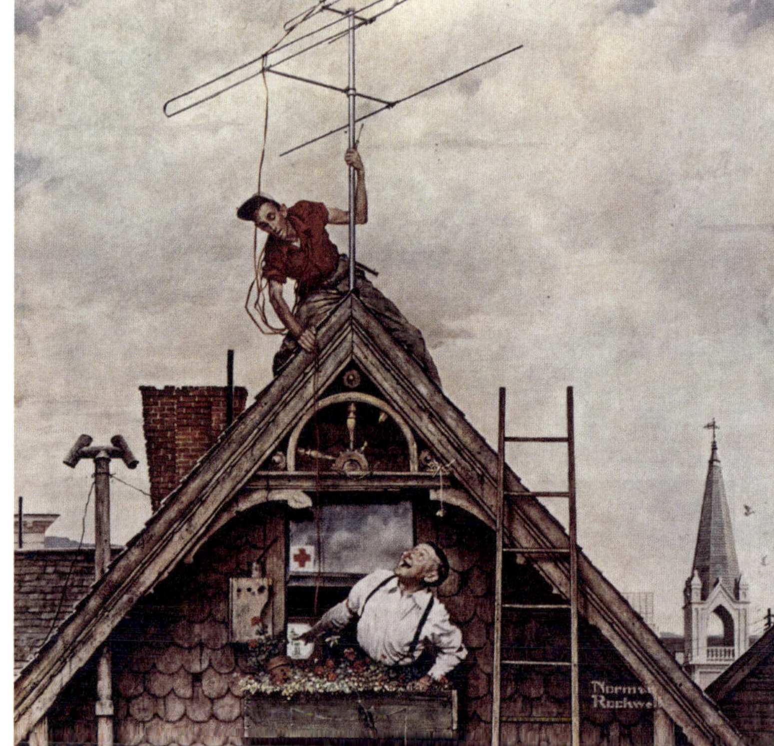

4.25. *New Television Antenna* (detail), 1949
Tear sheet, 14¼ × 11¼ in.
(36.2 × 28.6 cm)
Cover illustration for the *Saturday Evening Post*, November 5, 1949
RC.2007.1.258 (Gift of John A. and Laura C. Savio)

## Late Career: 1950–63

Rockwell's prodigious work for the *Post* continued through the 1950s. The Korean conflict, the excitement of the postwar economic boom, and the greater attention to politics fueled by mass media all provided inspiration to Rockwell as he painted his vision of America for the readers of the *Post*.

Yet by 1960, Rockwell's days at the *Post* were numbered, with the rise of television, a rapidly changing culture, the use of photography on magazine covers, and a turnover in *Post* staff from the men Rockwell had known and respected for decades. Ben Hibbs, Rockwell's editor since 1942, retired in 1962. In June of that year, Rockwell's longtime art director and his closest ally at the *Post*, Ken Stuart, was fired in a reorganization of the magazine. Stuart left behind a list of Rockwell's cover suggestions, which, to the artist's great surprise, were ignored. The incoming editors of the *Post* asked Rockwell to cease painting his popular idealized subjects—which had made him America's most beloved artist—and instead mostly compose portraits of politicians and celebrities.

In what Rockwell must have viewed as a demotion, the *Post* announced that their star cover artist of forty-six years was now a "portraitist."[9] Rockwell soon grew weary of his assignments to paint portraits of world leaders—such as one of John F. Kennedy, which would be reprinted for the issue following the president's assassination—and the increased oversight from the new editors. Rockwell finally expressed his feelings in a September 9, 1963, letter he wrote to the *Post*'s art editor, Asger Jerrild. "I have come to the conviction that the work I now want to do no longer fits into the *Post* scheme. . . . I don't want to retire, but I want to have freedom to do the work I wish. . . . It goes without saying this decision has not come easily, but I'm sure it is the right one for me."[10] His last work for the *Post* was the May 25, 1963, cover painting of Gamal Abdel Nasser, the president of Egypt.

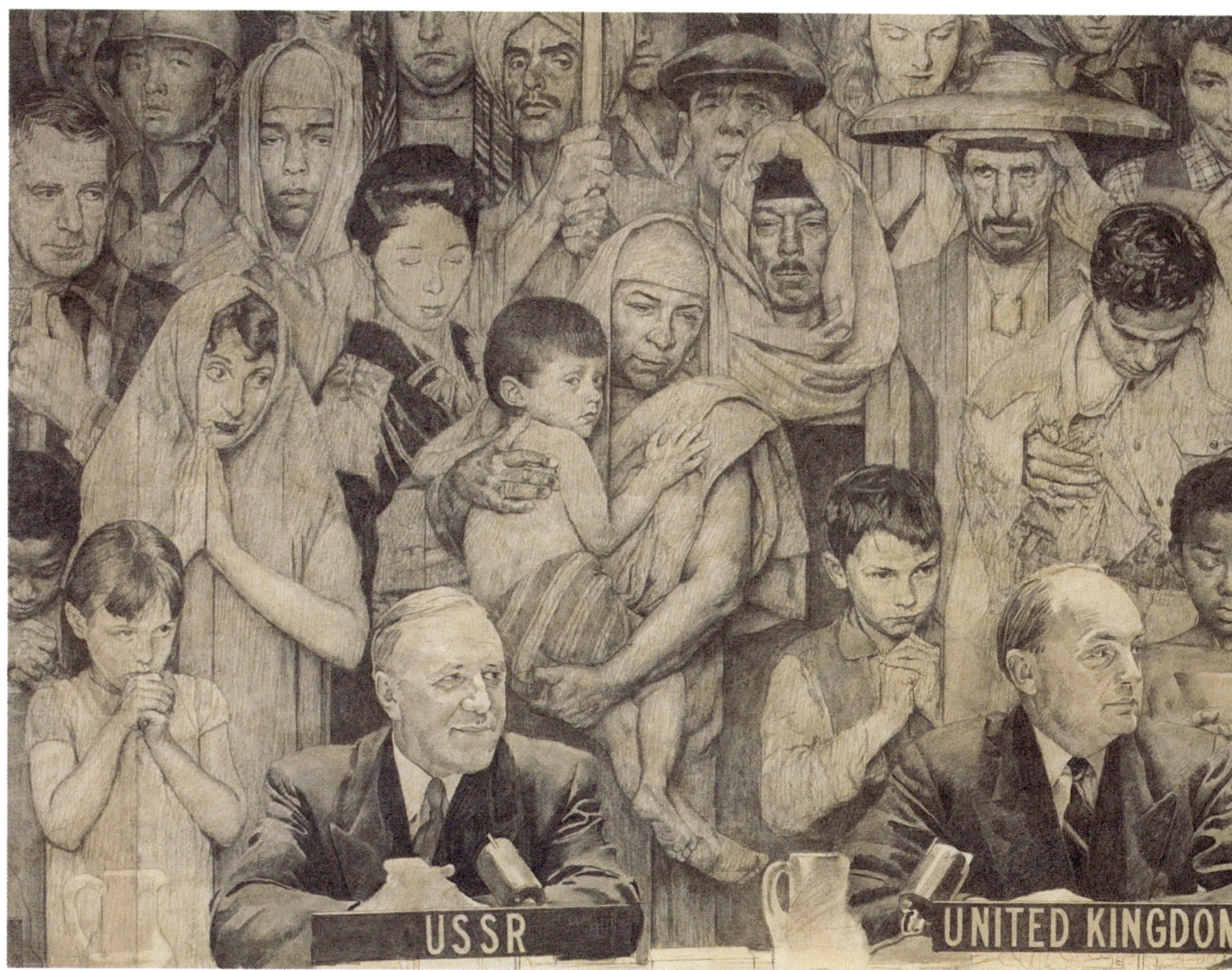


In 1953, Rockwell created a charcoal study titled *United Nations*, in which people from all the world's cultures and religions stand behind the members of the United Nations Security Council. Ben Hibbs and Ken Stuart at the *Post* supported Rockwell's idea and arranged for him to take photographs inside the U.N. Security Council chamber. The U.N. scheduled delegates from the permanent members of the council to be present for the photographs. Because the other delegates had not smiled, Rockwell had the interpreter ask the Russian delegate to remain serious. Nonetheless, his expression was the most positive, and Rockwell was forced to alter the expressions of the other men as a result.

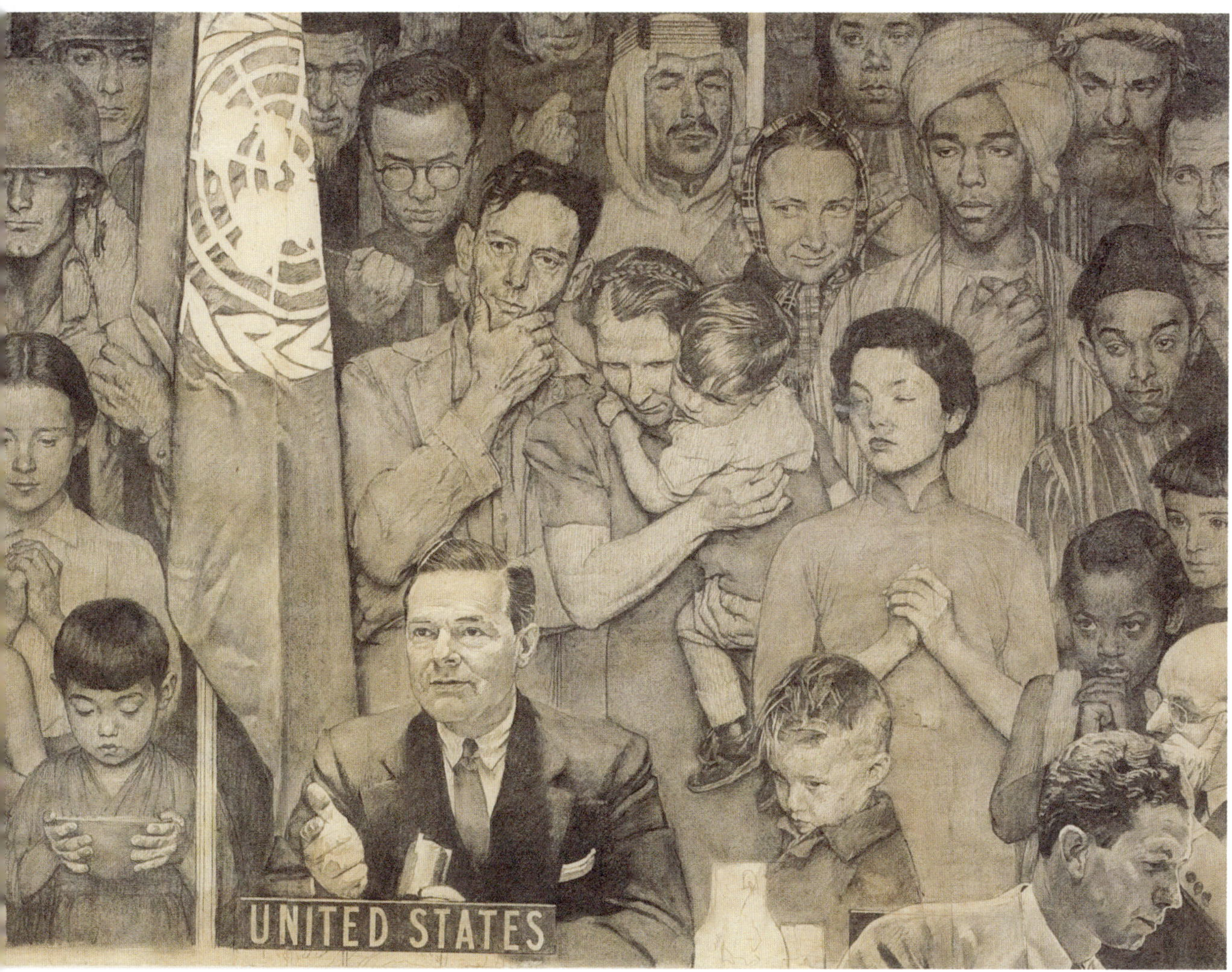


At his studio in Arlington, Rockwell spent a month taking photographs of nearly forty models to represent the various nations in the background of the work. He then spent another month working on the charcoal drawing, creating more than seventy background subjects. Rockwell had tried to accomplish a "big picture" painting that would change the world, but decided it was "just not my kind of picture."[11] Disappointed, he abandoned the work and moved on to other projects.

4.26. *United Nations*, 1953
Pencil and charcoal on paper,
27¼ × 73½ in. (69.2 × 186.7 cm)
NRACT.1973.113

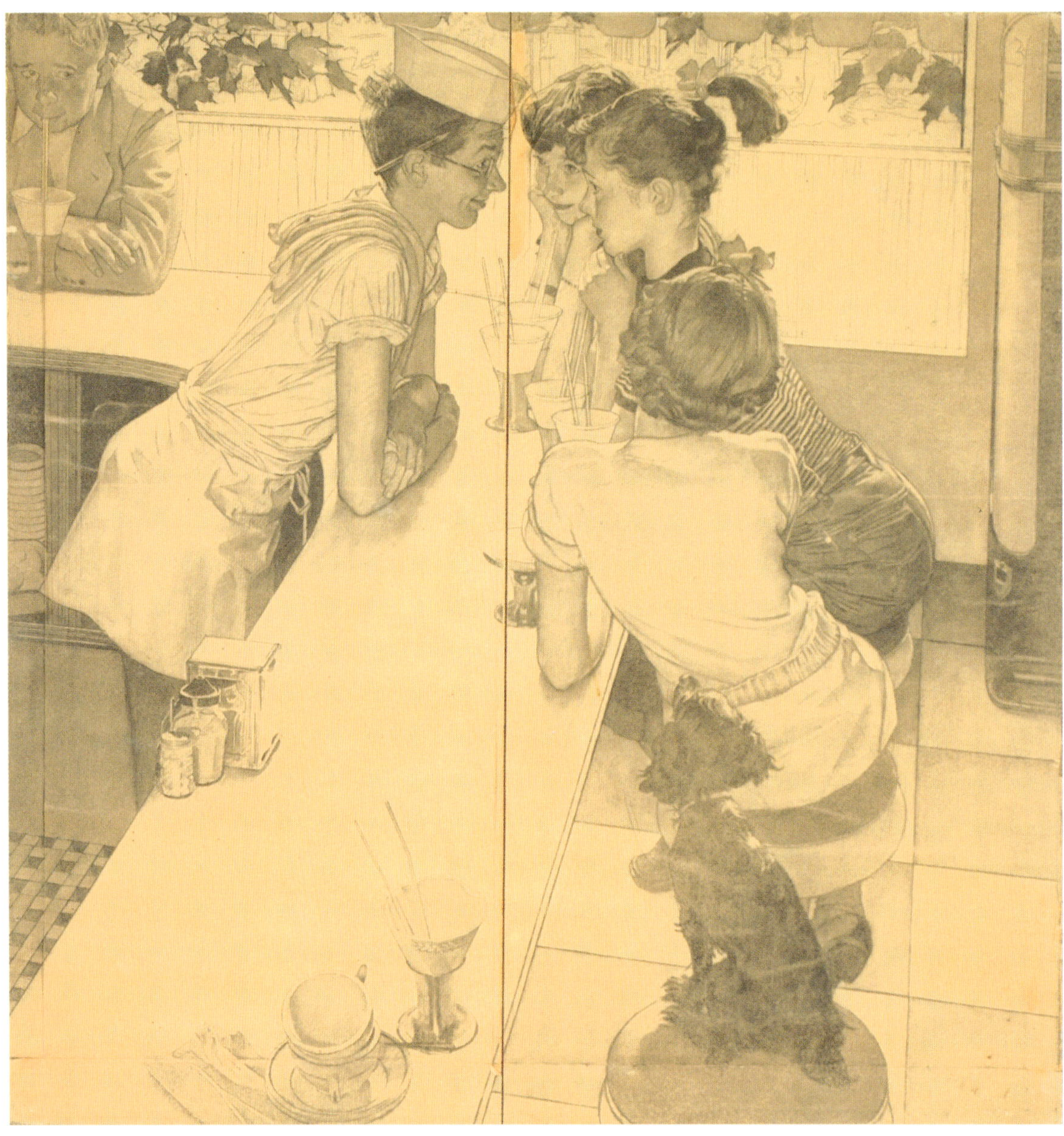

ABOVE
4.27. *Soda Jerk*, 1953
Charcoal and pencil on board, 35 × 33 in. (88.9 × 83.8 cm)
Cover study for the *Saturday Evening Post*, August 22, 1953
NRACT.1976.59

OPPOSITE
4.28. *Soda Jerk*, 1953
Oil on canvas
Cover illustration for the *Saturday Evening Post*, August 22, 1953
Whereabouts unknown

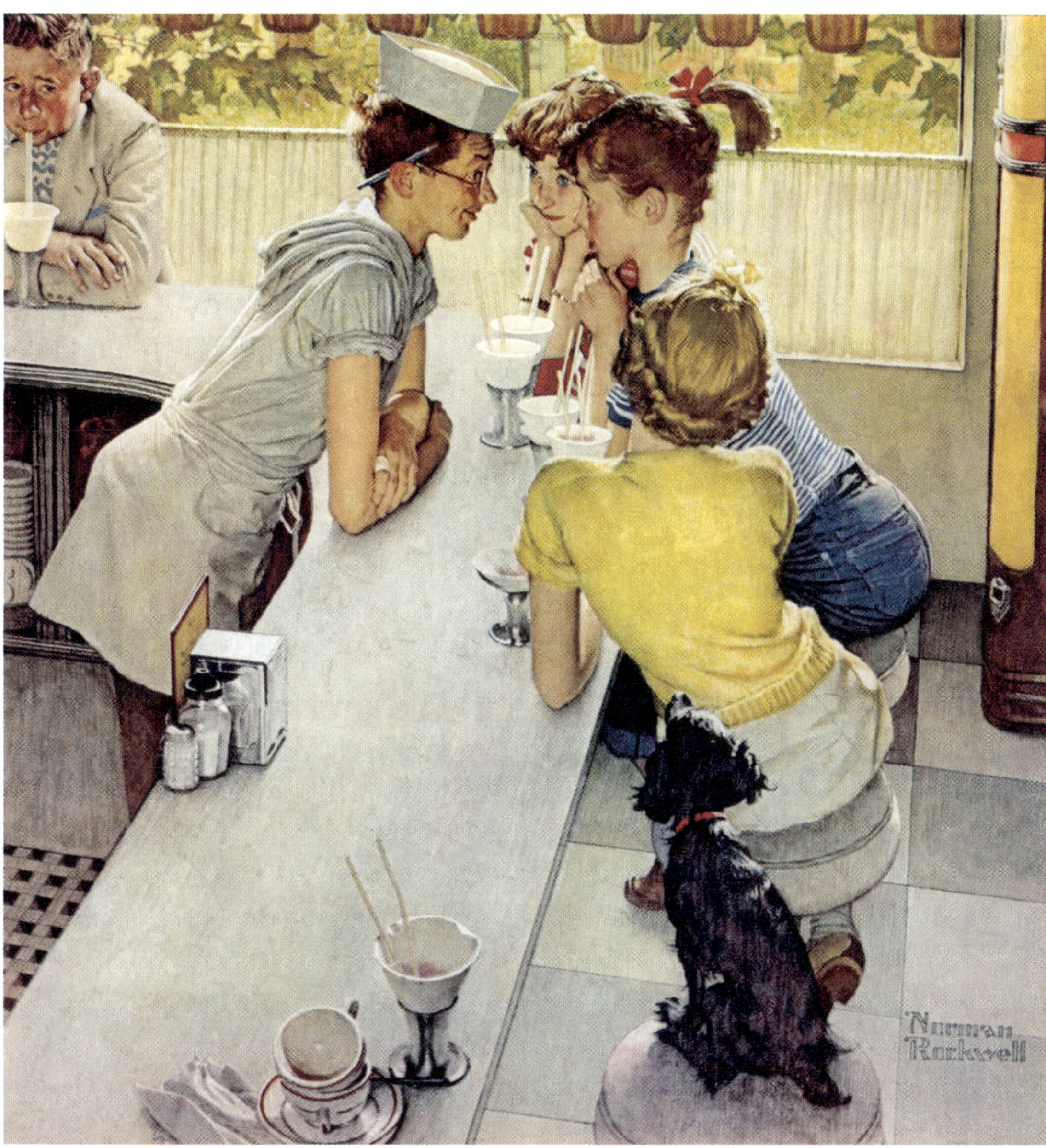


For this painting, one of his most popular, Rockwell brought his son Peter and a group of classmates home from school in Putney, Vermont, for the weekend to pose as models. The idea was based on Peter's own summer job as counter man at a soda fountain. Rockwell had each of his subjects photographed individually and then selected the best images for the final composition, placing them in a setting assembled from additional photographs taken in a local soda fountain.

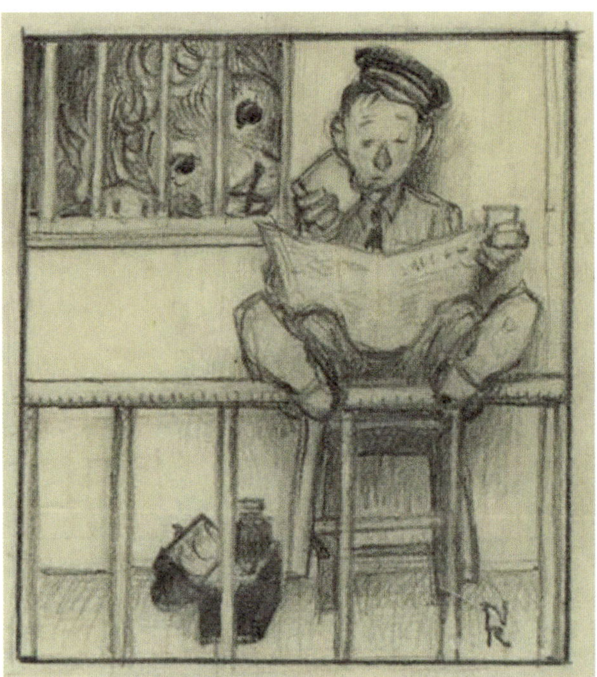

4.29. *Lion and Zookeeper*, 1954
Pencil on paper, 3½ × 3 in. (8.9 × 7.9 cm)
Cover study for the *Saturday Evening Post*, January 9, 1954
Private collection

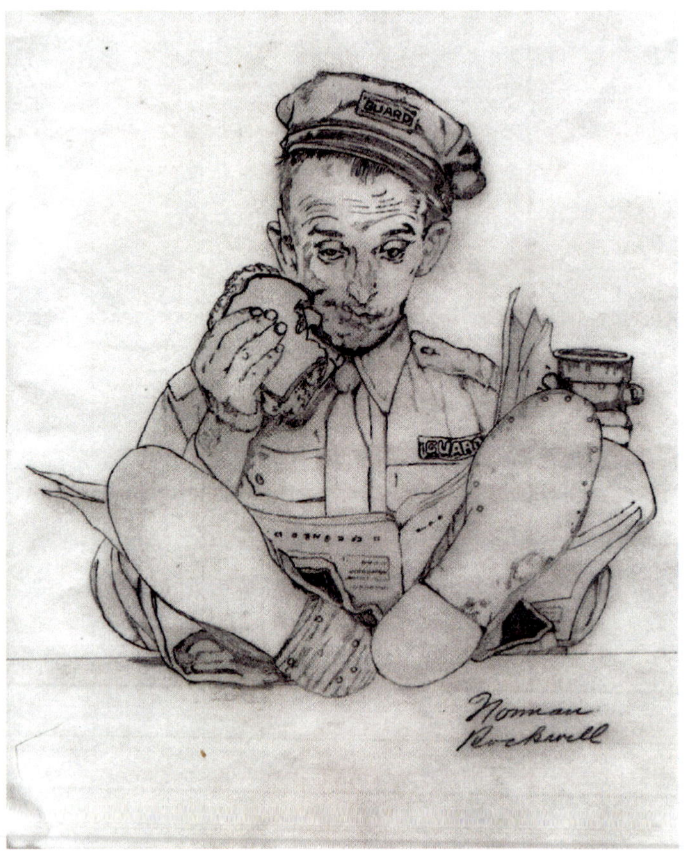


4.30. *Lion and Zookeeper*, 1954
Ink on paper, 11 × 8½ in. (27.9 × 21.6 cm)
Cover study for the *Saturday Evening Post*, January 9, 1954
Private collection

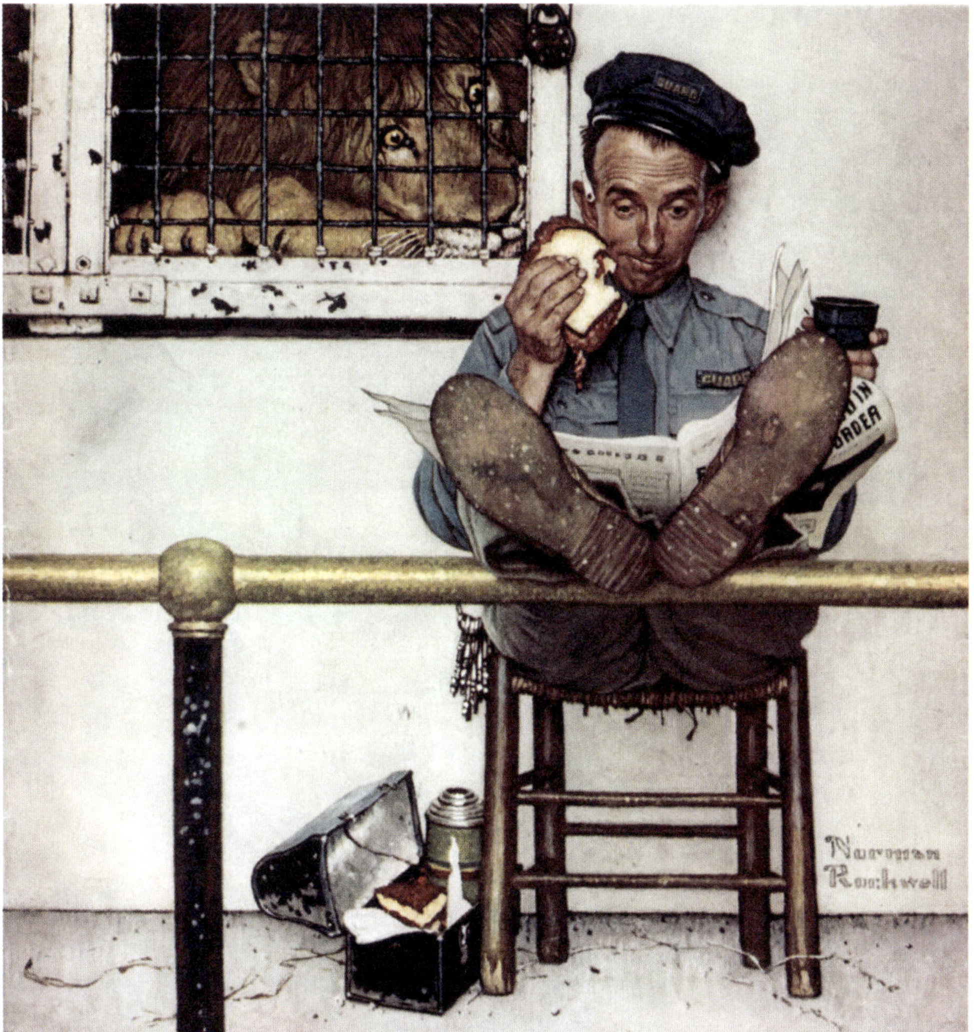


4.31. *Lion and Zookeeper* (detail), 1954
Tear sheet, 14¼ × 11¼ in. (36.2 × 28.6 cm)
Cover illustration for the *Saturday Evening Post*, January 9, 1954
RC.2007.1.275
(Gift of John A. and Laura C. Savio)

Reflecting on how he conceived of this work, Rockwell noted, "After three or four days of searching for ideas, I was sitting at my drawing board lacing up my tennis shoes and wondering if the rain would hold off long enough so that I could get in a set or two, when all of a sudden an idea for a *Post* cover strolled into my head. A zoo guard seated in front of a lion cage eating a sandwich, stuffed, overflowing, with red meat while the lion in the cage gazed hungrily, ravenously, and at the same time a little sadly, at the sandwich."[12]

The ink-on-paper drawing was likely the image Rockwell placed in his Balopticon to transfer the lines to canvas. Next, he would fill in all the details and complete the tonal work before beginning to paint.

Rockwell painted *Breaking Home Ties* both to manage his own feelings of loss and separation and to help others process their experiences of this common rite of passage. He recalled, "I was trying to express what a father feels when his son leaves home. Jerry, my oldest son, had enlisted in the Air Force; my younger sons, Tom and Peter, had gone away to school. Whenever I feel an idea strongly, I have trouble painting it. I keep trying to refine it, express it better."[13]

Rockwell explores what it would be like for a boy from a ranch in New Mexico to leave home. Experimenting with different versions, he chose the running board of an old truck over a railroad station bench and pictured a mournful collie instead of the boy's mother at his side. The boy model in the painting is Robert Waldrop, an Eagle Scout at the Philmont Scout Ranch in Cimarron, New Mexico, where Rockwell was visiting in 1953. While there, Rockwell also had photographs taken of a rural train station and an old pickup truck. The father is Floyd Bentley, a farmer in Arlington, Vermont. Rockwell noted, "As you can see, I could not decide on the proper setting. None seemed to convey the idea that the boy was leaving home to go to college. By the time I had discarded the third charcoal, I had begun to lose confidence in my original conception. . . . After trying the station platform, I returned to the original setting, substituting the trunk and signal lamp for the mailbag, the rail for the edge of the platform."[14]

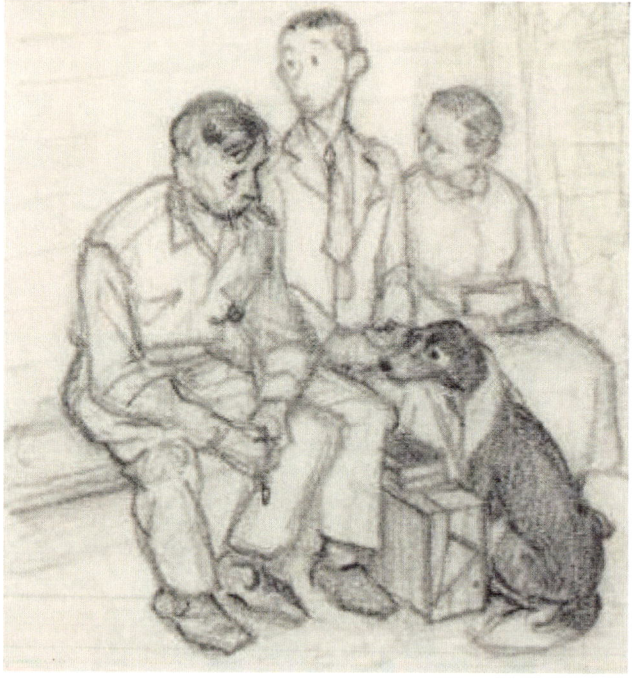

4.32. *Breaking Home Ties (Boy and Father Sitting on Truck)*, 1954
Pencil on paper,
3½ × 3¼ in. (8.9 × 8.3 cm)
Cover study for the *Saturday Evening Post*, September 25, 1954
Location unknown

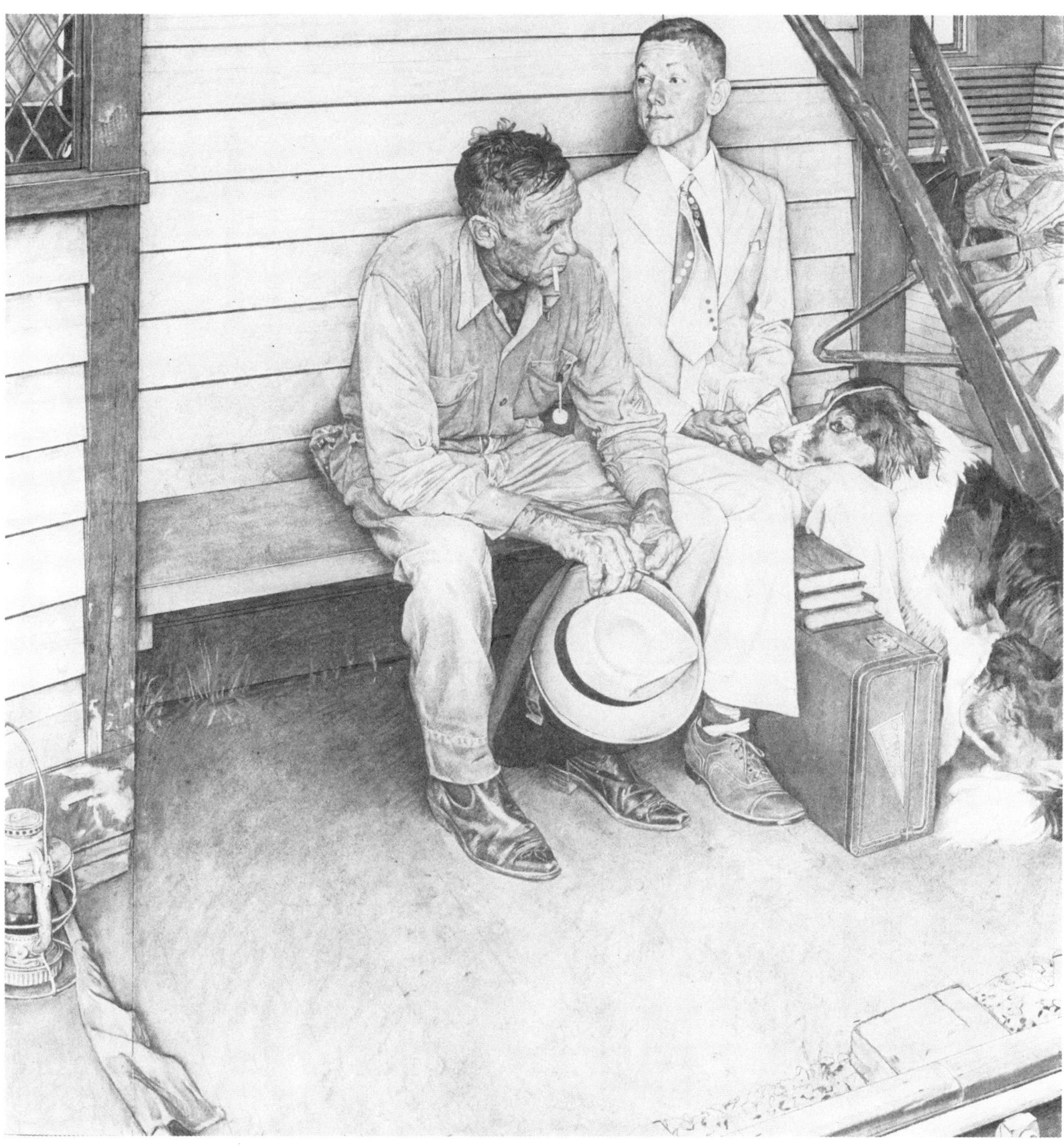

4.33. *Breaking Home Ties (Boy and Father Sitting on Truck)*, 1954
Pencil on paper, 47 × 36 in. (119.4 × 91.4 cm)
Cover study for the *Saturday Evening Post*, September 25, 1954
Private collection

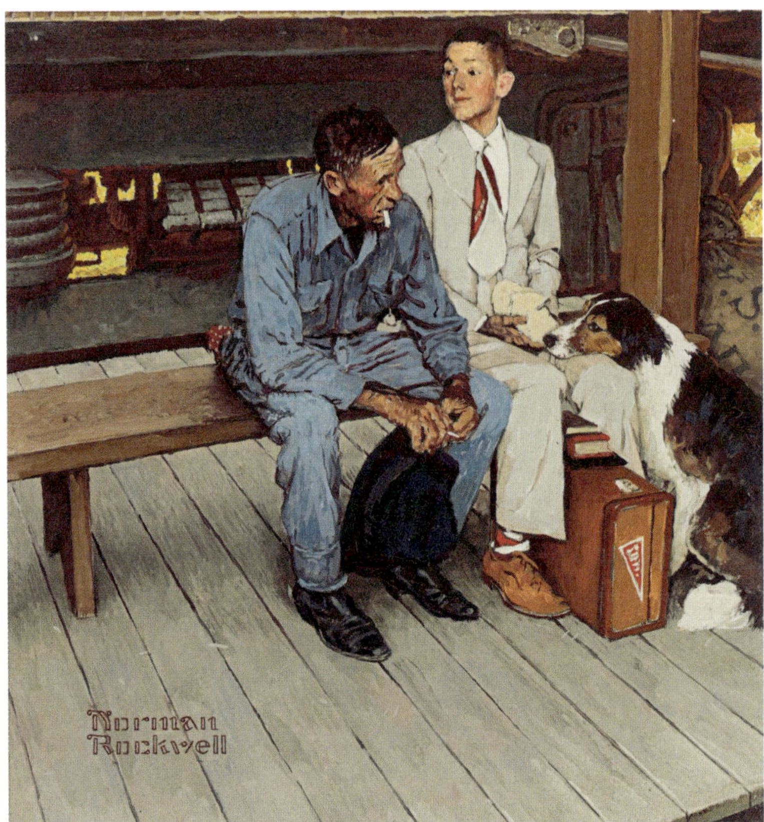


4.34. *Breaking Home Ties (Boy and Father Sitting on Truck)*, 1954
Oil on photograph
Color study for the *Saturday Evening Post*, September 25, 1954
Private collection

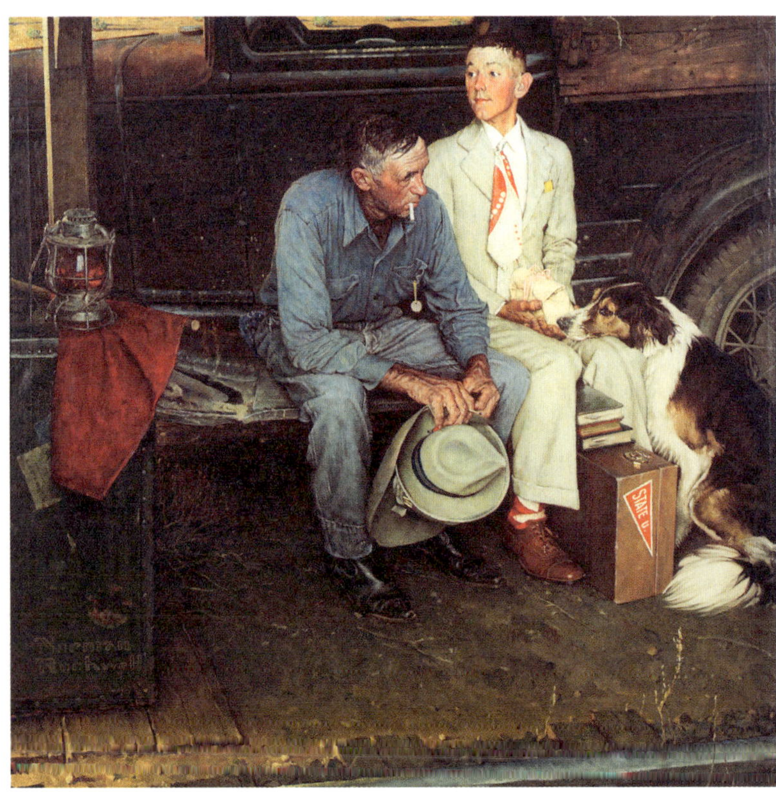

4.35. *Breaking Home Ties (Boy and Father Sitting on Truck)*, 1954
Oil on canvas, 44 × 44 in.
(111.8 × 111.8 cm)
Cover illustration for the *Saturday Evening Post*, September 25, 1954
Private collection

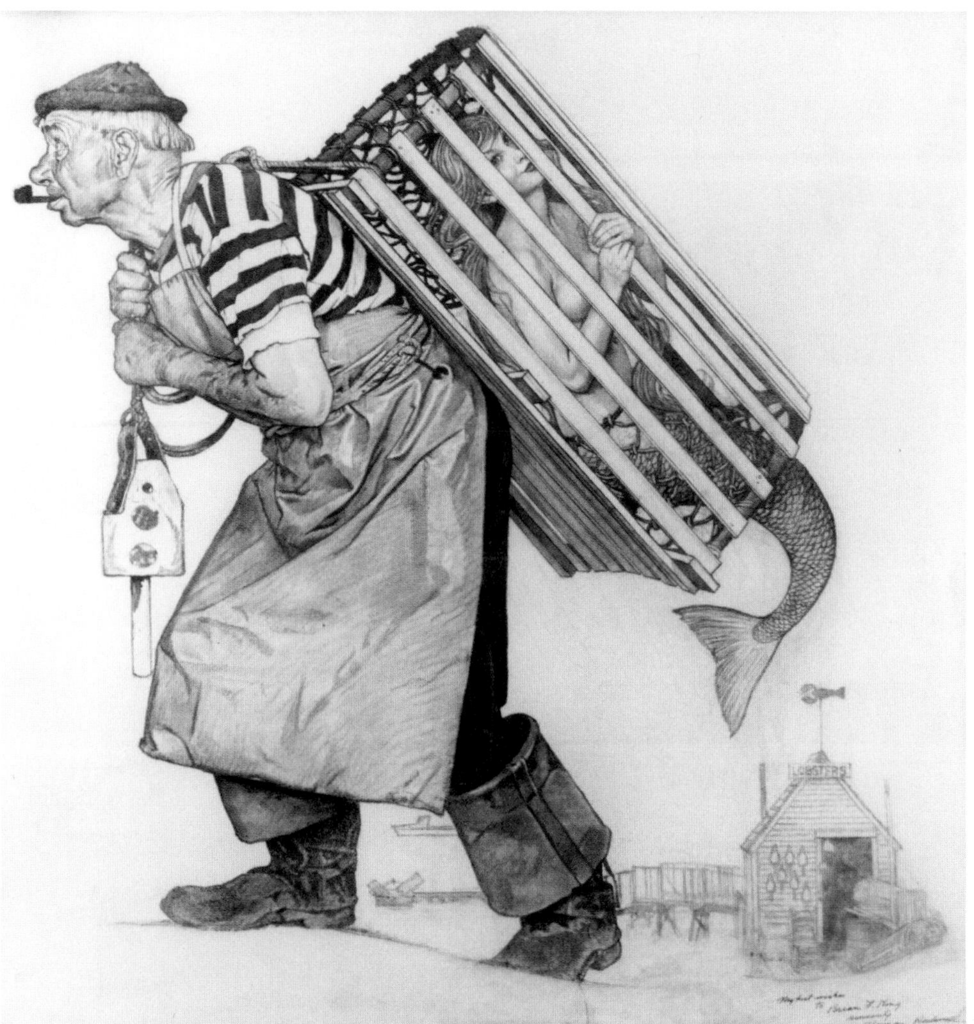


4.36. *Mermaid*, 1955
Charcoal on paper, 38 × 36¼ in. (96.5 × 92.1 cm)
Cover study for the *Saturday Evening Post*, August 20, 1955
Private collection

A seasoned angler returns home with the catch of the day in this lighthearted *Post* cover study, which is nearly identical to the final painting. Always a stickler for authenticity in his work, Rockwell contacted the New Rochelle Public Library to inquire about images of mermaids and lobster pots from their files. Fortunately, Rockwell was able to acquire authentic pots and fishing-related props from the Gloucester, Massachusetts, Chamber of Commerce. This drawing is one instance in which Rockwell hired a professional model instead of a neighbor, since she had to pose fully nude for several photographs. Although the cover may seem risqué for the time, the *Post* clarified that only one in twenty readers expressed concern. However, Rockwell did receive one letter of complaint, though in good fun, from the Lake Michigan Society for the Prevention of Cruelty to Mermaids.

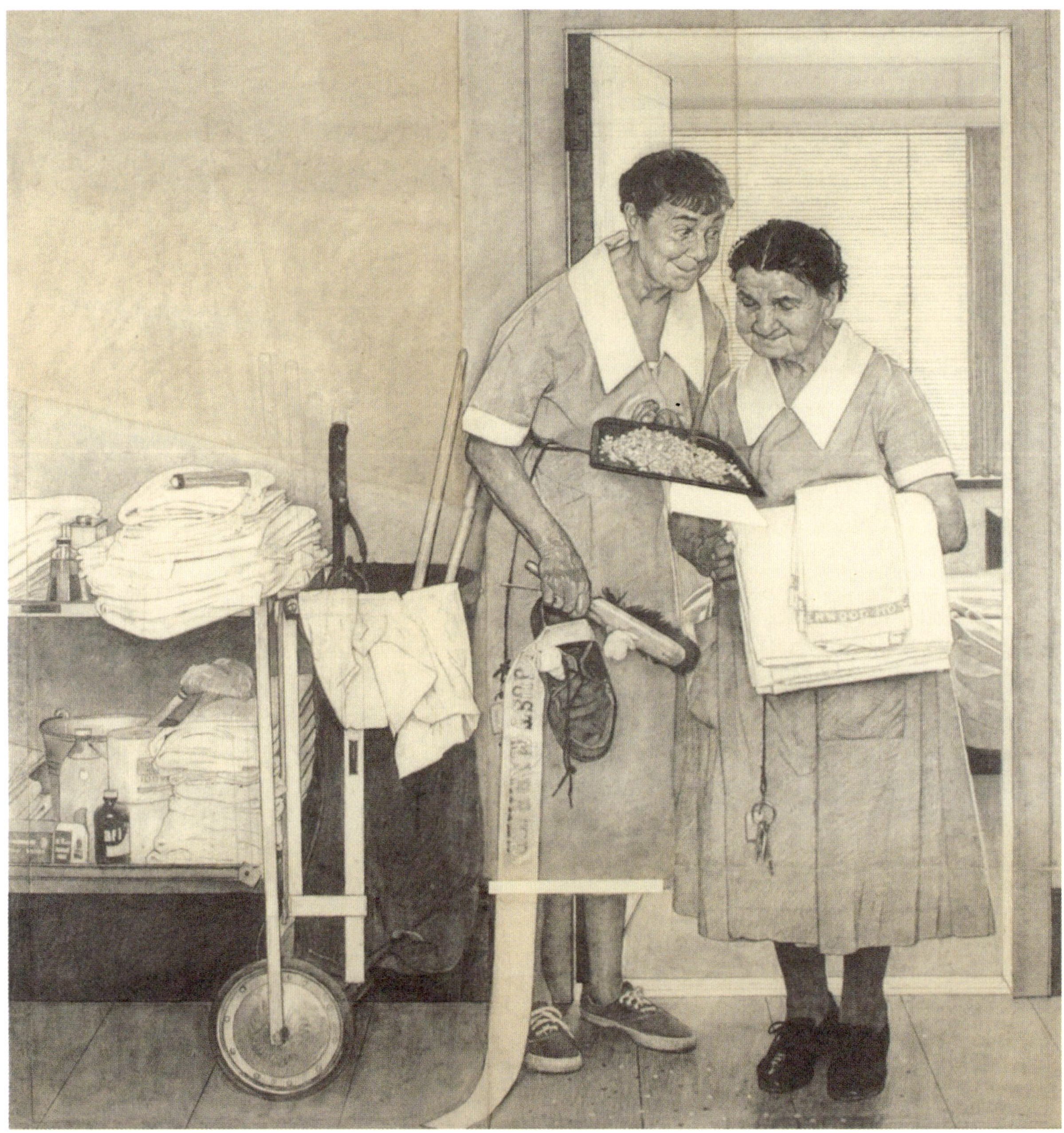

One of Rockwell's most ribald works, *Just Married*, alternatively titled *After the Honeymoon*, shows two housekeepers contemplating the events that occurred the previous night in a hotel room. Some of the reference photos for this work show a woman's shoe and a rose with loose petals in the dustpan. However, Rockwell removed the symbolic flower from the final painting, ensuring the cover would be more family friendly.

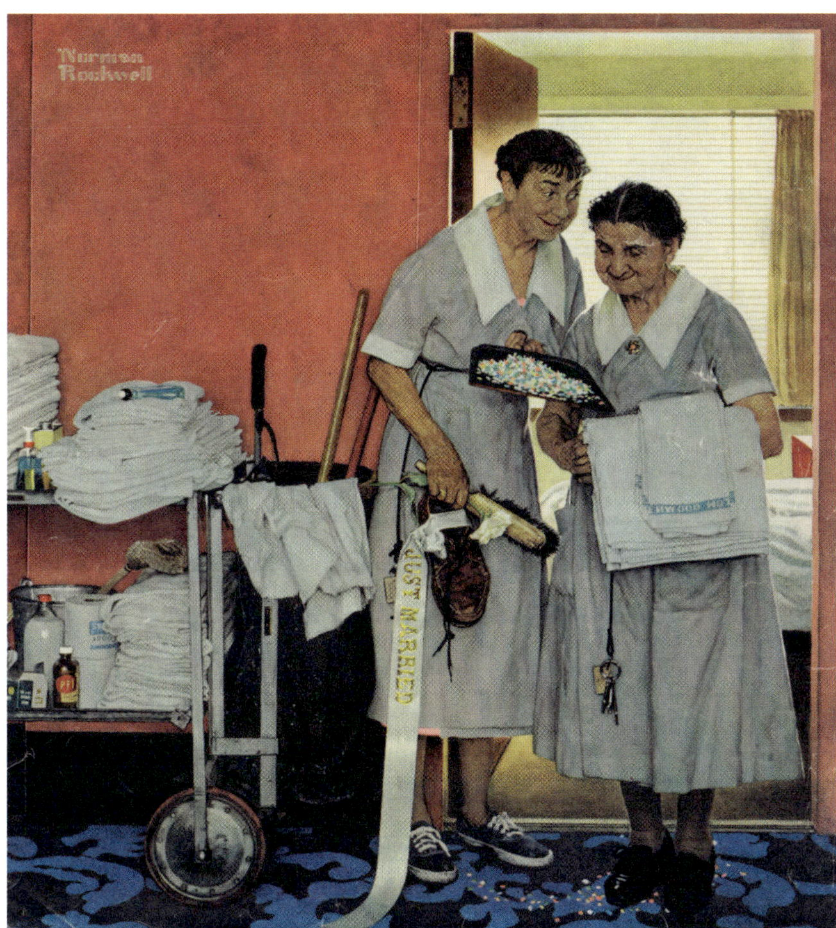


4.38. *Just Married* (detail), 1957
Tear sheet, 14¼ × 11¼ in.
(36.2 × 28.6 cm)
Cover illustration for
the *Saturday Evening Post*, June 29, 1957
RC.2007.1.291 (Gift of John A. and Laura C. Savio)

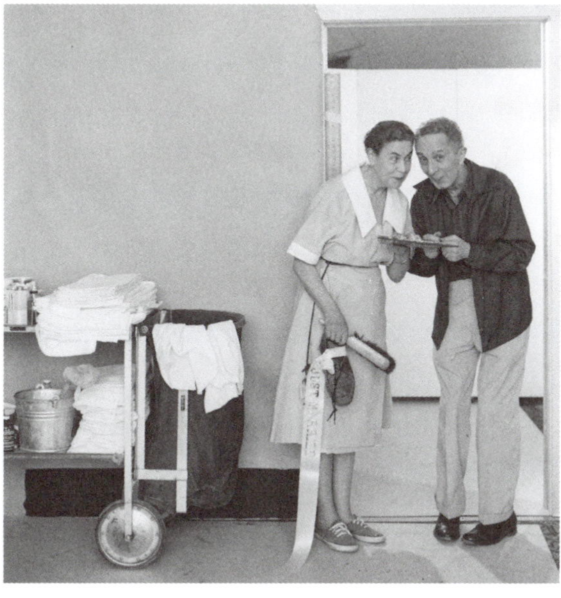

OPPOSITE
4.37. *Just Married*, 1957
Charcoal and pencil on board, 38 × 34½ in. (96.5 × 87.6 cm)
Cover study for the *Saturday Evening Post*, June 29, 1957
NRACT.1976.53

RIGHT
4.39. Bill Scovill (1915–1996)
Norman Rockwell posing with model for *Just Married*, 1957
Photograph (from negative)
ST19760.9360

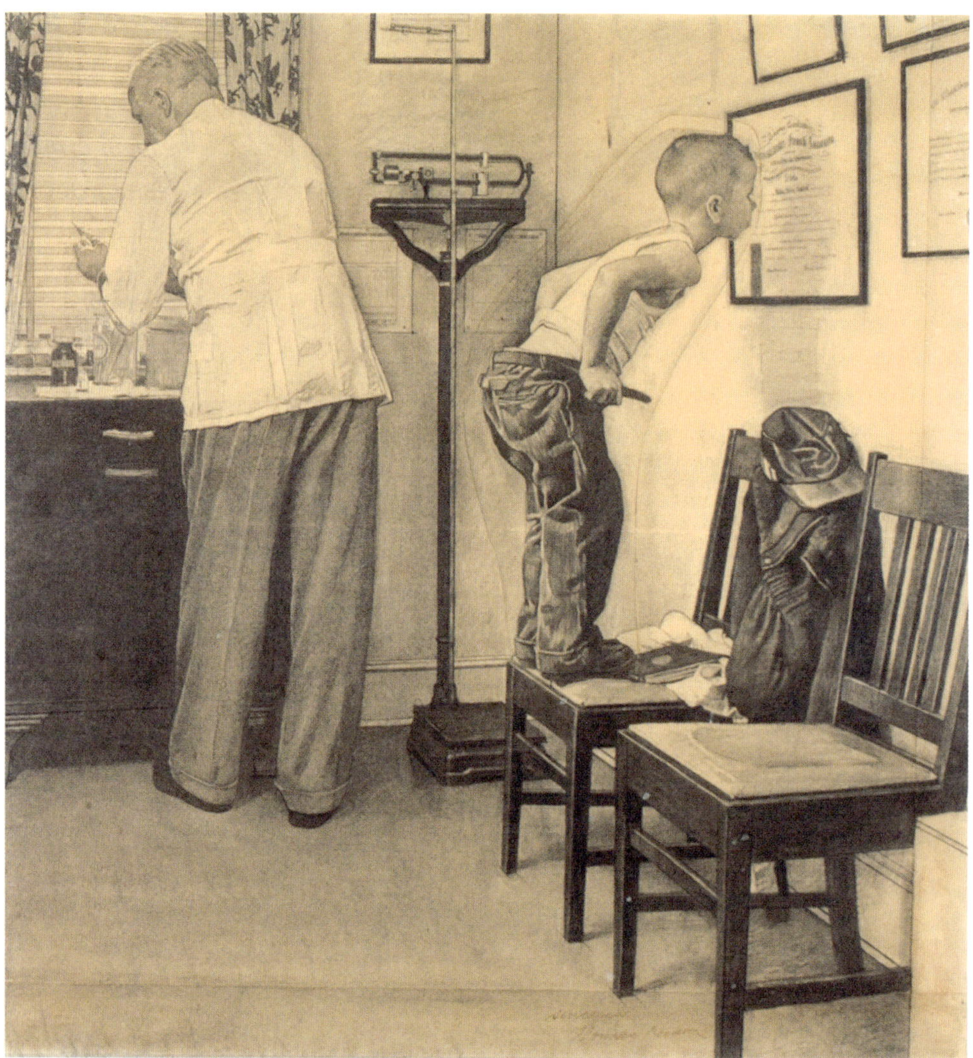

4.40. *Before the Shot*, 1958
Charcoal on paper,
30 × 26½ in. (76.2 × 67.3 cm)
Cover study for the *Saturday Evening Post*, March 15, 1958
NRM.1984.10

By 1958, Norman Rockwell had captured the idealized image of the family doctor in numerous illustrations for magazine covers and for pharmaceutical and life insurance advertisements. Aside from its overt humor, *Before the Shot* reflects the widespread use of penicillin in the 1950s, after it was first used to treat soldiers during World War II. The young model, Eddie Locke, was a Rockwell favorite who appeared in other significant works, including the 1958 *Post* cover *The Runaway*. *Before the Shot* was a complicated painting requiring photography, several drawings, and many color studies. Rockwell may have had some difficulty with this final draft, since the figure of Eddie Locke was drawn separately and then pasted onto the paper.

In 1960, Rockwell still felt strongly about the sentiment behind *United Nations*, the work he had left unfinished seven years before—and he had finally come up with an artistic solution. He began painting *Golden Rule* in 1961, repurposing images of some of the models from *United Nations* and finding additional models near his home in Stockbridge, Massachusetts, many of them local exchange students and visitors.

*Golden Rule* was reminiscent of Rockwell's Four Freedoms paintings and a precursor to the more timely subjects he would soon illustrate for *Look* magazine. A group of people of different religions and ethnicities serves as the backdrop for the inscription "Do unto others as you would have them do unto you." This simple phrase encapsulated the message Rockwell had wanted to express eight years before in *United Nations*.

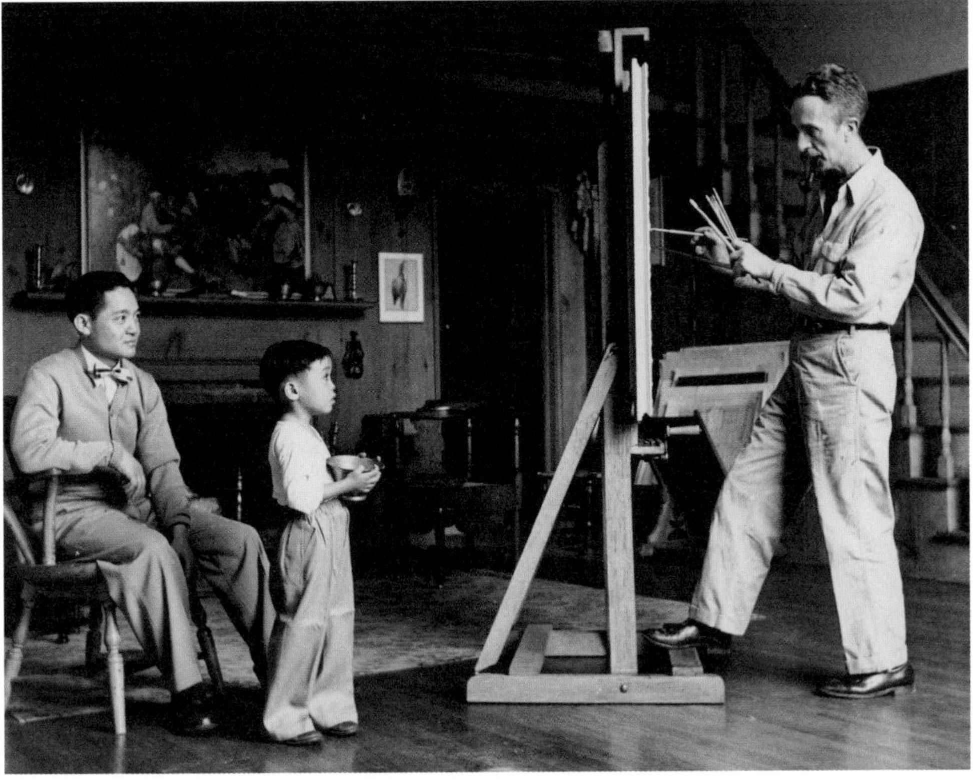

4.41. Reference photograph for *United Nations* and *Golden Rule*, 1953
Photograph (from negative)
ST.1976.20032.156.9

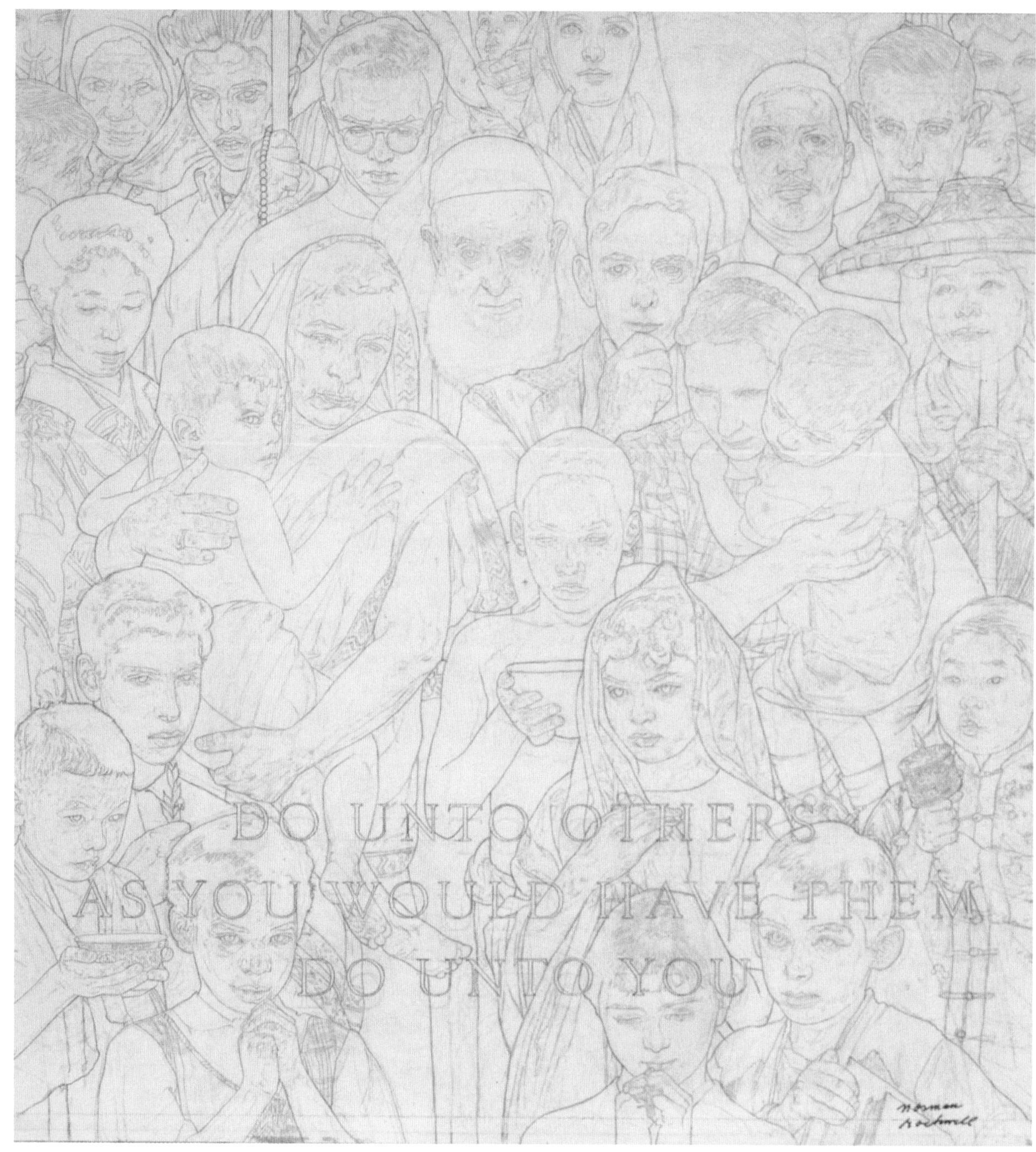


4.42. *Golden Rule*, 1961
Pencil on paper, 43 × 39¾ in.
(111.4 × 100.6 cm)
Cover study for the *Saturday Evening Post*, April 1, 1961
NRACT.1973.[illegible]

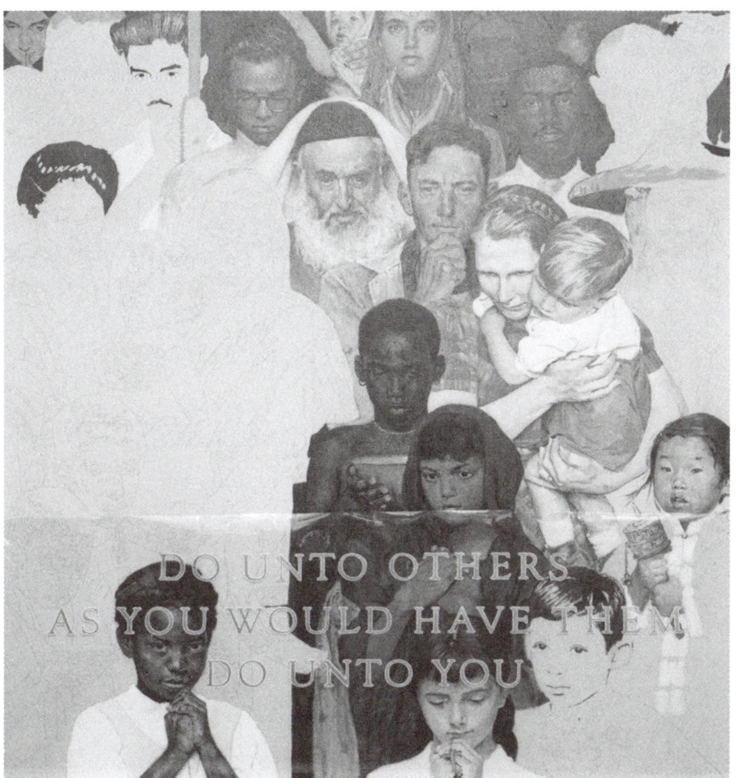


4.43. Bill Scovill (1915–1996)
Photograph of painting progress
for *Golden Rule*, 1960
Photograph (from negative)
RC.1997.3.134

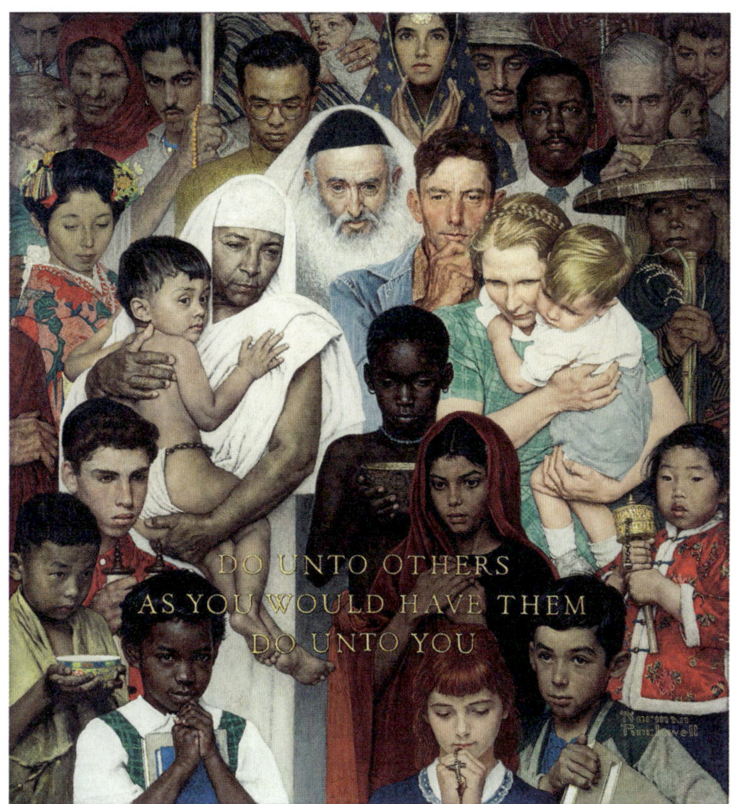


4.44. *Golden Rule*, 1961
Oil on canvas, 44½ × 39½ in. (113 × 100.3 cm)
Cover illustration for the *Saturday Evening Post*, April 1, 1961
NRACT.1973.010

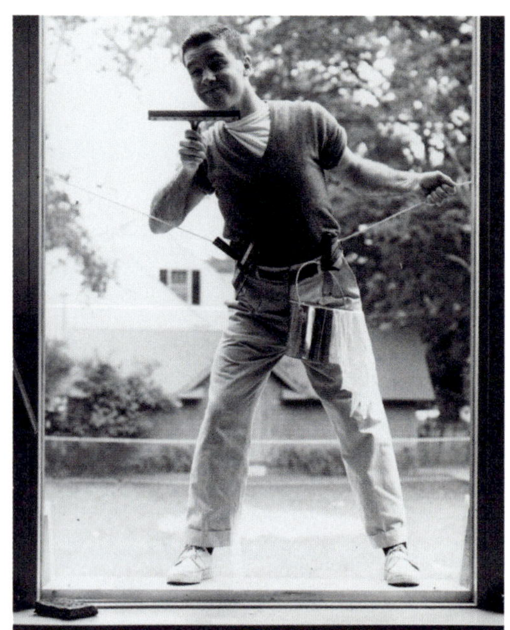

4.45. Bill Scovill (1915–1996)
Reference photograph for
*Window Washer*, 1960
Photographs (from negative)
ST.1976.20032.9.28

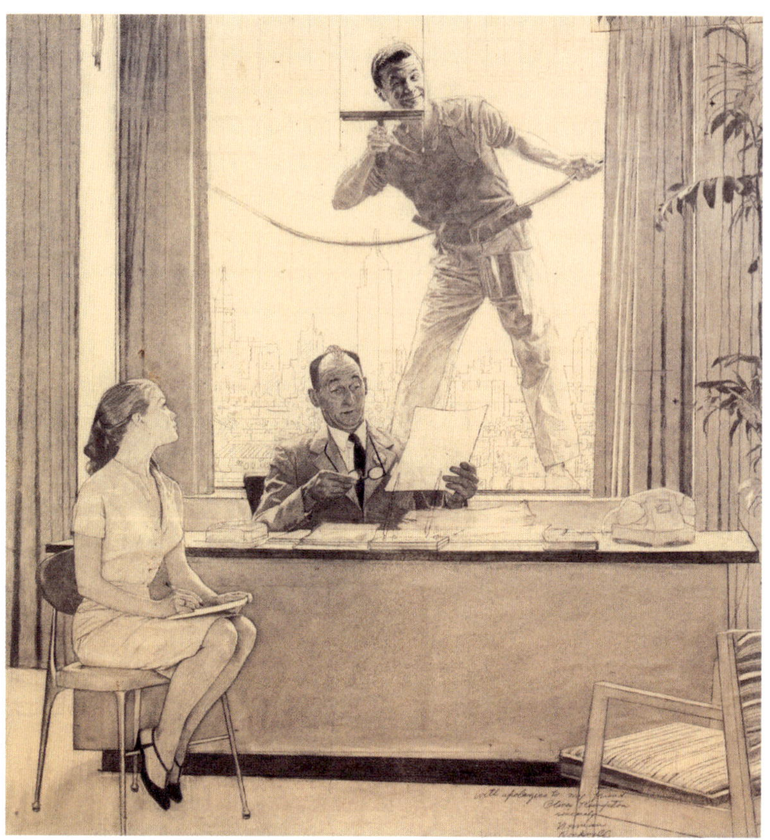

4.46. *Window Washer*, 1960
Charcoal on paper, 48 × 40 in.
(121.9 × 101.6 cm)
Cover study for the *Saturday Evening Post*, September 17, 1960
NRM.1991.02

For this tongue-in-cheek cover, Rockwell had models pose as window washers by standing on the windowsill outside his studio window. As was often the case, more than one model posed for each subject in the painting. Rockwell discussed the problems this occasionally caused: "I use one person, decide he's not right, and get another. But in the struggle with the picture I often forget to inform the first model that he is no longer being used. So he tells all his friends, 'Wait until you see me. I'm coming out on a *Post* cover next month. You watch for it. I'm the man holding the shovel.' Then the cover appears. He's not on it and is quite understandably embarrassed."[15]

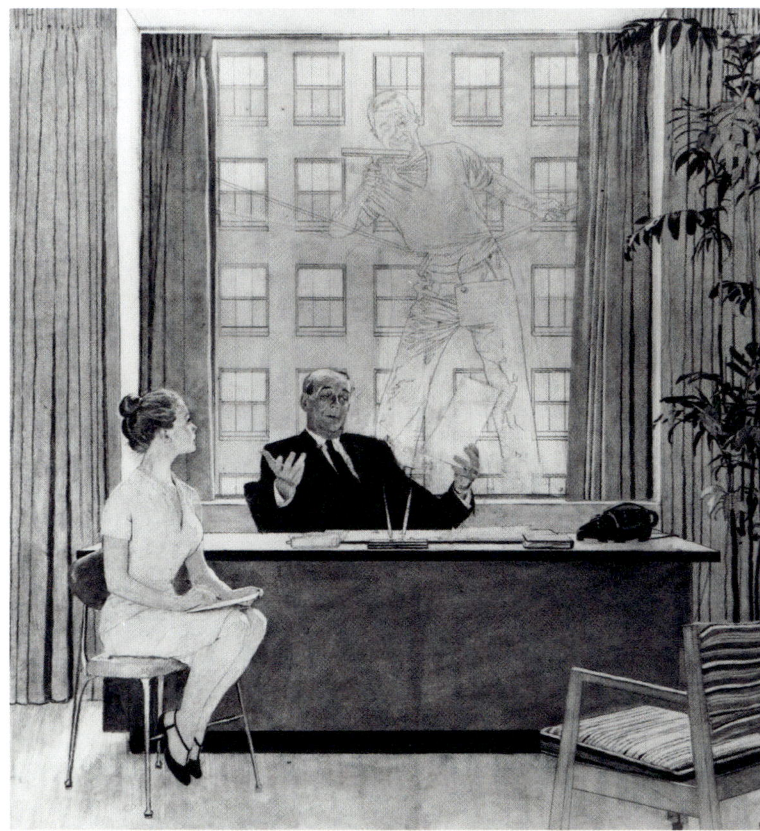

4.47. *Window Washer*, 1960
Charcoal on paper
Cover study for the *Saturday Evening Post*, September 17, 1960
Location unknown

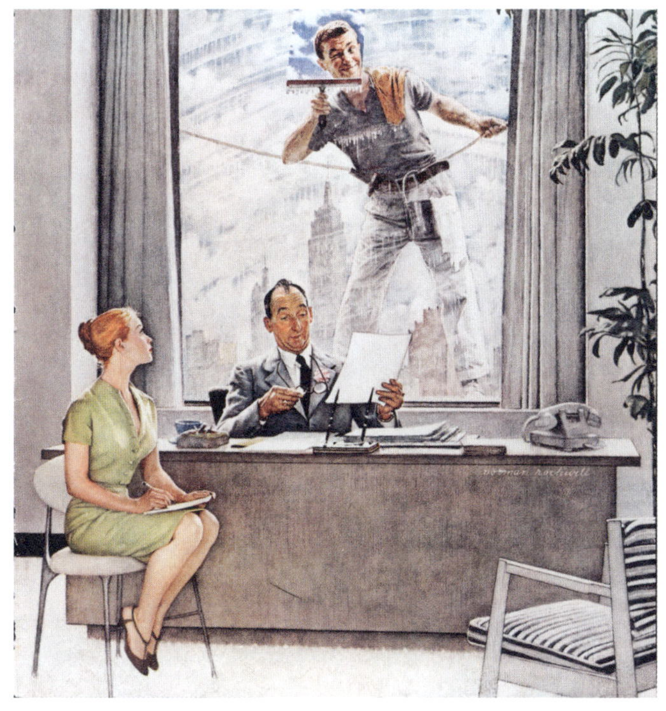

4.48. *Window Washer* (detail), 1960
Tear sheet, 14¼ × 11¼ in. (36.2 × 28.6 cm)
Cover illustration for the *Saturday Evening Post*, September 17, 1960
RC.2007.1.306 (Gift of John A. and Laura C. Savio)

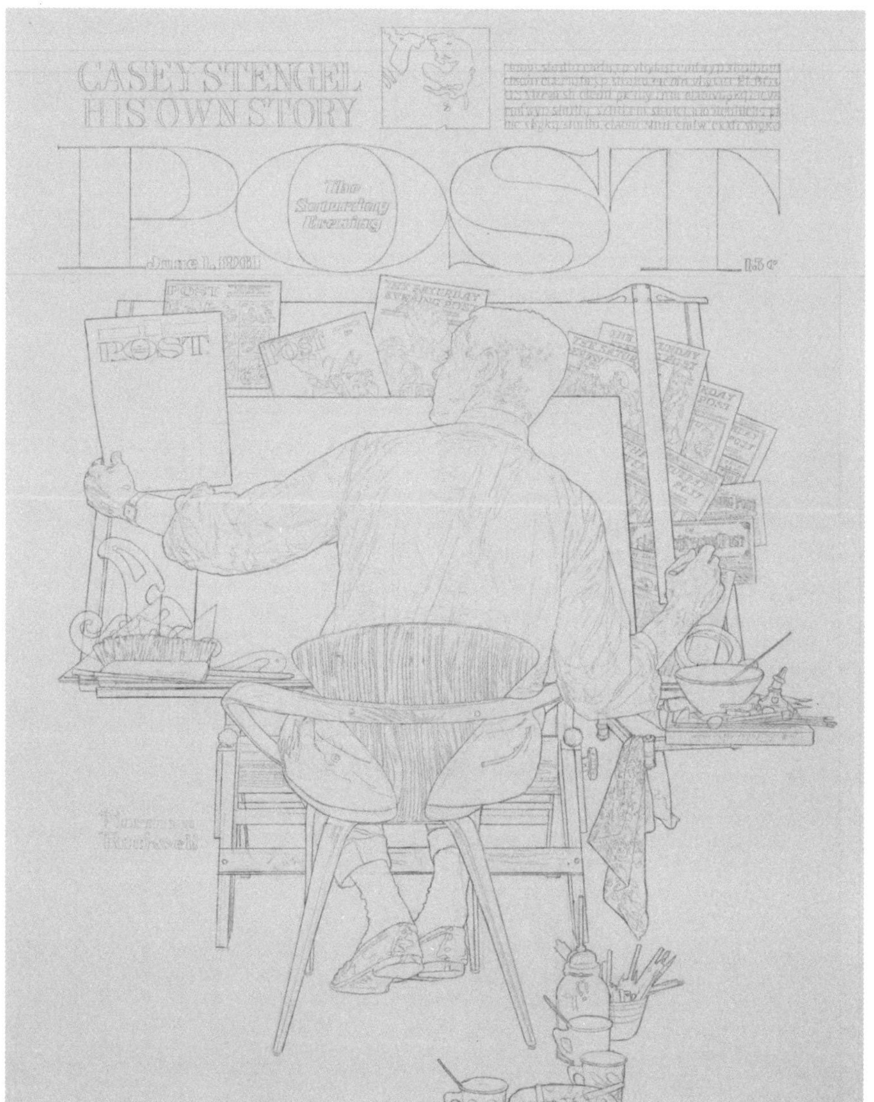


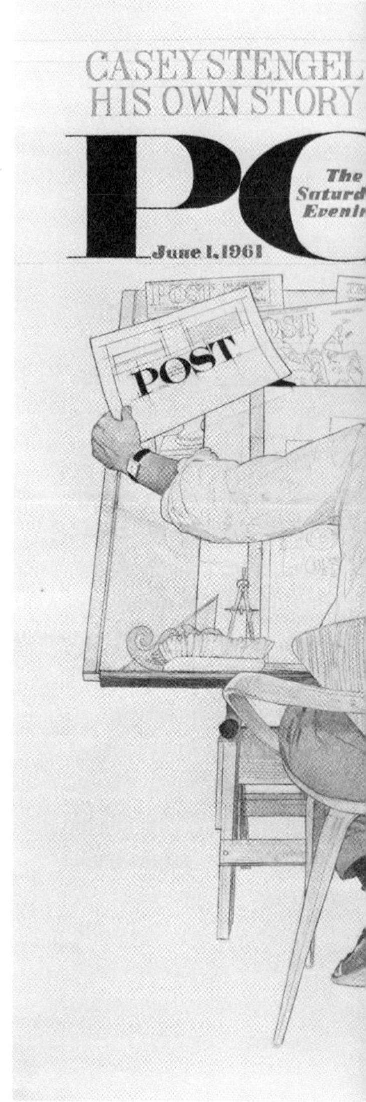


In 1961, the noted graphic designer Herbert Lubalin was hired to create a new, more contemporary logotype for the *Post*. To help readers accept the change, Rockwell was asked to paint the cover illustration for the first issue featuring the new design. His cover, also known as *Modernizing the* Post, shows Lubalin creating the logotype. Strewn over his drawing table are logos dating back to the beginning of the century. Reporting on the presentation of the cover to more than two hundred advertisers at the Savoy Hilton, the *Wall Street Journal* announced, "Saturday Evening Post's New Format Appears to Impress Advertisers." Just six months later, the magazine returned to its old format.

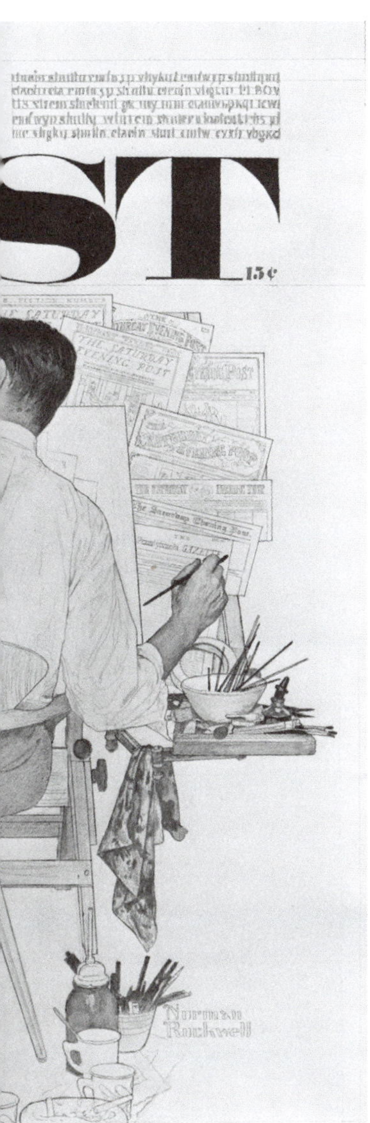

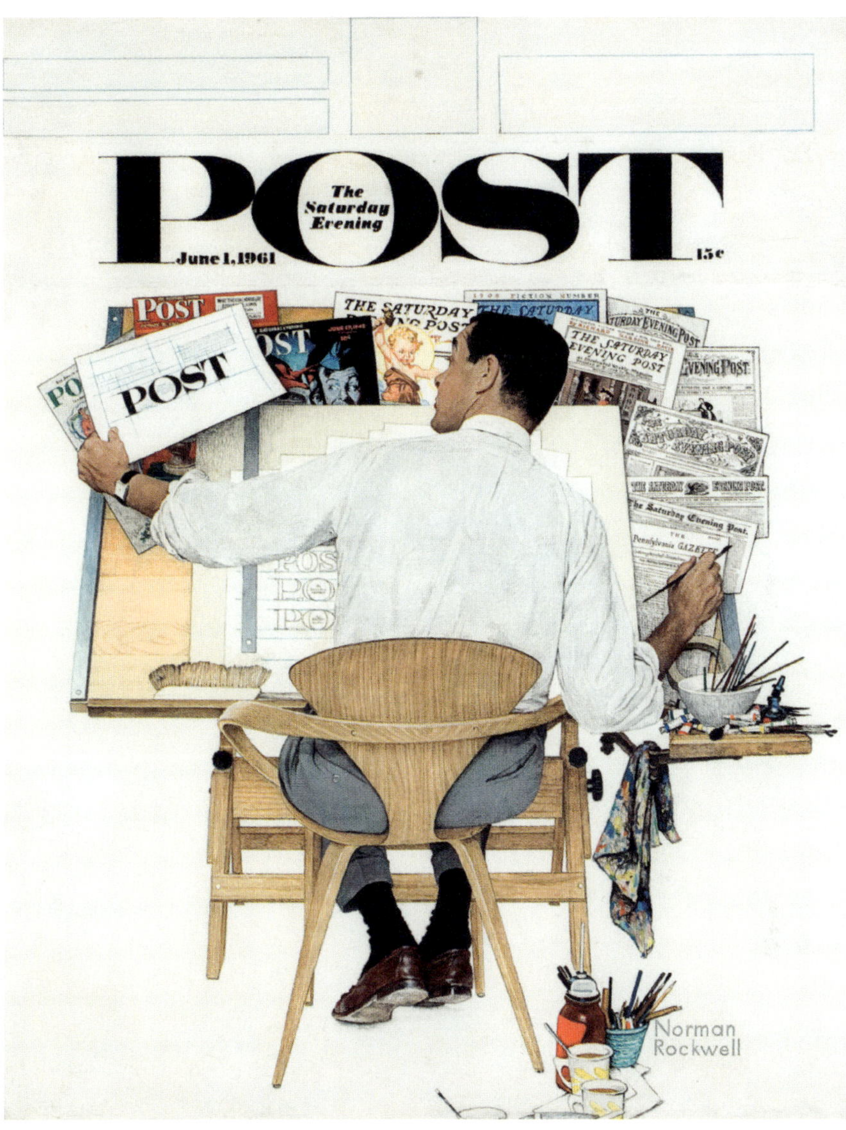


LEFT AND CENTER
4.49a–b. Bill Scovill (1915–1996)
Photographs of the drawing progress for *Lubalin Redesigning the* Post, 1961
Photographs (from negative)
RC.1997.3.230; ST1976.3560

RIGHT
4.50. *Lubalin Redesigning the* Post, 1961
Oil on canvas, 34 × 26½ in. (86.4 × 67.3 cm)
Cover illustration for the *Saturday Evening Post*, September 16, 1961
NRACT.1973.013

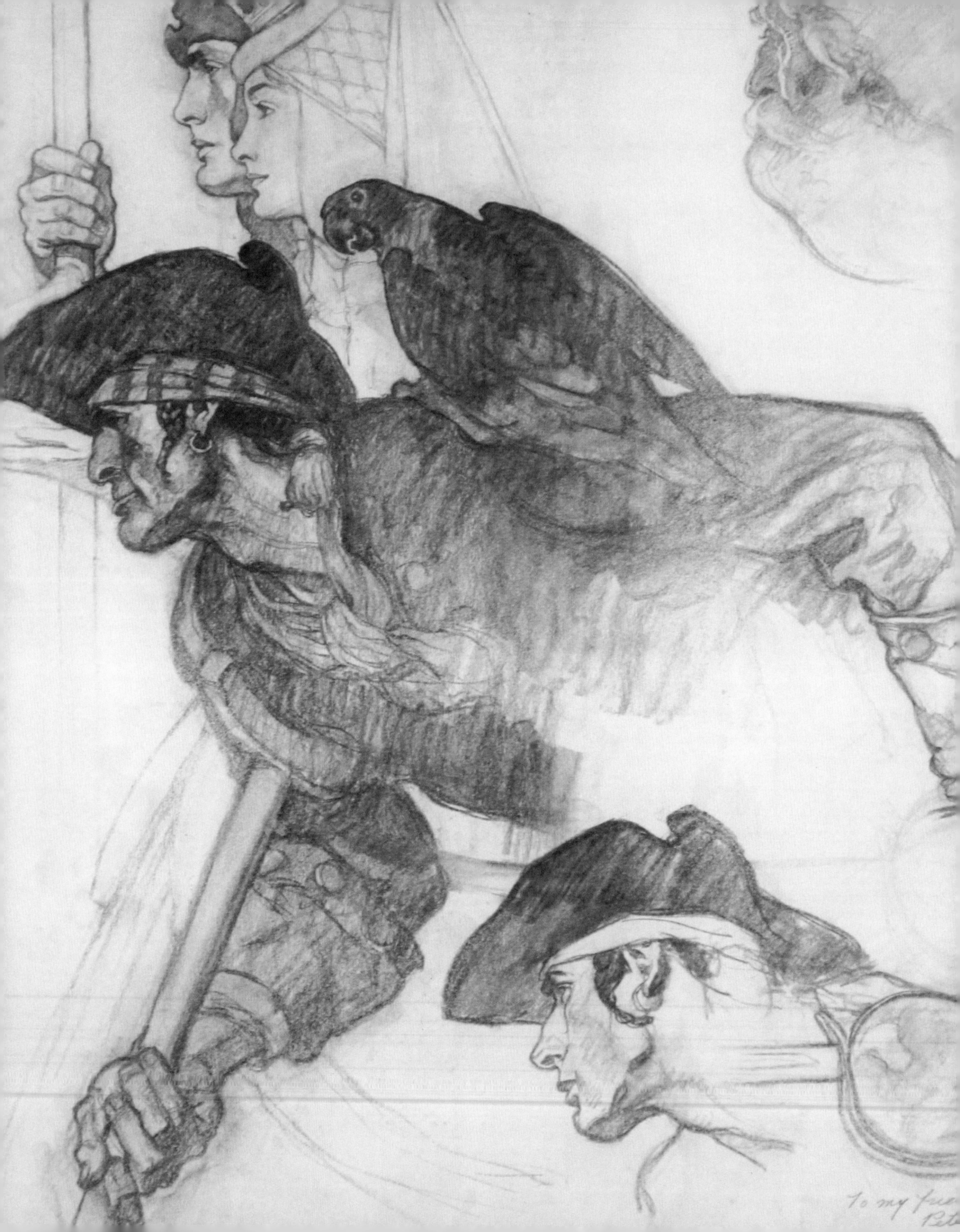
To my

# 5 Storytelling, Illustrations, and Classic Tales

STEPHANIE HABOUSH PLUNKETT

"My life work—and my pleasure—has been to tell stories to other people. I try to use each line, tone, color, and arrangement; each person, facial expression, gesture, and object in my picture for one supreme purpose—to tell a story and to tell it as directly, interestingly, and understandably as I can."

—Norman Rockwell[1]

Though Norman Rockwell preferred cover work to any other type of assignment, story illustration makes up a large body of Rockwell's art. Narrative texts by a wide range of authors, both famous and lesser-known, were the basis for thousands of illustrations. His interest in characterization and detail was perfectly suited to story illustration, which enhanced and expanded upon the written word in magazines and books. "An illustration is merely a scene from a story," Rockwell observed. "The characters and setting are fully developed by the author. So the illustrator

Detail of *The Land of Enchantment (Long John Silver)*, 1934
See plate 5.27.

has only to follow the story closely. His inspiration comes from the words, not, as in a *Saturday Evening Post* cover, from himself."[2]

Young people's adventure stories were an appropriate beginning for Rockwell, whose earliest illustrations appeared in *Boys' Life* and other children's publications when he was just a teenager. Through the 1940s, his art for published stories captivated countless readers of the *Post, American Magazine, Ladies' Home Journal,* and *Woman's Home Companion*. In the 1950s and early 1960s, Rockwell devoted himself more fully to cover illustration and accepted relatively few story assignments. But in the mid-1960s and 1970s, he illustrated his first children's picture book, and created a series of journalistic paintings for *Look*, departing from his fictional style. Politics, human rights, and man's journey to the moon would become his subjects, representing a turning point for the artist as a trusted visual commentator in an ever-changing world.

"I love to tell stories in pictures," Rockwell said. "For me, the story is the first thing and the last thing,"[3] and the framework upon which each illustration took shape. A consummate visual storyteller and a masterful draftsman and painter with a distinct, personal message to convey, Rockwell constructed fictional realities that offered a compelling picture of twentieth-century life. His seamless narratives seemed to ensure audience engagement with the publishers that commissioned his work, but the complexities of artistic production remained hidden to his enthusiasts, who were content to enjoy his art in finished form on the covers and pages of their favorite publications. What came between the first spark of an idea and a final Rockwell image was anyone's guess, and far more than readers would have ever imagined.

Conceptualization was central for Rockwell, who called the history of European art into play and employed classical painting methodology to weave contemporary tales inspired by everyday people and places. His richly detailed large-scale canvases and preparatory drawings offered far more than was necessary even by the standards of his profession. Each began with a single idea—and as in Rockwell's story illustrations, with an author's descriptive text. Sometimes hard to come by, strong picture concepts were indispensable for the artist, who, with an eye to graphic clarity, carefully balanced the integration of aesthetic and narrative elements in his art.

Just as in works of literature, character, plot, and setting play an important role for narrative artists—often in varying degrees depending upon the intent of their piece. Character is the "who," plot is the "what," and setting is the "where and when" of any visual story, and every artist has a different approach to incorporating these elements. Even before Rockwell had a clear picture concept, he had a general understanding of his subject as well as its emotional content. "If I have an illustration to do in a special setting, I always try to get the feel of the place," Rockwell wrote.[4]

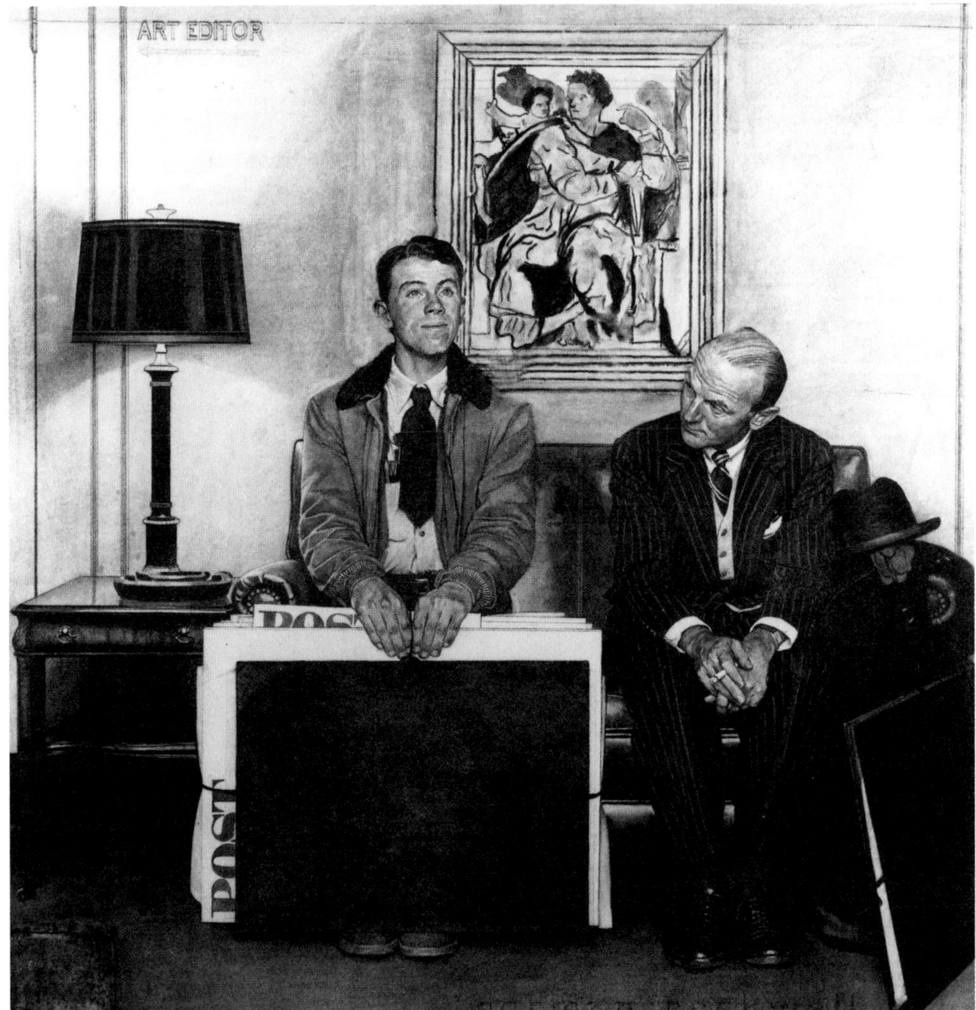


5.1. *Waiting for the Art Editor*, c. 1970
Charcoal on paper,
44½ × 41 in. (113 × 104.1 cm)
NRACT.1973.114

In *Waiting for the Art Editor* (plate 5.1), Rockwell tells his own story by recounting the experience of a young artist visiting the art editor of the *Post*, as he did in 1916, with portfolio in hand. After taking the train from New York to Philadelphia, home of the Curtis Publishing Company, Rockwell made his way to the sixth floor to see George Horace Lorimer (1867–1937), the *Post*'s powerful editor. But the artist arrived without an appointment, so newly installed art editor Walter H. Dower (1883–1934) reviewed Rockwell's work and presented it to Lorimer, who purchased two illustrations on the spot. Rockwell recalled that noted authors Irvin S. Cobb (1876–1944) and Samuel G. Blythe (1868–1947), who were in the reception room at the time, expressed amusement at the size of his massive portfolio.[5]

Seated in a well-appointed waiting room, the young artist has a wistful expression and is dressed in casual clothing, in contrast to the formal attire of the seasoned artist who warily looks on. In envisioning this scenario, Rockwell may have been thinking of friend, mentor, and New Rochelle, New York, neighbor J. C. Leyendecker (1874–1951), who was twenty years his senior and the *Post*'s most popular cover artist at the time. Here, both artists wait for the editor's review in a piece that also reveals Rockwell's appreciation for classical art and for the generations of artists who came before him. On the wall hangs a reproduction of the Old Testament *Prophet Isaiah* from Michelangelo's Sistine Chapel, c. 1511, which served as the inspiration for Rockwell's 1943 *Post* cover, *Rosie the Riveter*.

## Yankee Doodle

5.2. *The New Tavern Sign (Colonial Sign Painter)*, 1936
Oil on canvas, 30¼ × 54 in. (76.8 × 137.5 cm)
Illustration for the *Saturday Evening Post*, February 22, 1936, pp. 18–19
Private collection

George III (1738–1820) was the king of Great Britain and Ireland during the American Revolution. In *The New Tavern Sign*, a 1936 *Post* cover, Rockwell's colonial sign painter is intent upon replacing a tavern sign in the king's name with one honoring George Washington, the nation's first president (plate 5.2). Tavern signs originated from the practical need to identify businesses that provided entertainment and services to travelers—including food, drink, and lodging, as well as the feeding and stabling of horses. Many

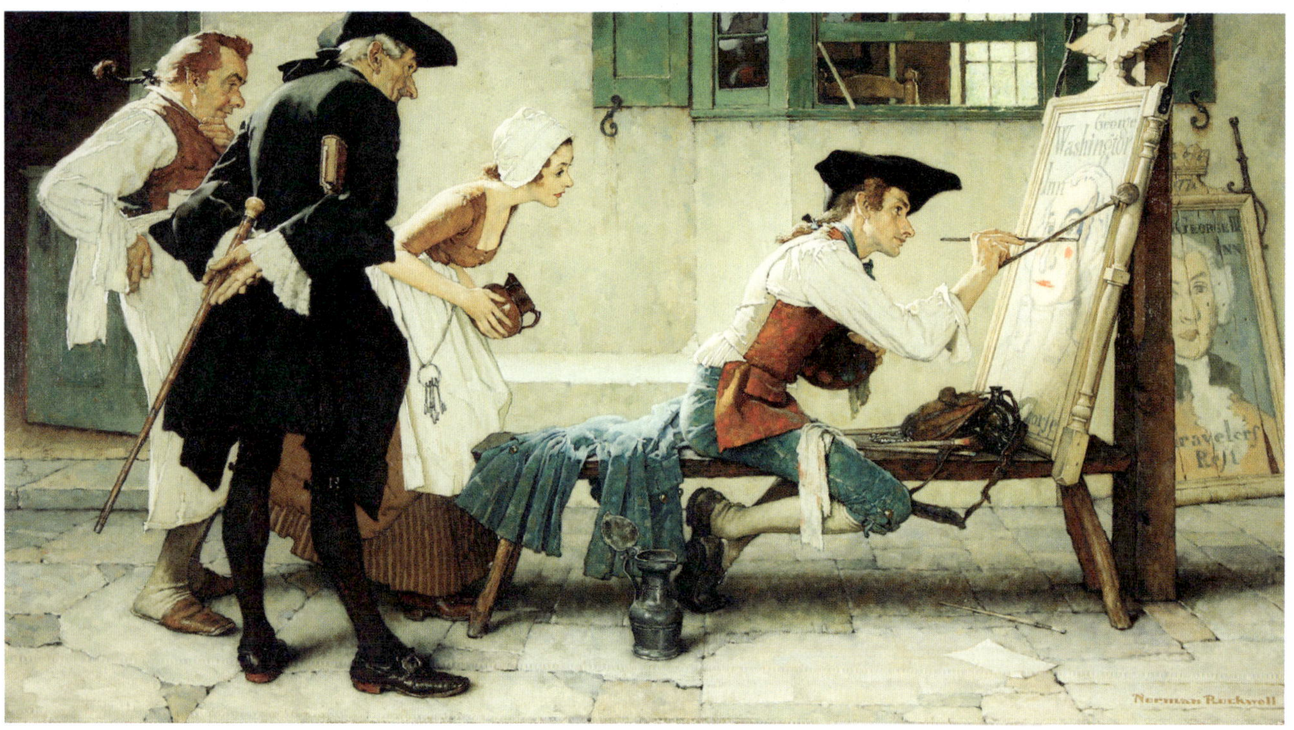

early sign painters were self-taught, or learned their craft as apprentices. Rockwell engaged a craftsman to build the wooden signs that are featured in this painting, harking back to earlier times.

Early in September 1937, a four-by-eleven-and-a-half-foot oil-on-canvas painting by Norman Rockwell was delivered to the taproom of the Nassau Tavern in Princeton, New Jersey. Rockwell's *New Tavern Sign* had caught the eye of Princeton architect Thomas Stapleton, who decided to commission Rockwell to paint a large oil for the taproom of the reconstructed 1756 Nassau Tavern at its new Princeton site. Rockwell enjoyed doing colonial subjects, and as Princeton was the site of a major Revolutionary War battle, a painting of Yankee Doodle was appropriate. The Tavern, relocated near its original site in a new town square known as Palmer Square, was part of a redevelopment project by Princeton University graduate Edgar Palmer, who began its planning in 1925 and financed the project in 1936. Rockwell's painting was placed behind the bar to be enjoyed by all the male guests, as the taproom was still "reserved for guests who may enjoy their wine in peace and speak freely of Politicks and such subjects of peculiar interest to the Male." Women were excluded until 1972.[6]

Rockwell researched and had made new costumes for his Hessian and British soldier models. He engaged his friend Fred Hildebrandt, a professional model and illustrator, to pose as Yankee Doodle. Work continued during the ensuing months. Rockwell completed a large Wolff pencil preliminary (plate 5.3) in preparation for the oil. He hired New Rochelle *Post* cover artist Walter Beach Humphrey to letter in the lyrics. Rockwell noted that he had never learned to letter well, so that whenever he needed text inscribed on his art, he called upon an expert to draw it. He then painted it to imbue it with his own artistic touch.

The tune of "Yankee Doodle" is said to derive from an English nursery rhyme. The nonsense lyrics were written in 1755 by British army physician Richard Shackburg to mock the disheveled colonials with whom the British served during the French and Indian War. During the Revolution it was appropriated by the colonists and became a favorite tune of colonial soldiers, who sang it in battle, in defeat, and in victory. The lyrics of a later chorus, used in Rockwell's depiction, are credited to Edward Bangs. In this preliminary, Rockwell used the word "went," but he changed it to "came" in the final oil painting. The term "Yankee" was used by the British as a derogatory term for a Puritan, a "doodle" was a simpleton, and "macaroni" was either the knot on which the feather was fastened or a dandyish young man, the latter being the common interpretation.

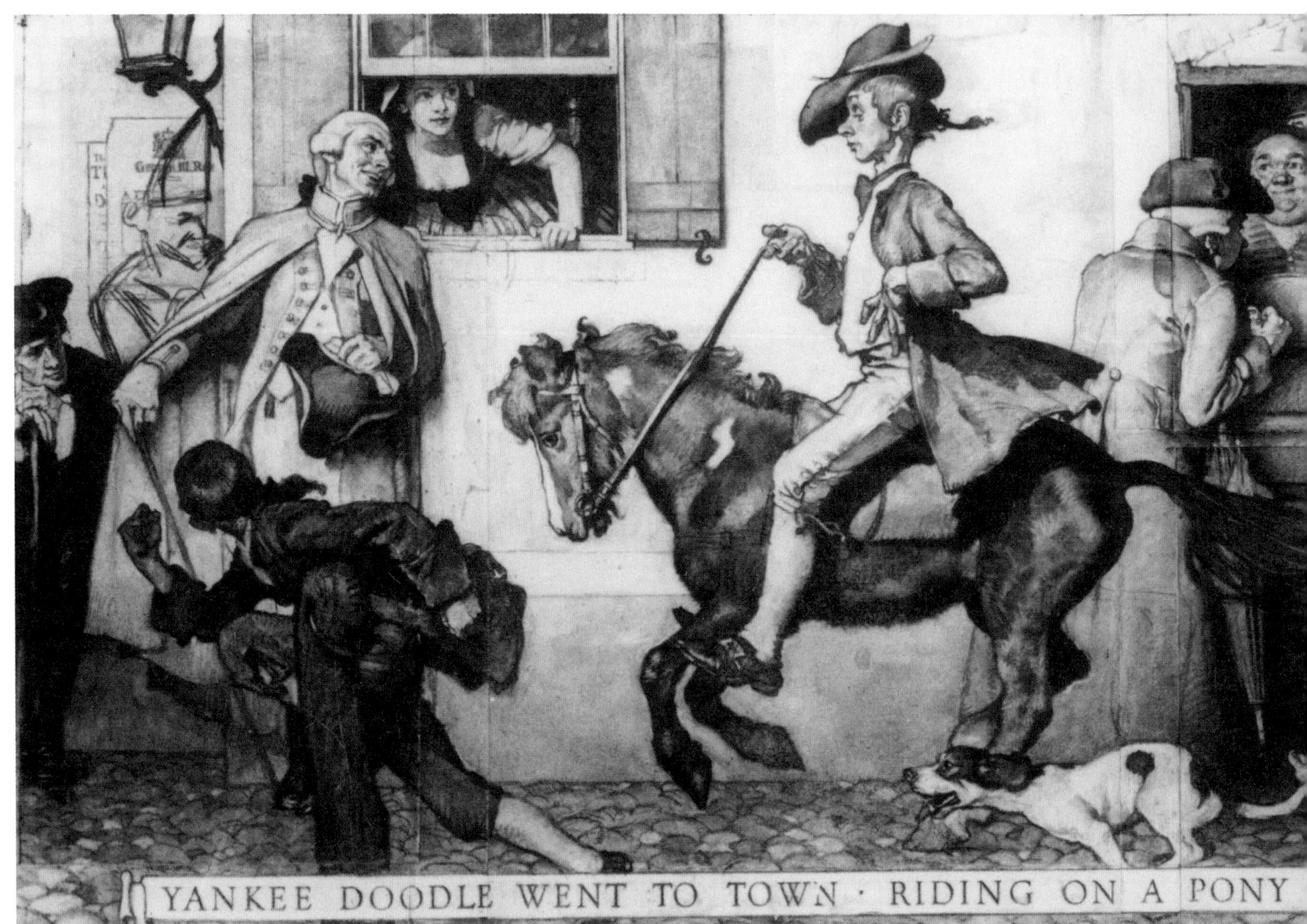


5.3. *Yankee Doodle*, 1937
Wolff pencil and charcoal
on paper mounted to board,
24½ × 72 in. (62.2 × 182.9 cm)
Preparatory mural drawing for Nassau
Tavern, Princeton, New Jersey
NRM.1981.01 (museum purchase)

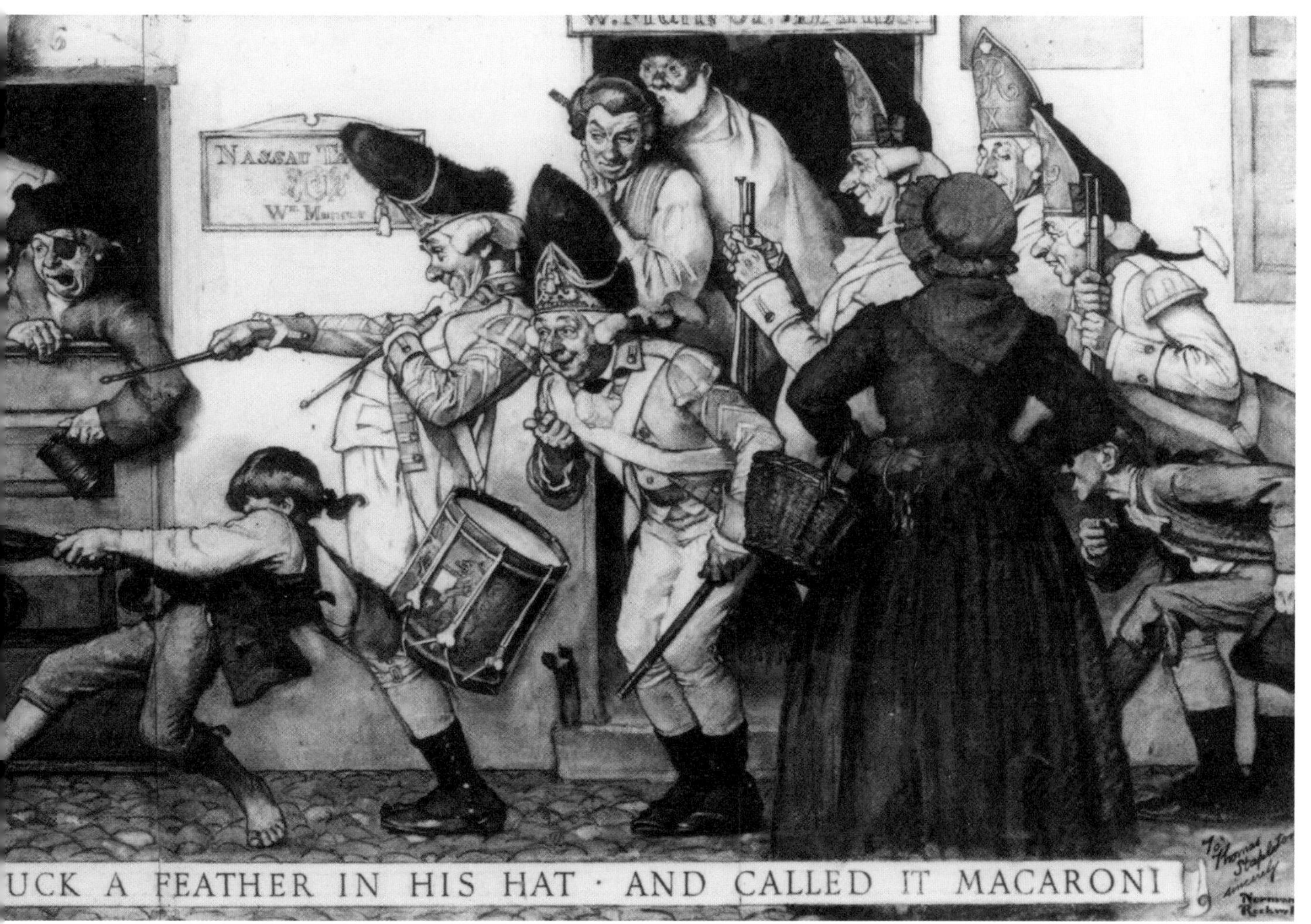
UCK A FEATHER IN HIS HAT · AND CALLED IT MACARONI

## Illuminating Alcott

Story and book illustrations comprised an important aspect of Rockwell's work in the 1930s. When *Woman's Home Companion* commissioned Rockwell to illustrate a biography of Louisa May Alcott (1832–1888), the author of *Little Women*, Rockwell went to the Alcott home in Concord, Massachusetts, where he made sketches of her bedroom and the attic where she used to write. "I had a real sense of the period; the old lamps and the lace curtains and hooked rugs and the Boston rocker really took me back," said Rockwell.[7] Rockwell executed both color and black-and-white illustrations for the article, and the latter are noteworthy examples of the artist's finished drawings intended for publication.

In *But It Was a Girl*, the writer, philosopher, and reformer Amos Bronson Alcott (1799–1888), with book in hand, peers at the infant Louisa. Rock-

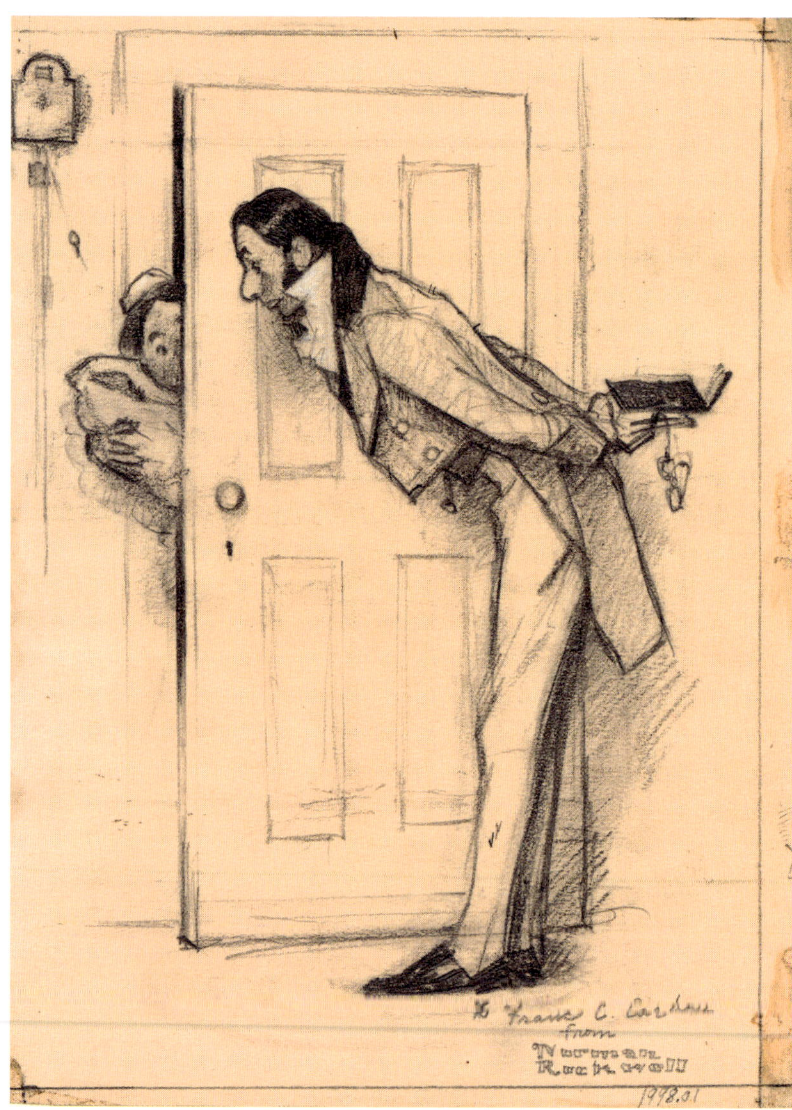

5.4. *But It Was a Girl*, 1938
Wolff pencil on paper,
8¾ × 6¾ in. (22.2 × 17.2 cm)
Study for Katharine Anthony, "The Most Beloved American Writer," *Woman's Home Companion*, March 1938
NRM.1998.01 (museum purchase)

well's charcoal study is fairly complete, but his final drawing for publication makes adjustments to Bronson Alcott's hairstyle and introduces such domestic elements as miniature portrait silhouettes and a period chair. The hands on the clock are more clearly delineated to indicate the time of the author's birth.

In this illustration, Rockwell stays fairly close to the writer's description of events while adding lighthearted humor. Amos Bronson Alcott and his wife Abba's first child was a girl, and they fully expected that their second would be a boy. "If the child was born on November twenty-ninth, [1832,] as it probably would be, it would have the same birthday as its father. The coming baby arrived just half an hour after midnight on the auspicious day. But it was a girl," wrote author Katharine Anthony.[8]

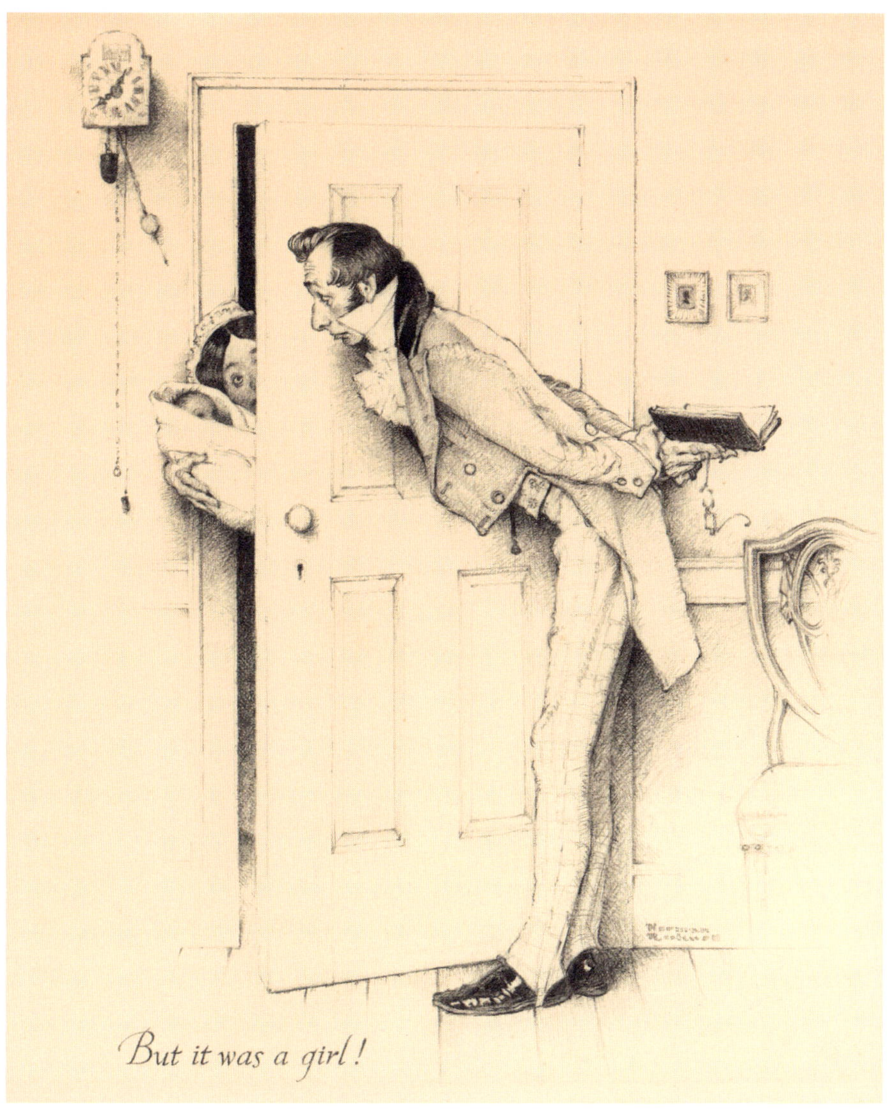


5.5. *But It Was a Girl*, 1938
Wolff pencil on paper, 13¼ × 10 in. (33.7 × 27.6 cm)
Illustration for Katharine Anthony, "The Most Beloved American Writer," *Woman's Home Companion*, March 1938
NRM.2000.02
(museum purchase)

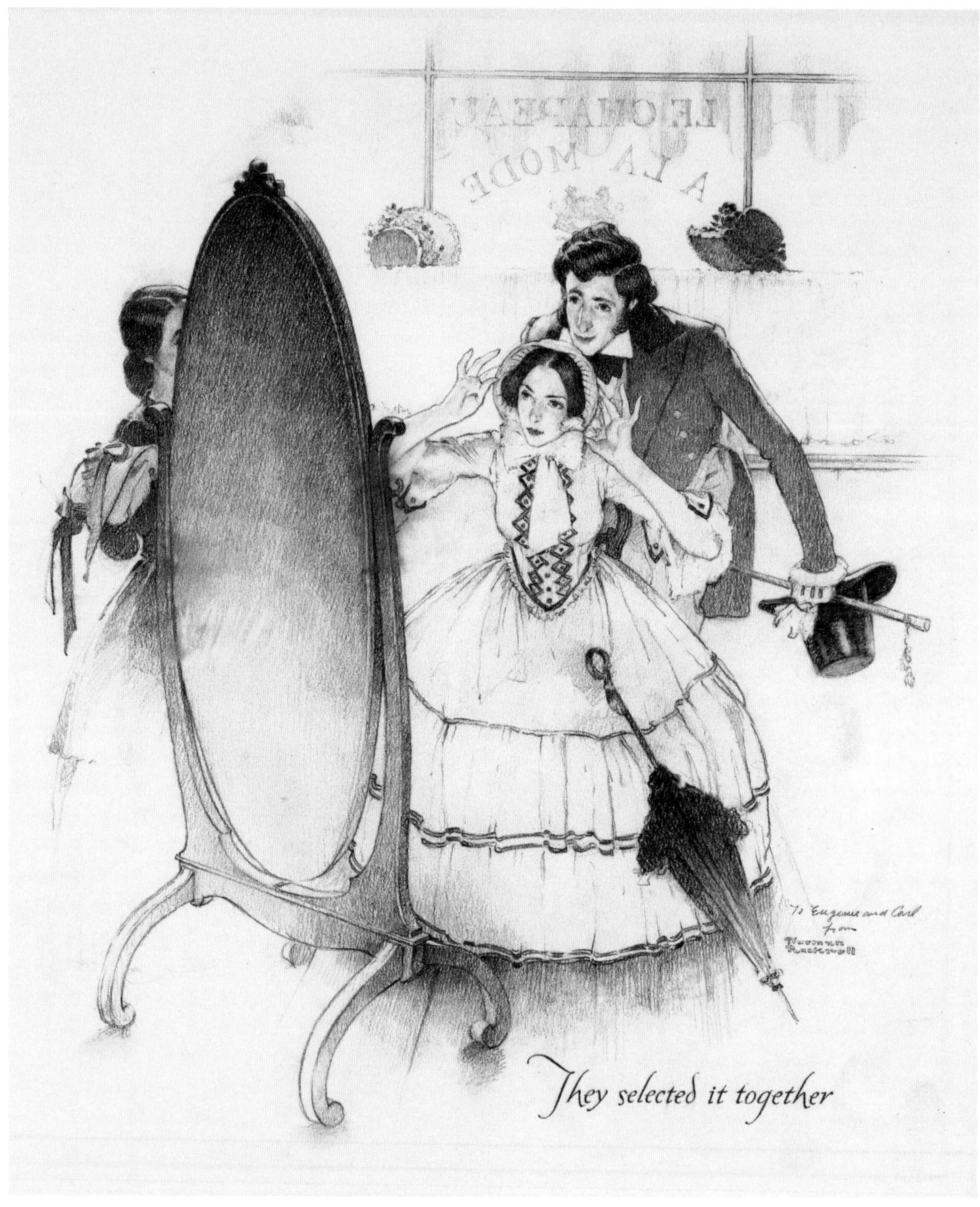


5.6. *They Selected It Together*, 1938
Wolff pencil on paper, 14½ x 12 in. (36.8 x 30.5 cm)
Illustration for Katharine Anthony, "The Most Beloved American Writer," *Woman's Home Companion*, April 1938, p. 11
NRM.1997.11 (museum purchase)

## In Mark Twain's Footsteps

To achieve authenticity in his illustrations for *The Adventures of Tom Sawyer*, Rockwell traveled to Hannibal, Missouri—Mark Twain's boyhood home. There, he visited Twain's house and the cave where Tom and Becky became lost. He even sketched the window from which the young Samuel Clemens used to climb, and purchased well-worn clothing from Hannibal residents to use in his artworks.

Rockwell was astounded by Twain's accuracy in describing Tom's famous escape from his bedroom window to meet up with Huckleberry Finn in chapter nine. Tom " 'was dressed and out of the window and creeping along the roof of the "ell" on all fours. He . . . then jumped to the roof of the woodshed and thence to the ground.' That's how Twain described it," Rockwell wrote. "When I visited the house he'd lived in . . . that was exactly what anyone would do if they left the bedroom by window."[9] Rockwell's Tom Sawyer wears suspenders and patched trousers, and is barefoot with a bandaged big toe. Twain's text reveals that Tom and Huck generally went barefoot, a detail that Rockwell and other illustrators have made sure to reflect in their art. Moonlight pervades the picture even in Rockwell's charcoal study, which set the composition, tonality, and details for his final painting, as was his general practice. In typical Rockwell fashion, this image features a frame within a frame, identifying Tom as the drawing's focal point.

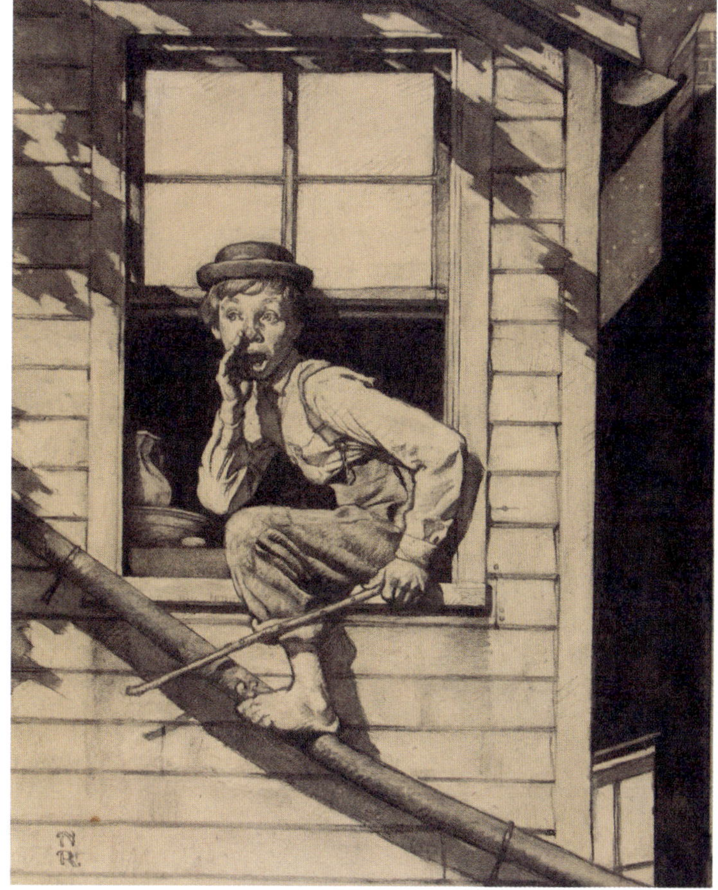

5.7. *He Meow'd with Caution Once or Twice* [Tom Sawyer Sneaking out the Window], 1936
Pencil and charcoal on paper, 24 × 18 in. (61 × 45.7 cm)
Study for Mark Twain, *The Adventures of Tom Sawyer* (New York: The Heritage Press, 1936)
Private collection

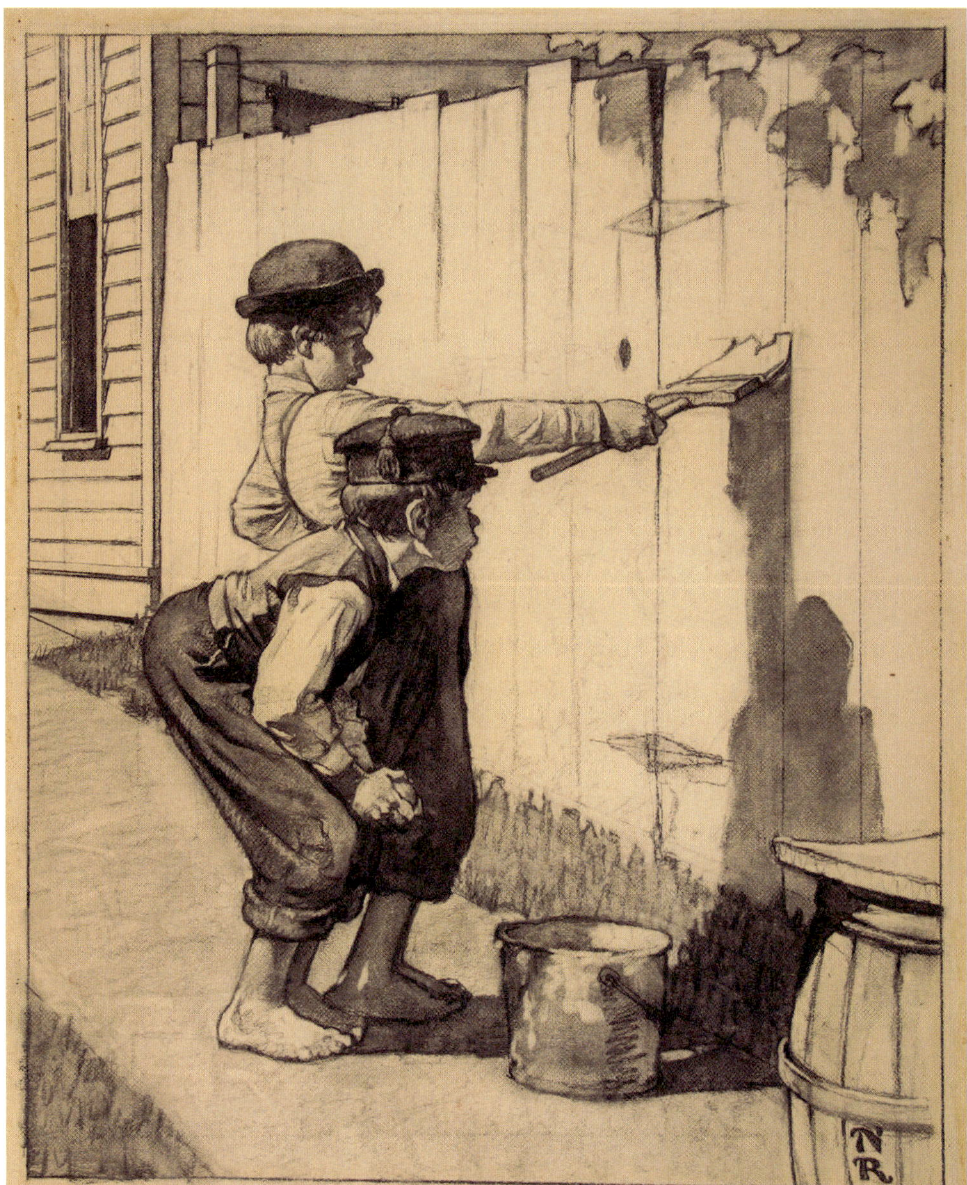


5.8. *Well, I Don't See Why I Oughtn't to Like It. Does a Boy Get a Chance to Whitewash a Fence Every Day?* [Tom Sawyer Whitewashing the Fence], 1936
Pencil and charcoal on paper, 24 × 18 in. (61 × 45.7 cm)
Study for Mark Twain, *The Adventures of Tom Sawyer* (New York: The Heritage Press, 1936)
Private collection

This drawing is a study for the book's color frontispiece, and is related to chapter two, "The Glorious Whitewasher." In the story, Tom Sawyer lures the boys of fictitious Saint Petersburg, Missouri, into whitewashing a fence—a task that he himself dreaded. Rockwell's model for Tom was young Richard Gregory of New Rochelle; he spent Saturdays for six uncomfortable months holding the poses for Rockwell's images. In the artist's drawing, the cast shadow created by young Ben Rogers's outstretched arm and Tom's intent posture and gaze establish a strong focal point for this work—Aunt Polly's whitewashed fence.

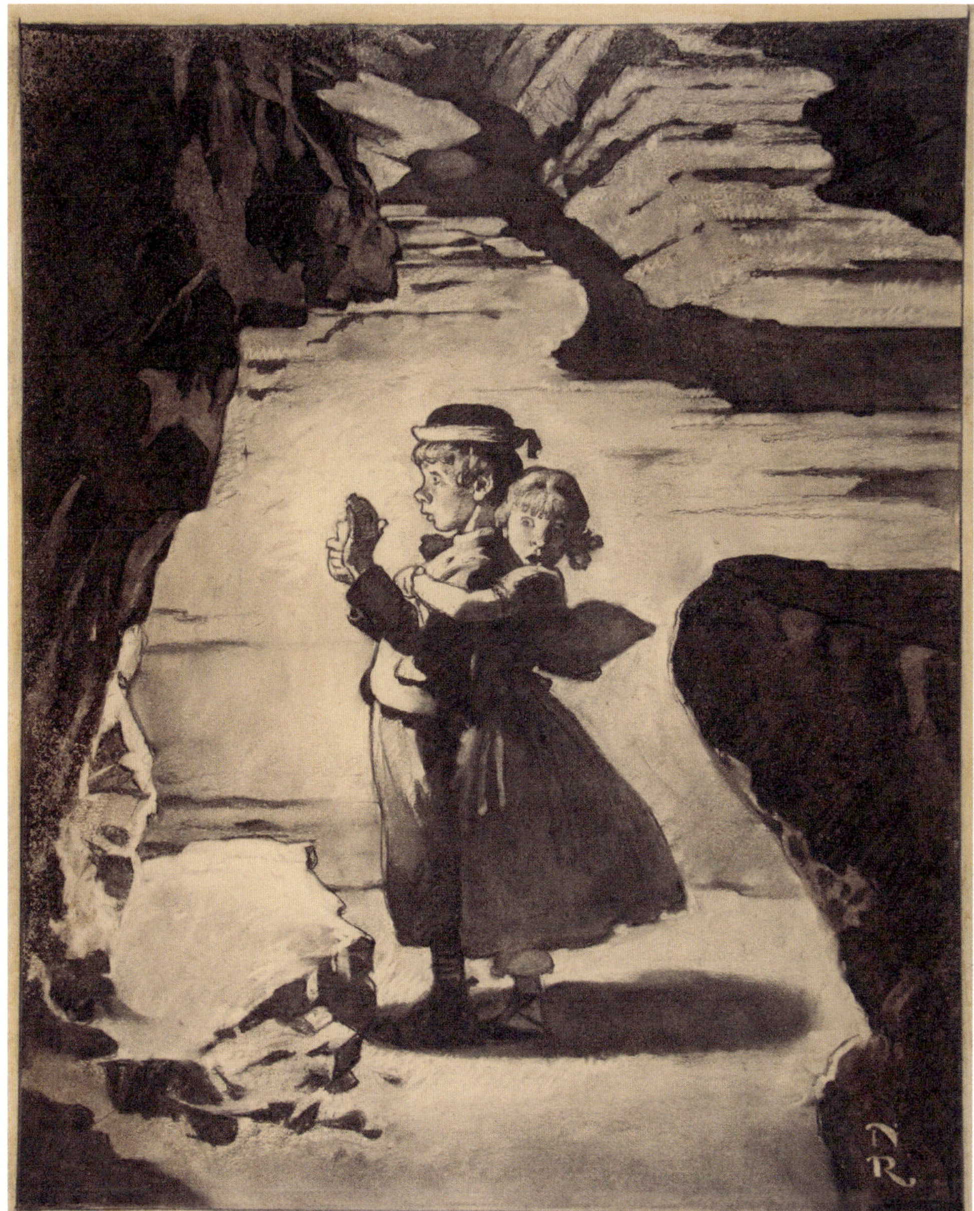

5.9. *Tom, Tom, We're Lost! We're Lost!* [Tom and Becky in the Cave], 1936
Pencil and charcoal on paper, 24 × 18 in. (61 × 45.7 cm)
Study for Mark Twain, *The Adventures of Tom Sawyer* (New York: The Heritage Press, 1936)
Private collection

An adventure clearly recalled by Rockwell was his visit to Five Points, an intersection of passages about a mile and a half into McDowell's Cave, the real-life inspiration for the McDougal's Cave in which Tom Sawyer and Becky Thatcher get lost. Instructed to come back at night to avoid tourists, he was left alone by the guide, who had to attend to his wife, who was giving birth. To stave off panic, he began to draw and before long made an important observation. He noted that other artists had painted the cave with stalactites hanging from the roof and sides. But Rockwell realized that the formations were actually horizontal, and in this drawing jutting ledges frame Tom and Becky, who are bathed in the light of a candle.

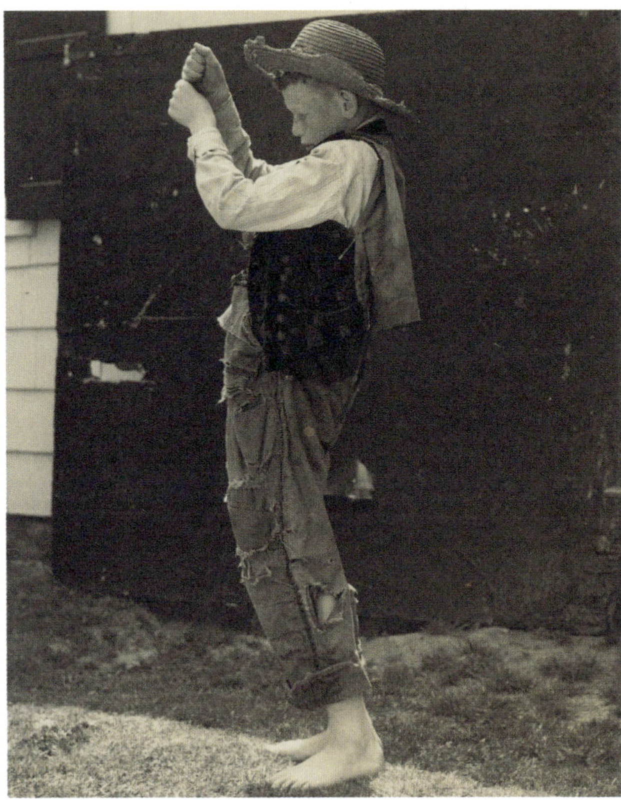

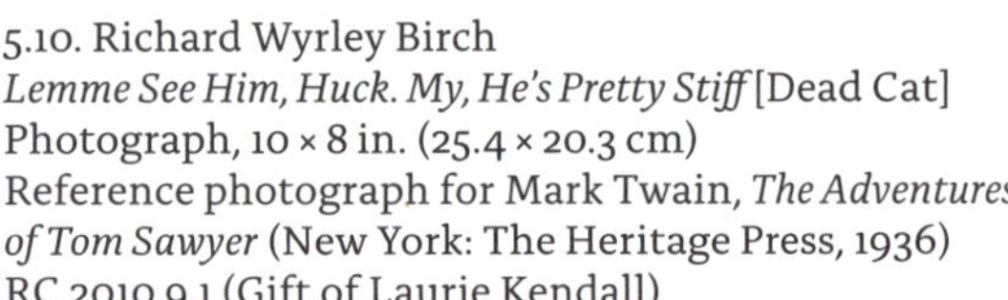

5.10. Richard Wyrley Birch
*Lemme See Him, Huck. My, He's Pretty Stiff* [Dead Cat]
Photograph, 10 × 8 in. (25.4 × 20.3 cm)
Reference photograph for Mark Twain, *The Adventures of Tom Sawyer* (New York: The Heritage Press, 1936)
RC.2010.9.1 (Gift of Laurie Kendall)

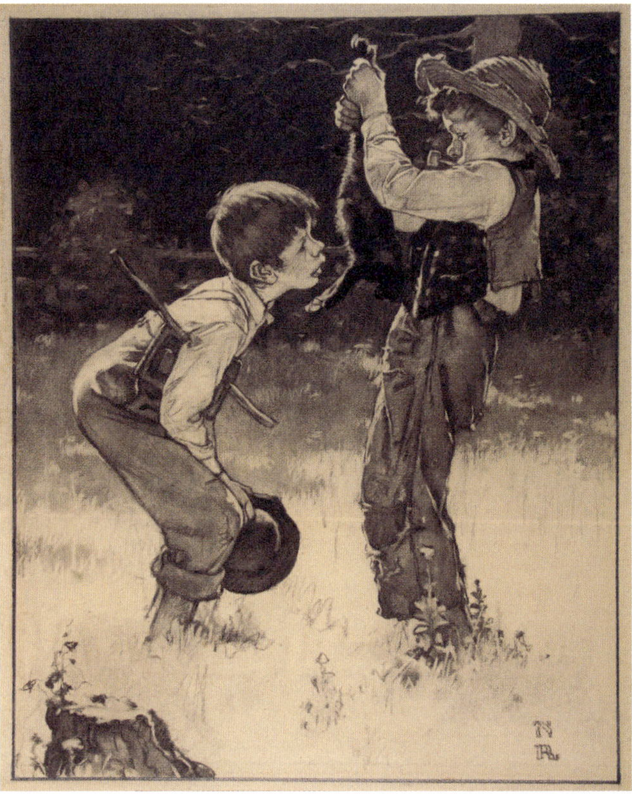

5.11. *Lemme See Him, Huck. My, He's Pretty Stiff* [Dead Cat], 1936
Pencil and charcoal on paper, 24 × 18 in. (61 × 45.7 cm)
Study for Mark Twain, *The Adventures of Tom Sawyer* (New York: The Heritage Press, 1936), 60
Private collection

In the 1930s, Rockwell began using photography as an integral part of his creative process. A deadline-driven artist, he was now able to cast the roles for his illustrations and direct model poses with great specificity. Richard Wyrley Birch lived in New Rochelle at the time and observed that Rockwell "was having trouble finding a photographer."[10] Commissioned to assist with *The Adventures of Tom Sawyer*, he continued to work with Rockwell as a photographer, model, and model scout until the artist moved to Arlington, Vermont, in 1939. Birch's photograph of a model posing as Huck Finn pretending to hold up a dead cat is one of the few surviving images from the series. As seen in the photo (plate 5.10) and related drawing (plate 5.11), Rockwell costumed his model according to Twain's description, wearing the cast-off clothing of a grown man.

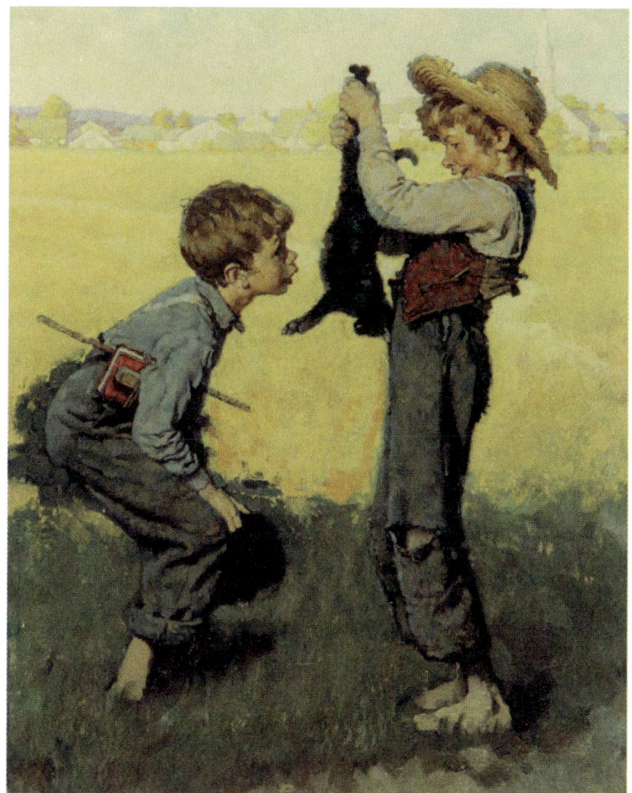

5.12. *Lemme See Him, Huck. My, He's Pretty Stiff* [Dead Cat], 1936
Oil on board, 30 × 26 in. (77.2 × 67 cm)
Color study for Mark Twain, *The Adventures of Tom Sawyer* (New York: The Heritage Press, 1936)
Collection of James Gurney

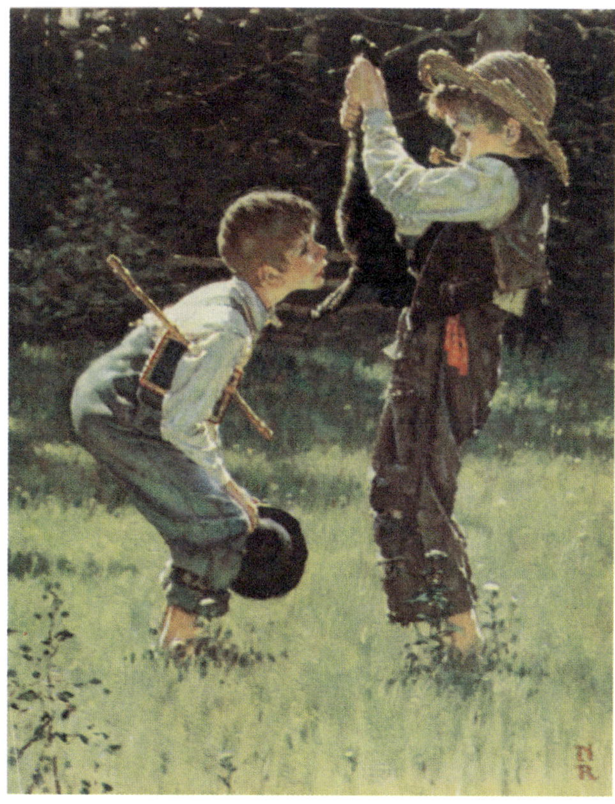

5.13. *Lemme See Him, Huck. My, He's Pretty Stiff* [Dead Cat], 1936
Oil on canvas, 25 × 20 in. (63.5 × 50.8 cm)
Illustration for Mark Twain, *The Adventures of Tom Sawyer* (New York: The Heritage Press, 1936)
Mark Twain Boyhood Home & Museum, Hannibal, Missouri

Created for "Tom Meets Becky," chapter six in the book, this image introduces readers to Huckleberry Finn, the unsupervised son of the town drunkard who is scorned by village parents and a hero to their children. Here, Huck is the bearer of a dead cat, which Tom studies intently. In his final painting (plate 5.12), Rockwell uses a lighting technique that is somewhat unusual for him, in which an edge effect from bright sunlight makes figures against a shaded background stand out. His impressionistic color study (plate 5.13), which also reflects the direction of his drawing, presents the opposite scenario—pictured in a sunlit field, the boys' silhouettes are emphasized by the shadowed outlines of their clothing.

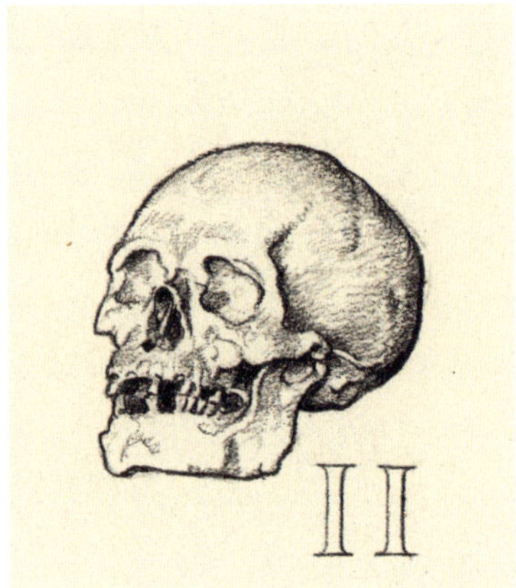


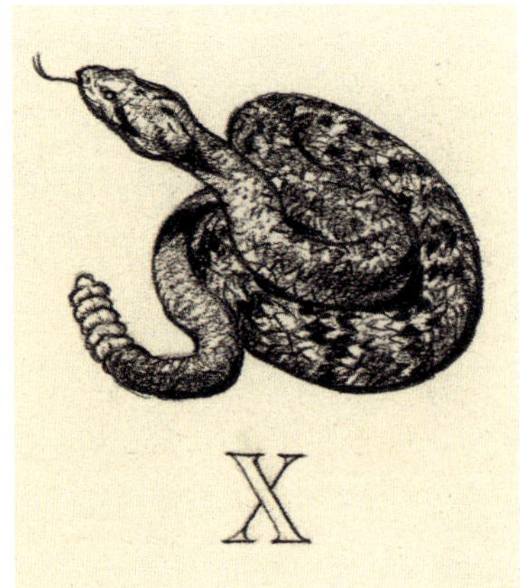


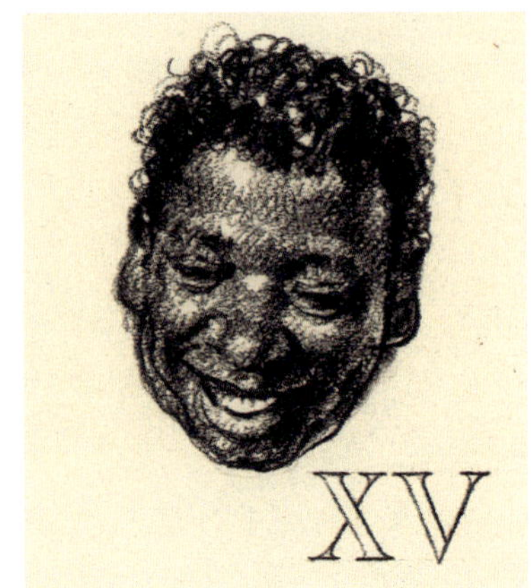


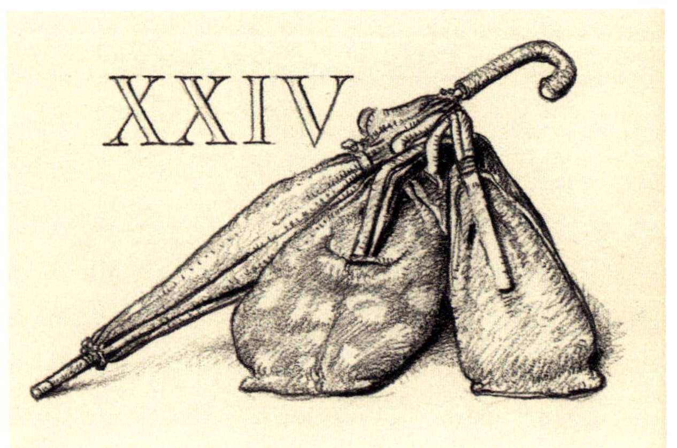


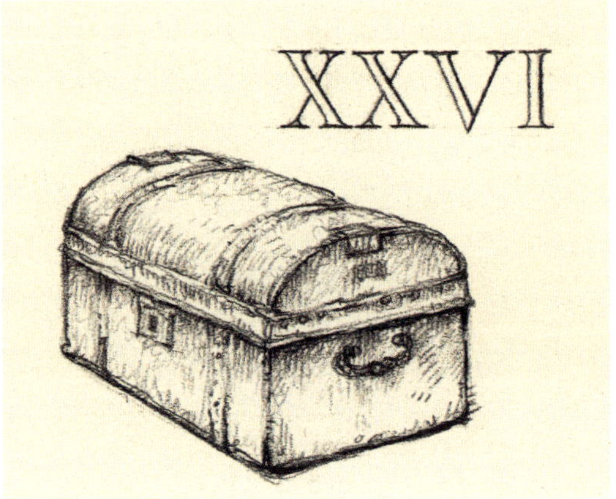


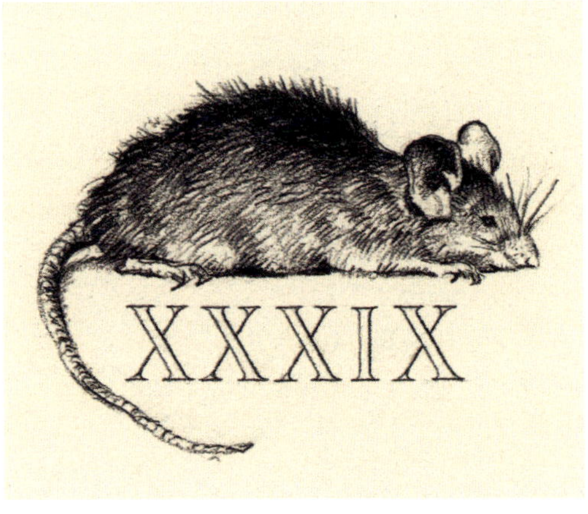


Rockwell's illustrations for *Tom Sawyer* and *Huckleberry Finn* included not only full-page color plates (eight per book) but also black-and-white drawings for the chapter headings, each intended to identify a unique story element with a singular image. Boldly and in some cases loosely drawn, Rockwell's chapter headings reflect both an ease with and mastery of his craft.

5.14a–f. Chapter heading illustrations for Mark Twain, *The Adventures of Huckleberry Finn* (New York: The Heritage Press, 1940)
Graphite on board, 5 × 5 in. (12.7 × 12.7 cm) each
Private collection

## A Horatio Alger Story

Norman Rockwell completed nearly three thousand images for publication, but less well known are the many images he created as preliminary studies. In some cases, a final image was never painted and the preliminary is the only record of Rockwell's idea. In 1945, the artist approached George Macy, publisher of the successful Rockwell-illustrated editions of *Tom Sawyer* and *Huckleberry Finn*, with an idea for a book for boys—an anthology of single chapters from popular boys' fiction. Rockwell prepared drawings for two of the proposed stories—*Phil the Fiddler* and *Little Lord Fauntleroy*. *Phil the Fiddler* was Horatio Alger Jr.'s 1872 attempt to expose and discredit the custom in Italy of selling boys as slaves to be brought to this country to work as street beggars for their owners. In December 1945, Macy wrote to Rockwell with enthusiasm about the project and scheduled publication for December 1947. An editor was assigned to do research for Rockwell and, in October 1946, sent him pictures of children and a copy of a Laura Caxton engraving of her interpretation of *Phil the Fiddler*. Rockwell posed a waiflike Vermont country boy as the child street musician. But this empathetically drawn portrayal of *Phil the Fiddler* was never painted. That year, Rockwell painted seven *Saturday Evening Post* covers, and was sent by the magazine around the country to document contemporary life in America through visual reports that were published in the magazine. His enthusiasm for new projects always propelled him through the idea stage, but with *Post* commissions taking precedence, new projects often were derailed.

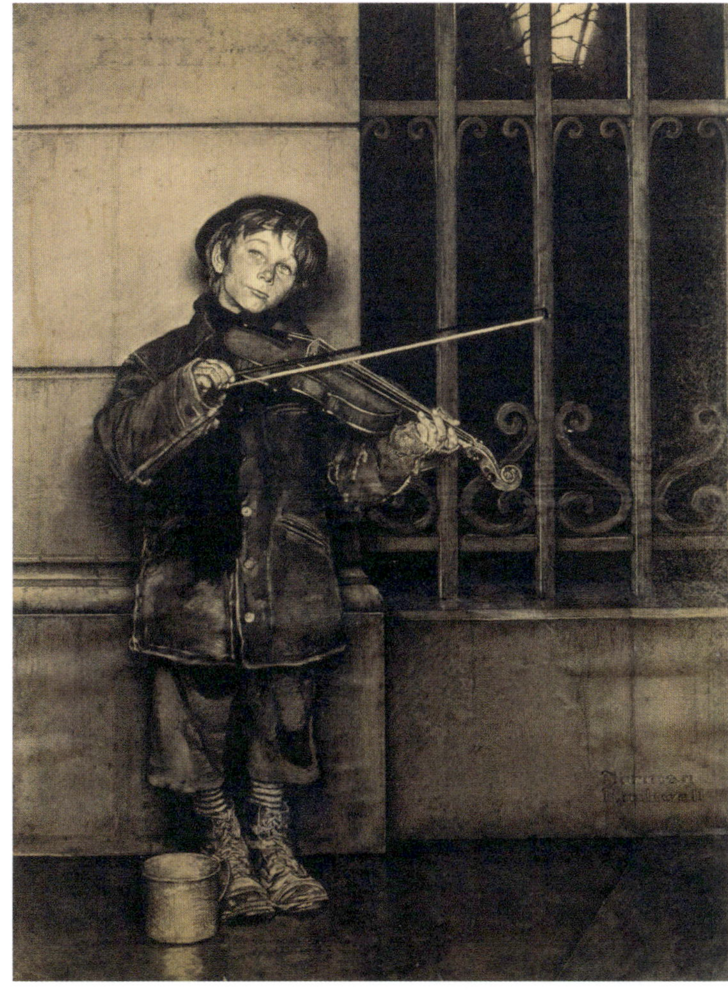

5.15. *Phil the Fiddler*, c. 1940
Charcoal on paper, 41 × 30 in.
(104.1 × 76.2 cm)
Unpublished drawing
NRACT.1973.109

## On Assignment for the Post

Between 1943 and 1948 the *Post* sent Rockwell on eight visits around the country to record the lives of representative Americans in a pictorial series. For each visual report, the artist produced multiple images in order to document contemporary life in America. He shared with *Post* readers what it was like to spend a night with paratroopers on a troop train; wait with reporters and photographers to see the president at the White House; apply at a ration board in Manchester, Vermont; vote at a polling station in Cedar Rapids, Iowa; visit a newspaper in Monroe County, Missouri; attend a one-room school in rural Carroll County, Georgia; spend a day with a family doctor in Arlington, Vermont; and make the rounds with a county agent in Jay County, Indiana.

When Rockwell visited the office of the *Monroe County Appeal*, a weekly newspaper in Paris, Missouri, he spent several days sketching the employ-

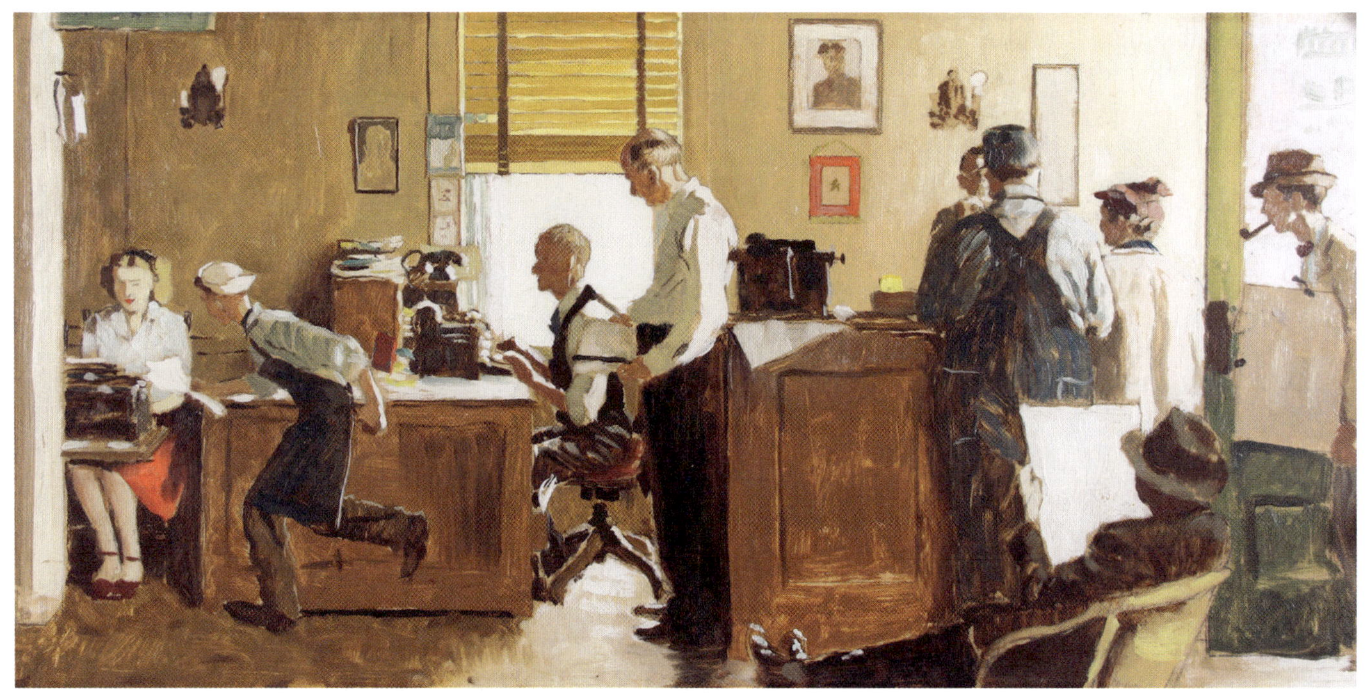

5.16. *Norman Rockwell Visits a Country Editor*, 1946
Oil on board, 12 × 23½ in. (30.5 × 59.7 cm)
Color study for Norman Rockwell, "Norman Rockwell Visits a Country Editor," *Saturday Evening Post*, May 25, 1946
NRACT.1973.122

ees there. The final painting depicts the staff doing Thursday's task, getting the paper to press. From left to right, secretary Fernelle Wood is typing copy as Dickie Wyatt, a printer's devil (or printing apprentice), runs by Jack Blanton, the editor of the paper for fifty-three years. He is putting the finishing touches on his editorial piece as printer Paul Nipps gauges the number of print lines it needs. At the counter, Malcolm Higgins, the city editor and a reporter, helps customers. Making a cameo appearance in the painting, Rockwell walks through the door with portfolio in hand.

As an interim step between Rockwell's drawing and his final painting, he would often create a color study that allowed him to establish his palette and pattern of light and color. The study was either painted on illustration board over a small-scale replica of a larger charcoal drawing, as seen in plate 5.16, or directly on a photograph of the drawing itself.

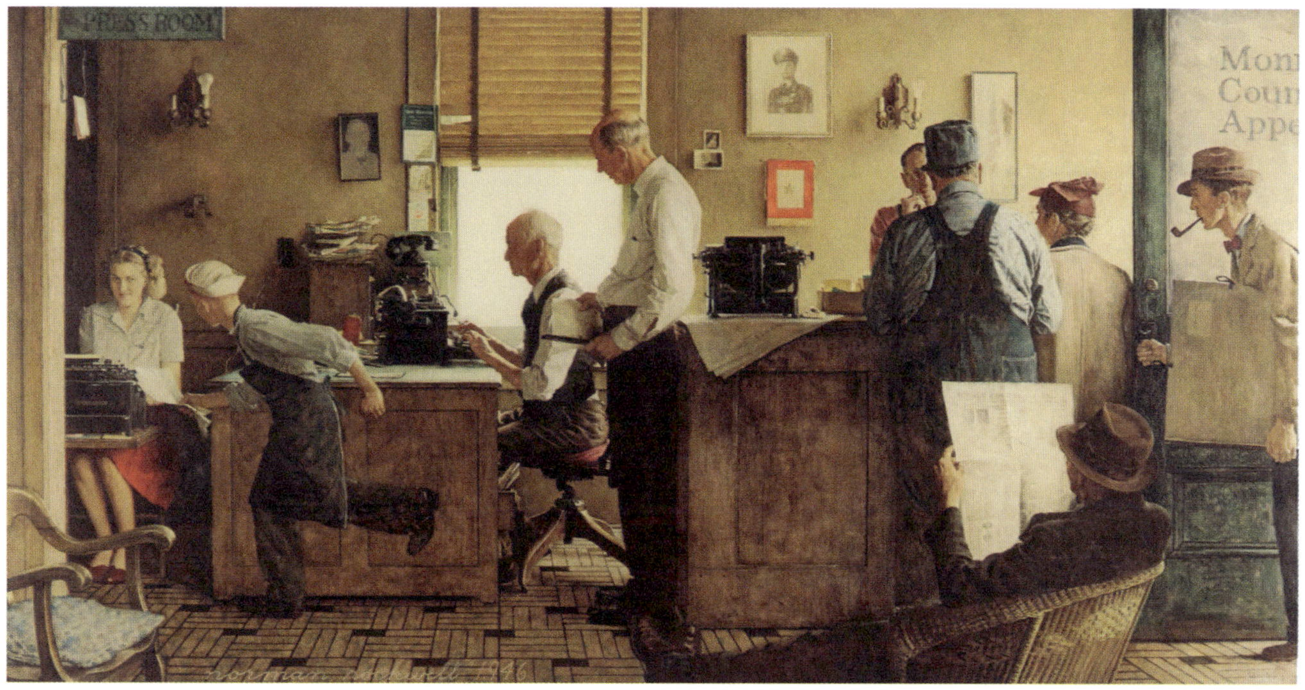


5.17. *Norman Rockwell Visits a Country Editor*, 1946
Oil on canvas, 40 × 66 in. (101.6 × 167.6 cm)
Illustration for Norman Rockwell, "Norman Rockwell Visits a Country Editor," *Saturday Evening Post*, May 25, 1946, pp. 24–25
Private collection

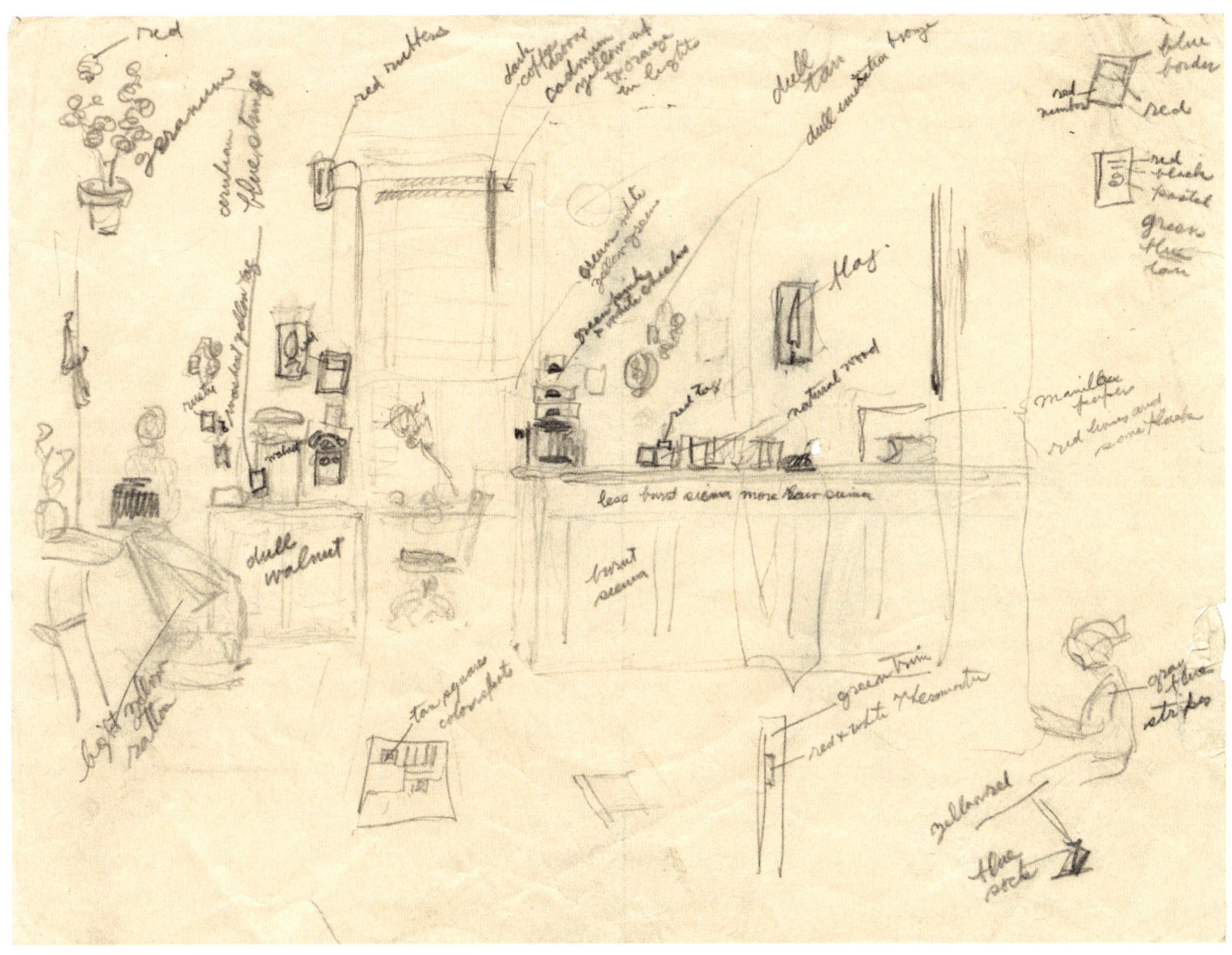


5.18. *Norman Rockwell Visits a Country Editor*, 1946
Pencil on paper, 8½ × 11 in. (21.6 × 28 cm)
On-site sketch for Norman Rockwell, "Norman Rockwell Visits a Country Editor," *Saturday Evening Post*, May 24, 1946
NRACT.1976.344

This sketch has notations on colors for possible future reference for the final illustration—from the dull walnut of the editor's desk to the room's touches of cerulean blue.

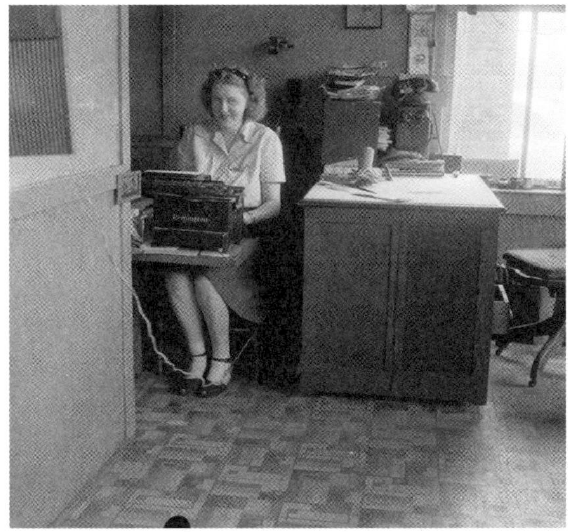

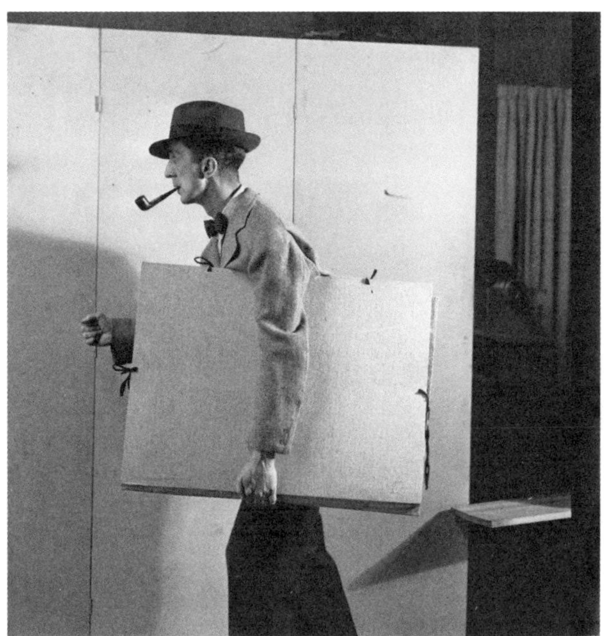

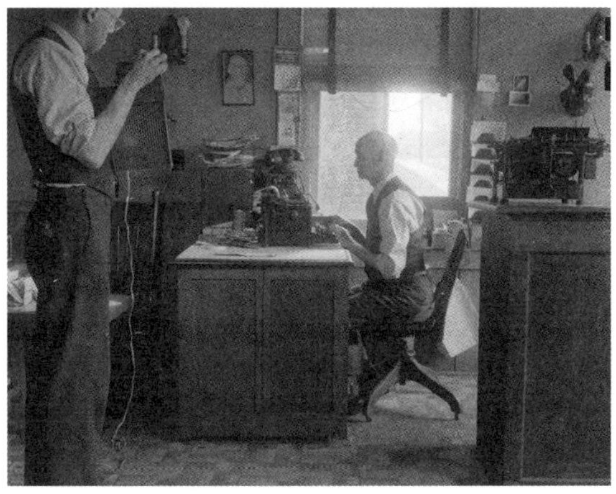

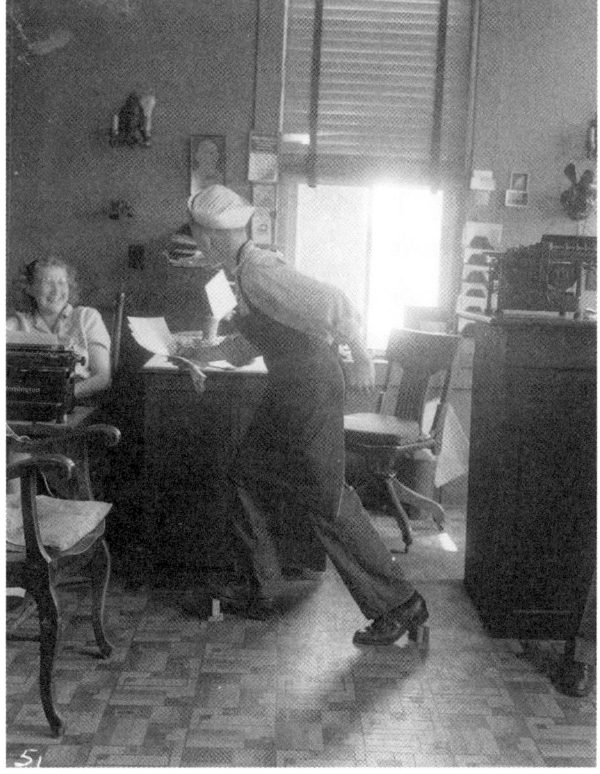

Rockwell carefully directed model poses and captured the details of characters and settings in a series of black-and-white photographs, important reference tools in the development of his art.

5.19a–d. *Norman Rockwell Visits a Country Editor*, 1946
Digital negatives, 4 × 5 in. (10.2 × 12.7 cm);
5 × 4 (12.7 × 10.2 cm); 4 × 5 in. (10.2 × 12.7 cm);
4¼ × 3¼ in. (10.8 × 8.3 cm)
Reference photographs for Norman Rockwell, "Norman Rockwell Visits a Country Editor," *Saturday Evening Post*, May 25, 1946
ST1976.6021, ST1976.6024, ST1976.6031, ST1976.6051

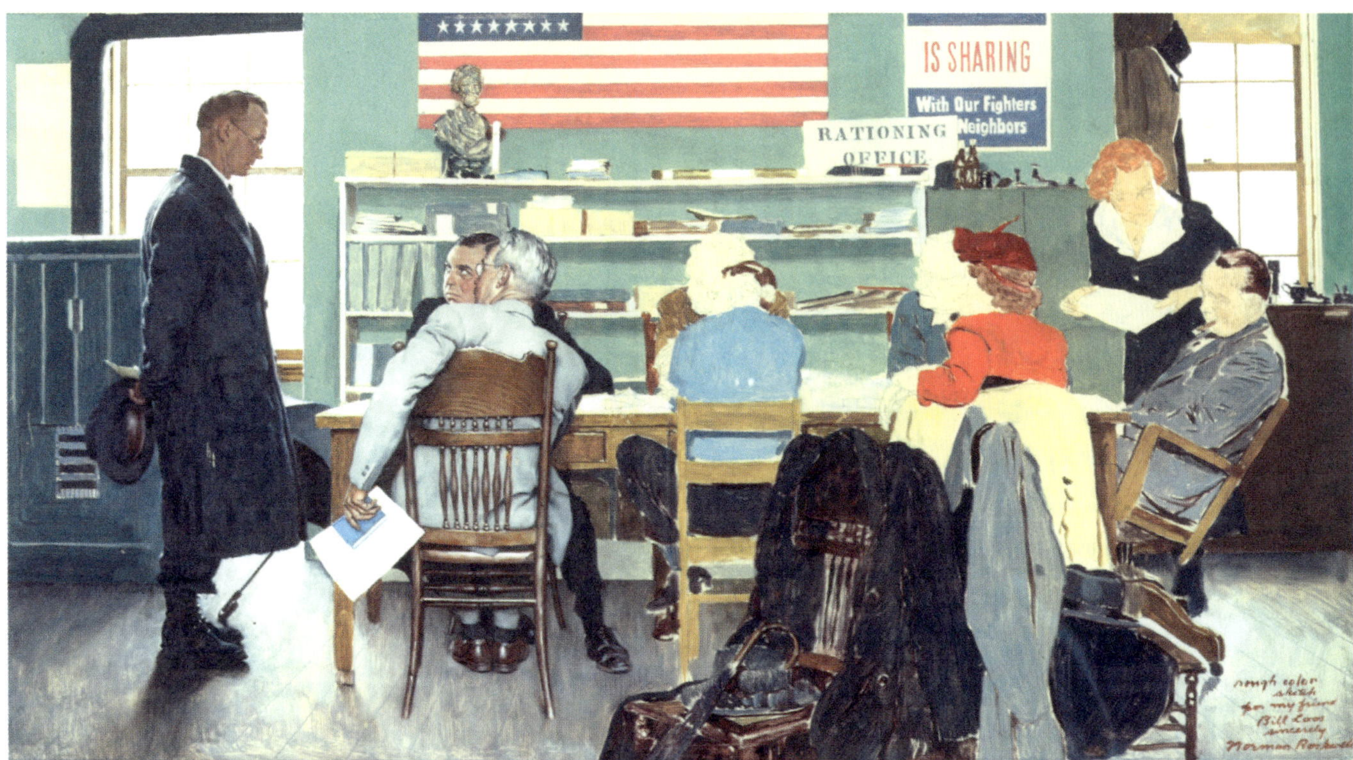


In the spring of 1942, volunteer ration boards were formed throughout the country to evaluate the claims of citizens who felt that their rations were insufficient. Rockwell used the board members and citizens of Manchester, Vermont, as models to document this wartime situation. This study reveals the artist's attention to the details of expression, gesture, color, and setting in his composition, though areas of the painting are finished to varying degrees. The artist's rough sketch is visible in the figures on the right side of the composition.

In Rockwell's main illustration in the *Post*'s double-page feature, the artist is seen seated in a chair on the left side of the image waiting to make his case to the ration board. A line of people from different walks with the same intent are also seen at the bottom of the page. These pencil studies present each citizen as an individual with a unique character, expression, and stance.

5.20. *Norman Rockwell Visits a Ration Board,* 1944
Oil on board, 28 × 45 in. (71.1 × 114.3 cm)
Color study for Norman Rockwell, "Norman Rockwell Visits a Ration Board," *Saturday Evening Post,* July 15, 1944
Private collection

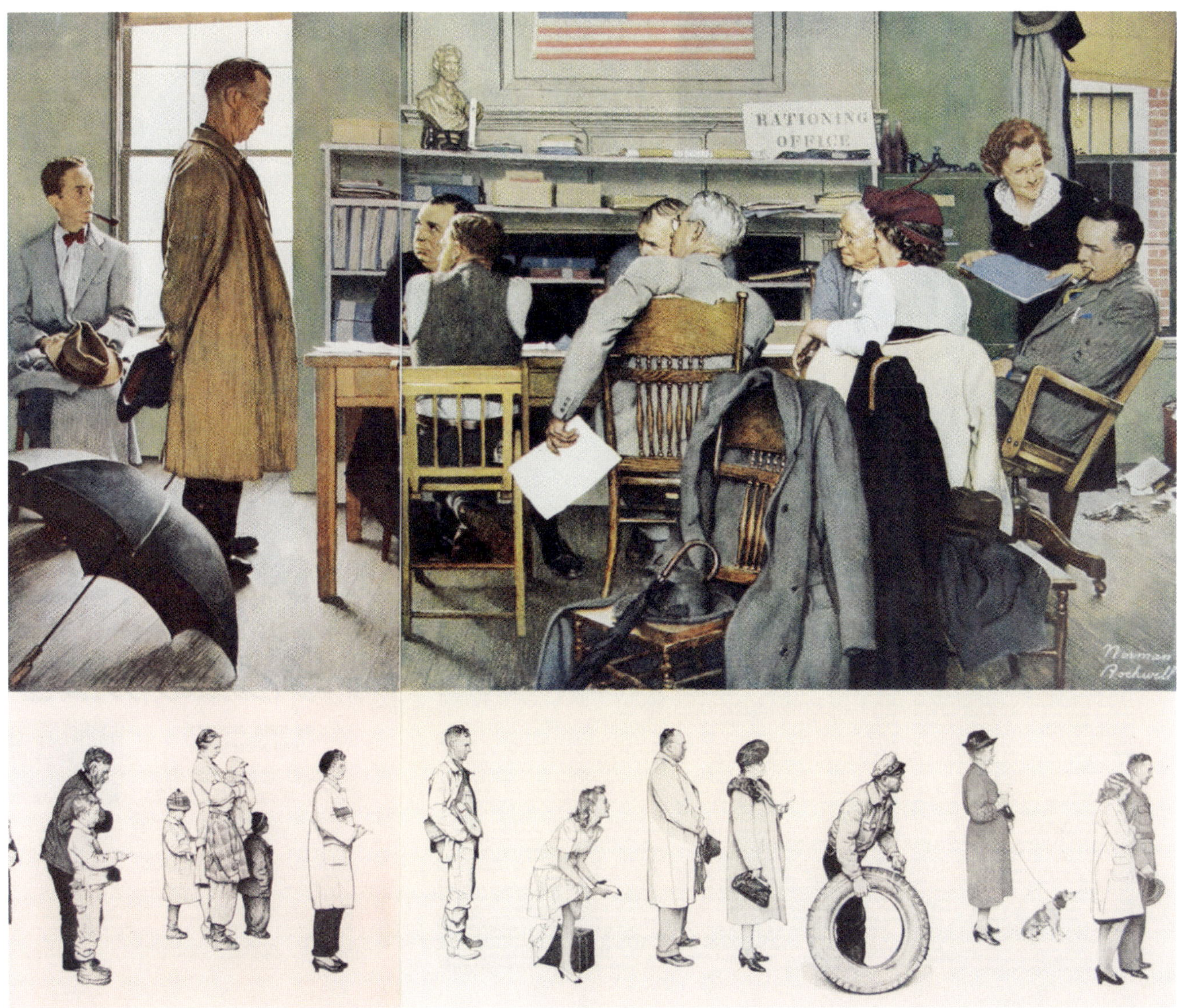


5.21. *Norman Rockwell Visits a Ration Board*, 1944
Tear sheet
Illustration for Norman Rockwell, "Norman Rockwell Visits a Ration Board," *Saturday Evening Post*, July 15, 1944
RC.2011.3.17.5

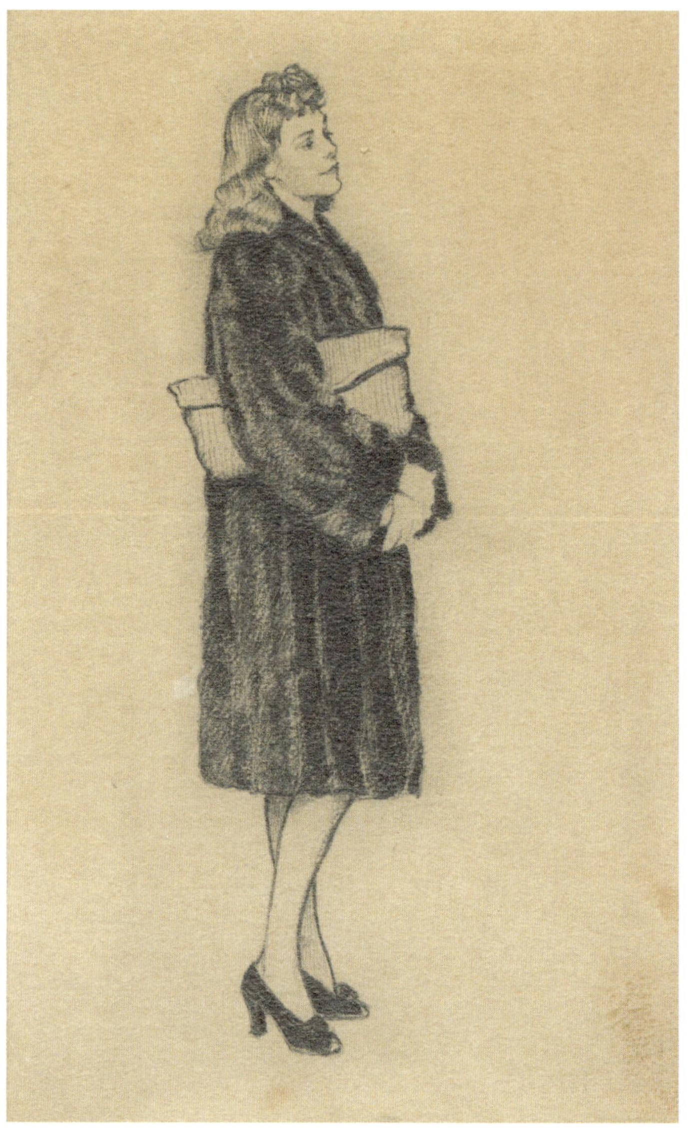

5.22. *"Waiting to Be Heard,"* 1944
Pencil on paper,
5¾ × 4½ in. (14.6 × 11.4 cm)
Illustration for Norman Rockwell, "Norman Rockwell Visits a Ration Board," *Saturday Evening Post*, July 15, 1944
NRM.2017.11 (Gift of Harry S. Forest)

The preparatory figure studies for *Norman Rockwell Visits a Ration Board* (plate 5.23) were among the materials used for his 1948 Famous Artists School course, How I Make a Picture. Though his final drawings (such as plate 5.22) were reproduced in his course book rather than the roughs seen here, Rockwell noted that he spent many hours looking for just the right models, important time spent in the creation of a final picture.

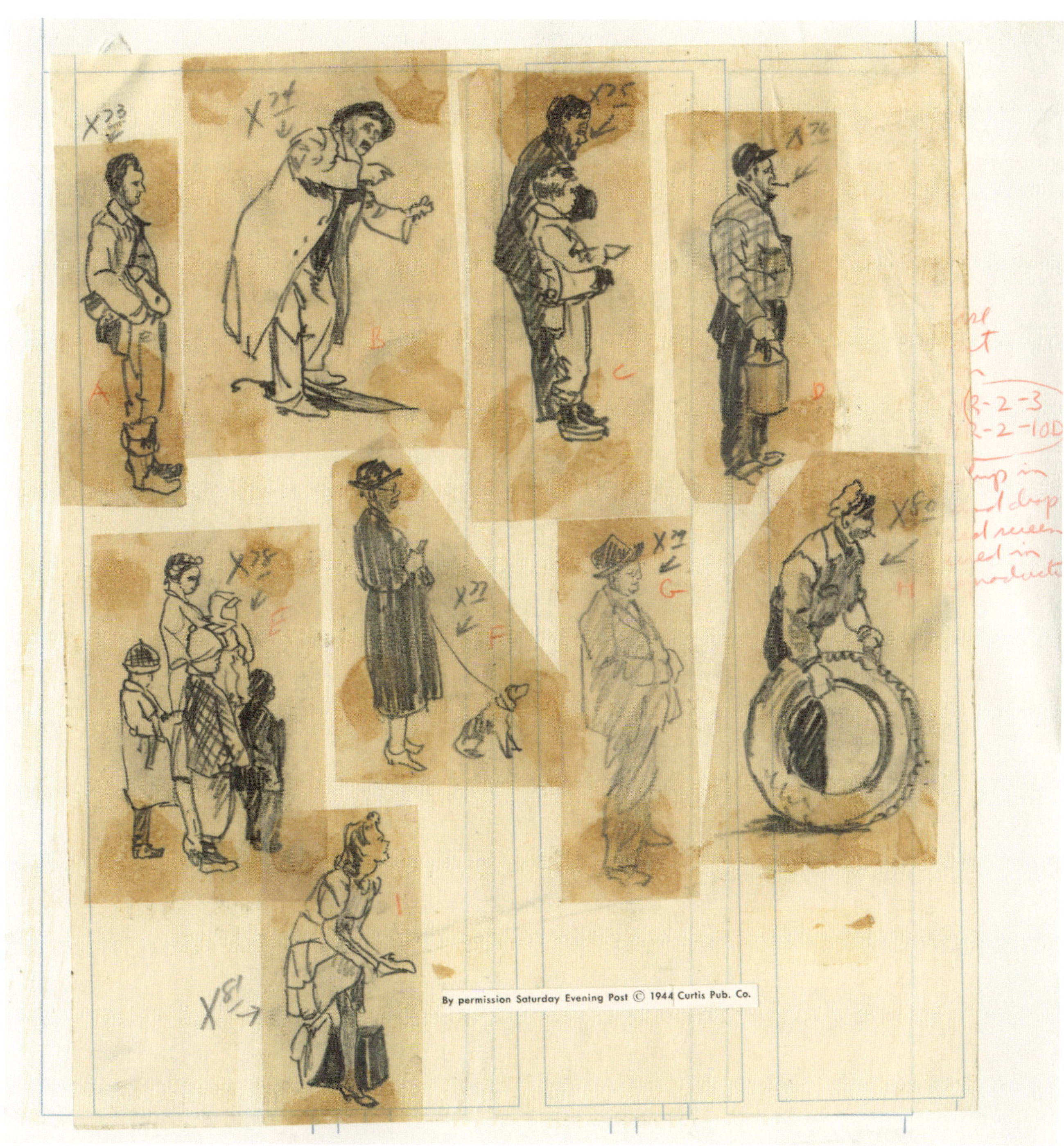


5.23. *Norman Rockwell Visits a Ration Board*, 1944
Pencil on paper, 13¾ × 21½ in. (34.9 × 54.6 cm) overall
Studies for Norman Rockwell, "Norman Rockwell Visits a Ration Board," *Saturday Evening Post*, July 15, 1944
NRM.2014.02.2071 (Robert E. Livesey/ Famous Artists School Collection)

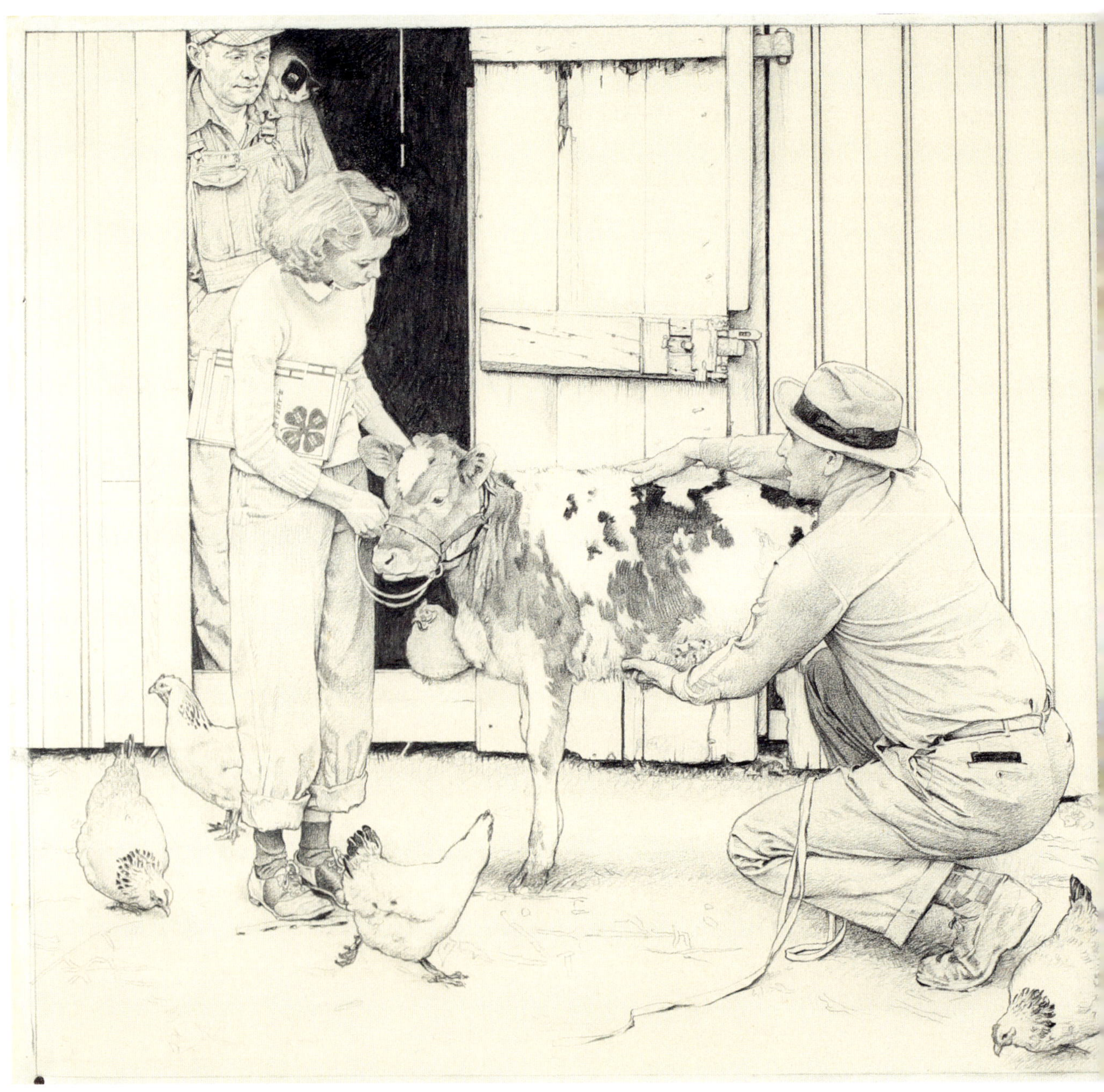

5.24. *Norman Rockwell Visits a County Agent*, 1948
Pencil on board, 15½ × 33 in. (39.4 × 83.8 cm)
Study for Norman Rockwell, "Norman Rockwell Visits a County Agent," *Saturday Evening Post*, July 24, 1948
NRACT.1973.116

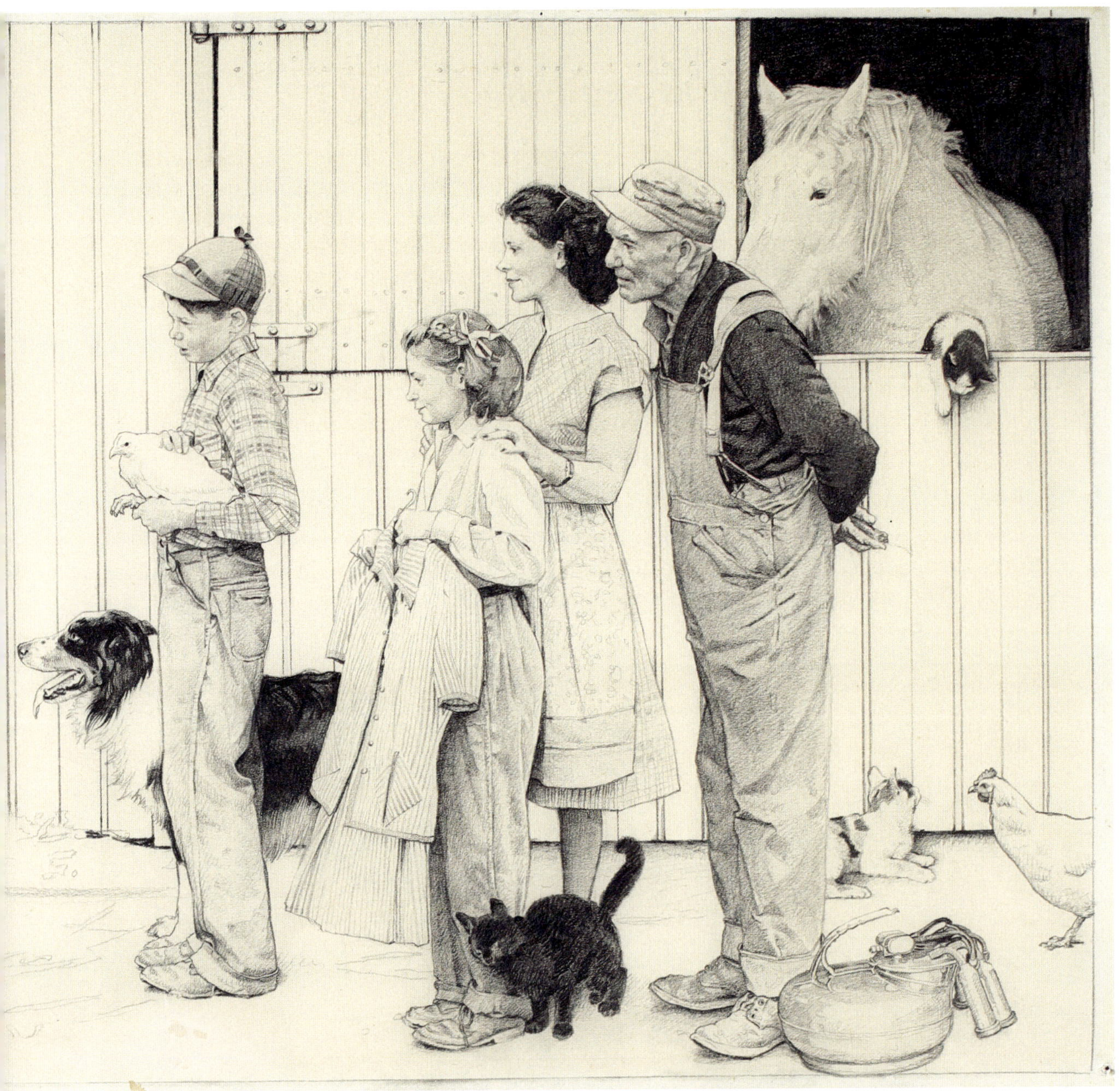

In creating this study, Rockwell captured County Agent Herald K. Rippey at work in the farming community of Jay County, Indiana. Rippey grew up on a farm and studied agriculture at Purdue University. His mission was to educate and aid farmers in creating and maintaining programs for better farming and living. In this drawing, all eyes are on Rippey, including those of the dog and horse in the stable. The artist uses a dark and light value pattern to move the viewer's eye across the composition.

## The Land of Enchantment

This painting, a flight of fancy inspired by works of classic fiction, appeared in the December 22, 1934, issue of the *Post*, though it was not originally intended for publication. Conceived in response to a commission that Rockwell received from a man who wished to hang it as an overmantel in his children's room, the project was curtailed when the financial crash of 1929 forced him to cancel his order. But the *Post* encouraged Rockwell to develop the idea, which became his first double-page spread for the magazine, and could be clipped from the magazine for framing. At the time, Rockwell lived in New Rochelle, New York, and displayed the painting at the town's library, where it hangs to this day in the Children's Room for public enjoyment.

In this rare, mural-size painting, Rockwell contrasts the worlds of fantasy and reality by surrounding two children who are engrossed in their books with a paler backdrop of storybook characters. Carefully inscribed are the names of many beloved characters from fairytales and fiction around a canvas perimeter, from Old King Cole to Rip Van Winkle, Alice in Wonderland, Little Red Riding Hood, Robinson Crusoe, the Cat and the Fiddle, and others.

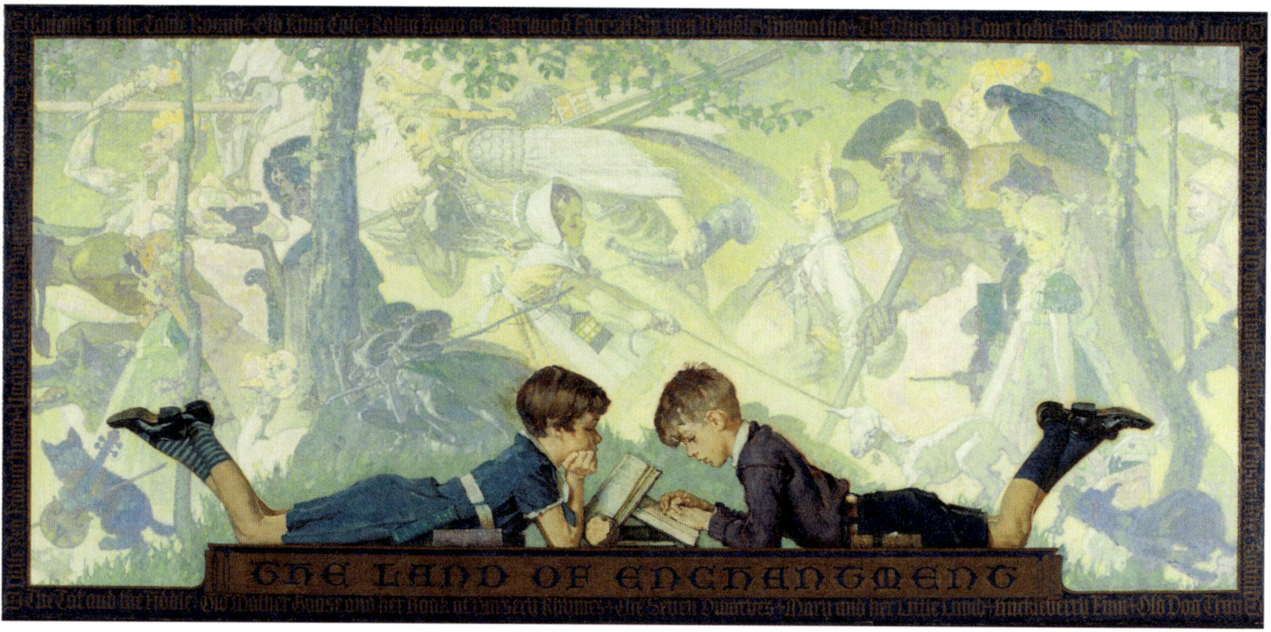


5.25. *The Land of Enchantment*, 1934
Oil on canvas, 37 × 76 in. (94 × 193 cm)
Illustration for the *Saturday Evening Post*, December 22, 1934
Collection of the New Rochelle Public Library, New Rochelle, New York

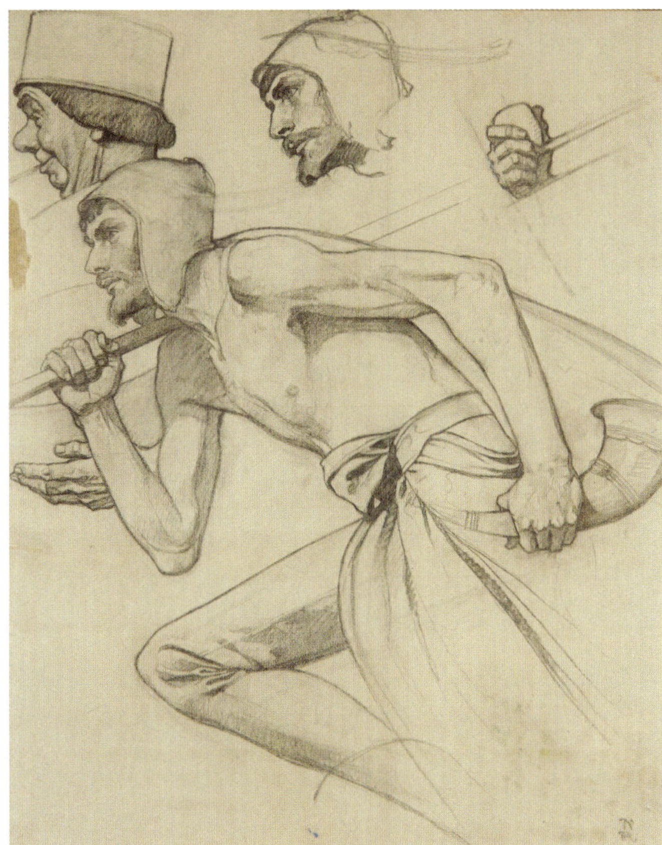

5.26. *The Land of Enchantment (Old King Cole and Robin Hood of Sherwood Forest)*, 1934
Charcoal and pencil on paper,
24½ × 19½ in. (62.2 × 49.5 cm)
Study for the *Saturday Evening Post*, December 22, 1934
NRM.1979.05 (museum purchase)

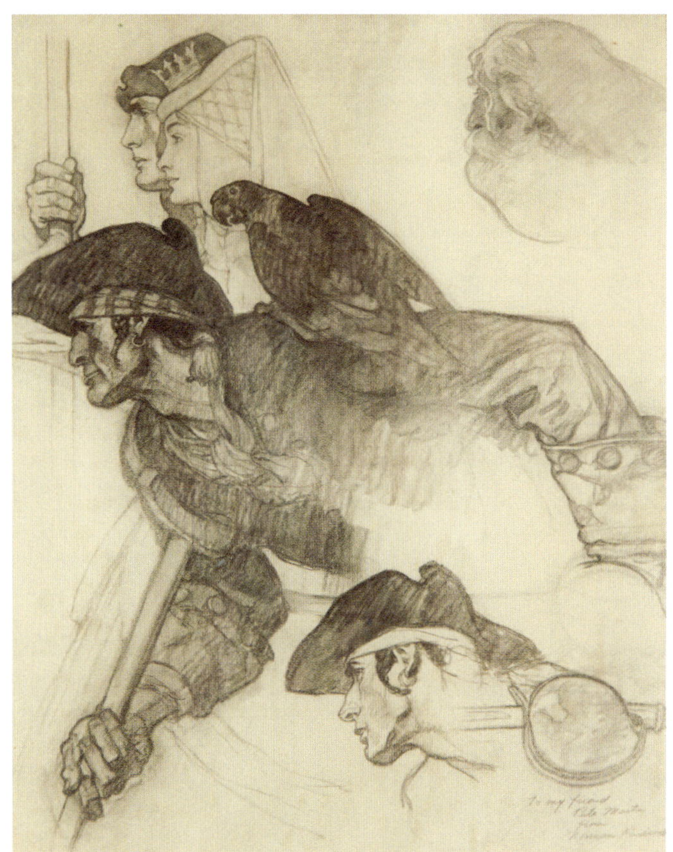

5.27. *The Land of Enchantment (Long John Silver)*, 1934
Charcoal and pencil on paper,
24½ × 19 in. (62.2 × 49.2 cm)
Study for the *Saturday Evening Post*, December 22, 1934
NRM.1979.06 (museum purchase)

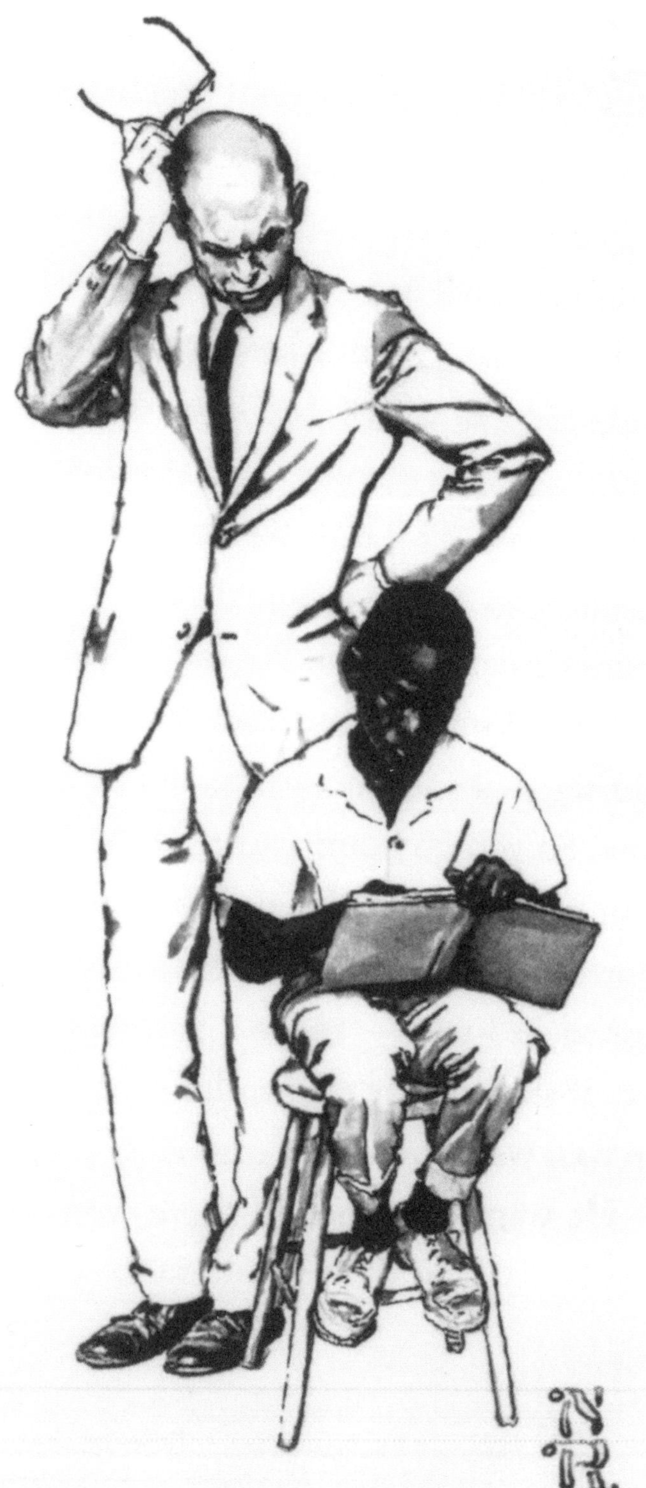

# A Reportorial Approach

After ending his forty-seven-year tenure with the *Saturday Evening Post* in 1963, Rockwell turned his attention to America's social concerns and adopted a pared-down reportorial approach to his art. In these drawings, he used a strong linear style and front-facing vignettes of the main characters in Dr. Robert Coles's *Dead End School,* which focuses on the subject of equity in education. In Coles's narrative, when a young African American student is to be sent from one overcrowded school to another, his mother organizes a protest, to the boy's chagrin. But her efforts result in change, when her son and other students are bused to better schools on the other side of the city.

LEFT
5.28. *The Principal Came Up Behind James,* 1968
Book plate
Illustration for Dr. Robert Coles, *Dead End School* (Boston: Little, Brown & Co., 1968), 41
Norman Rockwell Museum collection; Gift of John F. Butler Jr. in memory of John F. Butler Sr.

OPPOSITE
5.29. *This Is Our School,* 1968
Book plate, 8½ × 6½ in. (21.6 × 16.5 cm)
Illustration for Dr. Robert Coles, *Dead End School* (Boston: Little, Brown & Co., 1968), 61
Norman Rockwell Museum collection; Gift of John F. Butler Jr. in memory of John F. Butler Sr.

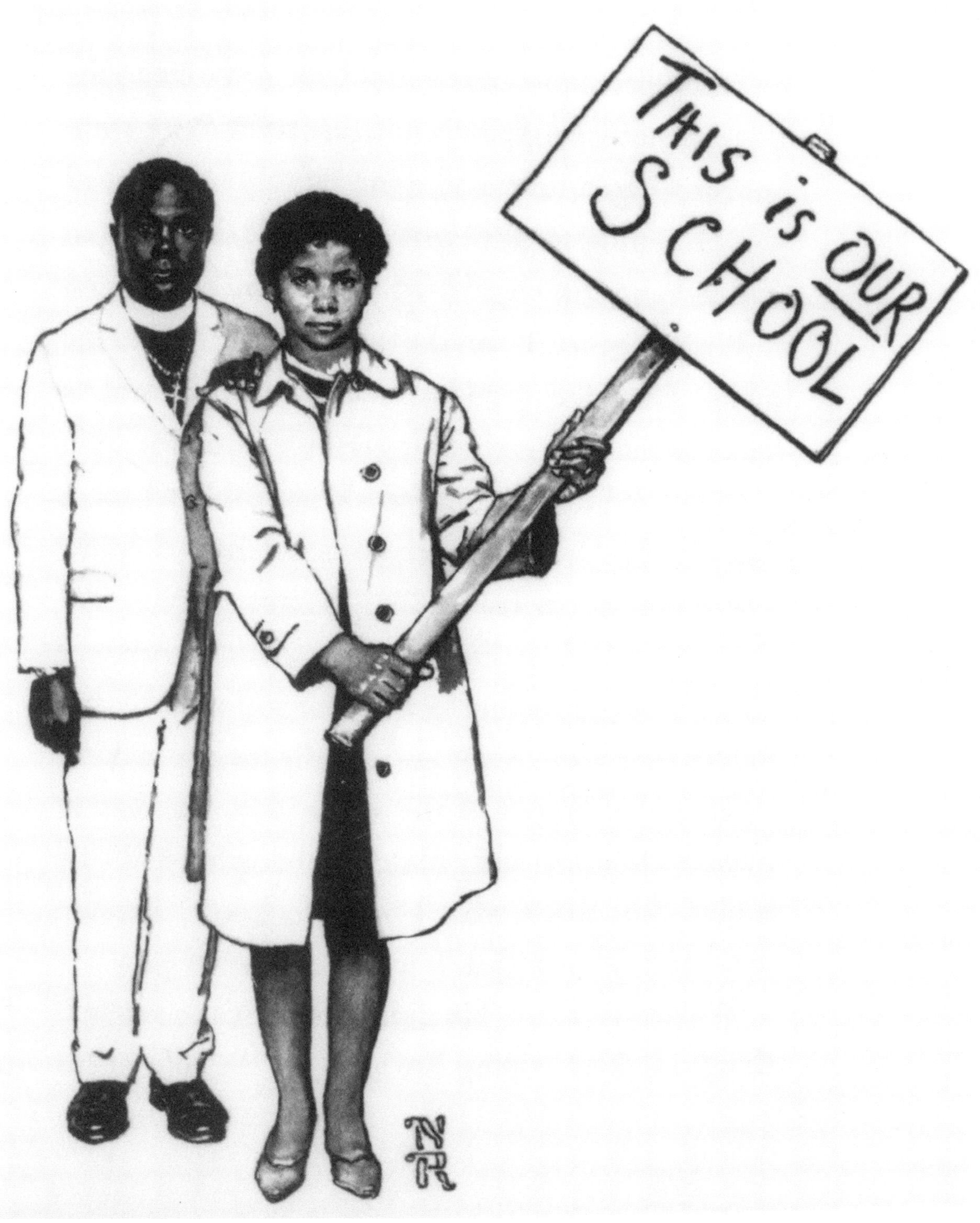
THIS IS OUR SCHOOL

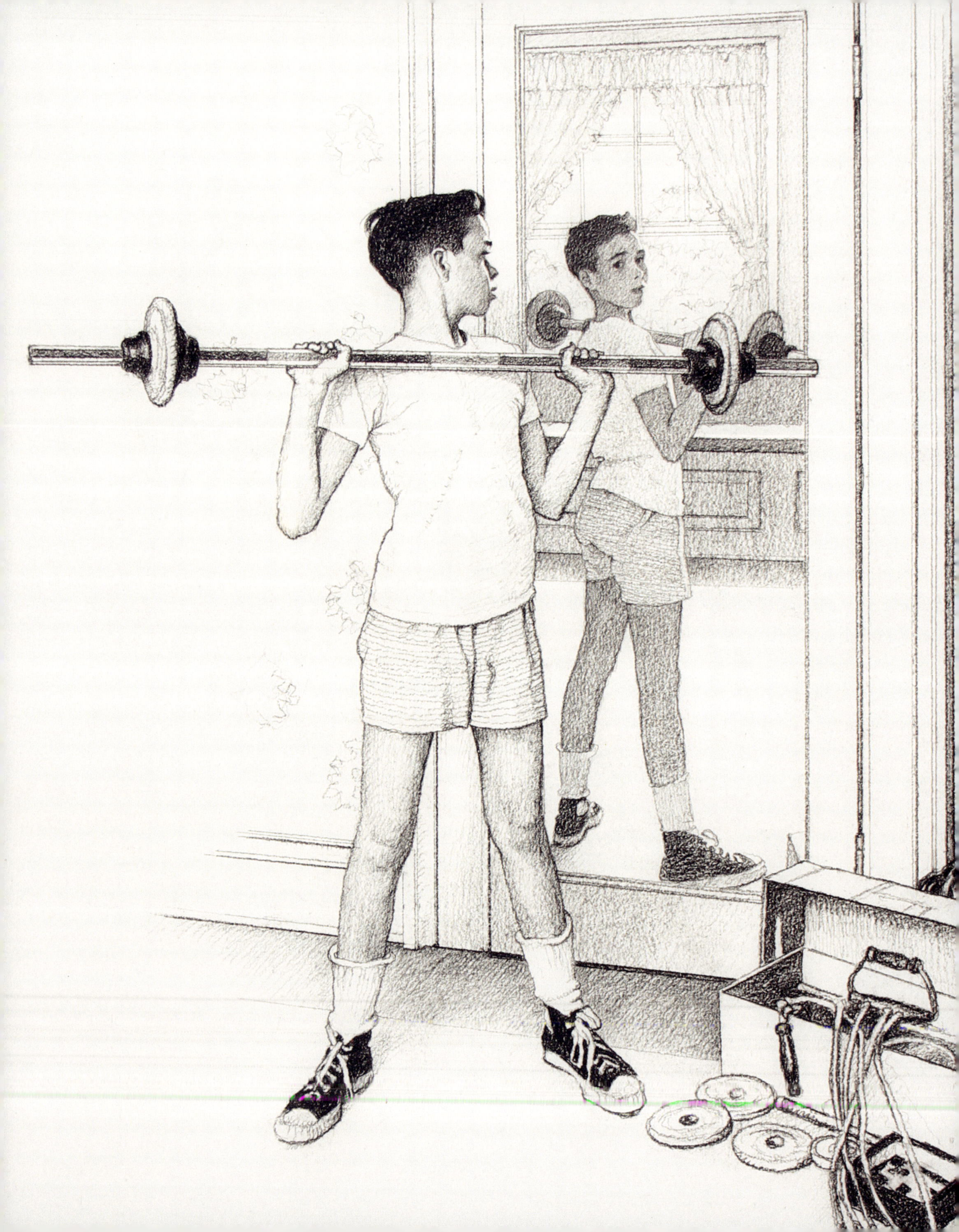

# 6 The Art of Persuasion: Drawings for Advertising

STEPHANIE HABOUSH PLUNKETT

"Over the years I've done many series of ads. But never under exclusive contract. . . . And I've tried to accept only those jobs which I believe I'll enjoy doing."

—Norman Rockwell[1]

While taking classes at New York's Art Students League in 1911 and 1912, Rockwell made a pact with his classmates never to do advertising jobs, which they considered more commercial than magazine illustrations. But the artist admitted that this promise was quickly broken. Rockwell's narrative style lent itself to advertising, and George Lorimer, editor of the *Saturday Evening Post,* advised him to charge double the fee that he received for a *Post* cover.

Detail of *Today He's Building Man-Sized Muscles . . .*, 1961
See plate 6.20.

Honesty, artistry, and integrity were qualities that were ascribed to Rockwell, making collaboration with the artist appealing for many companies. Descriptive words and phrases like "distinguished," "noted," "American legacy," "elegant taste and discrimination," "unexcelled craftsmanship," and "accustomed to the finest" made their way into advertisements that showcased Rockwell's art. During his prolific career, he accepted commissions from more than one hundred and fifty corporations, including Edison Mazda Lamp Company, Ford Motor Company, Pan American World Airways, Twentieth Century–Fox Film Corporation, Budweiser, Del Monte, and Sun-Maid.

Rockwell categorized advertising illustration into two types—the direct approach, a picture of the target audience enjoying the product; and the institutional approach, an image showcasing the company's good will. He opined that some commissions limited the illustrator's originality due to the advertising agency's layout requirements and was disheartened when his artwork required changes. As Rockwell gained success, he felt less need to accept advertising assignments and concentrated on cover- and story-illustration work, which allowed him more creative freedom. This helps explain why Rockwell produced fewer finished preparatory drawings for his advertising illustrations than for his magazine covers—though ad work was an important part of the artist's financial equation, his streamlined process allowed him to get back to the work that meant the most to him.

## Cream of Kentucky Whiskey

Beginning in the 1930s, Rockwell produced a group of ads for Cream of Kentucky whiskey produced by Schenley Distilleries, a New York–based company with a distillery in Lawrenceburg, Indiana. Most of the images for these ads were quick pencil or charcoal portraits of well-known male personalities or commonly recognized characters, such as the mythical Uncle Sam made famous by his fellow illustrator James Montgomery Flagg (1877–1960). In this drawing, the artist used white opaque (watercolor) gouache to change the contour of the character's face rather than taking time to do the piece over from scratch.

6.1. *Uncle Sam*, 1947
Charcoal and gouache on paper,
13 × 11¾ in. (34 × 29.8 cm)
Advertising illustration for the
Schenley Distillers Company
NRM.1984.02 (museum purchase)

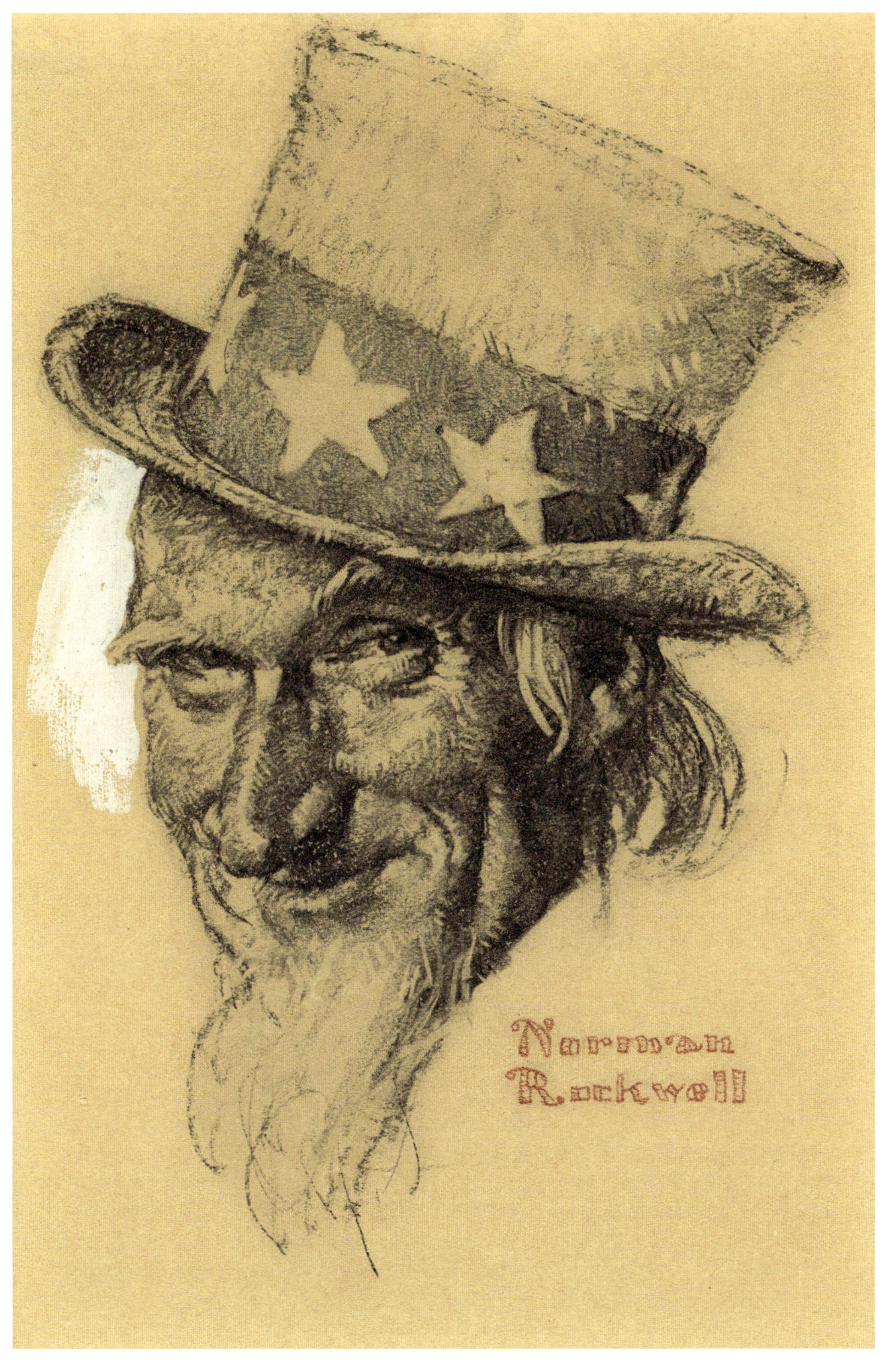
Norman
Rockwell

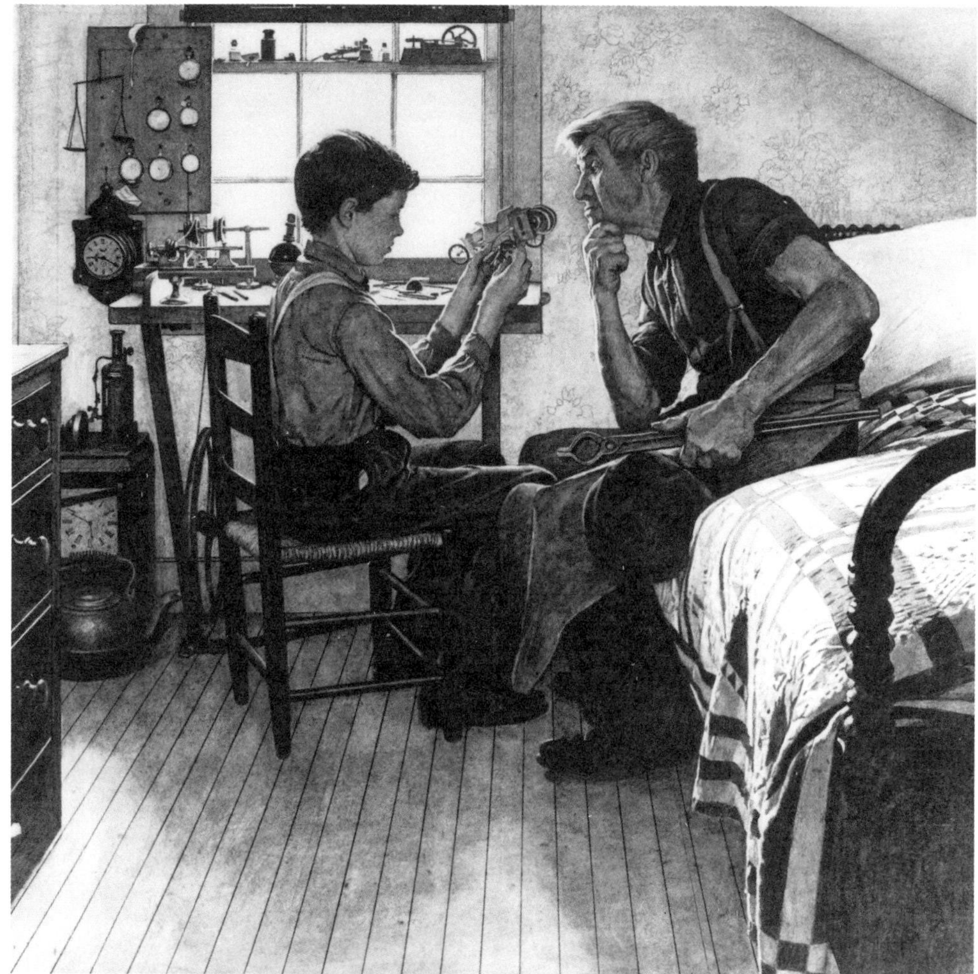

6.2. *Henry Ford, the Boy Who Put the World on Wheels (The Inventor)*, c. 1952
Charcoal and graphite on paper, 36¼ × 35¾ in. (92.1 × 90.8 cm)
Study calendar illustration for Ford Motor Company's fiftieth anniversary
NRACT.1973.121

## Ford Motor Company

Norman Rockwell's perfectionism and care in all aspects of picture-making led him to spend extensive time on research, seeking the perfect elements and details to enhance the story he wished to tell. This commission for the Ford Motor Company commemorates the company's fiftieth anniversary, offering Rockwell the opportunity to showcase his well-tuned abilities as a nostalgic storyteller. In the beautifully rendered tonal drawing, young Henry Ford, at his work bench in Dearborn, is shown working on a windup model of a precursor to his Model T that would change the way America and the world would travel in the twentieth century. Rockwell's drawing is typical of the high degree of finish he employed before beginning

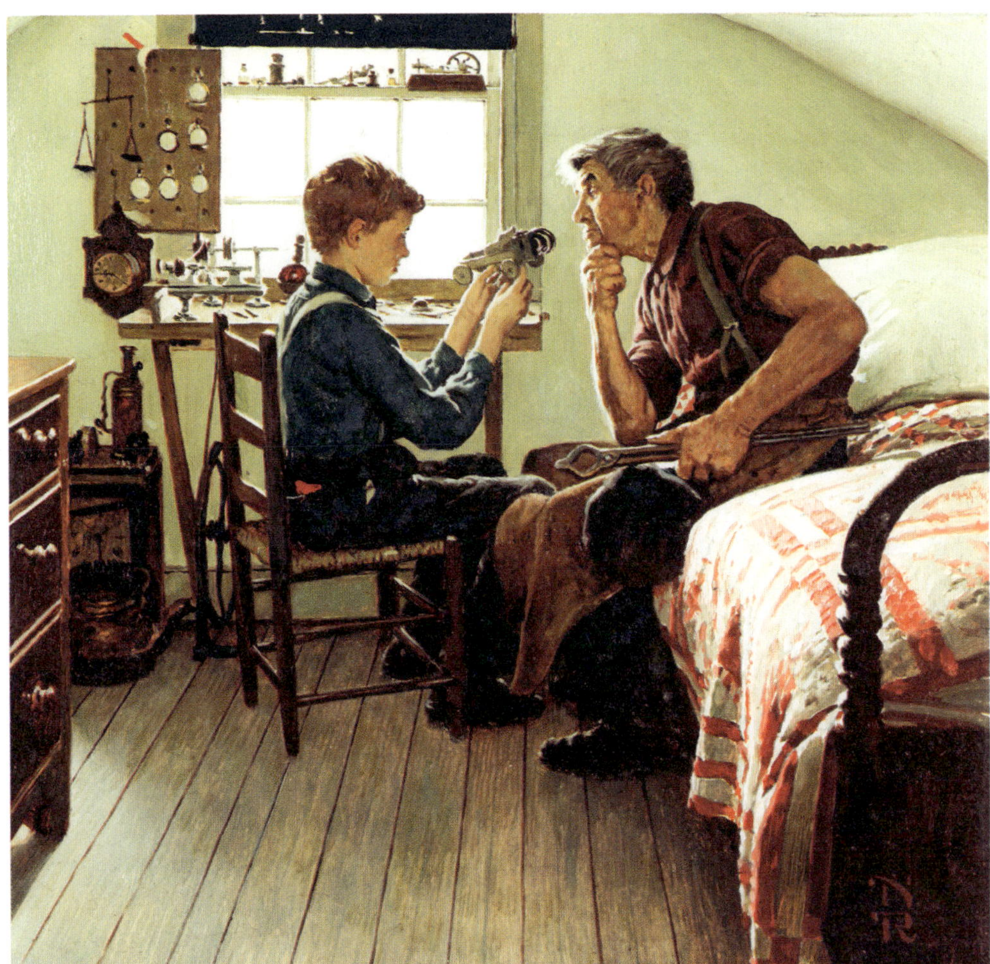

6.3. *Henry Ford, the Boy Who Put the World on Wheels (The Inventor)*, c. 1952
Oil on board, 14½ × 15 in. (36.8 × 38.1 cm)
Calendar illustration for Ford Motor Company's fiftieth anniversary
The Henry Ford Museum, Dearborn, Michigan; Gift of Ford Motor Company

a work in color, the full value rendering finalizing all the elements of the composition.

Rockwell was commissioned by Ford to create six paintings—four of these were to be used as calendar illustrations—but for promotional purposes, he was asked to do smaller versions of the same images. After working on the first full-size painting, Rockwell realized that he would never have enough time to finish three more large oils and asked Ford's vice president, Ben Donaldson, if he would accept his studies as final art. Rockwell wrote, convincingly, that he would do everything he could to make them complete in themselves, and Donaldson accepted his proposal.

# Around the World for Pan Am

In 1955, Rockwell was asked to do illustrations for a Pan American World Airways (Pan Am) ad campaign to encourage round-the-world travel by American tourists. The airline, which began service in 1927, was, in 1947, the first to offer commercial, round-the-world service. Pan Am wanted to emphasize the time savings of air travel, and the number and variety of their routes—by 1956 they were flying to eighty countries. A great lover of travel, Rockwell enthusiastically embraced his new assignment. He visited thirteen countries over the course of two months, recording on the pages of his sketchbook the people and scenes he witnessed in Paris, Barcelona, Rome, Istanbul, Beirut, Karachi, Calcutta, Varanasi, Yangon, Bangkok, Hong Kong, Tokyo, and Hawaii. By integrating American tourists within some of these scenes, he made travel to foreign countries seem familiar, and shaped people's expectations of how they might experience diverse cultures.

The simply drawn tourists in this composition are contrasted with a richly detailed view of a Karachi street packed with people and animals going about their daily routines, reflecting the artist's deep interest in his subject.

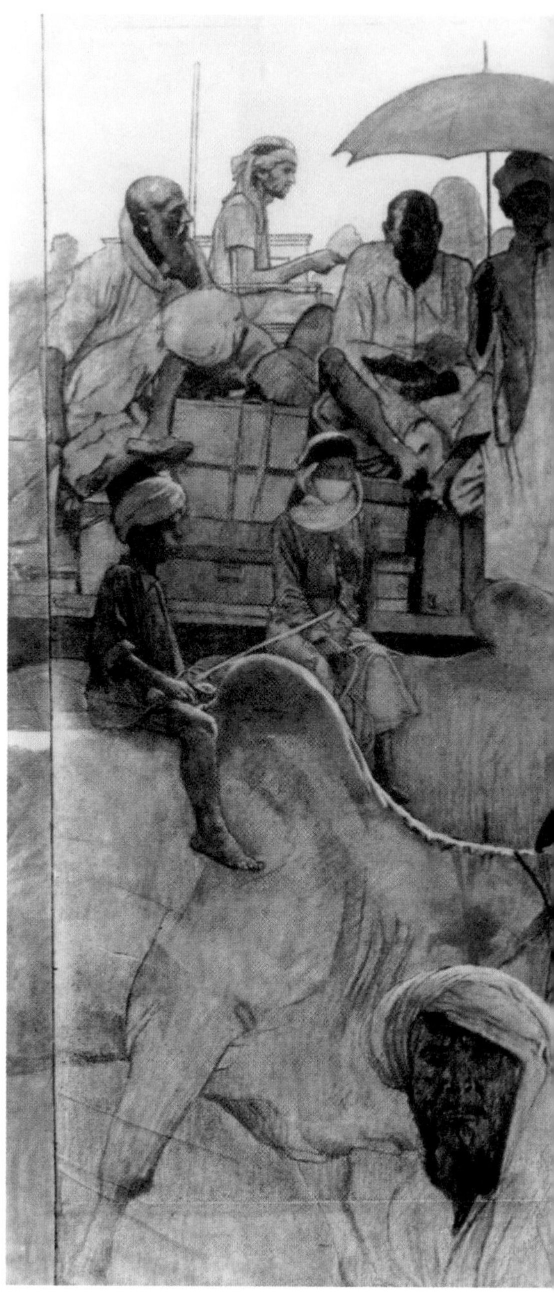

6.4. *Karachi, Pakistan*, 1955
Charcoal on paper, 45 × 71½ in.
(114.3 × 181.6 cm)
Study for Pan American World Airways, Inc., *Pan American Was My Magic Carpet around the World* advertising campaign
NRACT.1973.112

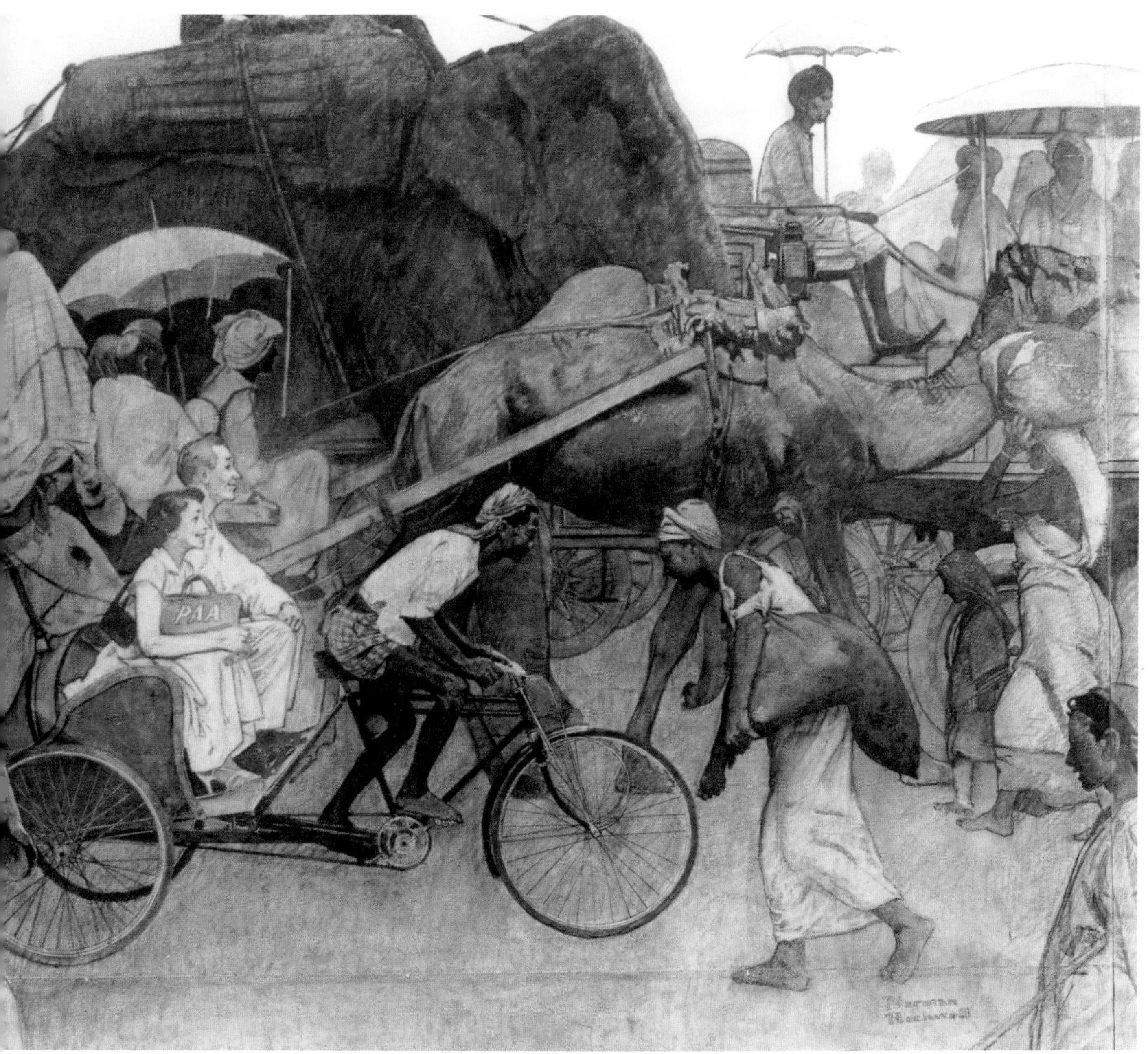
P.A.A.
Norman
Rockwell

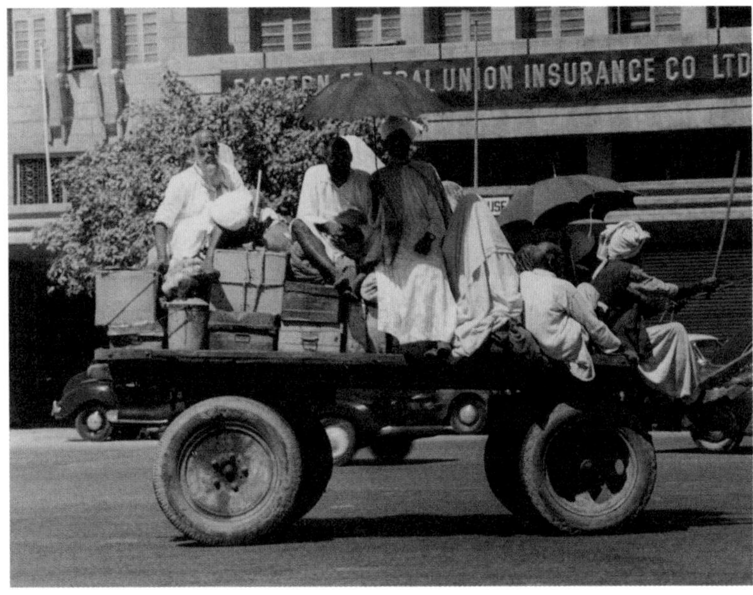


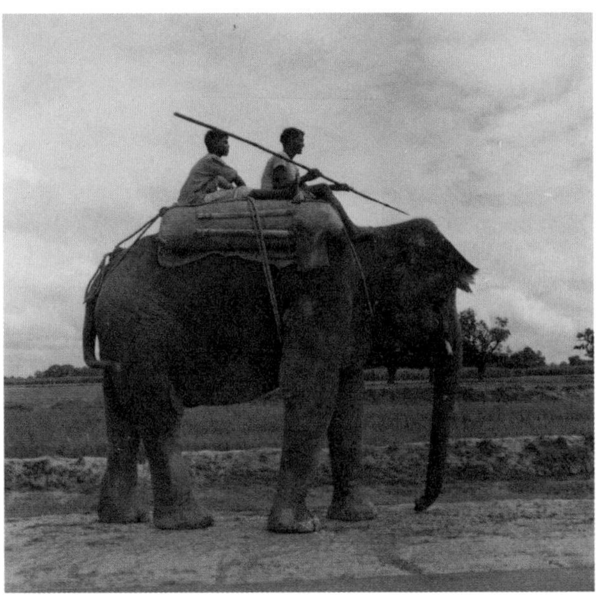

6.5. Chester "Blackie" Kronfeld (1913–1962)
*Travelers on Vehicle in Karachi, Pakistan*, 1955
Photograph, 8 × 10 in. (20.3 × 25.4 cm)
Reference photograph for Pan American World Airways, Inc., *Pan American Was My Magic Carpet around the World* advertising campaign
ST.1976.20032.184.2

6.6. Chester "Blackie" Kronfeld (1913–1962)
*Elephant in Karachi, Pakistan*, 1955
Photograph, 8 × 10 in. (20.3 × 25.4 cm)
Reference photograph for Pan American World Airways, Inc., *Pan American Was My Magic Carpet around the World* advertising campaign
ST.1976.20032.111.1

On September 2, 1955, Norman Rockwell boarded a Pan Am Clipper at Idlewild Airport in New York with photographer Chester "Blackie" Kronfeld and J. Walter Thompson advertising agency art director Walter C. House. Kronfeld took photographs at each location for Rockwell's reference; the two photographs above were combined in Rockwell's Karachi drawing.

A photograph by Rockwell's longtime assistant Louis Lamone shows the artist sketching in his Main Street Stockbridge studio with his Karachi drawing tacked up beside him. On top of it is a print of Toulouse-Lautrec's 1895 painting *Marcelle Lender Dancing the Bolero in "Chilpéric."* The artist often took inspiration from the masters, and in this case, he may have been studying the dynamic flow of form in Lautrec's work as he considered his own.

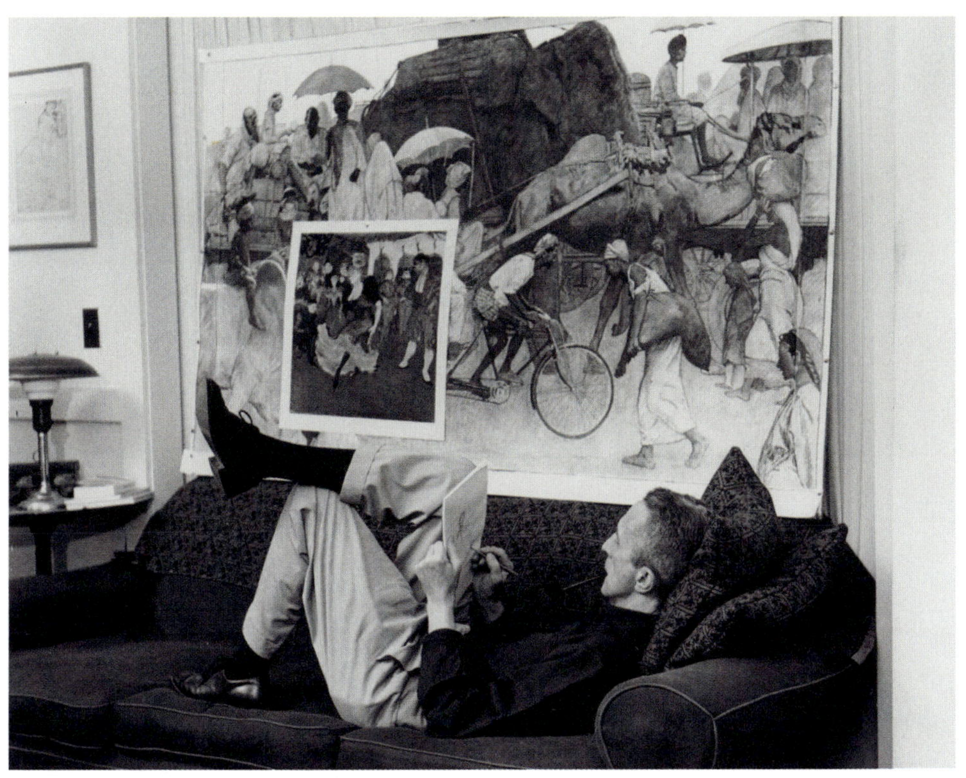

LEFT
6.7. Louis Lamone
(1918–2007)
*Norman Rockwell Sketching (Karachi Drawing over Sofa)*, 1956
Photograph, 8 × 10 in.
(20.3 × 25.4 cm)
ST.20032.178.293

BELOW
6.8. *Pan American Was My Magic Carpet around the World*
Tear sheet, 11 × 16 in.
(27.9 × 40.6 cm)
Advertising illustration for Pan American World Airways, Inc., *Saturday Evening Post*, March 17, 1956
RC.2011.3.9.27

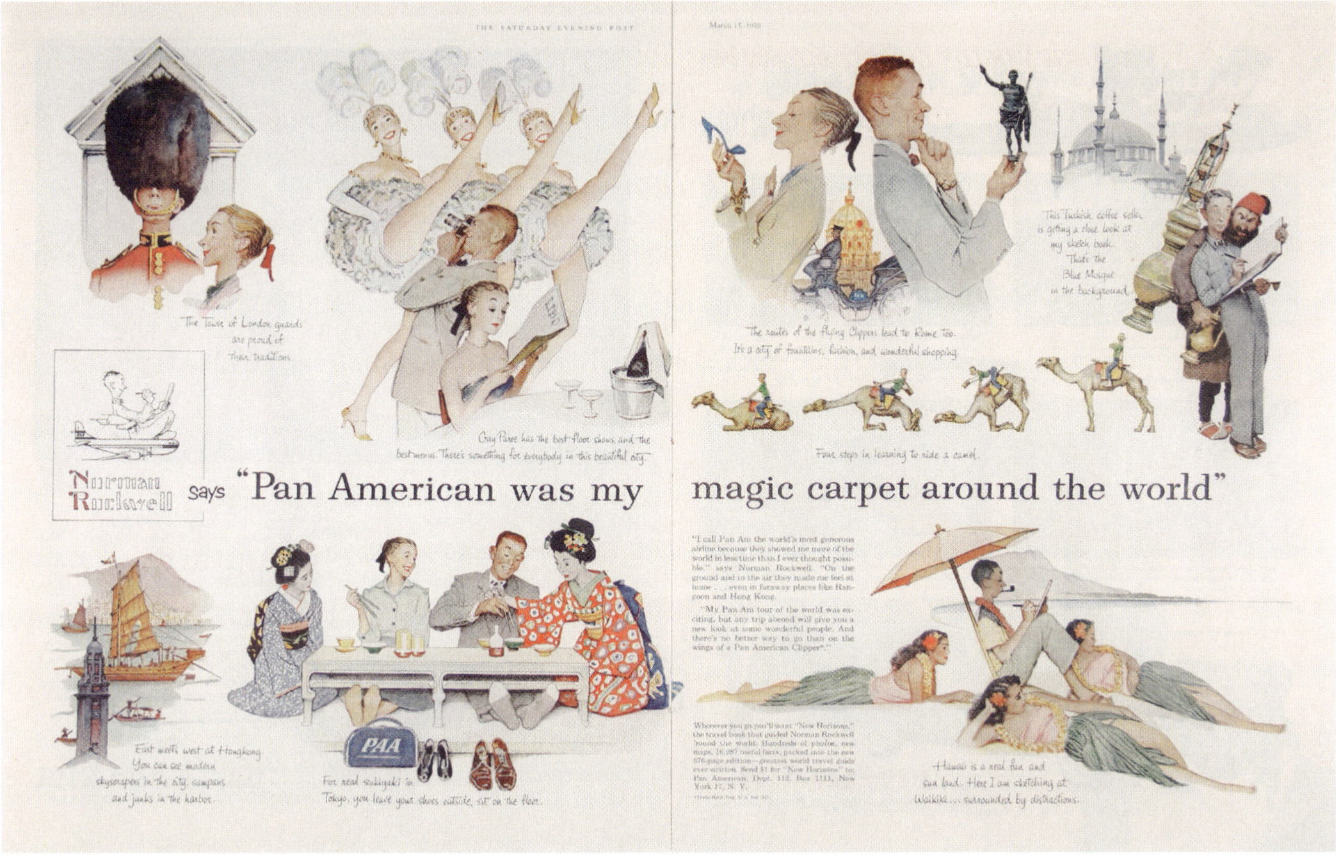

The Tower of London guards are proud of their traditions

Gay Paree has the best floor shows and the best menus. There's something for everybody in this beautiful city.

The routes of the Flying Clippers lead to Rome too. It's a city of fountains, fashion, and wonderful shopping.

This Turkish coffee seller is getting a close look at my sketch book. That's the Blue Mosque in the background.

Four steps in learning to ride a camel.

Norman Rockwell says "Pan American was my magic carpet around the world"

"I call Pan Am the world's most generous airline because they showed me more of the world in less time than I ever thought possible," says Norman Rockwell. "On the ground and in the air they made me feel at home . . . even in faraway places like Rangoon and Hong Kong.

"My Pan Am tour of the world was exciting, but any trip abroad will give you a new look at some wonderful people. And there's no better way to go than on the wings of a Pan American Clipper*."

East meets west at Hongkong. You can see modern skyscrapers in the city, sampans and junks in the harbor.

For real sukiyaki in Tokyo, you leave your shoes outside, sit on the floor.

Wherever you go you'll want "New Horizons," the travel book that guided Norman Rockwell 'round the world. Hundreds of photos, new maps, 16,287 useful facts, packed into the new 576-page edition—greatest world travel guide ever written. Send $1 for "New Horizons" to: Pan American, Dept. 112, Box 1111, New York 17, N. Y.

Hawaii is a real fun and sun land. Here I am sketching at Waikiki... surrounded by distractions.

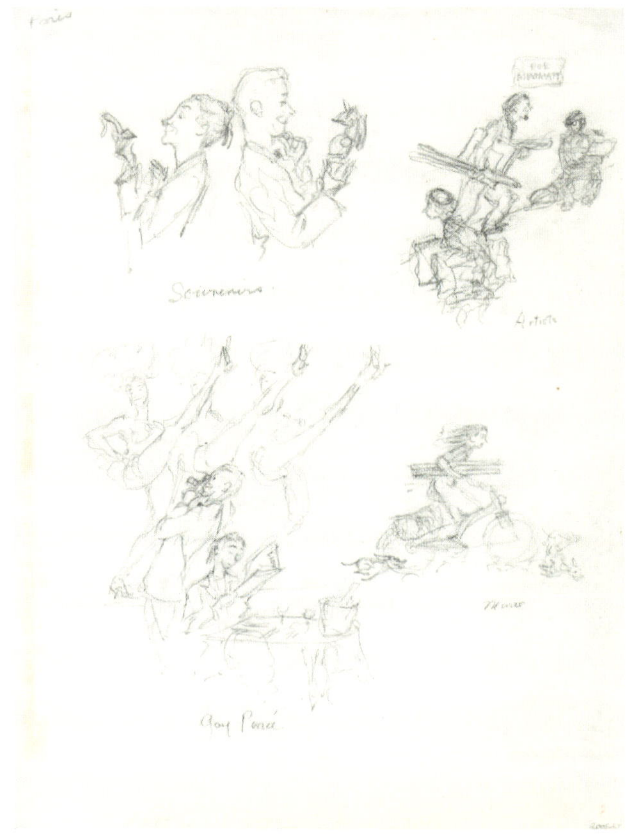


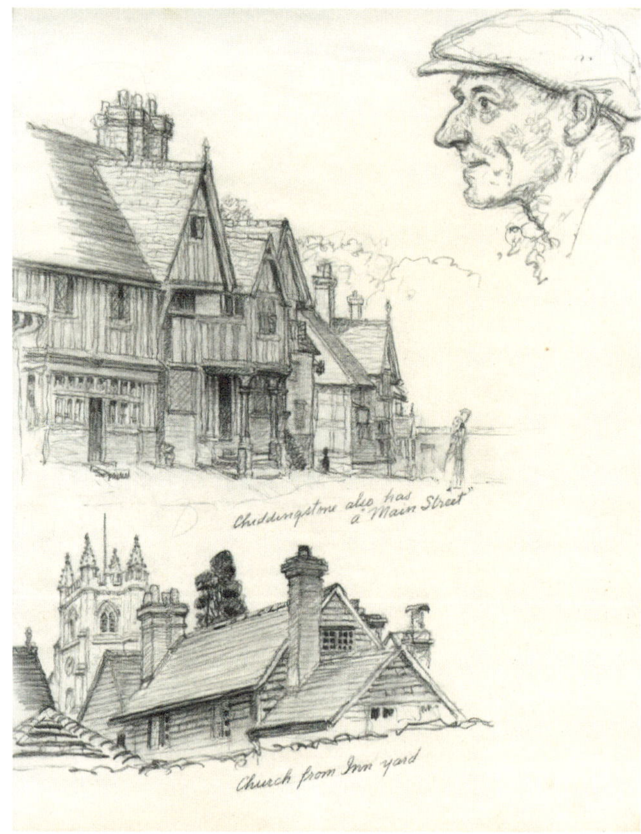


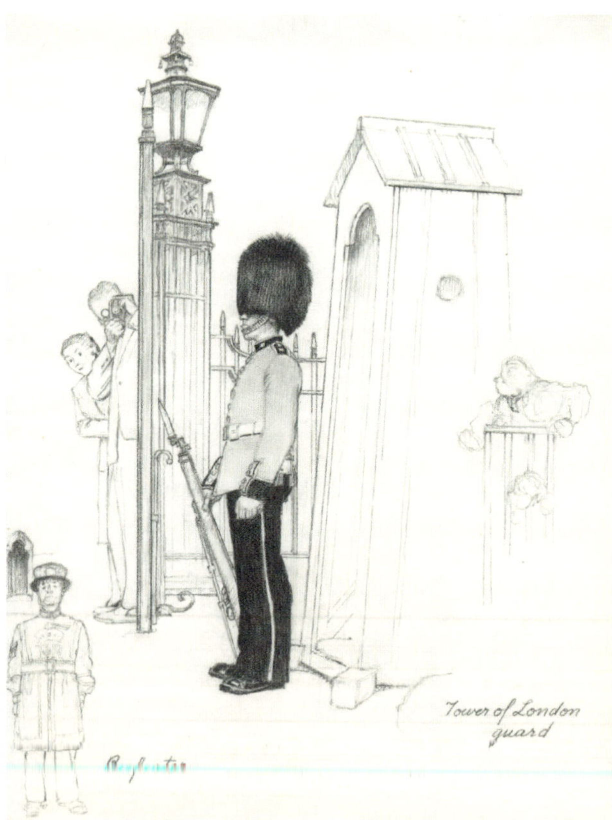


Rockwell's whimsical approach to his illustrations for Pan Am sent the message that tourists could safely experience exotic locales and new situations. Appearing in *Life*, the *Saturday Evening Post*, and *Holiday*, the ads ran throughout 1956. His "round-the-world spread" (plate 6.8) was a "solid hit," according to the J. Walter Thompson ad agency, which handled the account. However, Rockwell referred to this project

THIS SPREAD
Sketchbook drawings for Pan American World Airways, Inc., *Pan American Was My Magic Carpet around the World* advertising campaign
Wolff pencil on paper, 16½ × 13 in. (41.9 × 34.6 cm) each

TOP LEFT
6.9. *Gay Paree (Paris, France)*, 1955
NRM.2006.27 (Gift of Shirlee and Salvatore F. Scoma)

TOP RIGHT
6.10. *Chiddingstone, England*, 1955
NRM.2006.35 (Gift of Shirlee and Salvatore F. Scoma)

LEFT
6.11. *Beefeater, Tower of London Guard*, 1955
NRM.2006.49 (Gift of Shirlee and Salvatore F. Scoma)

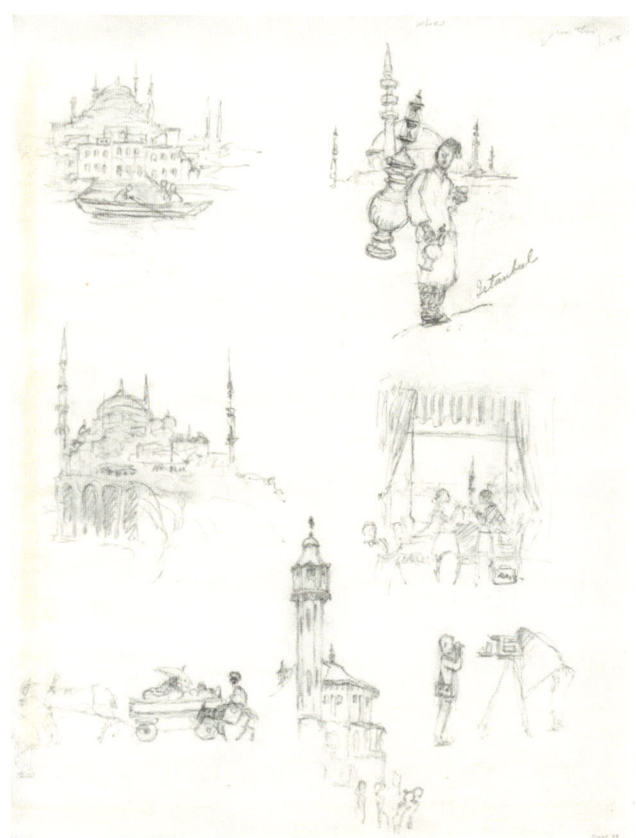


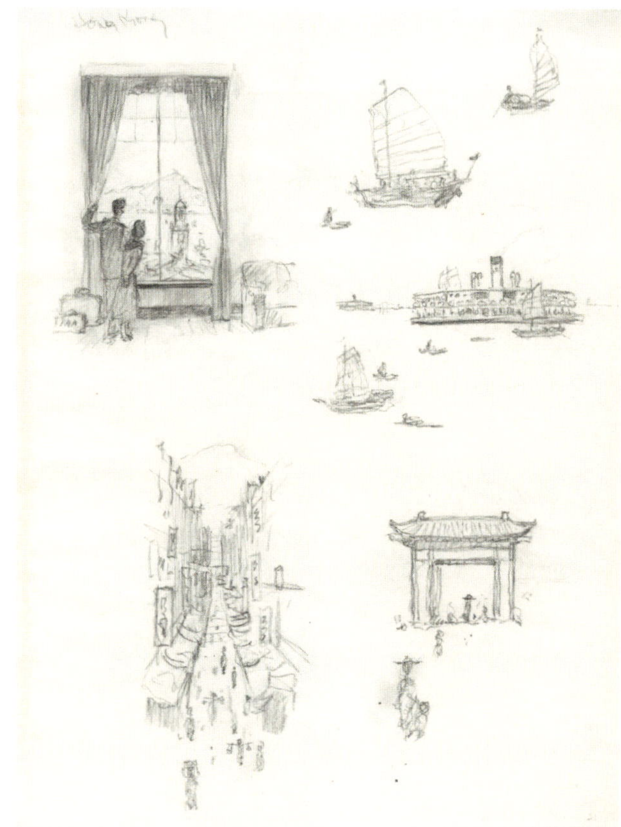

as his “most disappointing fiasco.”[2] When he returned home and submitted his sketchbook, it was rejected. “Oh, I did a few ads. Nothing to justify the time and money which had been spent, though,” he wrote, noting that Pan Am did not want pictures of foreign lands and people. “‘Those would only frighten tourists,’ they said, ‘we want pictures of smart-looking tourists sunning on smart beaches in front of smart hotels.’ If I have any more wide-ranging fiascos like that one I’ll have to go live in a closet,” he said.[3]

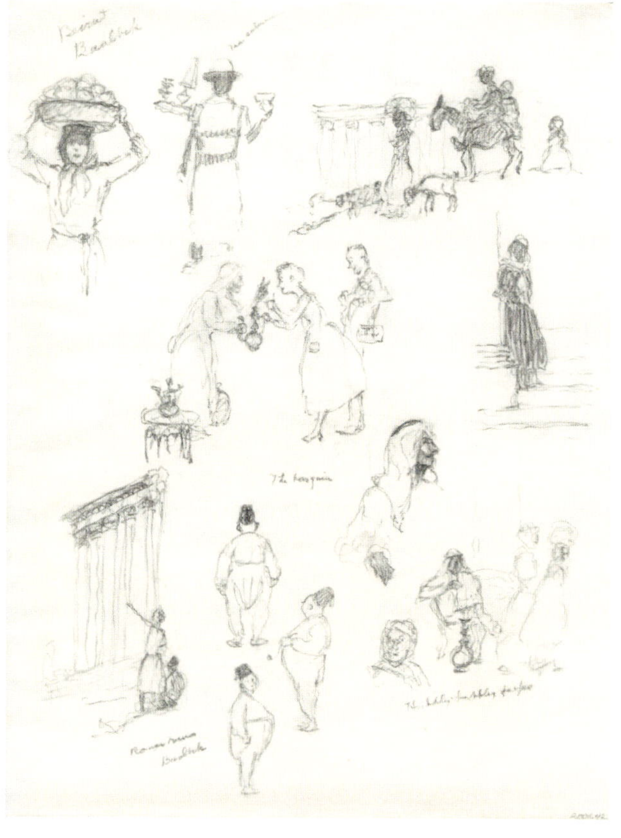

TOP LEFT
6.12. *Istanbul, Turkey*, 1955
NRM.2006.33 (Gift of Shirlee and Salvatore F. Scoma)

TOP RIGHT
6.13. *Hong Kong*, 1955
NRM.2006.39 (Gift of Shirlee and Salvatore F. Scoma)

RIGHT
6.14. *Beirut and Baalbek, Lebanon*, 1955
NRM.2006.42 (Gift of Shirlee and Salvatore F. Scoma)

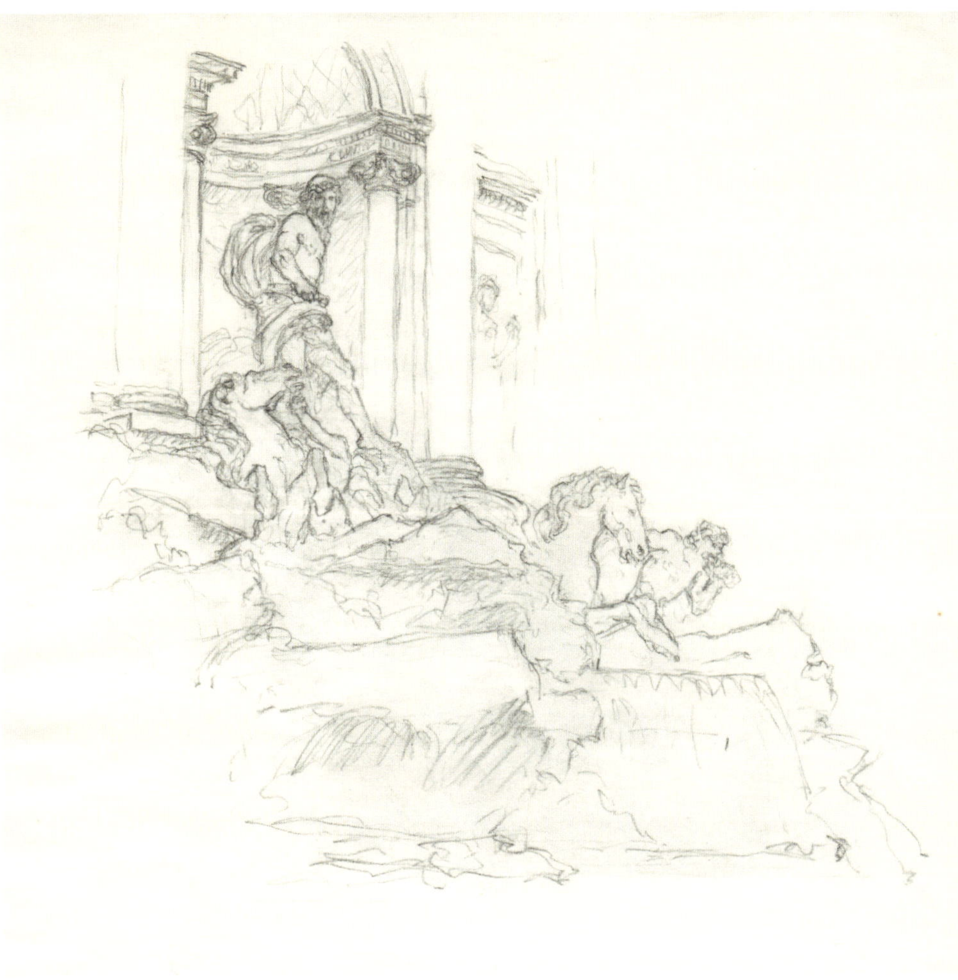

6.15. *Trevi Fountain, Rome*, 1955
Wolff pencil on paper,
16½ × 13 in. (41.9 × 34.6 cm),
Sketchbook drawing for Pan American World Airways, Inc., *Pan American Was My Magic Carpet around the World* advertising campaign
NRM.2006.53 (Gift of Shirlee and Salvatore F. Scoma)

Before leaving for Europe on his Pan Am trip, Rockwell spent three days in Hartford, Connecticut, visiting his wife, Mary, who had been hospitalized there. When approached by a reporter, he kept the matter to himself, and replied that he was there to limber up his sketching arm in preparation for his upcoming assignment. In a letter to his therapist, Erik Erikson, written from Paris, Rockwell notes that his greatest disappointment was not having sufficient time to sketch on location, saying "our stops are so short that I must make the 'sketch' book mostly from photos we are taking." Aside from experiencing some anxiety when trying to locate his hotel in Paris at night, he writes, "In fact I feel fine and [am] loving it."[4]

An inveterate traveler who depicted famous cities such as London, Rockwell visited Rome only briefly during his round-the-world trip for Pan Am, but he would come to know the city very well. The artist's youngest son, Peter Rockwell (1936–2020), a sculptor, moved to Rome in 1961 and Rockwell visited him there, taking in the sights and sounds of the city through the years. After spending time with his in-laws, who were living near Pisa at the time, Peter and his wife, Cynthia, went to Rome, where they planned to live for six months. Unable to find a furnished apartment for that length of stay, "we rented an unfinished apartment for a year. And that began the extension of our six months," he said.[5] Peter remained in Rome throughout his life, where he lived, worked, and raised a family.

## The Family Life Series for the Massachusetts Mutual Insurance Company

Between 1952 and 1963, the Massachusetts Mutual Life Insurance Company (Mass Mutual) of Springfield, Massachusetts, amassed an impressive collection of original artworks by Norman Rockwell. These black-and-white line drawings, created with soft 3B or 4B pencils, or pencil and Conté crayon on paper, portrayed families in every stage of life and were commissioned by the company for a national advertising campaign designed for a white middle-class audience. Accompanied by narrative text offering compelling reasons to purchase life insurance—especially to protect loved ones—Rockwell's drawings were widely circulated in such leading magazines as the *Saturday Evening Post*, *Time*, *Newsweek*, and *Readers' Digest*, which each had subscription rates in the millions. "The copy was to be short," said art director Julian Watkins of J. Walter Thompson, the New York advertising agency that handled the account. "The picture was to dominate the page. The ads were to be merchandised as mailers and posters." At midcentury, Rockwell was a respected brand, and his name "was to be the most important thing."

The artist's illustrations for Mass Mutual were so well received that the company made their collection of original drawings available for exhibition at museums throughout the country. In addition, reproductions were circulated as a premium to attract buyers and enhance the popular appeal of the product, free of charge. These vivid portrayals of life's memorable moments featured many of Rockwell's neighbors, and the artist himself, as models in the series.

In 1983, Mass Mutual generously donated its collection of original drawings to two Massachusetts museums—the Norman Rockwell Museum in Stockbridge and the Connecticut Valley Historical Museum in Springfield (now the Springfield Museums), where they remain preserved for future generations. Numbering eighty-three in all, they constitute one of the largest groups of advertising images created by Rockwell for any single company.

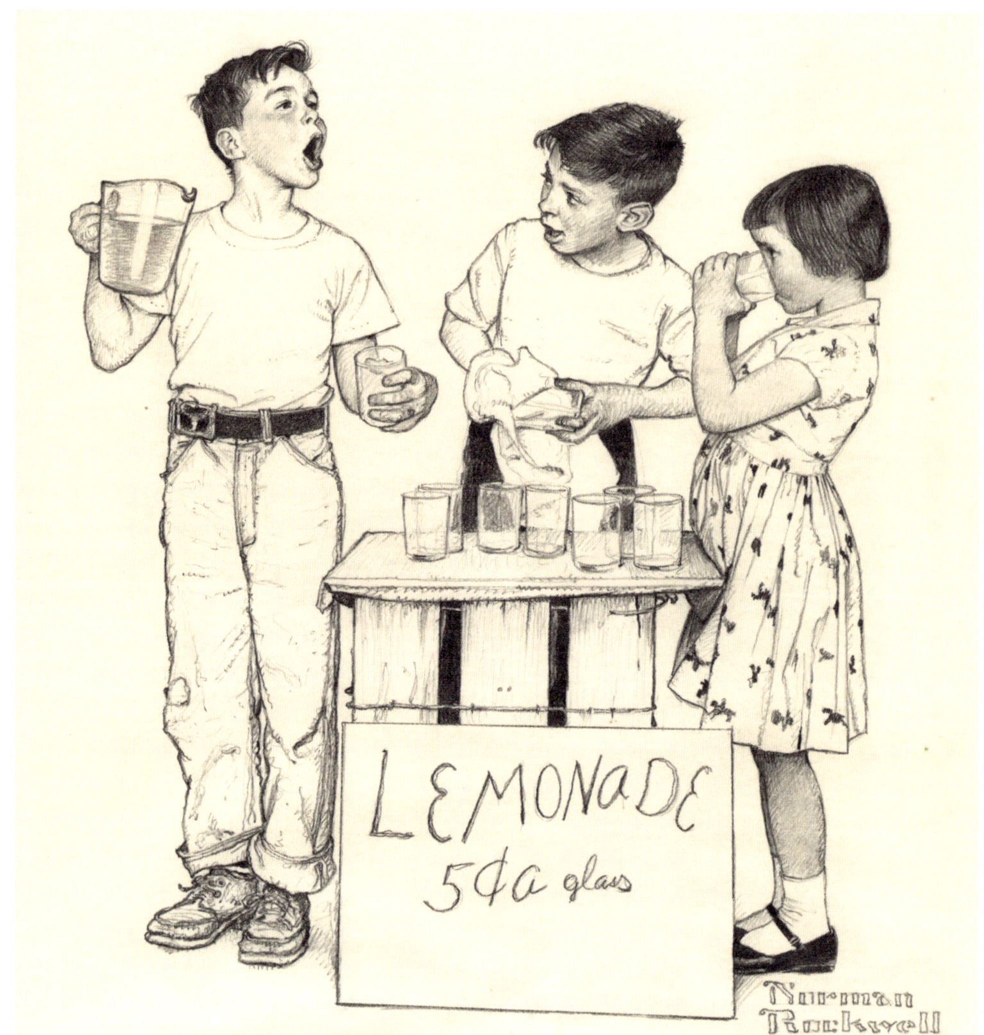


6.16. *Lemonade Stand,* 1955
Pencil on paper, 13 × 12 in.
(33 × 30.5 cm)
Illustration for
Massachusetts Mutual
Life Insurance Company
NRM.1983.32 (Gift of
Massachusetts Mutual
Life Insurance Company)

Rockwell's animated portrayal of children selling and enjoying lemonade (plate 6.16) would have been familiar to many in the 1950s, whether they hailed from urban or rural environs. The artist's drawings were designed to appeal to a broad populous by capturing human experiences that many in Mass Mutual's target audience would recognize and identify with. From the 1880s through the mid-twentieth century, lemonade stands were fixtures across the United States, a means by which children could venture out as entrepreneurs to earn money for themselves and a variety of causes. This advertisement's text emphasizes the importance of supporting children's growth by ensuring their financial stability: "Every youngster wants to assert himself . . . to do things on his own. You want your boy to make good all through life . . . and you'd like to give him a head start in a realistic way." Traditional male and female gender roles are evident in many Mass Mutual ads, which portray men as breadwinners and women as stay-at-home

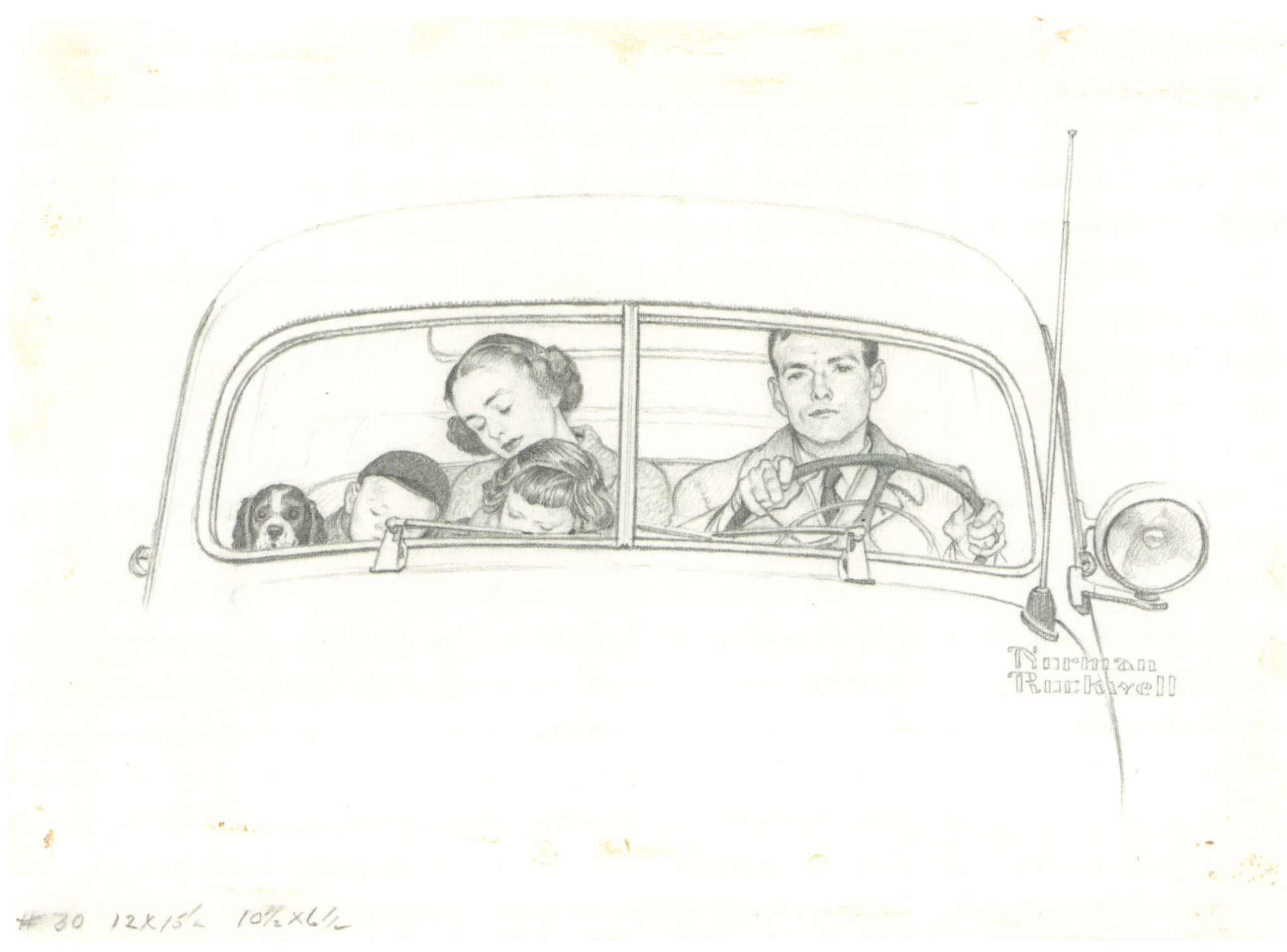


6.17. *Family in Automobile*, 1954
Pencil on paper, 7½ × 11½ in. (19.1 × 29.2 cm)
Illustration for Massachusetts Mutual Life Insurance Company
NRM.1983.18 (Gift of Massachusetts Mutual Life Insurance Company)

mothers—messaging that underscores prevailing attitudes of the time. Each ad closes with an invitation to learn more about available insurance policies from "your Mass Mutual man."

Created before 1968 when seatbelts became mandatory in all vehicles manufactured in the United States, another Mass Mutual drawing (plate 6.17) pictures a family of four, and their dog, traveling together in the front seat of their car. In the 1950s, 65 percent of all children under the age of fifteen were being raised in traditional breadwinner-homemaker families.[6] The ad's text and illustration both emphasize the confidence placed in husband and father, who will do all that he can to see his family safely through the years. Clearly and simply delineated, Rockwell's linear drawing is easily read and uses a pattern of light and dark to create visual interest. The artist's name, located just beneath the antenna on the driver's side, is a selling point and a prominent element within the composition.

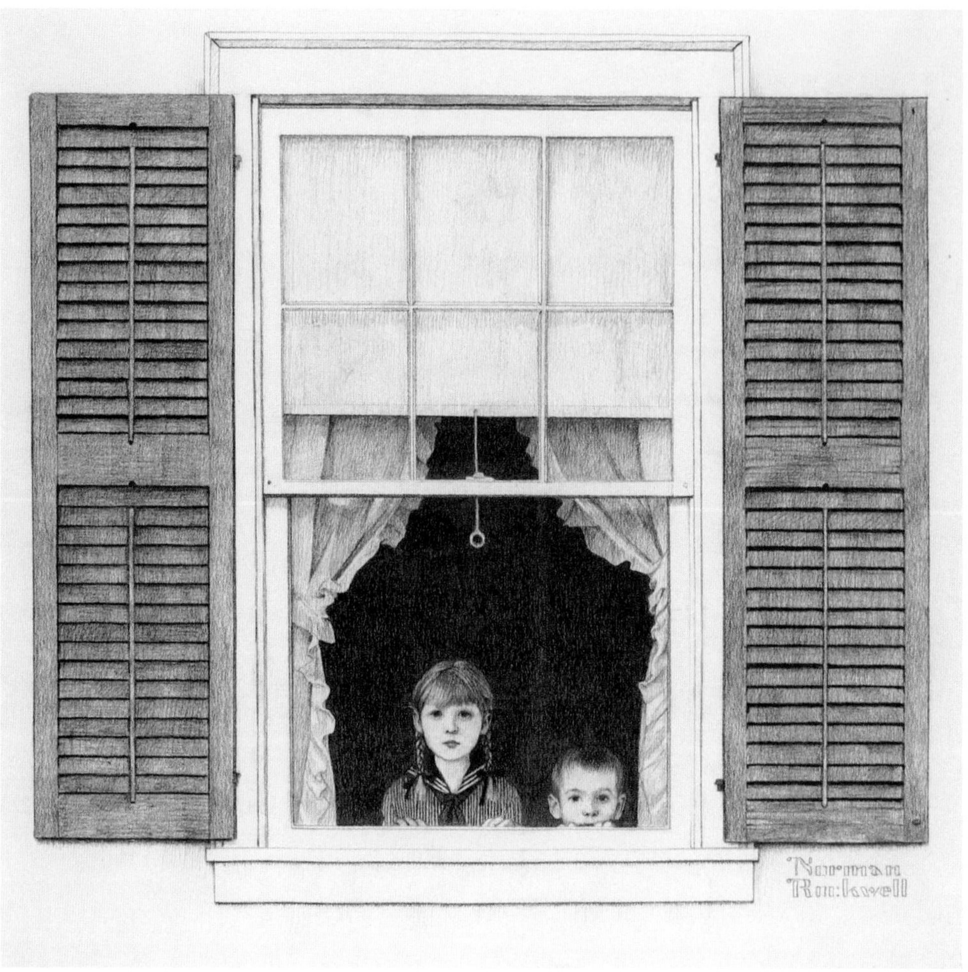


6.18. *Can Children Understand Why . . . ?*, 1959
Pencil on paper,
16 × 16 in. (40.6 × 40.6 cm)
Illustration for Massachusetts Mutual Life Insurance Company, 1959
NRM.1983.12 (Gift of Massachusetts Mutual Life Insurance Company)

Rockwell frames the forlorn faces of two young children in a darkened window, echoing the feeling of this advertisement's text: "Can children understand 'why' . . . when mother must take a job? Can they feel her love, as strong as ever, even when her work makes their day long, her homecoming late?" (plate 6.18). Though the ad compelled fathers to purchase life insurance to ensure that their wives could remain at home with the children if they died, it was likely meant to tug at the heartstrings of mothers who came upon it in the popular magazines of the day. In the 1950s, just one in three women worked outside the home, such as the nurse featured in a 1958 Mass Mutual drawing (plate 6.19), but by the end of the twentieth century, that number had risen to three in every five.[7] The U.S. Bureau of Labor Statistics states that in 2019, 57 percent of women over the age of sixteen were in the work force.

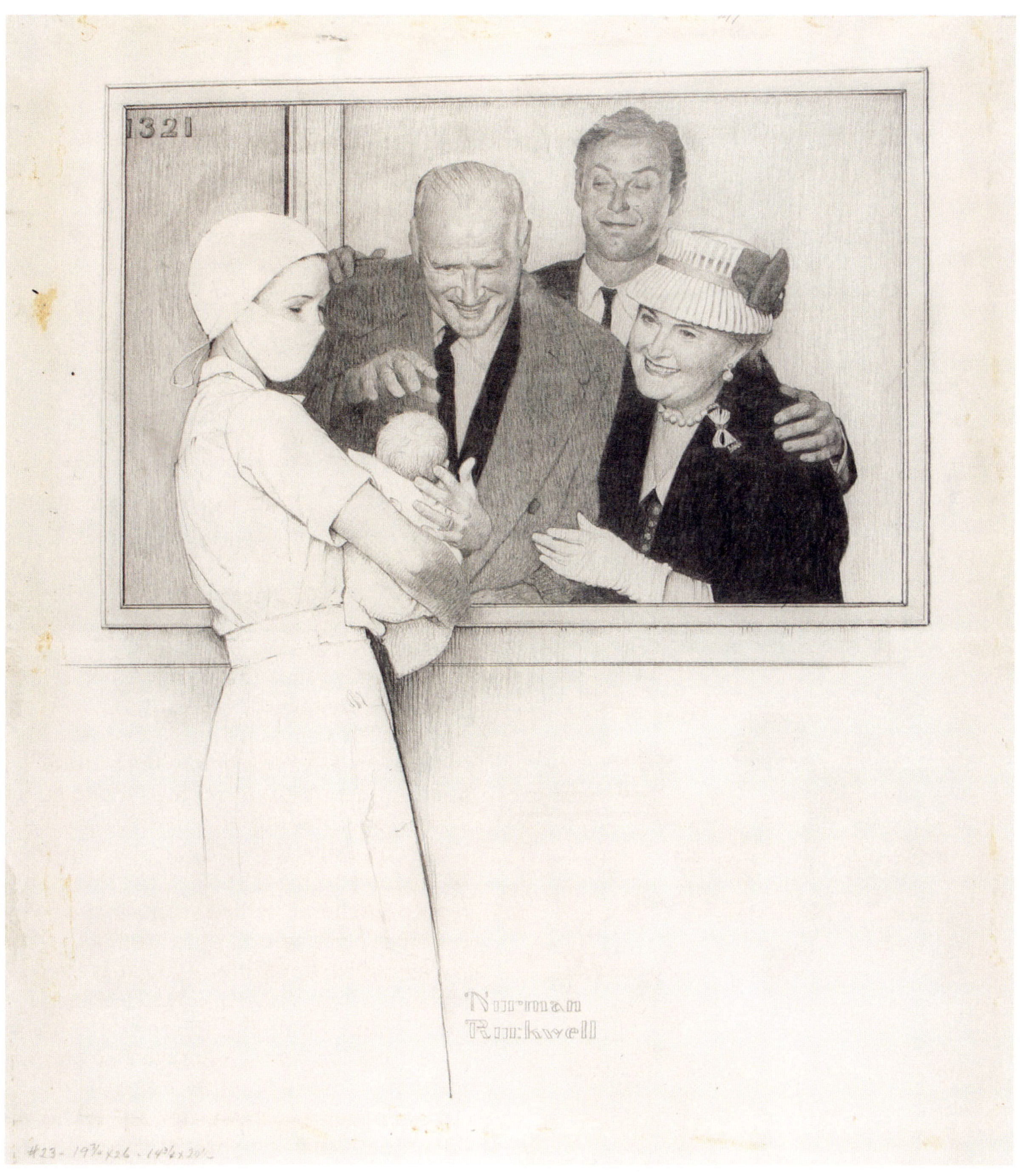


6.19. *Maternity Scene*, 1958
Pencil on paper, 19 × 15¾ in. (48.3 × 40 cm)
Illustration for Massachusetts Mutual
Life Insurance Company
NRM.1983.36 (Gift of Massachusetts
Mutual Life Insurance Company)

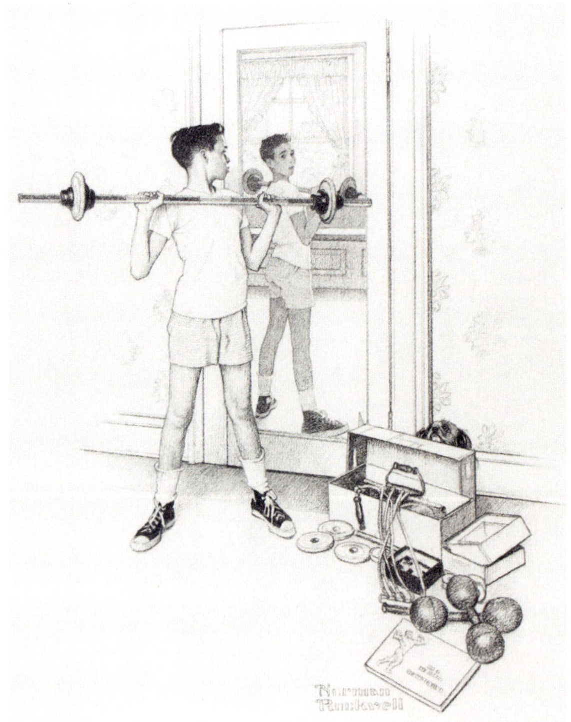

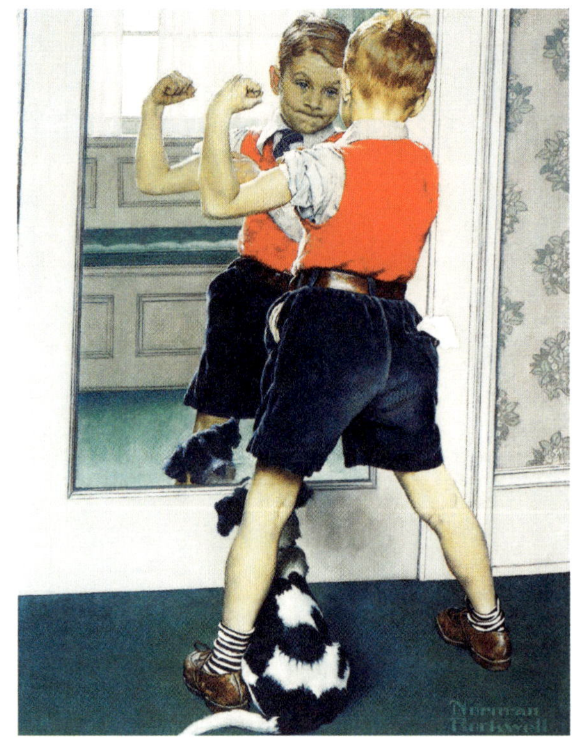

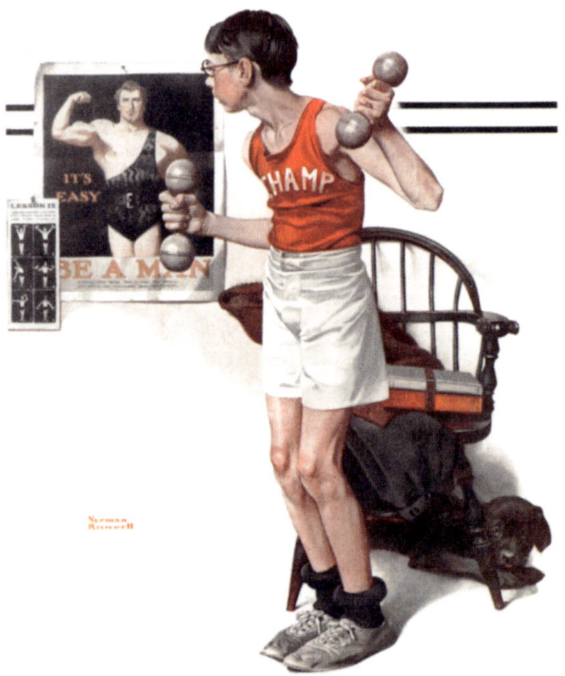


It was not unusual for Rockwell to repurpose picture concepts for different clients at different times. In one 1961 Mass Mutual ad (plate 6.20), a young man intent on building his physique is surrounded by an array of equipment that will help him do so, if only he can stick with the plan outlined in the instructional book on the floor. This repetitive theme, which seems inspired by Rockwell's perception of himself as a gangly, awkward, nonathletic youth, is also evident in a 1941 vitamin advertisement for the Upjohn Company (plate 6.21) and in *Boy Lifting Weights (It's Easy to Be a Man)*, a 1922 cover for the *Post* (plate 6.22).

In another Mass Mutual ad, Rockwell documents his own participation in the democratic process by picturing himself as a rare individual who is undecided in his vote (plate 6.23). The artist sometimes made cameo appearances in his art, and

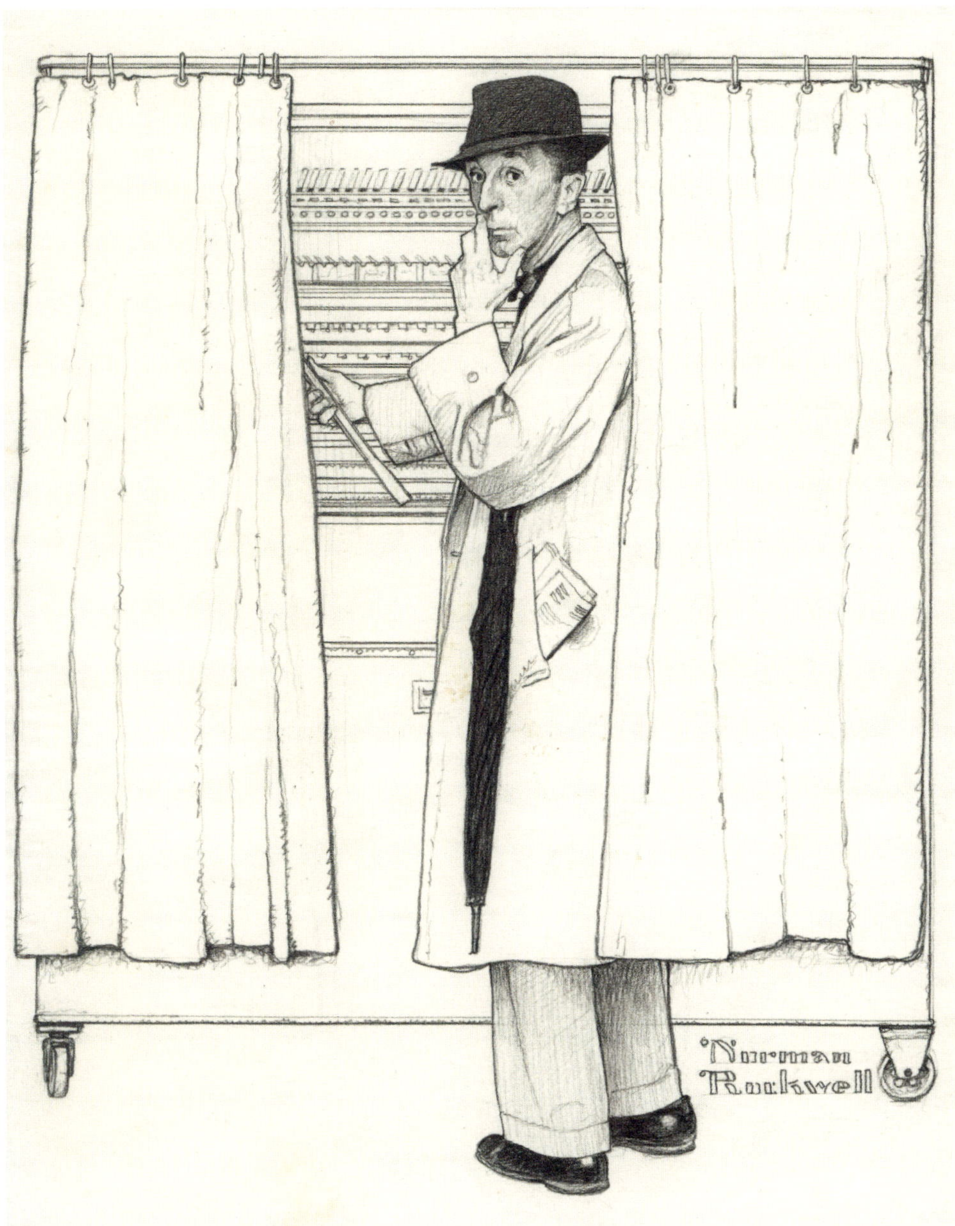


OPPOSITE TOP LEFT
6.20. *Today He's Building Man-Sized Muscles. Tomorrow He'll Be Building His Career*, 1961
Pencil on paper, 19 × 15½ in. (48.3 × 39.4 cm)
Illustration for Massachusetts Mutual Life Insurance Company
NRM.1983.10 (Gift of Massachusetts Mutual Life Insurance Company)

OPPOSITE TOP RIGHT
6.21. *The Muscleman*, 1941
Oil on canvas, 34¾ × 24 in. (88.3 × 62.6 cm)
Advertising illustration for the Upjohn Company
Location unknown

OPPOSITE BOTTOM
6.22. *Boy Lifting Weights (It's Easy to Be a Man)*, 1922
Tear sheet, 14¼ × 11¼ in. (36.2 × 28.6 cm)
Cover illustration for the *Saturday Evening Post*, April 29, 1922
RC.2007.1.46 (Gift of John A. and Laura C. Savio)

LEFT
6.23. *Norman Rockwell in a Voting Booth*, 1961
Pencil on paper, 13¼ × 10¼ in. (33.7 × 26 cm)
Illustration for Massachusetts Mutual Life Insurance Company
NRM.1983.39 (Gift of Massachusetts Mutual Life Insurance Company)

drew and painted many of the major candidates of his day without specific mention of his political viewpoints. In 1960, he met and painted presidential candidates John F. Kennedy and Richard Nixon for covers of the *Post*. Following Kennedy's assassination in 1963, Rockwell's portrait of the president appeared in memoriam—the last Rockwell illustration to be published in the magazine.

# Her First Watch

Intergenerational scenes were a mainstay in Rockwell's lifestyle advertisements, just as they were in his editorial work. This drawing of a father and daughter proudly selecting the girl's first watch presents the experience as a milestone to be emulated by postwar consumers. Commissioned by the Swiss Federation of Watch Manufacturers, the final illustration was published in the *Saturday Evening Post* on March 12, 1955, with the goal of promoting the acquisition of imported Swiss watches by an increasingly affluent American public.

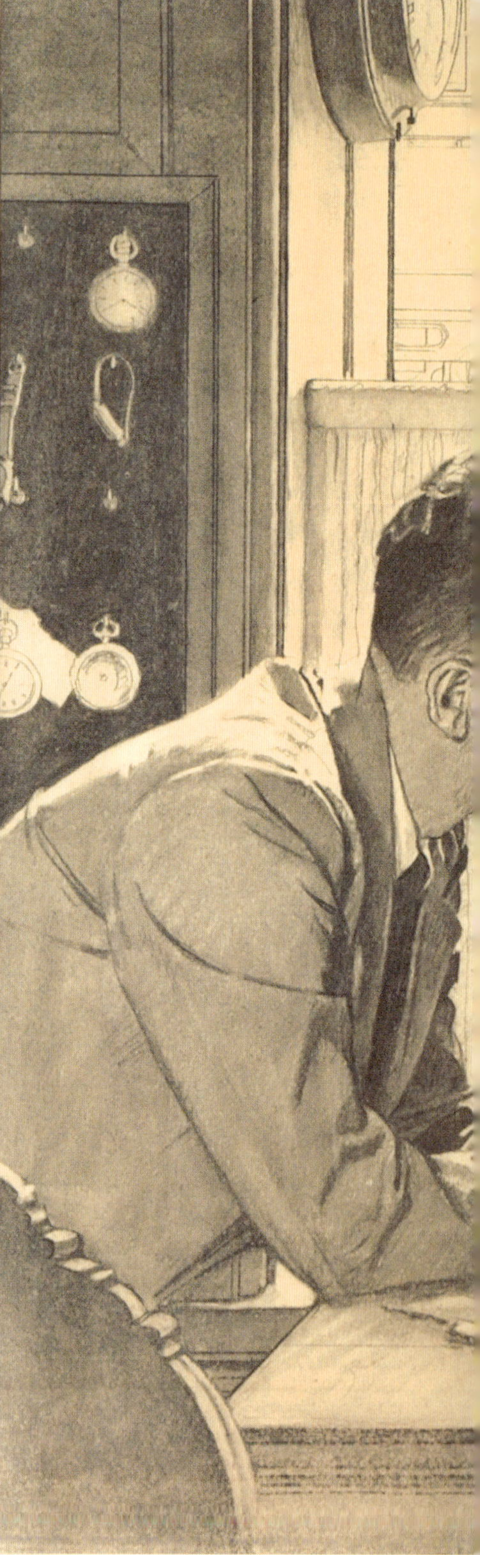

6.24. *The Jewelry Shop*, c. 1955
Pencil and charcoal on paper,
21 × 25 in. (53.3 × 63.5 cm)
Study illustration for the Swiss
Federation of Watch Manufacturers
NRACT.1976.48

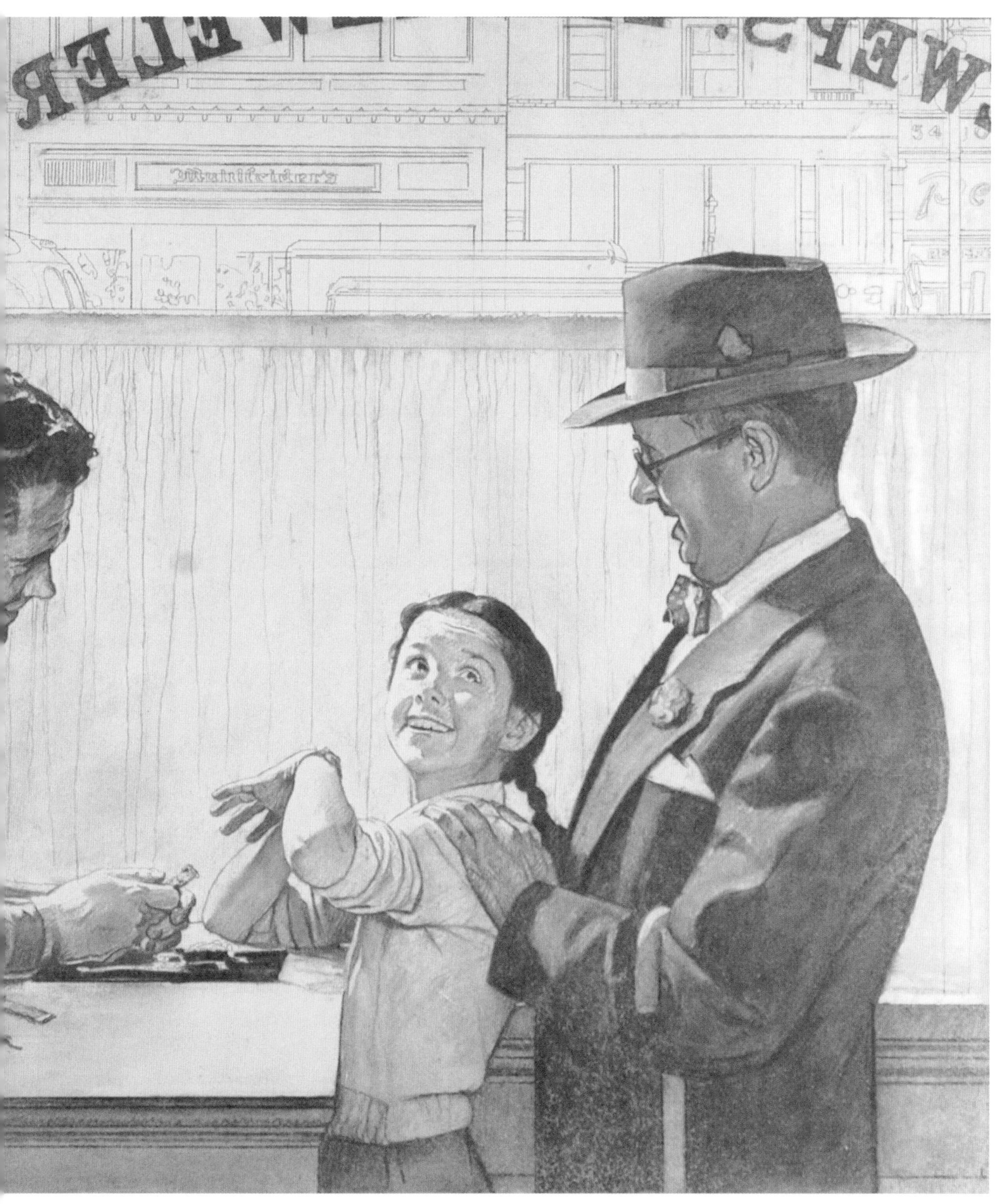

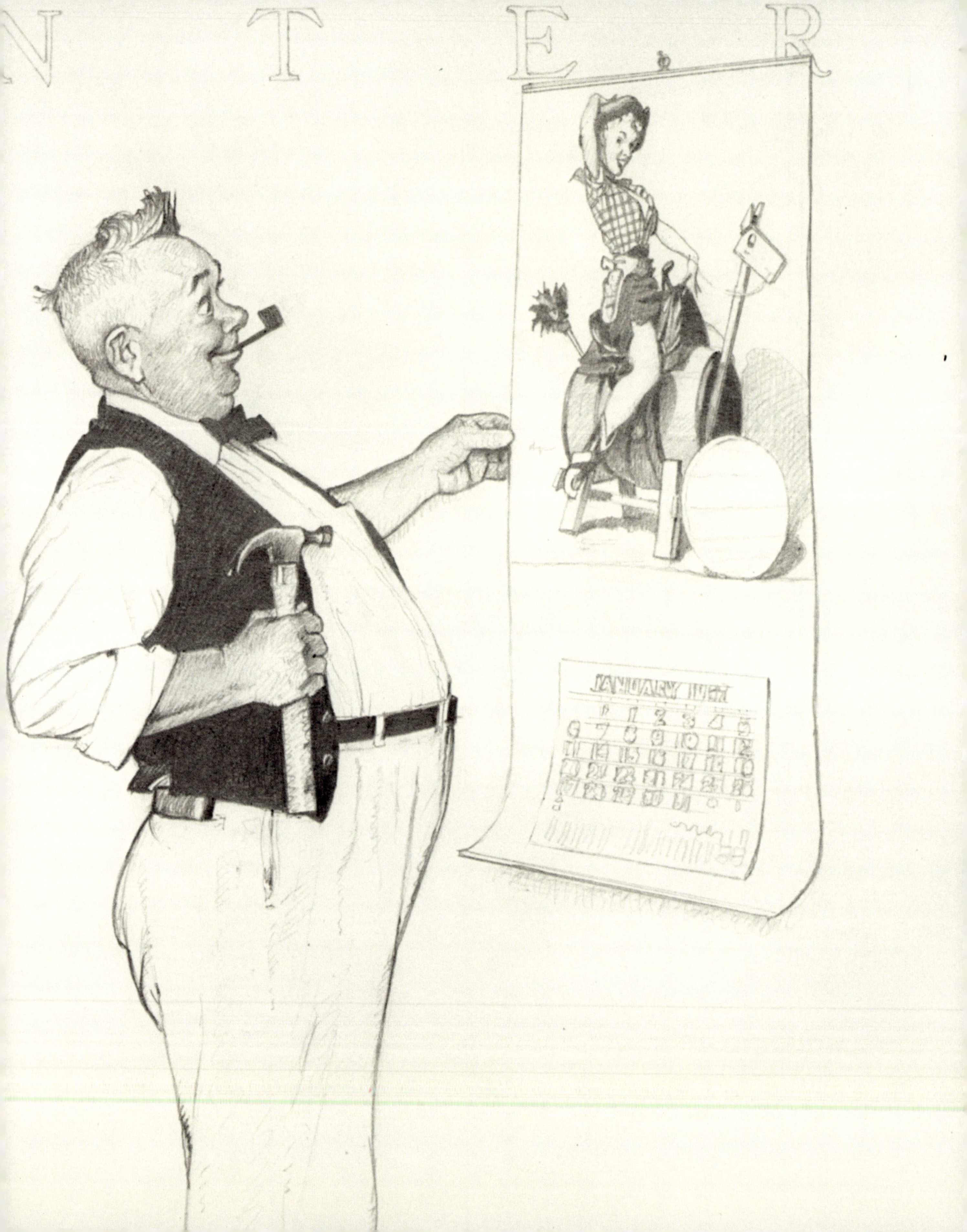
N T E R
JANUARY

# 7 Around the Year: Rockwell's Calendar Illustrations

JESSE KOWALSKI

The modern American calendar industry got its start in 1888, when Edmund Burke Osborne and Thomas D. Murphy established the first art calendar factory in Red Oak, Illinois. Initially their goal was to raise funds for the new county courthouse by publishing a calendar featuring an illustration of the courthouse along with ads for local businesses; they sold the calendar to those businesses, who in turn distributed it to their customers as a promotional item. The idea proved successful, and soon developed into the familiar model of the advertising calendar: an at-

Detail of study for *Tender Years: New Calendar*, 1955
See plate 7.17.

tractive color illustration to be hung on the wall, customized with the name and address of a local business, with tearaway calendar pages affixed at the bottom.

In 1895, a former salesman for the Thomas D. Murphy company, one Herbert H. Bigelow, moved to St. Paul, Minnesota, and established the firm of Brown & Bigelow, which soon became the nation's biggest producer of calendars. Brown & Bigelow were selling millions of calendars annually by the 1920s, with artwork commissioned from many of the leading illustrators of the day, including Maxfield Parrish and Andrew Loomis. It would seem almost inevitable that a rising star like Norman Rockwell would come to the firm's attention. Interestingly, however, Rockwell's relationship with Brown & Bigelow was at first indirect, through one of his earliest clients, the Boy Scouts of America.

## Rockwell and the Boy Scouts

Rockwell's relationship with the Boy Scouts of America began when the organization was still in its infancy. In 1912, only two years after the organization was founded, they hired the eighteen-year-old artist to create a series of pen-and-ink drawings for *The Boy Scout's Hike Book*. *Boys' Life*, the weekly magazine of the Boy Scouts of America, had just expanded to national circulation. After only six months of working for the magazine, Rockwell was promoted to art director and given a salary of fifty dollars per month. He was responsible for producing cover art, illustrating one story per issue, and acquiring and editing the interior artwork. Rockwell began his tenure at the *Saturday Evening Post* in 1916 and resigned from his salaried position at *Boys' Life* the next year, but he continued to include images of Scouts on *Post* covers and in the monthly magazine of the American Red Cross.

In 1923, a Brown & Bigelow executive noticed that the Boy Scouts had made several successful fundraising drives using reproductions of Rockwell's Red Cross paintings. The firm saw great potential in an annual Boy Scout calendar illustrated by Rockwell. In gratitude for his early break and the valuable experience he gained with the Boy Scouts of America, Rockwell made a lifelong commitment to them, producing fifty-one illustrations for Brown & Bigelow's highly successful Boy Scout calendar from 1925 to 1976. The artist's sixty-five-year relationship with this venerable organization became the longest association of his career. Ironically, neither Rockwell nor his three sons were ever Boy Scouts. The models were not typically Scouts either, but local boys Rockwell knew, though the Boy Scouts sent perfectly pressed uniforms every year in anticipation of Rockwell's next submission.

For each calendar, the Boy Scouts developed several ideas for Rockwell to consider—the organization always requested that artists portray the

Scouts according to the rules of the Scout Law, which prescribes values such as trustworthiness, loyalty, cheerfulness, and bravery. Rockwell would counter with suggestions until they reached a mutual decision. The artist would then create a charcoal drawing to be approved by the organization. Chief Scout Executive James West was particular about the representation of Scouts in the paintings, and at times he would send a trusted staff member to Rockwell's studio during the painting process to ensure the subject met the Scouts' strict standards. Rockwell would present the completed painting to West, who would then call in several staff members to pick apart the work in front of the artist. Naturally, numerous errors were found—in the way the neckerchief was tied, the girth of the Boy Scout, the age of the boy, or placement of the subjects. Rockwell waited patiently until they had talked among themselves, ultimately determining the artwork was exactly what they wanted.

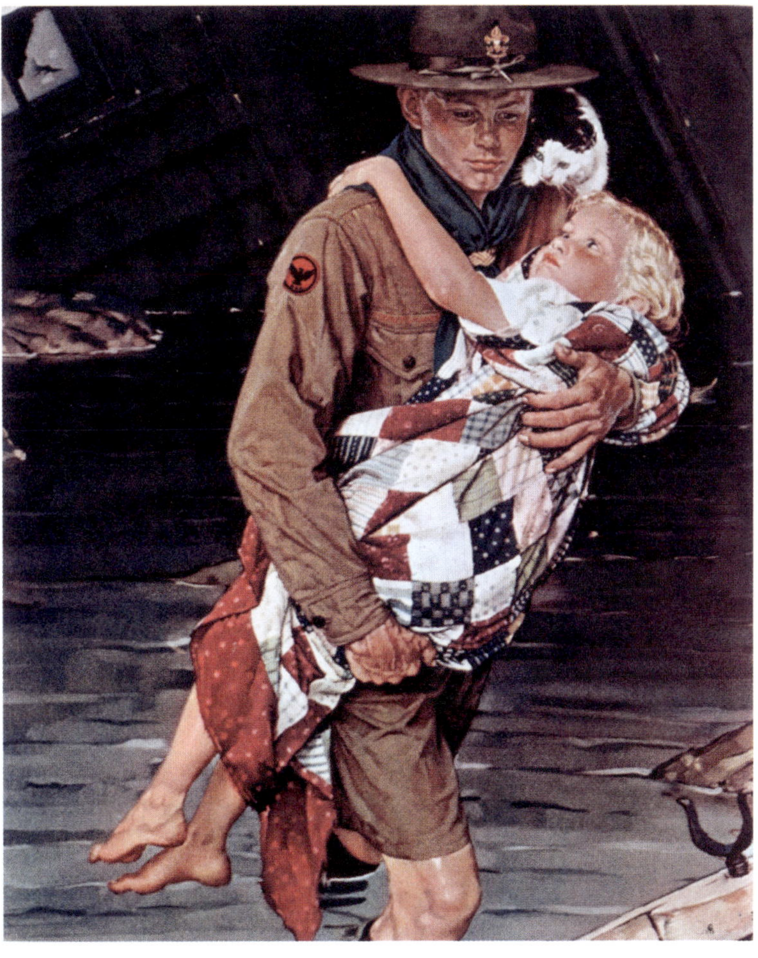

Beginning in 1929, Rockwell devised a more suitable arrangement: for all future Boy Scout calendars, he would deliver the artwork to Brown & Bigelow rather than the Boy Scout headquarters. Nevertheless, of all Rockwell's clients, the Boy Scouts continued to demand the most changes to his work. Rockwell often had to redraw studies or repaint portions of canvasses, which necessitated shipping the artwork back and forth from Brown & Bigelow to Rockwell until it was approved—the painting for the 1941 calendar, titled *A Scout Is Helpful*, was no exception (plate 7.1). Rockwell's first version showed the Scout in long pants that were wet from the knees down. The Boy Scouts' editor asked Rockwell to put the young man in short pants, as Scouts were supposed to appear presentable at all times.

7.1. *A Scout Is Helpful*, 1939
Oil on canvas, 34 × 24 in. (86.4 × 61 cm)
Illustration for Boy Scouts of America 1941 calendar
NRM.1988.10

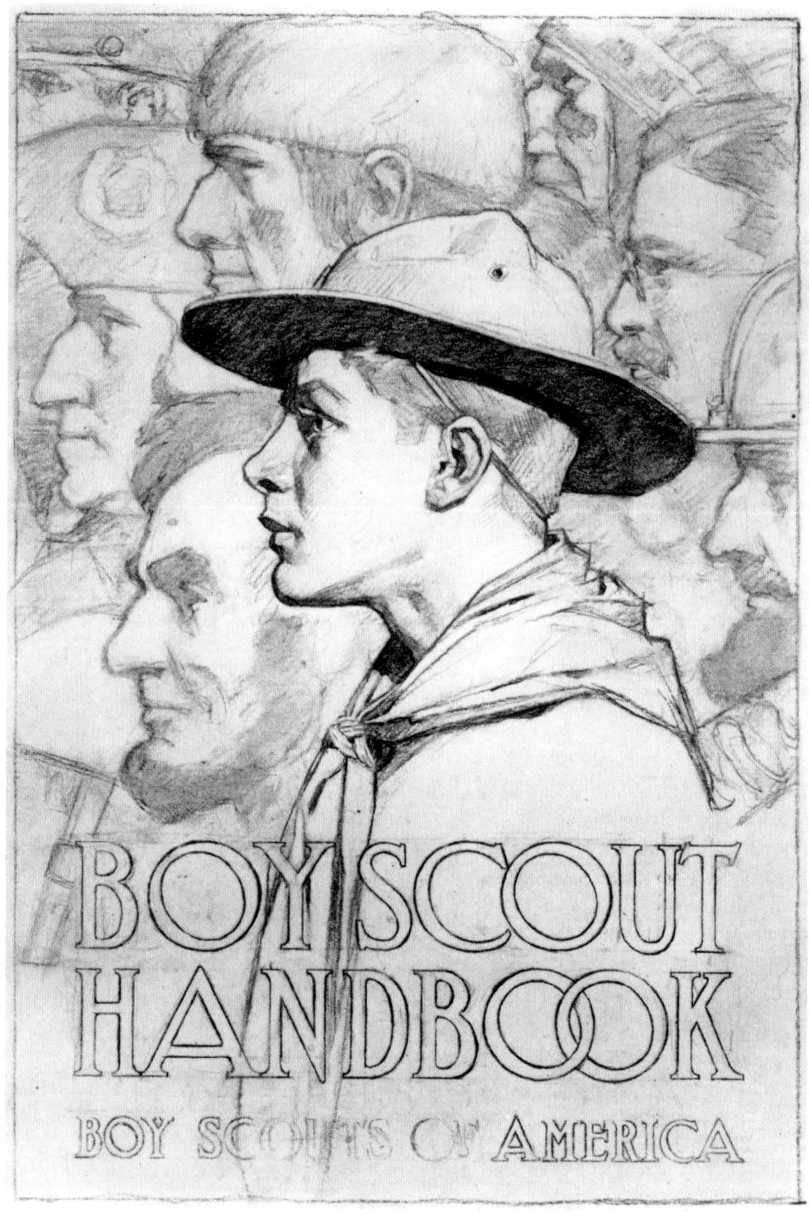


7.2. *Spirit of America*, 1927
Charcoal on paper
Study for *Boy Scout Handbook* (3rd edition), 1927; illustration for Boy Scouts of America 1929 calendar
Location unknown

One of Rockwell's most notable works to appear on the Boy Scout calendar was *Spirit of America*, which features a Scout standing with American luminaries, such as George Washington, a frontiersman, an unnamed Native American, Teddy Roosevelt, Charles Lindbergh, and Abraham Lincoln—Rockwell's favorite historical figure. There are some minor differences between the drawing and the finished painting. In the painting, the Scout has better posture, which doubtless reflects the ideals of the organization. The profiles in the painting appear closer, and some are not as apparent as they

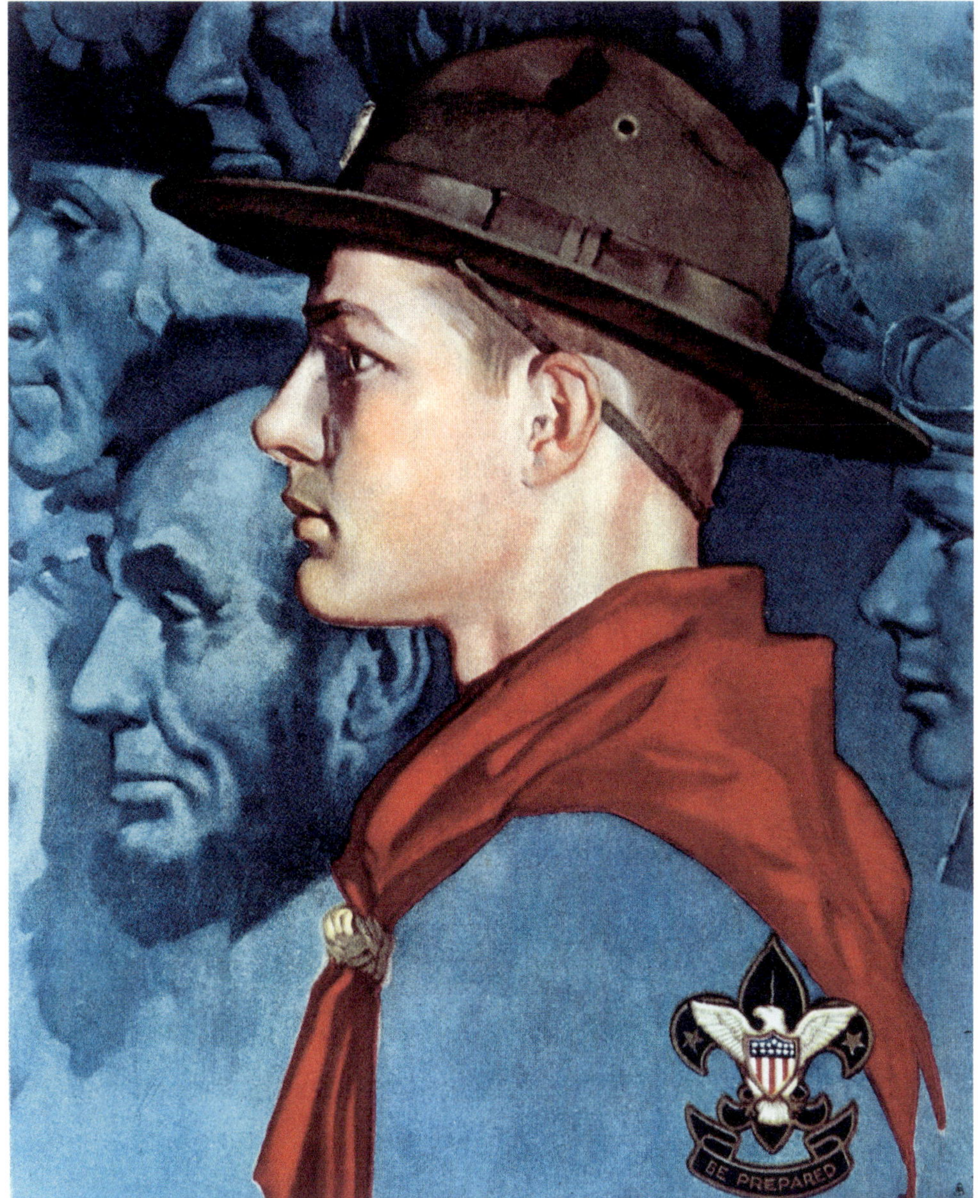


7.3. *Spirit of America*, 1927
Oil on canvas, 20 × 16 in.
(50.8 × 40.6 cm)
Cover illustration for
*Boy Scout Handbook*
(3rd edition), 1927;
illustration for Boy Scouts
of America 1929 calendar
Private collection

are in the drawing, such as the Native American man, while others have been omitted altogether.

The image was so beloved that the Boy Scouts displayed it on the cover of their handbook from 1927 to 1940. However, they were not the only ones overjoyed with Rockwell's Boy Scout illustrations. In the first few years of production, Brown & Bigelow sold the Boy Scout calendar to an estimated two million households.

As with his *Post* covers, Rockwell put a great deal of time and care into drafting his Boy Scout calendar illustrations before he painted the final version. *The Adventure Trail,* which was made for the 1952 Boy Scout calendar and was also used on the cover of *Boys' Life,* exemplifies Rockwell's detailed process from charcoal to pencil to paint. The drawings reveal the addition of quintessential Scout apparatus at the time, including a helmet, a flashlight, and even a hand ax. In the final version, the leader wears more regalia, and he is holding an arrowhead rather than pointing in the opposite direction.

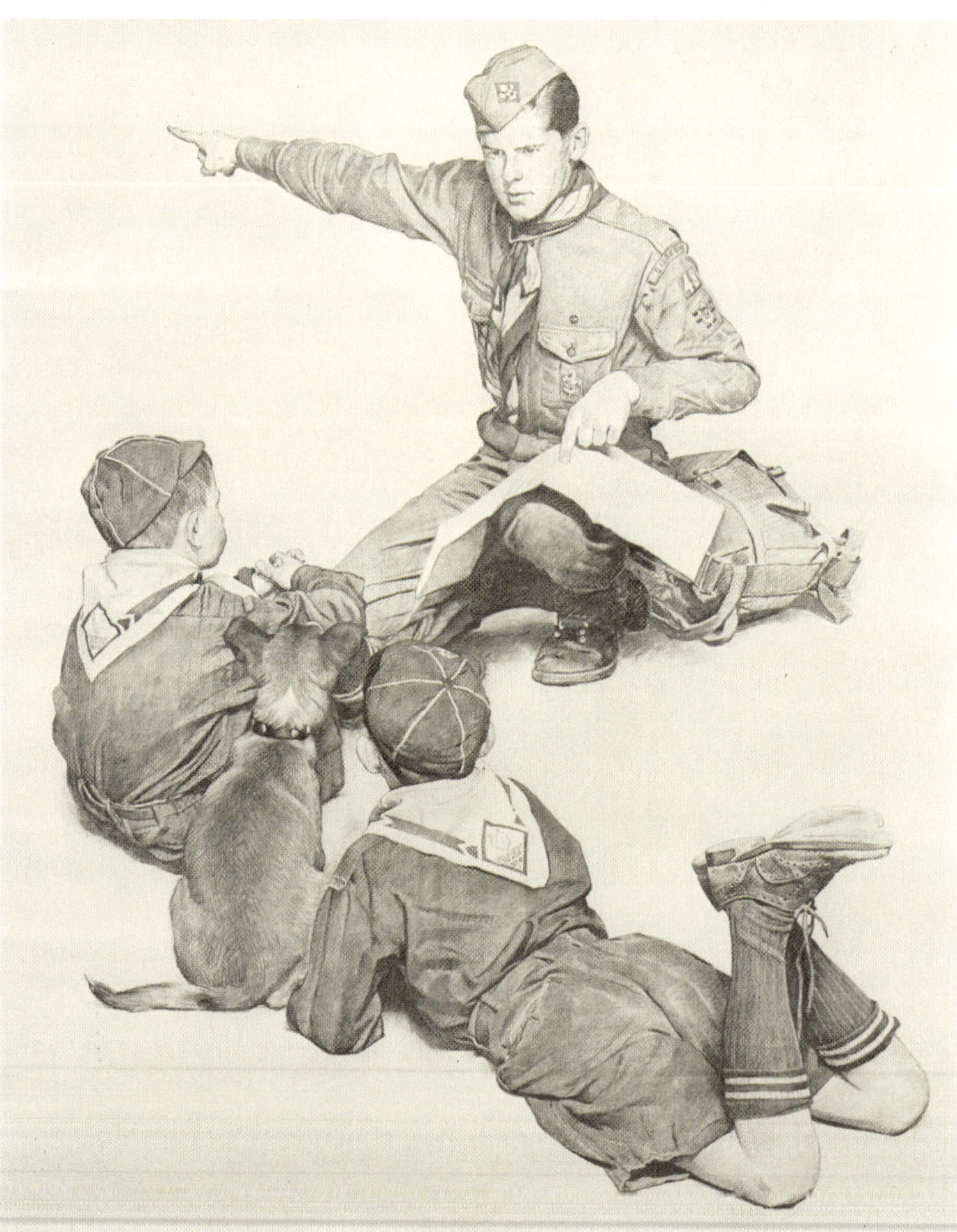

7.4. *The Adventure Trail,* 1952
Charcoal on paper
Study for Boy Scouts of America 1952 calendar
Location unknown

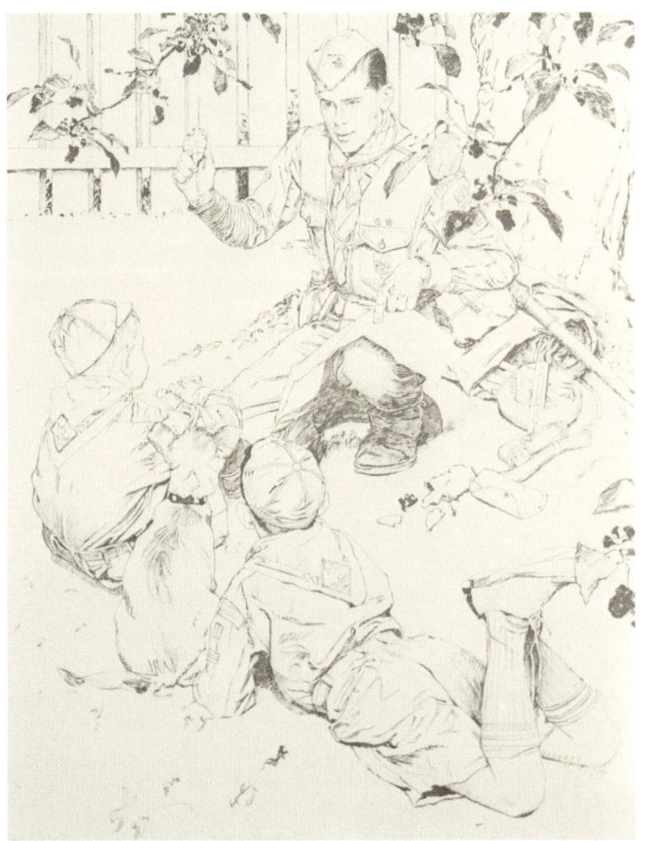

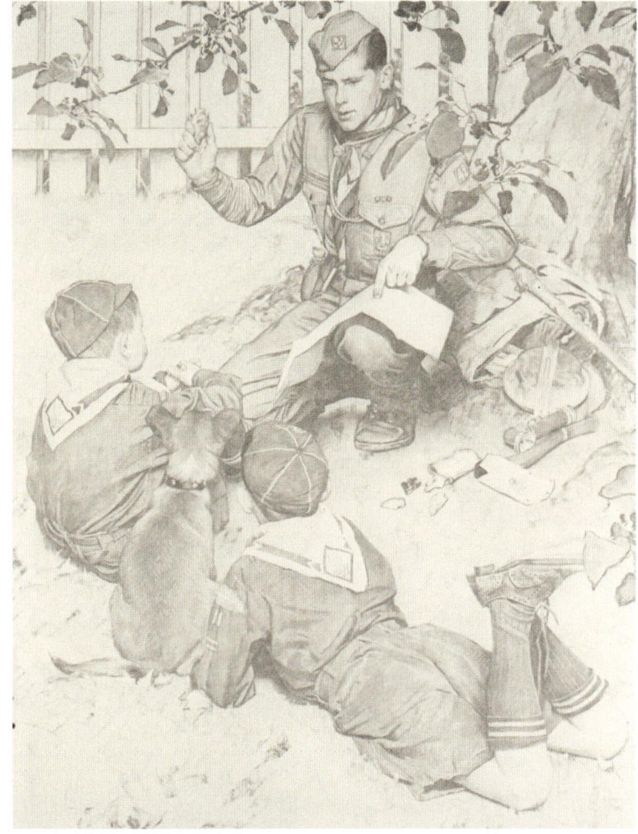

ABOVE LEFT
7.5. *The Adventure Trail*, 1952
Pencil on paper
Study for Boy Scouts of America 1952 calendar
Location unknown

ABOVE RIGHT
7.6. *The Adventure Trail*, 1952
Charcoal on paper
Study for Boy Scouts of America 1952 calendar
Location unknown

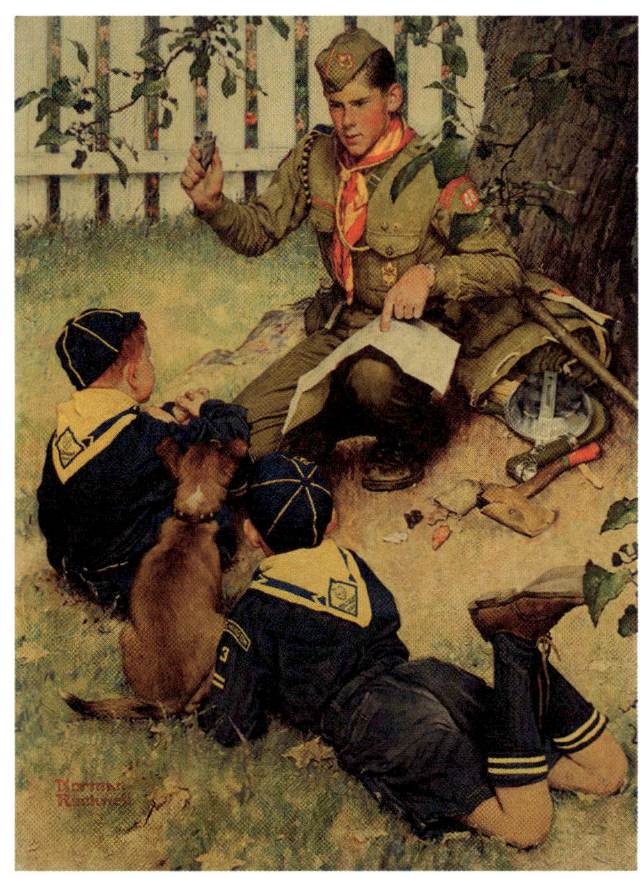


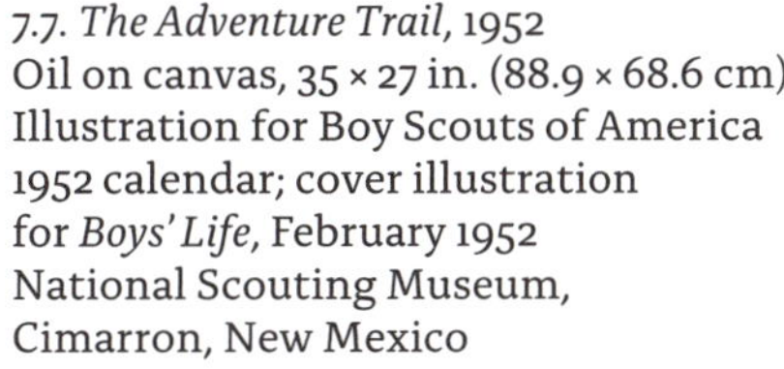
7.7. *The Adventure Trail*, 1952
Oil on canvas, 35 × 27 in. (88.9 × 68.6 cm)
Illustration for Boy Scouts of America 1952 calendar; cover illustration for *Boys' Life*, February 1952
National Scouting Museum, Cimarron, New Mexico

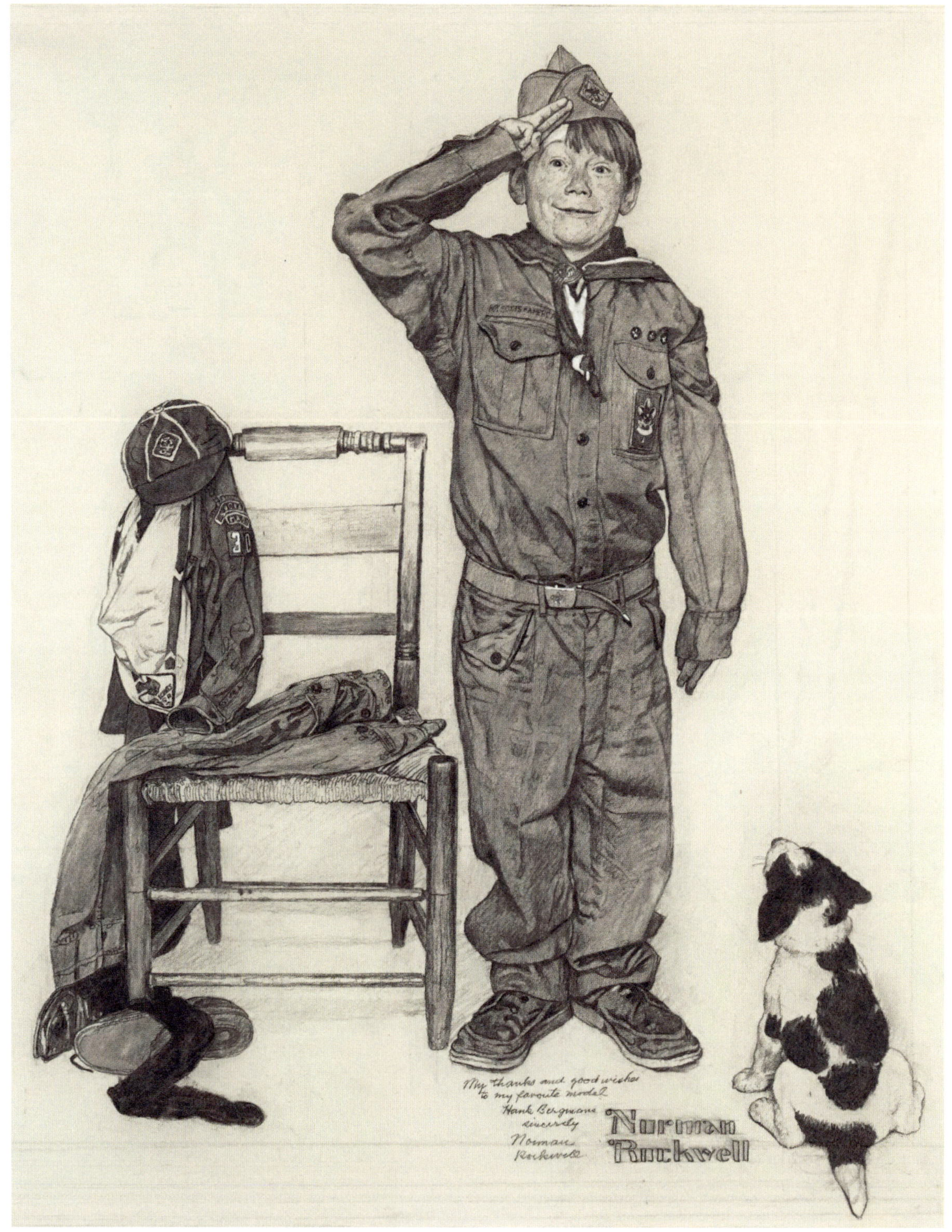


7.8. *Can't Wait*, 1970
Charcoal on paper, 39 × 31½ in. (99.1 × 80 cm)
Study for Boy Scouts of America 1972 calendar;
autographed for the model, Hank Bergmans
Private collection

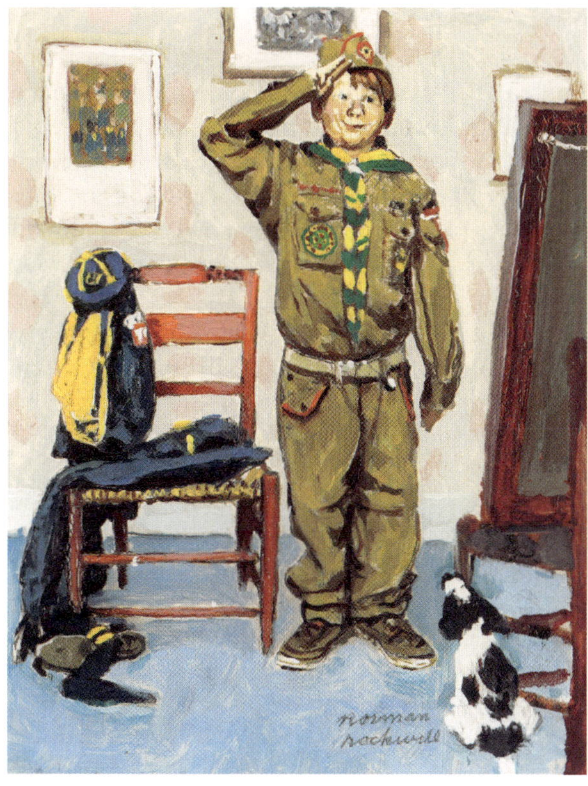

7.9. *Can't Wait*, 1970
Oil on board, 10 × 7½ in.
(25.4 × 19.1 cm)
Color study for Boy Scouts
of America 1972 calendar
Private collection

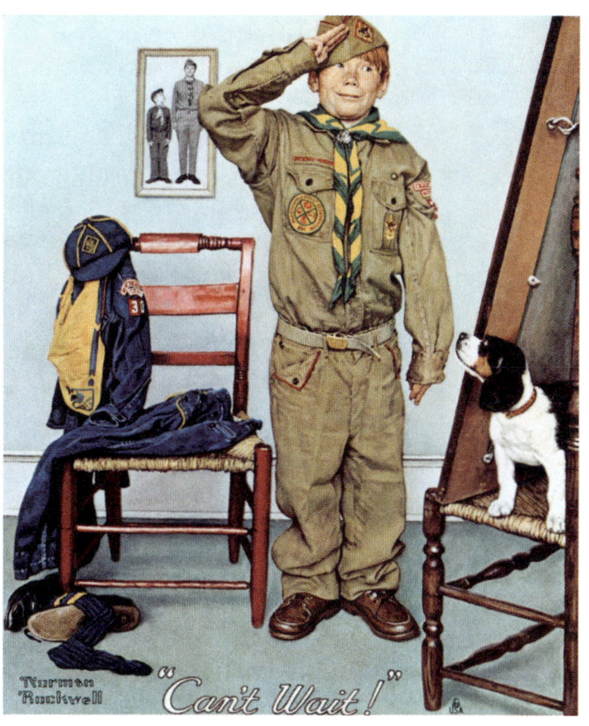


7.10. *Can't Wait*, 1970
Oil on canvas, 40 × 32 in. (101.6 × 81.3 cm)
Illustration for Boy Scouts of
America 1972 calendar
National Scouting Museum,
Cimarron, New Mexico

Bittersweet paintings of children growing up were a hallmark of Rockwell's work. One of his final Scout paintings, *Can't Wait*, is an especially poignant example. In this illustration, featuring model Hank Bergmans, a young boy has set aside his Cub Scout uniform and is trying on his older brother's Boy Scout uniform. The theme changed substantially from the charcoal drawing to the color study to the final painting. In the completed work, the Scout admires himself in the propped-up mirror. At the same time, his gaze and that of his pet dog are focused on the picture on the wall, which depicts the Cub Scout looking up to his big brother, the Boy Scout. This is an example of how Rockwell was able to insert thoughtful narratives in his Boy Scout paintings that would be both relatable and inspirational to their young audience.

## The Four Seasons Calendars

Norman Rockwell had been illustrating the Boy Scout calendar for more than twenty years when Brown & Bigelow asked him whether he would paint calendars they could use for advertising—at this time, Rockwell was already viewed as an iconic American painter for his work for the Boy Scouts, the *Saturday Evening Post*, and numerous other clients. Rockwell agreed, and in 1948, he began painting a series of calendars for Brown & Bigelow called the Four Seasons, in which he created an image for winter, spring, summer, and autumn. In Rockwell's Four Seasons illustrations, he deviated from his standard formula for *Post* covers, since each image would be on view in the home or business for three months. The images he painted were lighthearted, comical, and episodic as the subjects switched from season to season.

During 1964, the final year of original Four Seasons calendars—the company would later continue to reprint Rockwell's calendar illustrations—sales surpassed even those of the Boy Scout calendar. Since their publication, the Four Seasons images have remained popular, appearing not only on calendar reprints, but on greeting cards, display plates, Christmas ornaments, and other collectibles.[1]

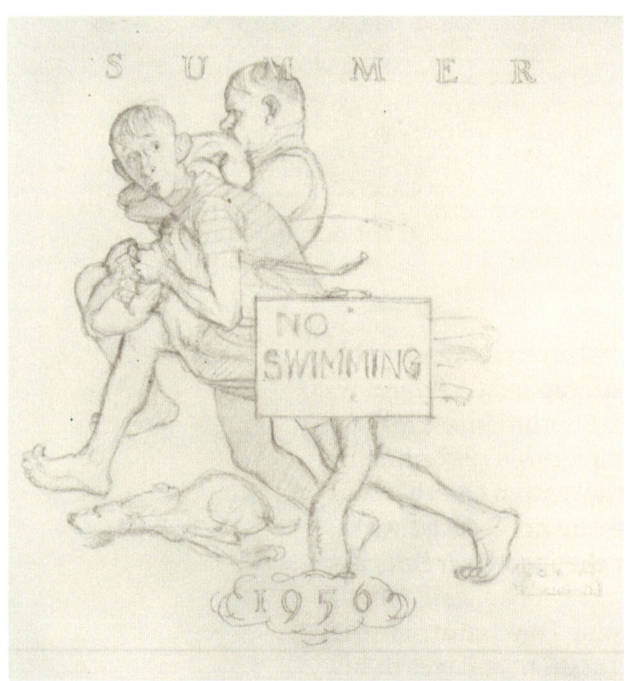


7.11. *Two Old Men and Dog: No Swimming*, 1956
Pencil on paper
Study for Four Seasons calendar, summer 1956
Private collection

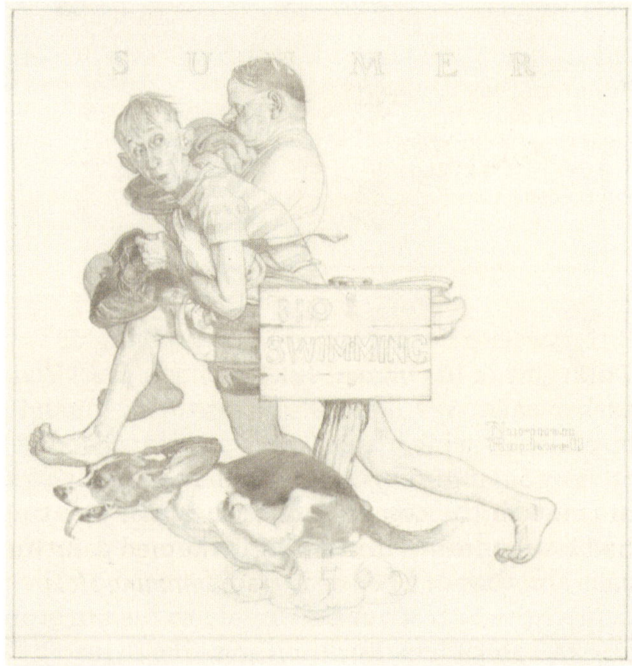


7.12. *Two Old Men and Dog: No Swimming*, 1956
Pencil on paper
Study for Four Seasons calendar, summer 1956
Private collection

7.13. *No Swimming*, 1921
Oil on canvas, 25¼ × 22¼ in.
(64.1 × 56.5 cm)
Cover illustration for the *Saturday Evening Post*, June 4, 1921
NRACT.1973.015

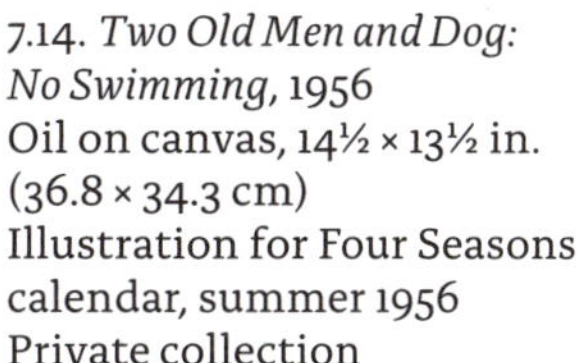

7.14. *Two Old Men and Dog: No Swimming*, 1956
Oil on canvas, 14½ × 13½ in.
(36.8 × 34.3 cm)
Illustration for Four Seasons calendar, summer 1956
Private collection

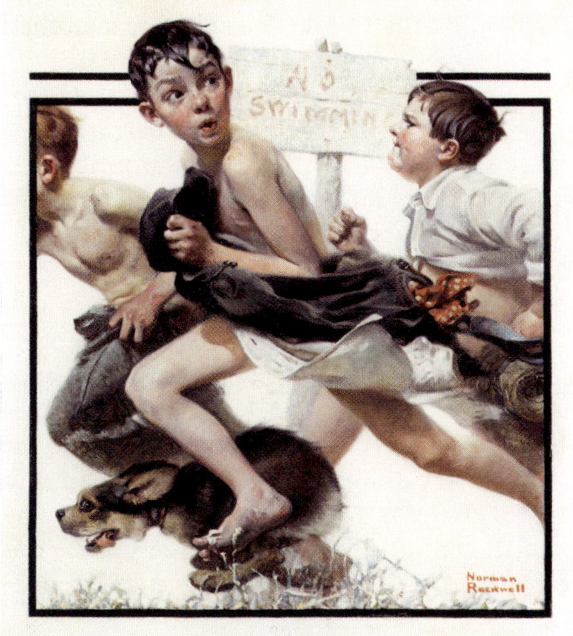


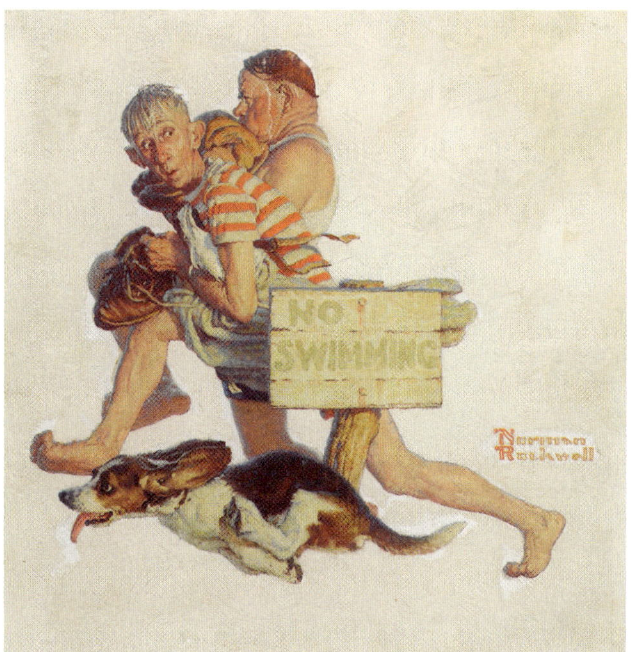


Throughout his career, Rockwell often revisited themes he had used in earlier paintings. This is evident in his illustrations for the Four Seasons calendars, such as *Two Old Men and Dog: No Swimming* from 1956, a playful recreation of his popular *No Swimming* painting that appeared on the cover of the *Saturday Evening Post* in 1921. The two old men in the 1956 painting had also appeared in a similarly themed painting for the 1950 Four Seasons calendar, *Two Old Men and Dog: Swimming Hole*.

The initial sketch differs in several respects from the final painting: the dog will end up on the other side of the men, the signpost will evolve from a crooked branch to a worn log, and the closer man's back leg will be extended (much longer than it would be in reality).

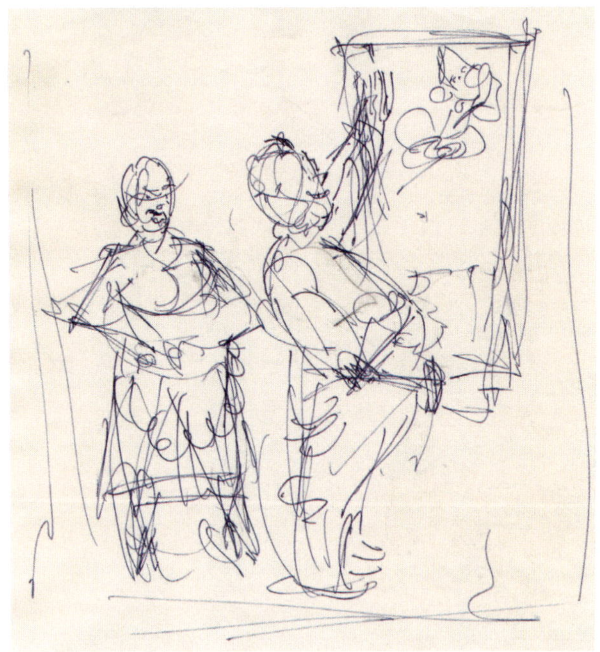

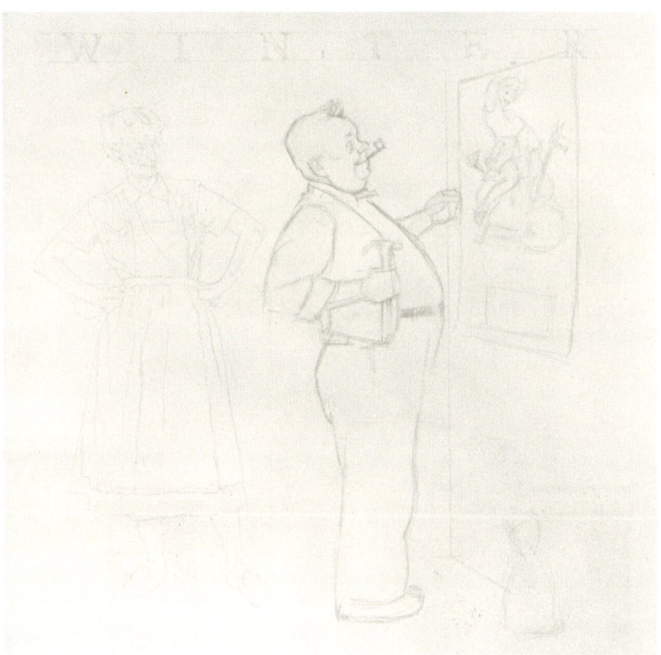


ABOVE LEFT
7.15. *Tender Years: New Calendar*, 1956
Ink and pencil on paper, 10 × 7½ in. (25.4 × 19.1 cm)
Study for Four Seasons calendar, winter 1957
NRACT.1976.185

ABOVE RIGHT
7.16. *Tender Years: New Calendar*, 1955
Pencil on paper
Study for Four Seasons calendar, winter 1957
Private collection

The process of creating *Tender Years: New Calendar* was a little unorthodox for Rockwell, since he made an early sketch with what appears to be a ballpoint pen (plate 7.15). Rockwell usually drew rough early sketches like this with pencil, though he would use pencil and charcoal for the subsequent series of sketches and studies. Rockwell's depiction of an older man and his loving wife went through several changes during its development. The artist made numerous sketches of the couple, first in ink, then pencil and charcoal, until he captured the connection between a long-married husband and wife.

Dozens of photographs of local models were taken for this illustration, and a handful were used to create the final setup for the drawing that formed the basis of the painting. In the source photographs, the placeholder for the wall calendar was actually Rockwell's 1956 Brown & Bigelow calendar. In order to provoke a laugh from the model, Rockwell pasted a comical photograph of Oliver Kempton, a local schoolteacher from Stockbridge, Massachusetts, posing in a ballerina costume over the calendar. The calendar in the final painting features pinup artist Gil Elvgren's painting *Sitting Pretty* (1955).

7.19a–b. Reference photograph (and detail) for Four Seasons calendar, winter 1957, 1955
Photograph (from negative)
ST1976.4225 (detail)

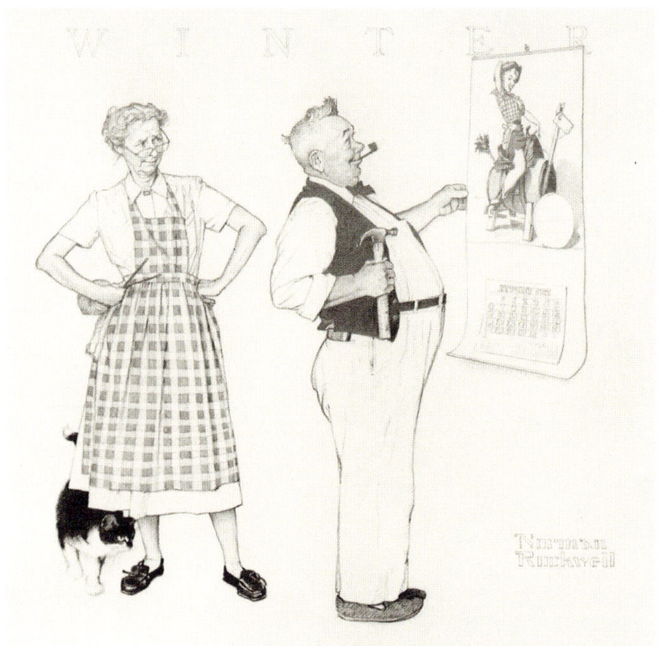


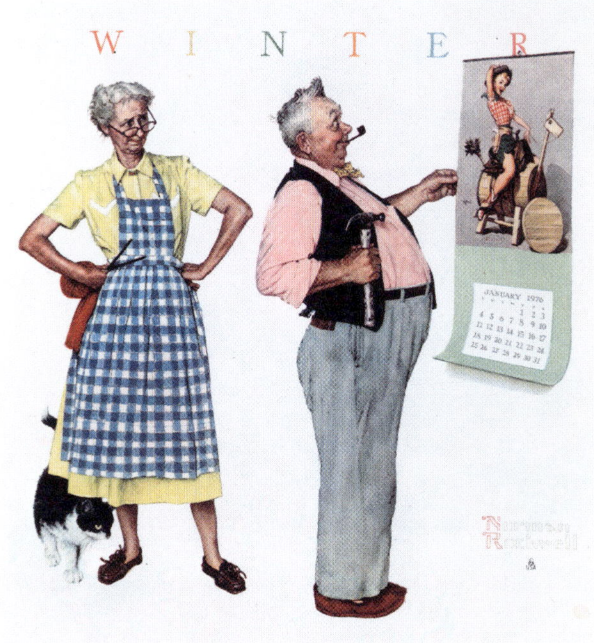


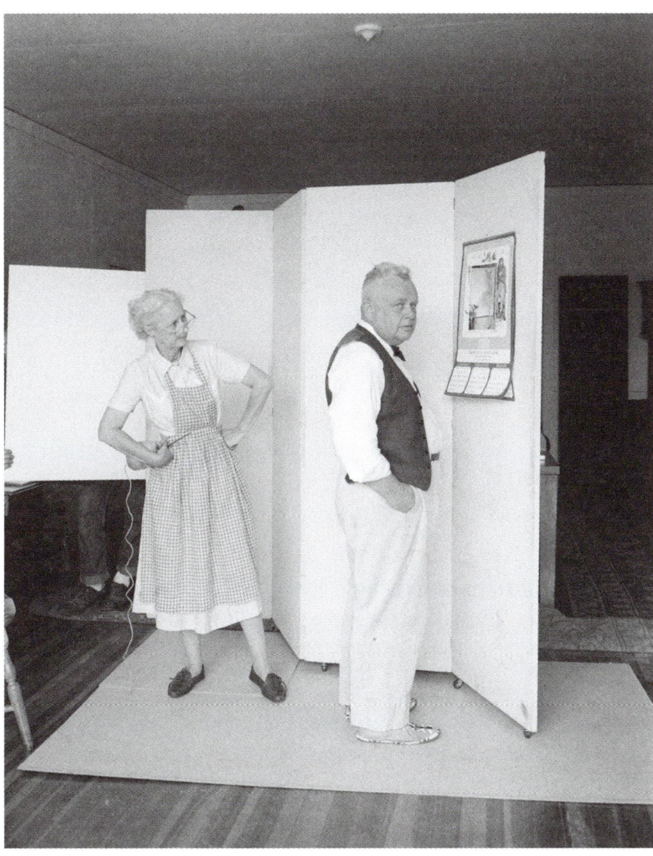

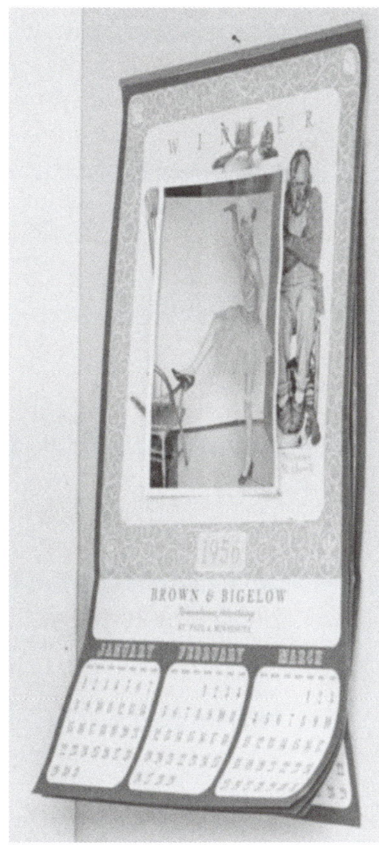


ABOVE LEFT
7.17. *Tender Years: New Calendar*, 1955
Pencil on paper, 14¾ × 14¾ in. (37.5 × 37.5 cm)
Study for Four Seasons calendar, winter 1957
Private collection

ABOVE RIGHT
7.18. *Tender Years: New Calendar*, 1955
Oil on canvas, 18 × 18 in. (45.7 × 45.7 cm)
Illustration for Four Seasons calendar, winter 1957
Private collection

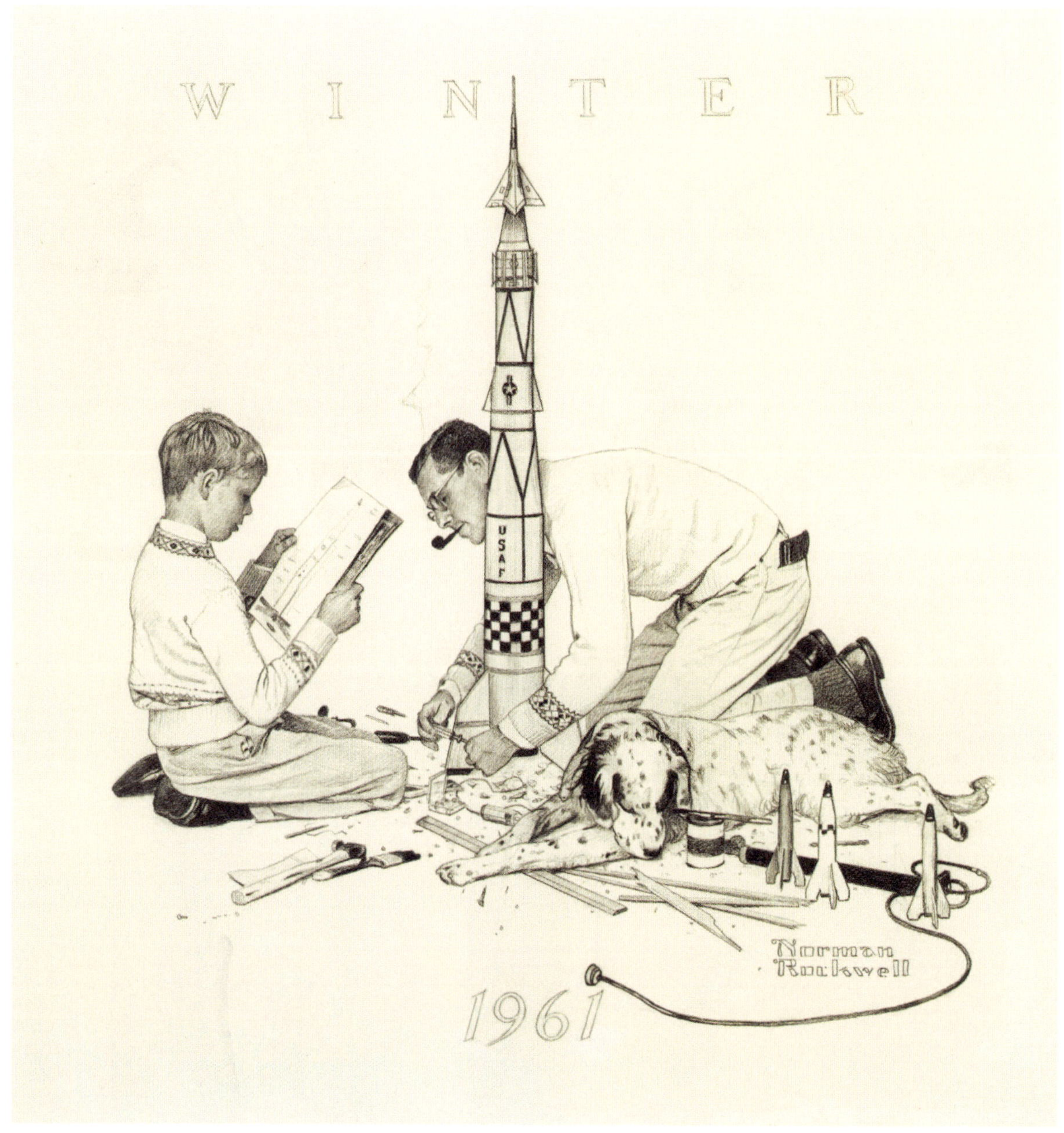


ABOVE
7.20. *Father and Boy: Rocket Ship*, 1961
Pencil on paper, 21½ × 20 in. (54.6 × 50.8 cm)
Unpublished study for Four Seasons calendar, winter 1961
Private collection

OPPOSITE
7.21. *Father and Boy: Church*, 1961
Pencil on paper, 21½ × 20 in. (54.6 × 50.8 cm)
Study for Four Seasons calendar, spring 1961
Private collection

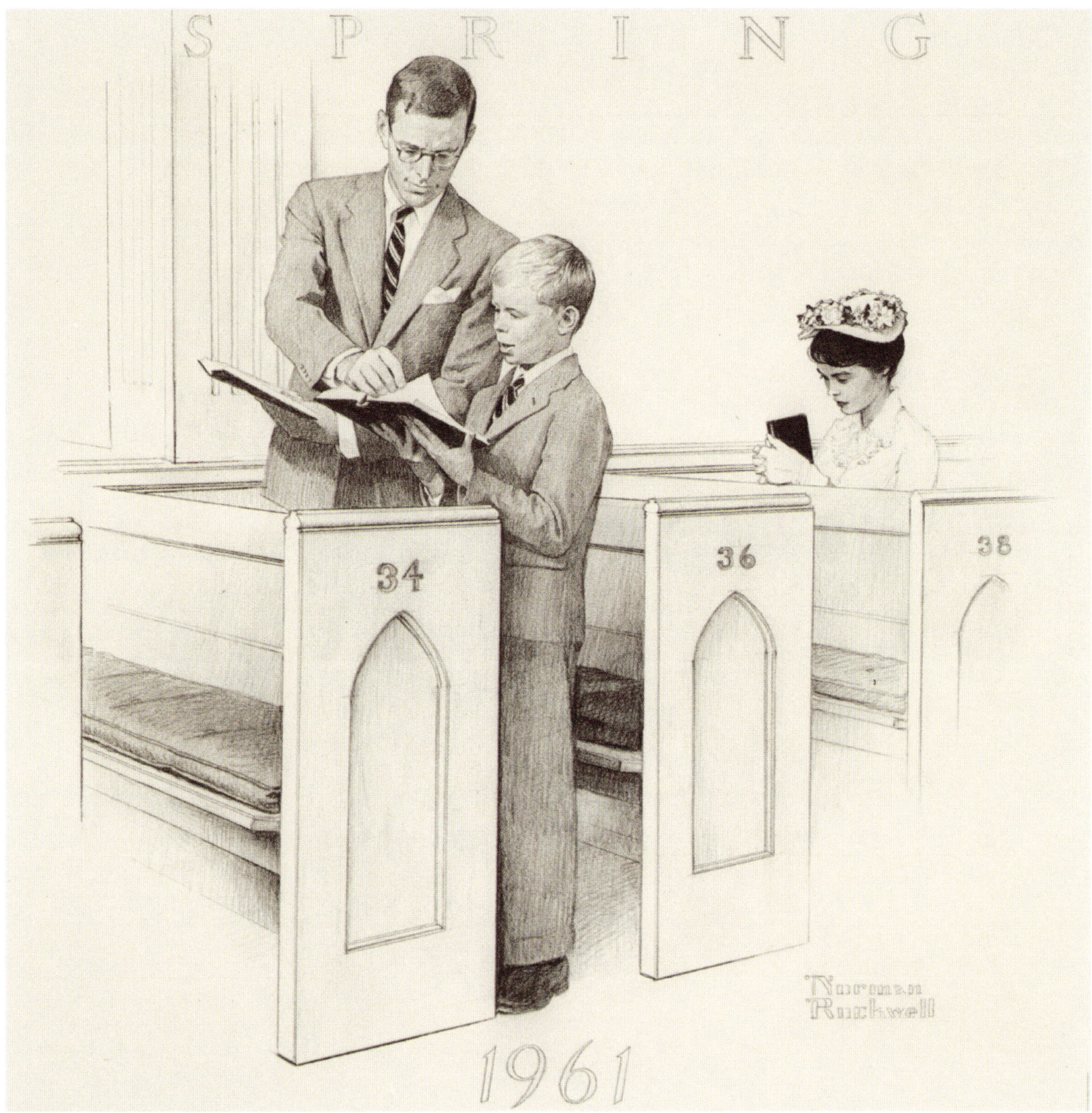


Of all the drawings Rockwell made for the Four Seasons calendars, perhaps none are as perfectly executed as those for the Father and Boy series of 1961. Rockwell may have felt nostalgic for his own childhood, or considered how his own children would soon be entering their thirties. The drawings are exquisite and poignant—arguably better than the final paintings. The following year, Rockwell's Four Seasons calendar paintings would follow a similar theme, titled Boy and Father.

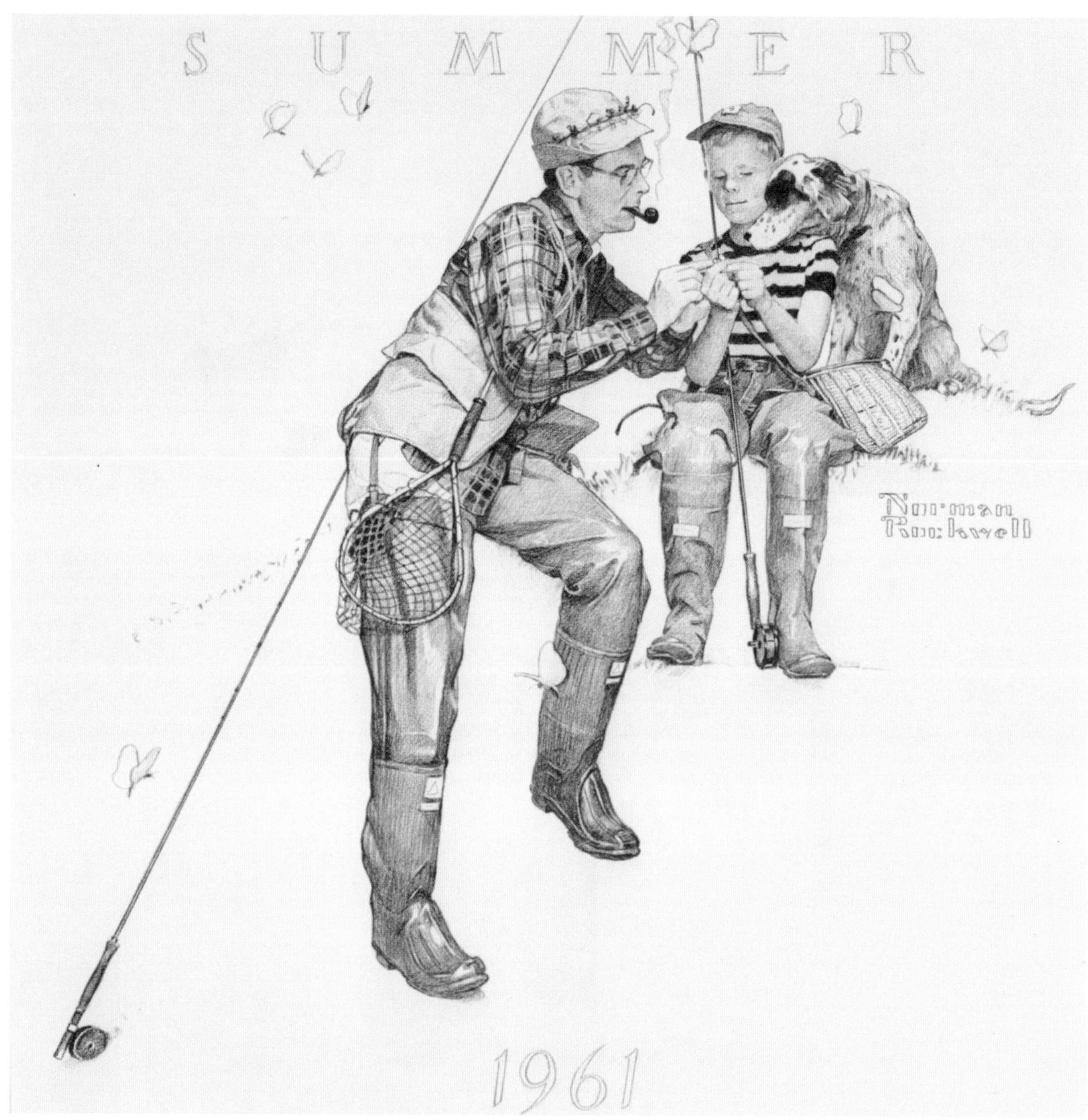


7.22. *Father and Boy: Fishing*, 1961
Pencil on paper, 21½ × 20 in. (54.6 × 50.8 cm)
Study for Four Seasons calendar, summer 1961
Private collection

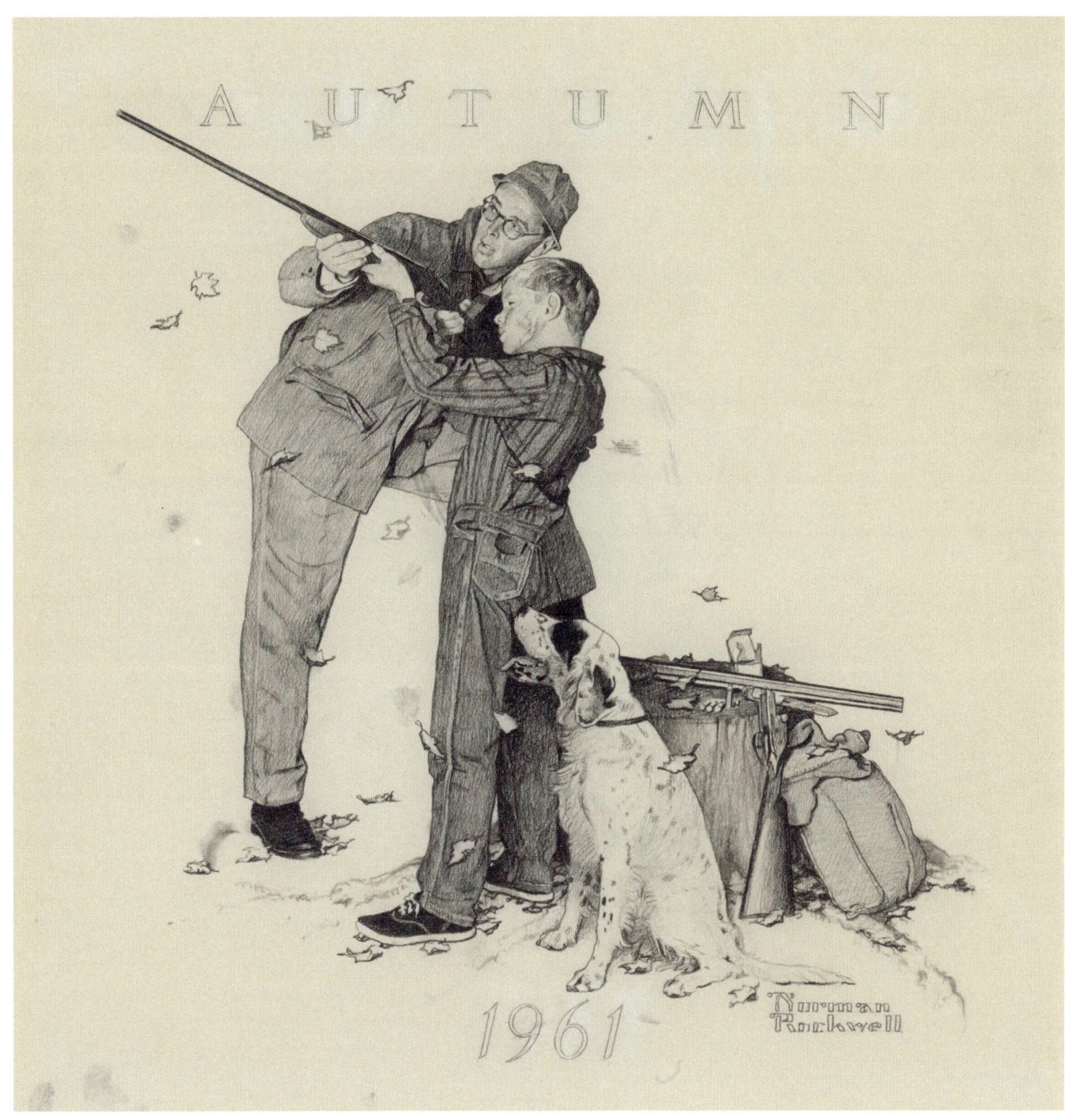


7.23. *Father and Boy: Hunting*, 1961
Pencil on paper, 21½ × 20 in. (54.6 × 50.8 cm)
Study for Four Seasons calendar, autumn 1961
Private collection

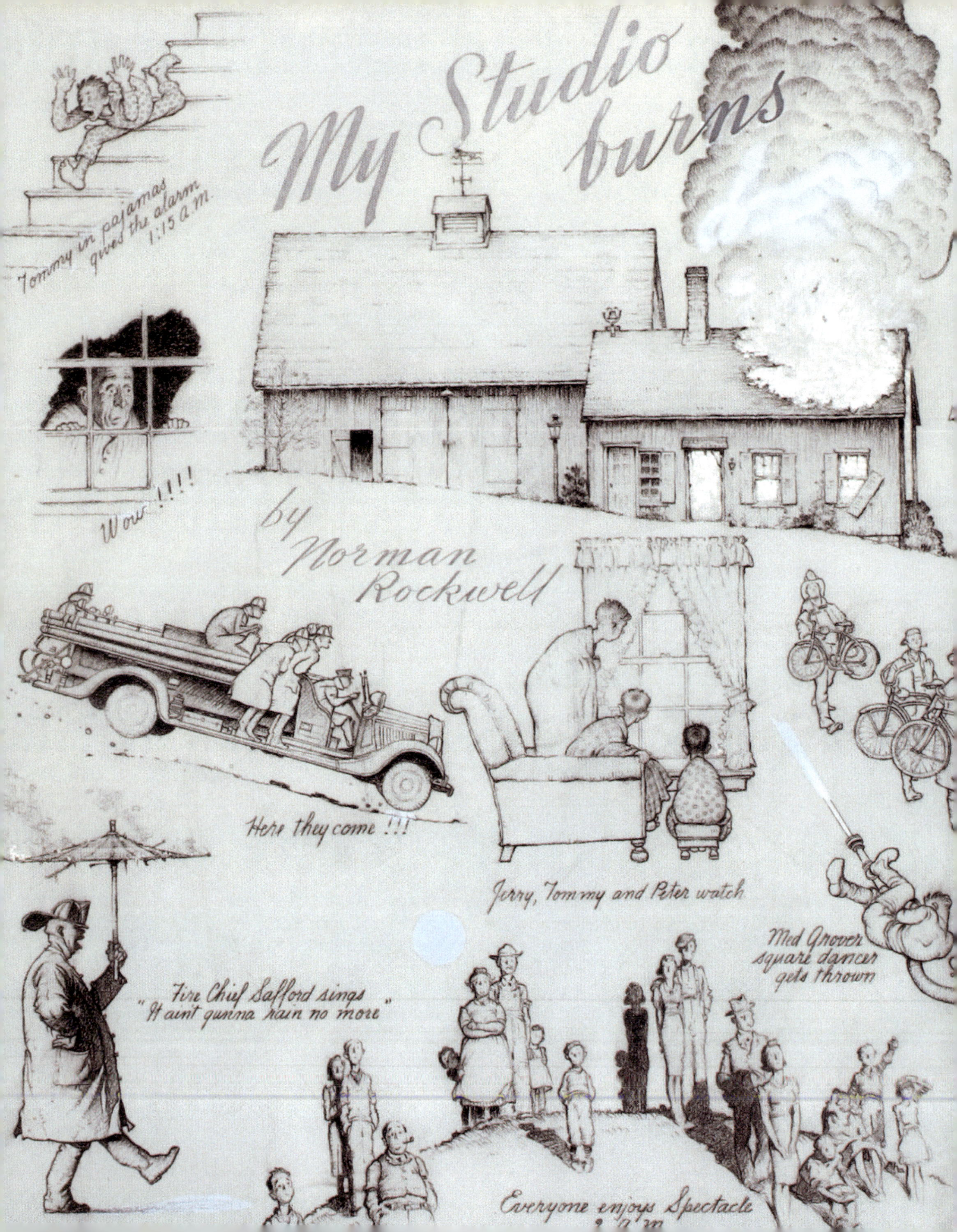
My Studio burns
Tommy in pajamas gives the alarm 1:15 A.M.
Wow!!!!
by Norman Rockwell
Here they come!!!
Jerry, Tommy and Peter watch
Med Grover square dancer gets thrown
Fire Chief Safford sings "It aint gunna rain no more"
Everyone enjoys Spectacle

# 8 Comics, Caricatures, and Illustrated Letters

JESSE KOWALSKI

Humor and wit were central aspects of Norman Rockwell's character. From his caricatures drawn for the navy during the closing months of World War I to his first *Saturday Evening Post* cover in 1916, and throughout the rest of his life, Rockwell filled a societal niche by providing levity during times of great strife.

Detail of *My Studio Burns*, 1943
See plate 8.7.

Humor, indeed, is a worthy goal of art. In the 1941 film *Sullivan's Travels*, a cornball film director seeks to make a "serious" film that portrays the sorrows of humanity. However, once he hits rock bottom and joins a room

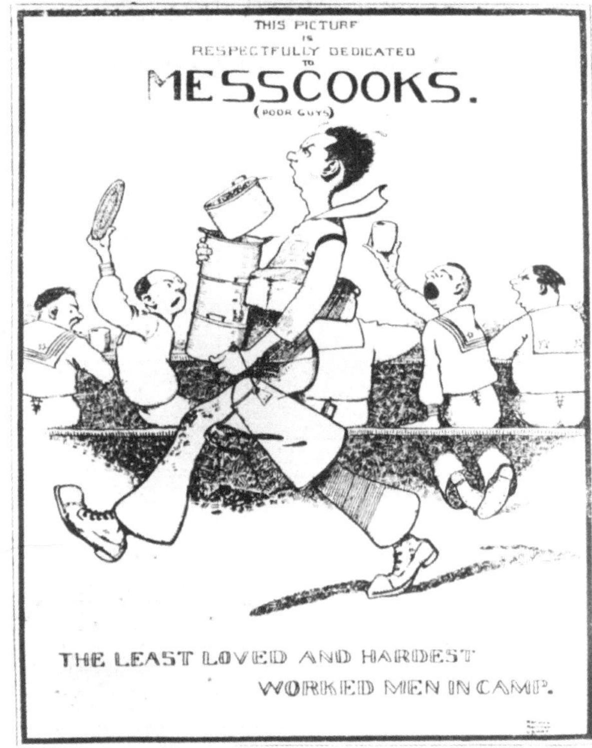


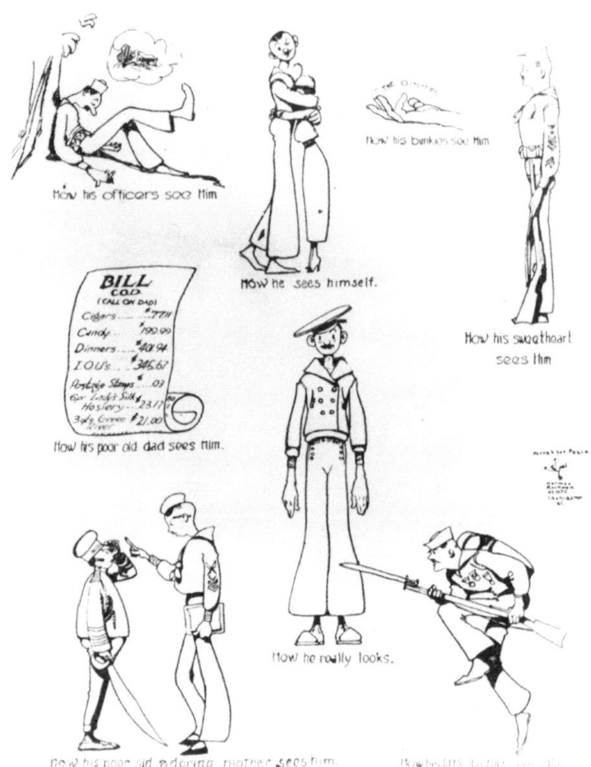


LEFT
8.1. *Mess Cooks*, 1918
Tear sheet
Illustration for *Afloat and Ashore*, November 13, 1918
Whereabouts unknown

RIGHT
8.2. *Navy Seaman*, 1918
Tear sheet
Illustration for *Afloat and Ashore*, November 20, 1918
Whereabouts unknown

full of convicts who are laughing at a Mickey Mouse short film, he realizes, "There's a lot to be said for making people laugh. Did you know that's all some people have? It isn't much, but it's better than nothing in this cock-eyed caravan."[1] The great Cubist painter Pablo Picasso declared, "The purpose of art is washing the dust of daily life off our souls."[2]

## Humor in Dark Times

Feeling a sense of duty to fight for his country during the first World War, Norman Rockwell planned to enlist in the navy. Though at twenty-three years of age he was older than many enlisting sailors, it was neither his age nor his lack of physical fitness that prevented him. He was underweight, but determined to find a way to pass the physical.

In his 1960 autobiography, Rockwell recalled:

> In June 1917 [when I tried to enlist in New Rochelle,] the doctors rejected me. I was seventeen pounds underweight for my height and age. I

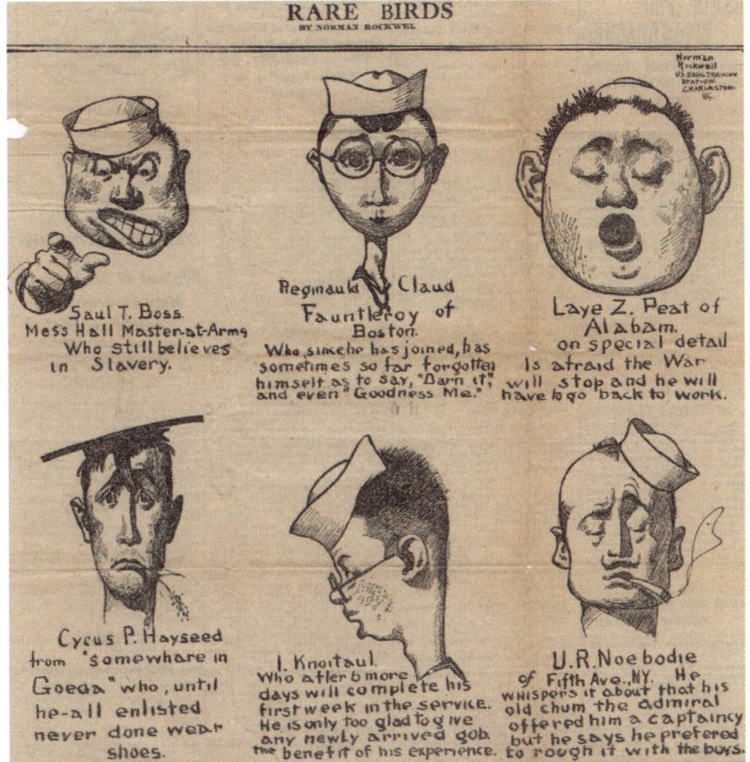


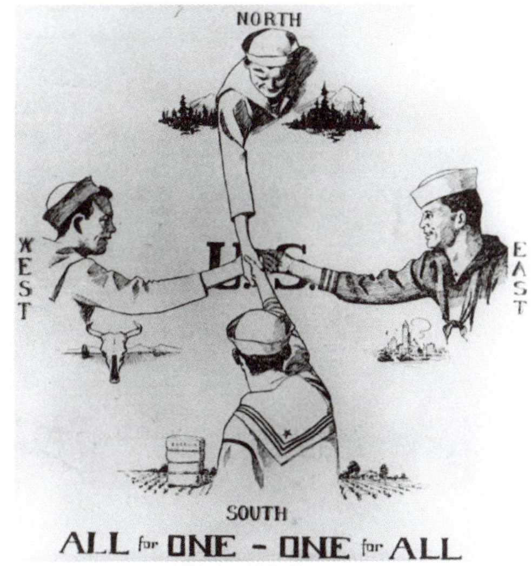


LEFT
8.3. *Rare Birds,* 1918
Tear sheet
Illustration for *Afloat and Ashore,* October 16, 1918
Whereabouts unknown

ABOVE
8.4 *All for One—One for All,* 1918
Tear sheet
Illustration for *Afloat and Ashore,* November 13, 1918
Whereabouts unknown

> caught a train back to New York. Maybe the doctors at the enlistment center at City Hall would accept me. . . . The yeoman who weighed me . . . [said], "You're underweight. . . . You really want to get in?" I told him I did. . . . He led me into a dark drafty little office and explained my problem to a doctor. . . . "Norm's an artist. . . . If we get him in they'll give him a special assignment, painting the insignia on airplane wings or something. It won't matter if he's underweight."[3]

The doctor agreed to waive ten pounds off the weight requirement if Rockwell accepted "the treatment," which consisted of eating seven pounds of bananas and doughnuts the doctor supplied to him. Quickly consuming pounds of food, Rockwell continued to miss the mark for the first few weigh-ins. Finally, Rockwell stood on the scale to find he weighed seven pounds heavier, and "the doctor and [the yeoman] congratulated each other."[4]

On August 23, 1918, Rockwell was stationed at the Charleston Naval Shipyard in South Carolina. His commanding officers made note of his lanky

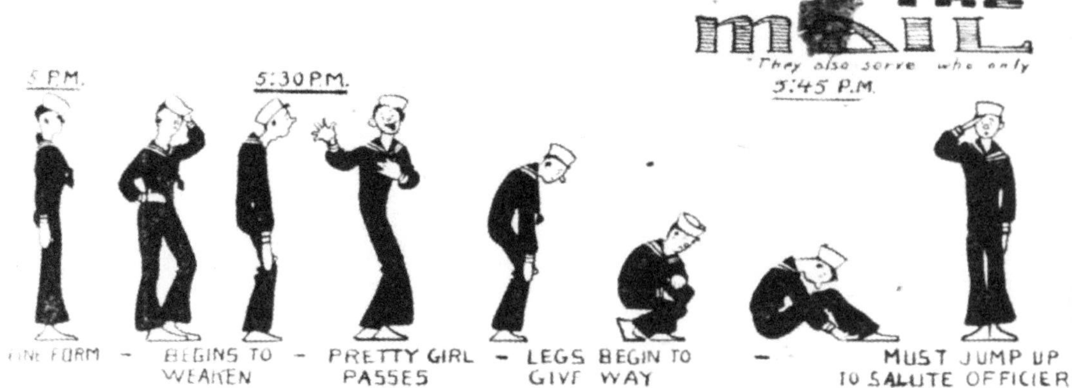


ABOVE
8.5. *Mail Line*, 1918
Tear sheet
Illustration for *Afloat and Ashore*, November 13, 1918
Whereabouts unknown

RIGHT
8.6. *Is This You?*, 1918
Tear sheet
Illustration for *Afloat and Ashore*, October 30, 1918
Whereabouts unknown

physique and were wise to assign him duties that showcased his artistic abilities. He was given the title of "Landsman Quartermaster Painter and Varnisher," which sounds more elevated than his actual assignment: drawing cartoons and caricatures for the shipyard's newspaper, *Afloat and Ashore* (plates 8.1–8.6).

Rockwell was required to spend just two days each week working on the newspaper, and the other days were his to freely draw, as long as the artwork was related to the navy. He spent this time creating magazine covers for publication and drawing portraits of sailors and officers, which he noted "made [his] life less complicated."[5] Prior to being discharged on November 12, 1918, Rockwell received a special request to paint portraits of the naval base's commander, Mark St. Clair Ellis, and his wife.

Not only was Rockwell able to provide humor to a world in turmoil, but he was also able to turn his personal troubles into moments of drollery. In the middle of the night on May 15, 1943, his son Tom awoke to see the artist's Arlington, Vermont, studio in flames. Tom banged on his father's bedroom door yelling, "Pop, the studio's on fire." Because the phone was wired through the studio, the line was already dead and Rockwell couldn't call for help.

Sending his hired man to the nearest neighbor to summon the fire department, Rockwell dashed to the studio to see what he could save. Suddenly, rifle cartridges and shotgun shells kept in a drawer in the studio started ex-

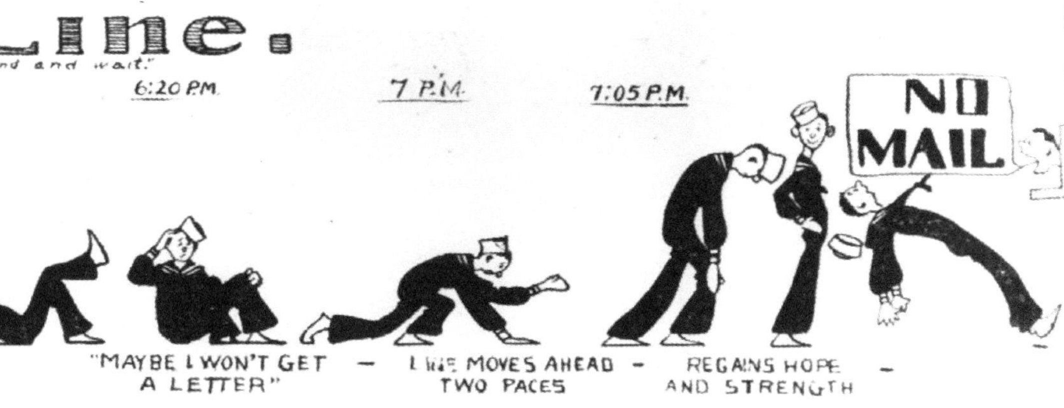


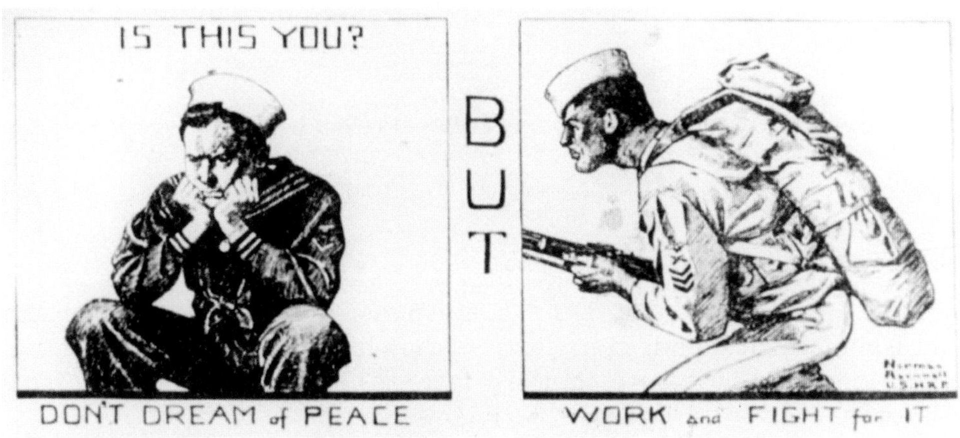


ploding. Rockwell and his family could only stand and watch while flames consumed the studio and most of the adjacent barn (plate 8.7).

Lost were a dozen of Rockwell's favorite paintings, numerous drawings and correspondence, a collection of costumes, props, artist materials, reference files, prints, books, antique guns, and the artist's favorite pipes. Rather than rebuild, Rockwell bought a house nearer to town and hired a carpenter to construct a new studio. That summer, while his new studio was built, Rockwell shared Mead Schaeffer's studio. Schaeffer, a good friend and fellow *Post* cover artist who lived nearby, joked that Rockwell was so convincing in his rationalization of how the setback had been beneficial by forcing him to reexamine his work that Schaeffer was nearly convinced to burn down his own studio.[6]

In the book *Norman Rockwell: Illustrator*, the author notes that the Society of Illustrators subsequently sent Rockwell a complete set of reproductions of his artwork.[7]

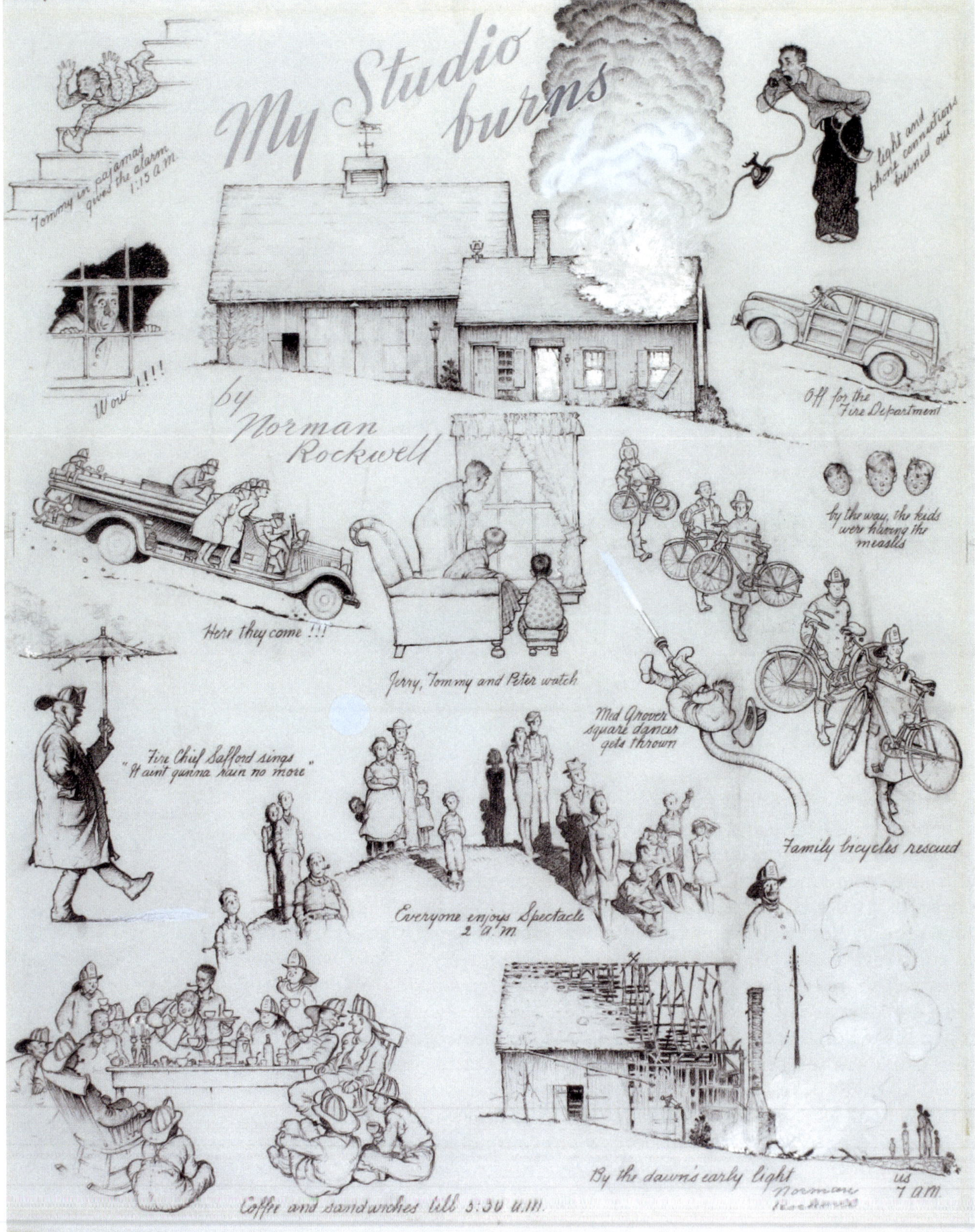
My Studio burns
by Norman Rockwell
Tommy in pajamas gives the alarm 1:15 a.m.
lights and phone connections burned out
Wow!!!!
Off for the Fire Department
Here they come!!!
Jerry, Tommy and Peter watch
by the way, the kids were having the measles
Fire Chief Safford sings "It aint gunna rain no more"
Mel Grover square dancer gets thrown
Family bicycles rescued
Everyone enjoys Spectacle 2 A.M.
By the dawn's early light
us 7 A.M.
Norman Rockwell
Coffee and sandwiches till 5:30 a.m.

## Insightful Caricatures

*Norman Rockwell: Illustrator* was the first major book detailing the life and work of the artist. It was a collaboration between publisher Arthur Guptill and Rockwell himself, with the artist contributing commentary and nearly one hundred caricatures, in which he humorously addressed subjects such as his daily life, insecurities, hectic work schedule, and difficulty in locating good models, in addition to a number of self-portraits (plates 8.8 and 8.9). The book, published by Watson-Guptill Publications, Inc., was released in 1946. Though some events may be exaggerated, it remains a valuable insight into the artist at his prime. The book's dust jacket declares, "This is a great book about a great illustrator—Norman Rockwell, painter to America's millions. . . . The author takes us on visits to the lovely Vermont home where we meet the artist, who, we are not surprised to discover, is the genial, philosophic human being his *Saturday Evening Post* covers have prepared us to expect."[8]

OPPOSITE
8.7. *My Studio Burns*, 1943
Pencil on illustration board, 21½ × 17 in. (54.6 × 43.2 cm)
Story illustration for the *Saturday Evening Post*, July 17, 1943
Private collection

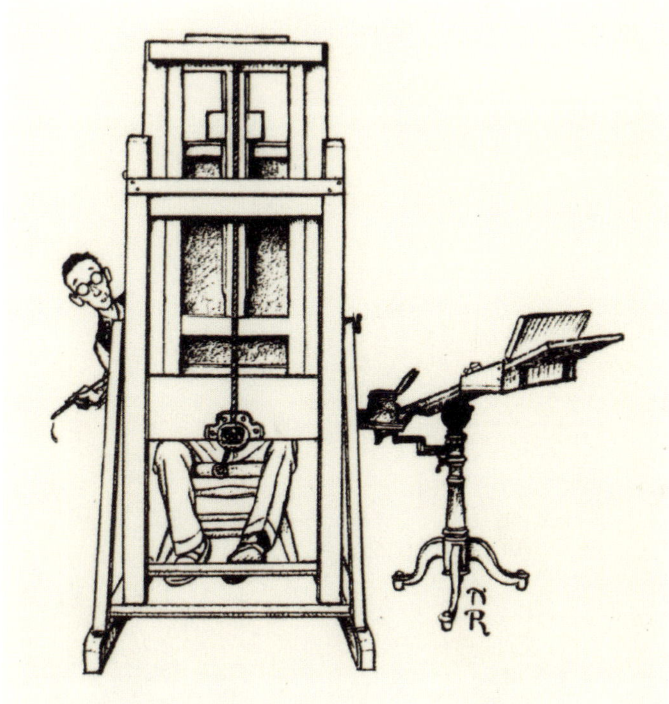

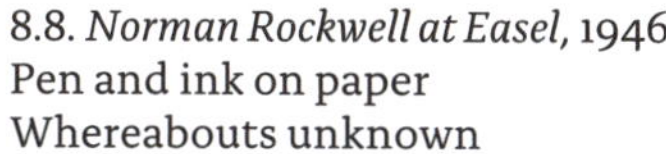

8.8. *Norman Rockwell at Easel*, 1946
Pen and ink on paper
Whereabouts unknown

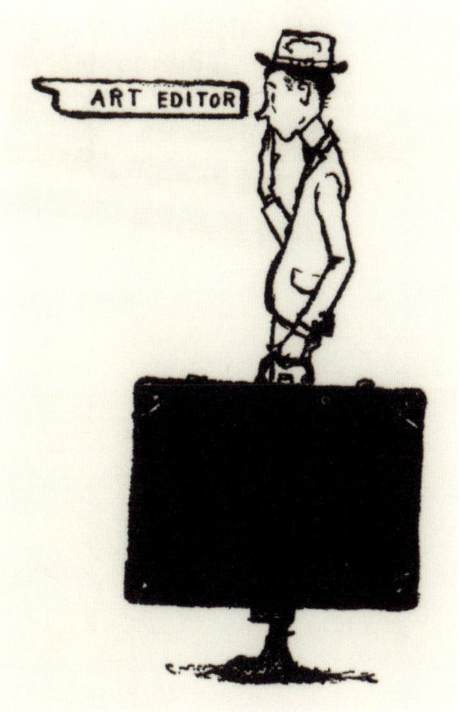


8.9. *The Art Editor's Office*, 1946
Pen and ink on paper
Whereabouts unknown

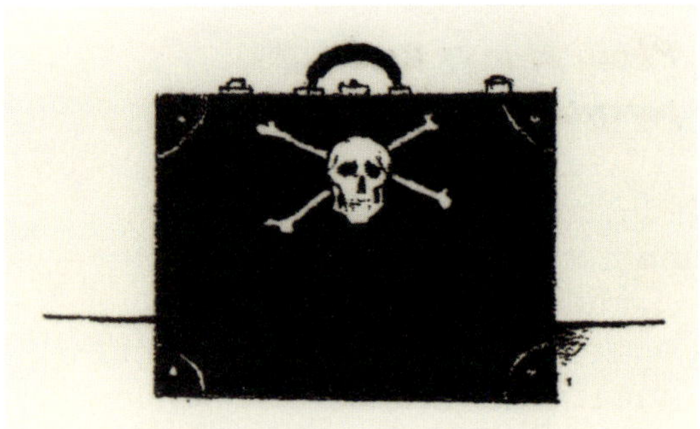

8.10. *Skull and Crossbones*, 1946
Pen and ink on paper
Whereabouts unknown

In *Skull and Crossbones*, Rockwell depicts the case he had custom built to carry his paintings for his unscheduled introduction to the *Saturday Evening Post*. In the *Post*'s waiting room, writer Irvin S. Cobb joked, "Young man . . . is that a coffin?" Rockwell assured him it was not. Cobb replied, "That's good. We were afraid you had a body in it."[9]

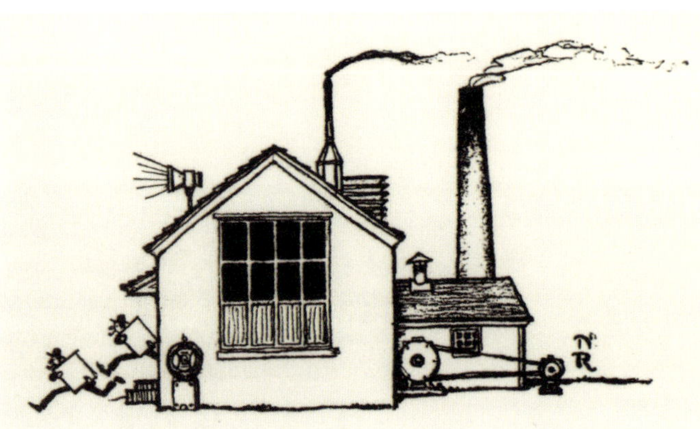

With smokestacks burning, engines running, horns blaring, and men running out with finished artwork, Rockwell represents his studio as an assembly line in *Norman Rockwell Studio*.

8.11. *Norman Rockwell Studio*, 1946
Pen and ink on paper
Whereabouts unknown

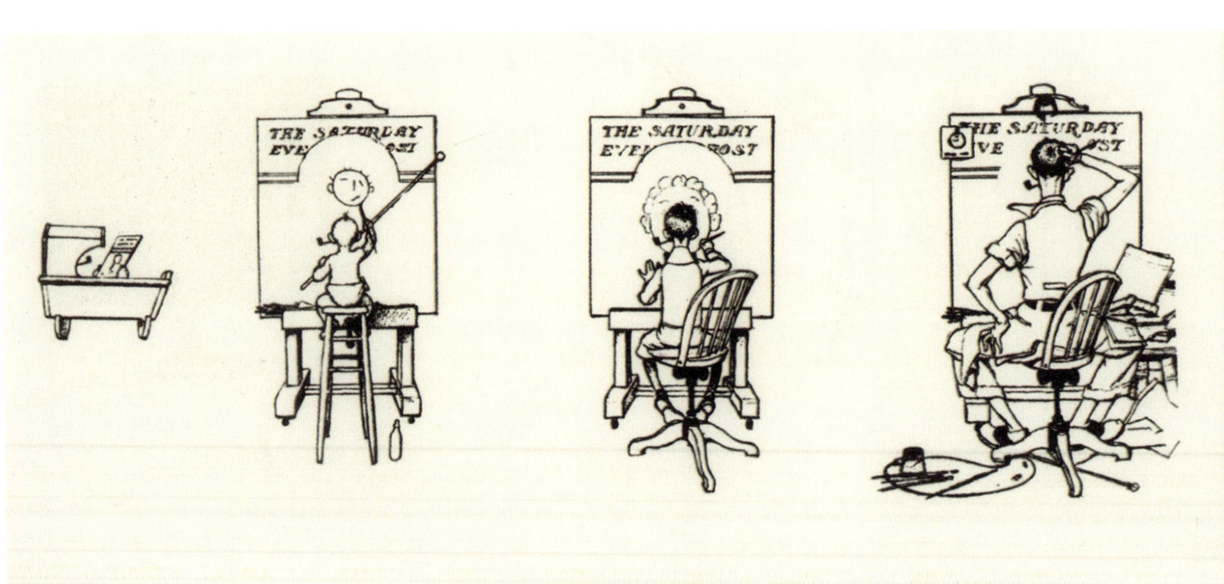

In the chapter "Thirty Years of Rockwell *Post* Covers," Rockwell comments on the *Artist Facing Blank Canvas (Deadline)* self-portrait (plate 8.12) that appeared on the cover of the October 8, 1938, issue of the *Post* and referenced in the 1946 drawing *Norman Rockwell from the Cradle to the Grave* (plate 8.13): "In agony of soul this cover was done, because the most terrible thing an illustrator has to face is a deadline. Often it is a case of either getting a picture in on time—not done as well as you like—or of doing it well and being too late to have it published. This portrait is reasonably accurate."[10]

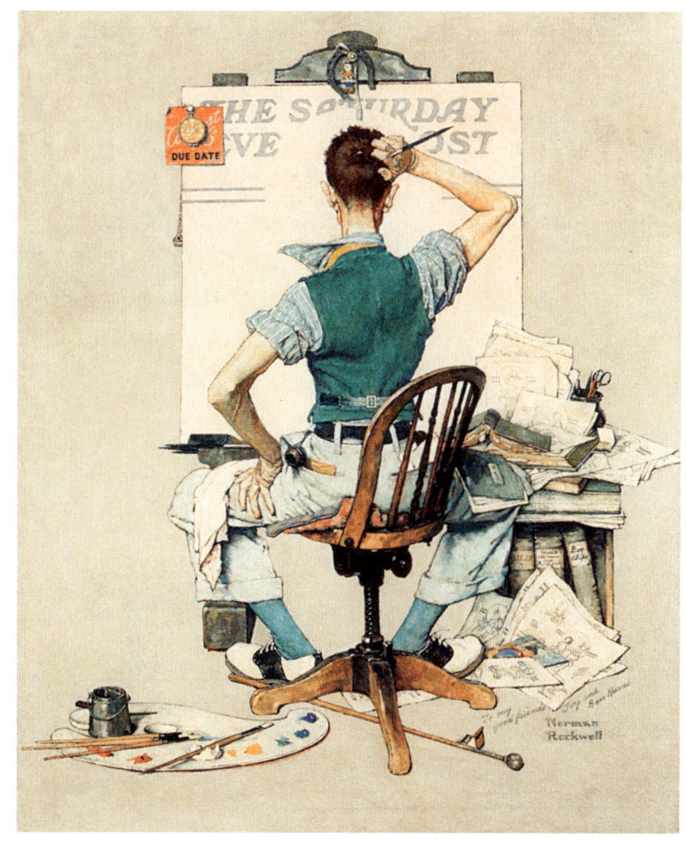


8.12. *Artist Facing Blank Canvas (Deadline)*, 1938
Oil on canvas, 38½ × 30½ in. (97.8 × 77.5 cm)
Illustration for the *Saturday Evening Post*, October 8, 1938
NRACT.1973.4

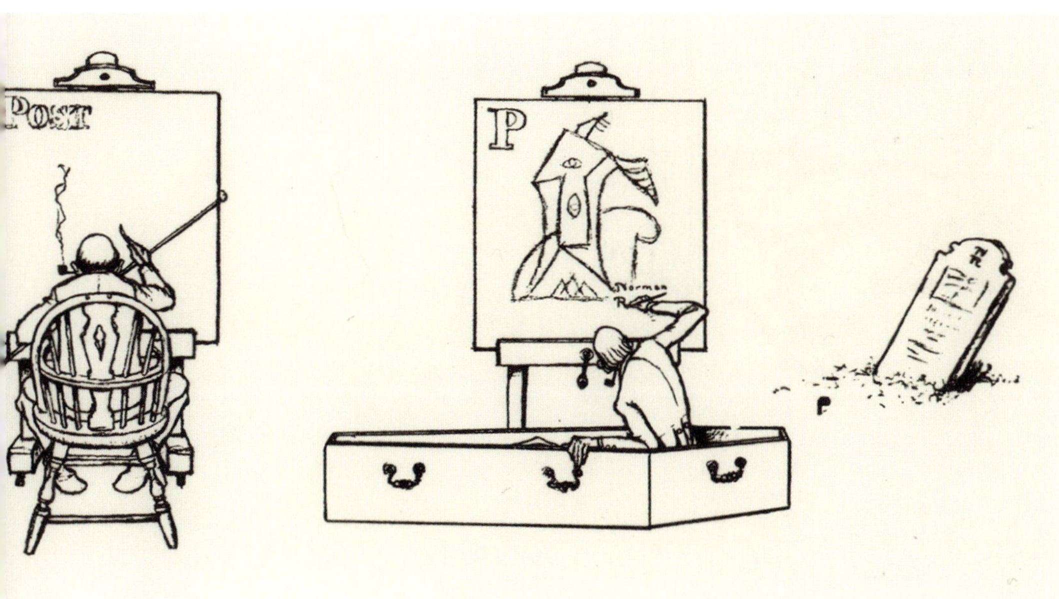


8.13. *Norman Rockwell from the Cradle to the Grave*, 1946
Wolff pencil on posterboard, 8 × 34 in. (20.3 × 86.4 cm)
Private collection

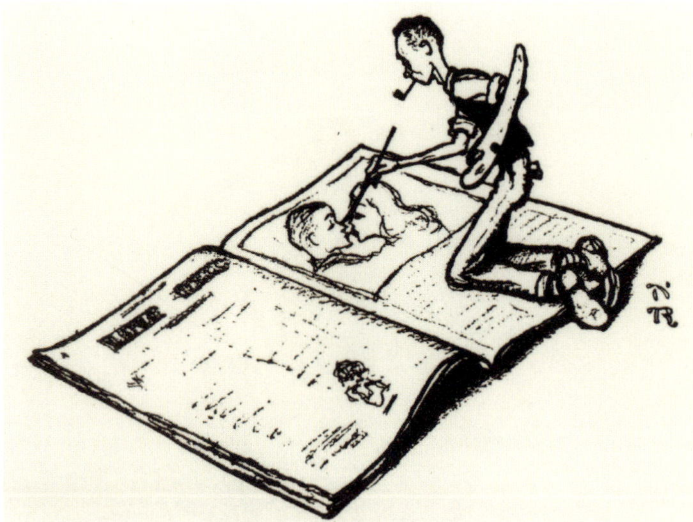

Regarding story illustration, Rockwell notes, "It is more difficult to make an illustration than to paint a cover, as you must customarily interpret the author's text."[11]

8.14. *Norman Rockwell: Magazine Illustrator*, 1946
Pen and ink on paper
Whereabouts unknown

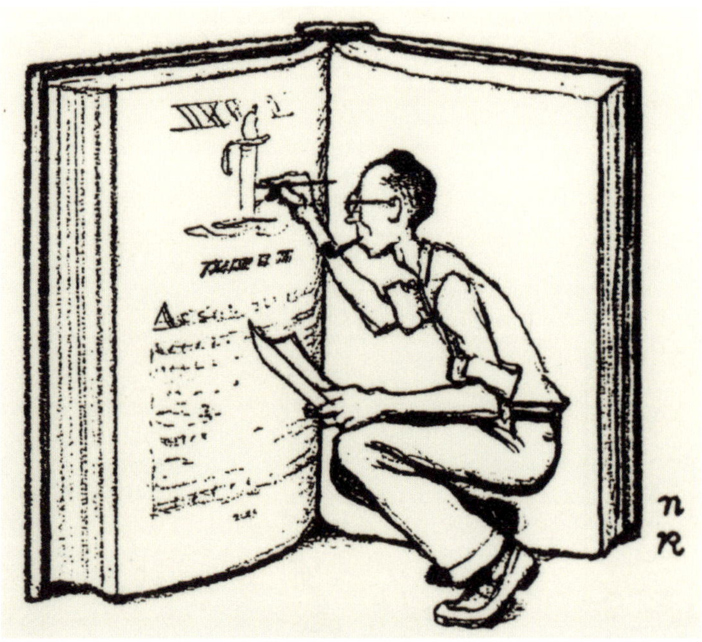

Rockwell says of his book illustrations: "It's fun to do a really good book, but only the best titles give me satisfaction. Mark Twain's *Tom Sawyer* and *Huckleberry Finn* are of the type I enjoy."[12]

8.15. *Norman Rockwell: Book Illustrator*, 1946
Pen and ink on paper
Whereabouts unknown

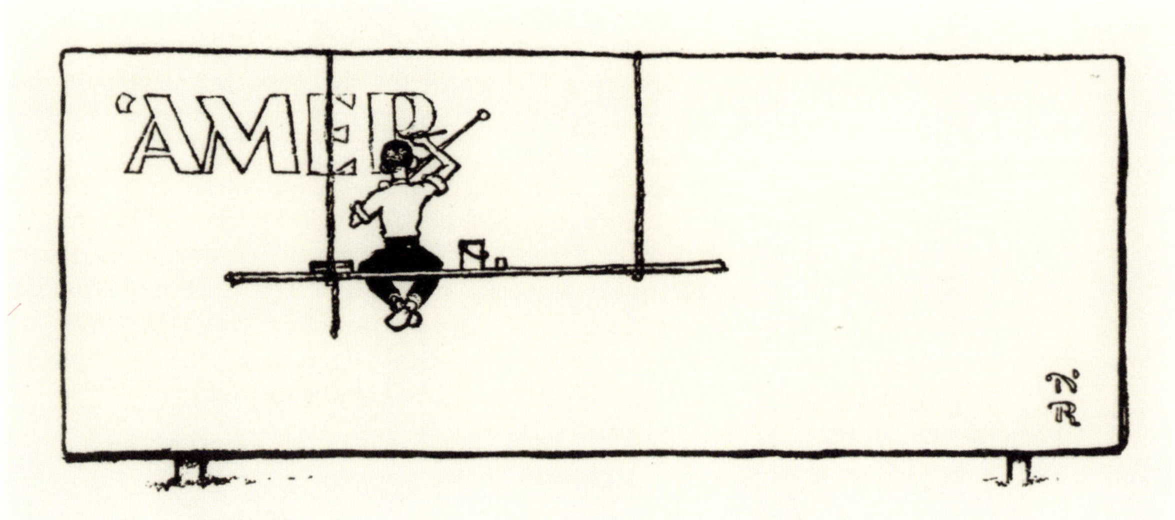


*Norman Rockwell Painting Billboard* marks the beginning of the chapter titled "Advertising Art." Rockwell remarks on the large fees he commands for advertising work, noting he charges double the amount for ads than for magazine covers since the corporations can afford the larger fees.[13]

ABOVE
8.16. *Norman Rockwell Painting Billboard*, 1946
Pen and ink on paper
Whereabouts unknown

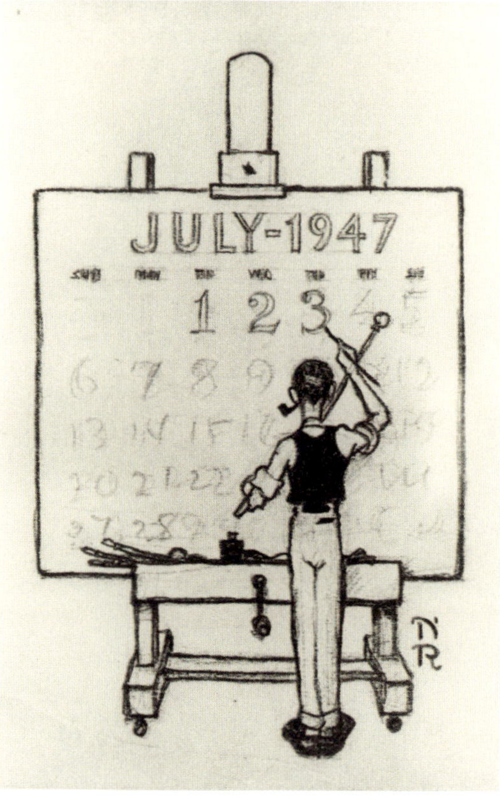


By the time he drew *Norman Rockwell Painting Calendar* in 1946, Rockwell had been illustrating calendars for the Boy Scouts for more than twenty years, and would continue to do so for thirty more.

8.17. *Norman Rockwell Painting Calendar*, 1946
Charcoal on paper, 5 × 4 in. (12.7 × 10.2 cm)
Private collection

Norman Rockwell's 1960 autobiography, *My Adventures as an Illustrator*, was an ideal follow-up to *Norman Rockwell: Illustrator*. Typically reserved, Rockwell would open himself up to the world for the first time in this book. In May 1957, he was approached by an editor from the publisher Doubleday about Rockwell creating an autobiography. The editor in chief, Ken McCormick, sent a Dictaphone machine to Rockwell in the hope that he would start to record his thoughts in short order, and planned for a ghostwriter to sort out the details. After several months with no progress, Rockwell's son Tom stepped in as a coauthor of sorts. They decided Norman would record his memories on the Dictaphone and Tom would organize the thoughts into a cohesive narrative. Rockwell began using the Dictaphone in April 1959 and used it regularly throughout that summer.[14]

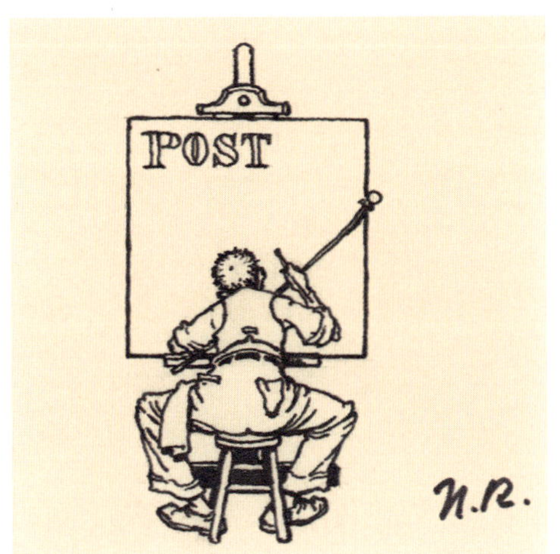


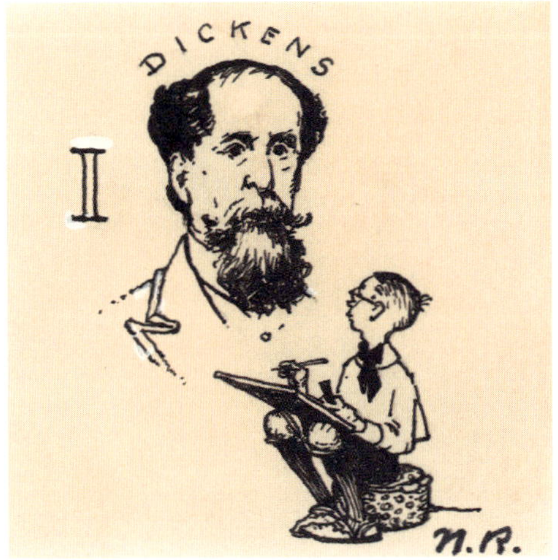


LEFT
8.18. *"Still Going Strong,"* 1960
Ink on paper, 5½ × 5 in. (14 × 12.7 cm)
Private collection

RIGHT
8.19. *"Scairt as a Rabbit, Bold as a Bear,"* 1960
Ink on paper, 5½ × 5 in. (14 × 12.7 cm)
Private collection

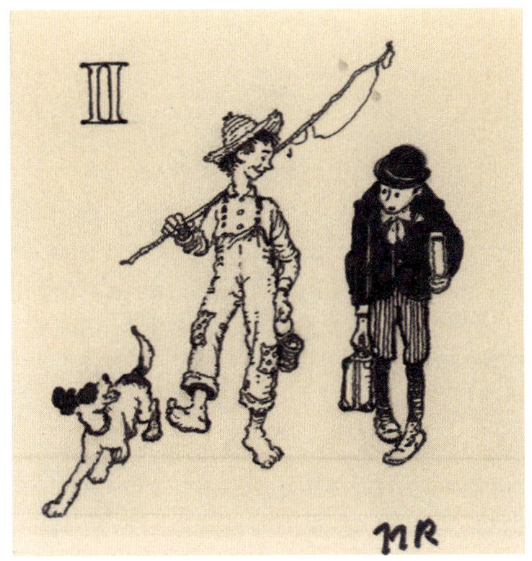


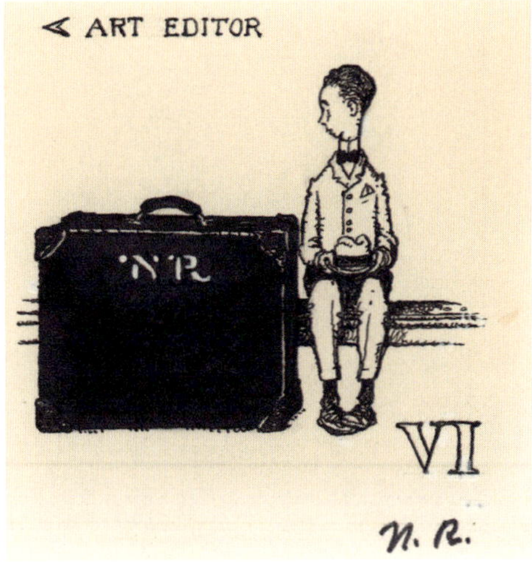


LEFT
8.20. *"I Sign My Name in Blood,"* 1960
Ink on paper, 5½ × 5 in. (14 × 12.7 cm)
Private collection

RIGHT
8.21. *"Great Expectations,"* 1960
Ink on paper, 5½ × 5 in. (14 × 12.7 cm)
Private collection

As with *Norman Rockwell: Illustrator* fourteen years prior, Rockwell included caricatures in his autobiography, though these sketches tended to be less lighthearted and more focused on specific events, reflecting their purpose as chapter headings (plates 8.18–8.23). After all, while he was recalling the highlights of his life, Rockwell was now sixty-five years old, working in a field that had substantially changed since he began at the *Post* more than forty years before. Norman Rockwell completed his recording on August 19, 1959, leaving Tom to finish writing the book. Sadly, six days later, his wife of twenty-eight years, Mary Rockwell, passed away. Rockwell dedicated the book, "To Mary, whose loving help has meant so much to me." The *Post* began printing excerpts from the completed book in its February 13, 1960, issue, and Norman Rockwell's life would soon enter a new phase.

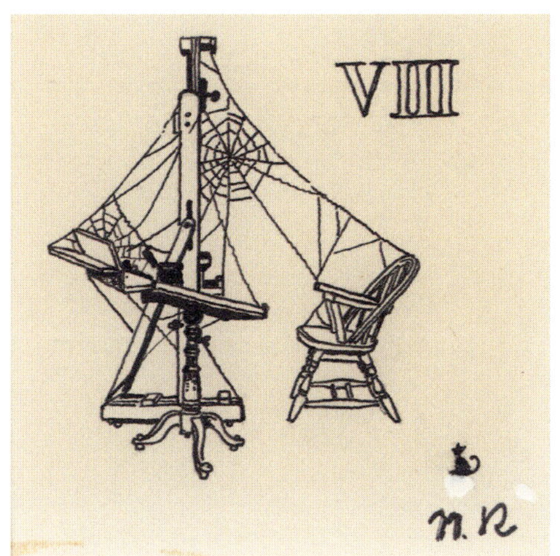


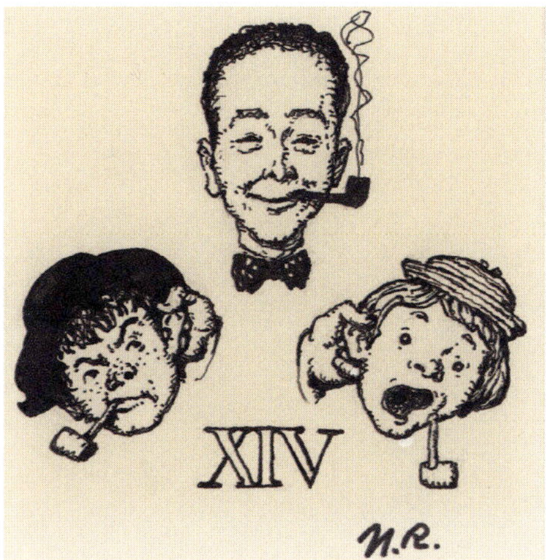


LEFT
8.22. *"Lost—$10,000,"* 1960
Ink on paper, 5½ × 5 in.
(14 × 12.7 cm)
Private collection

RIGHT
8.23. *"Trials, Tribulations, and Twain,"* 1960
Ink on paper, 5½ × 5 in.
(14 × 12.7 cm)
Private collection

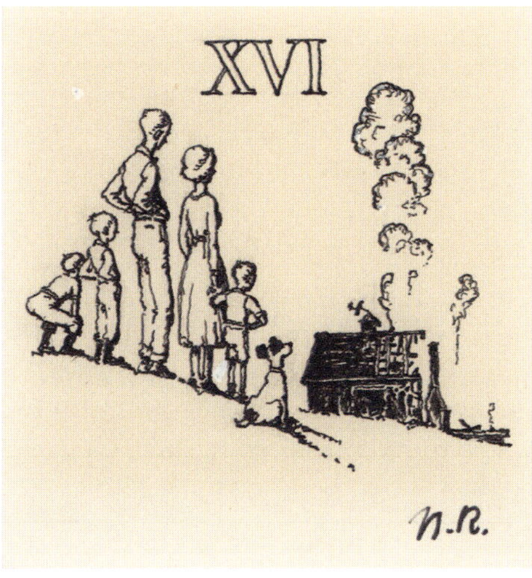


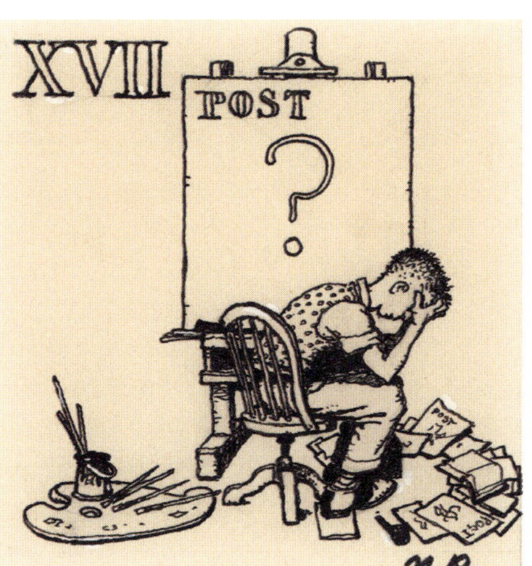


LEFT
8.24. *"I Rise from the Ashes,"* 1960
Ink on paper, 5½ × 5 in.
(14 × 12.7 cm)
Private collection

RIGHT
8.25. *"Flops!,"* 1960
Ink on paper, 5½ × 5 in.
(14 × 12.7 cm)
Private collection

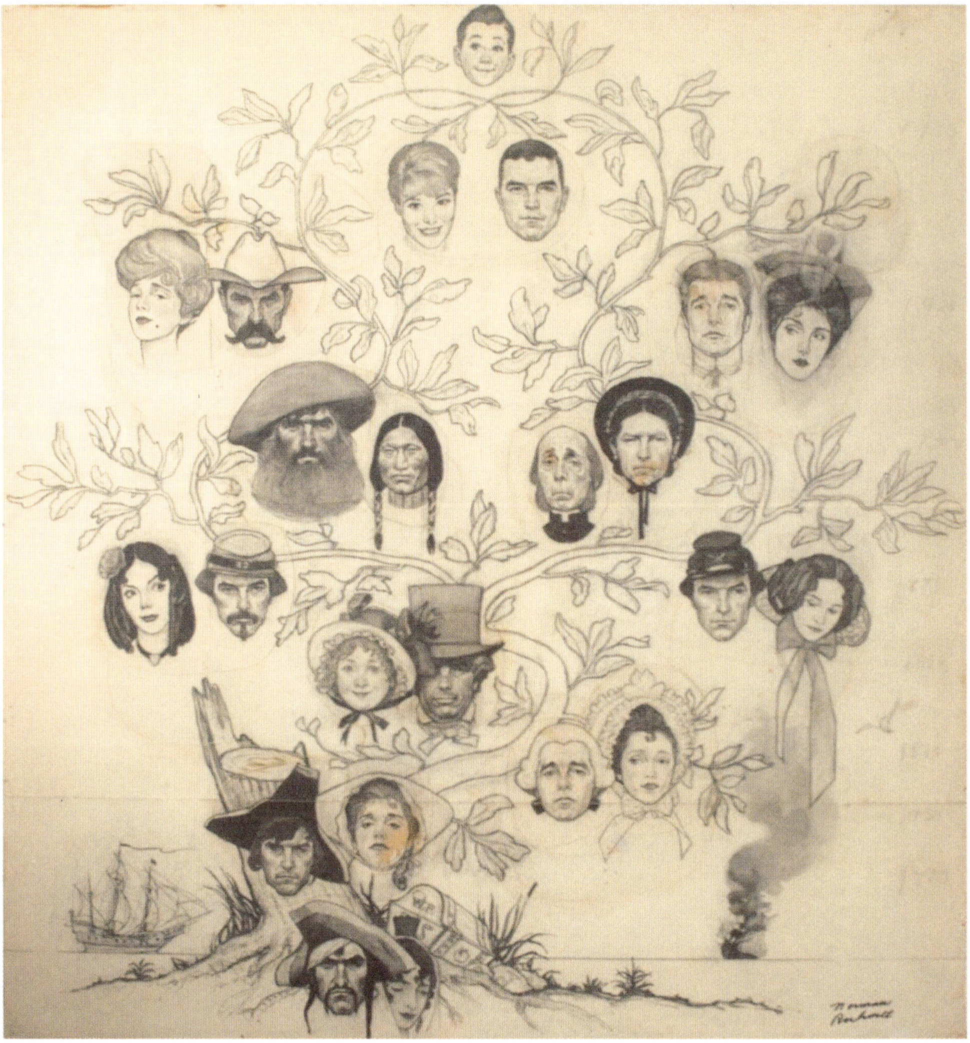

8.26. *Family Tree*, 1959
Charcoal on paper, 45½ × 42 in. (115.6 × 106.7 cm)
Cover study for the *Saturday Evening Post*, October 24, 1959
NRACT.1973.007a

BELOW
8.27. *"I Paint Another* Post *Cover,"* 1960
Ink on paper, 5½ × 5 in. (14 × 12.7 cm)
Chapter heading illustration for *My Adventures as an Illustrator* (Garden City, NY: Doubleday, 1960)
Private collection

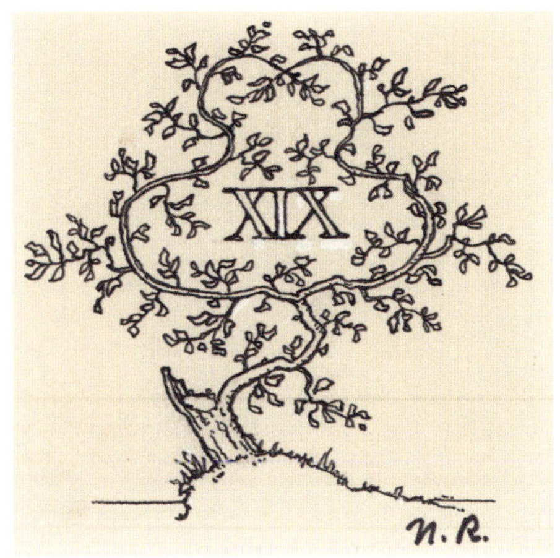


For a book about his life, a painting of a family tree seemed apt for the final chapter of Rockwell's autobiography. The chapter's title was "I Paint Another *Post* Cover" (plate 8.27), and indeed Rockwell did paint a family tree, but perhaps the pressure of documenting such an event caused Rockwell to be dissatisfied with its progress. He spent the summer of 1959 trying to perfect the work (plate 8.26), but had not finished the piece when he stopped recording his autobiography. Rockwell completed the work shortly after and *Family Tree* appeared on the cover of the *Post* on October 24, 1959.

## Rockwell Tackles Franklin's Wit

Shortly after Rockwell ended his association with the *Saturday Evening Post* in 1963, Heritage Press commissioned him to illustrate a special edition of Benjamin Franklin's *Poor Richard's Almanack*, originally published by Franklin on December 19, 1732, under the pseudonym Richard Saunders. Heritage Press had previously worked with Rockwell, who illustrated their publications of *The Adventures of Tom Sawyer* (1936) and *The Adventures of Huckleberry Finn* (1940). The 1964 release of Franklin's book included six color plates by Rockwell, in addition to thirty-eight small pen-and-ink drawings he created (plates 8.28–8.36), each tied to a related witticism attributed to Benjamin Franklin.[15] Incidentally, Franklin published the book in the same building where he published his magazine, the *Pennsylvania Gazette*. The magazine ceased publication in 1800, but in 1821 the building reopened as the printing press for a new periodical, the *Saturday Evening Post*.

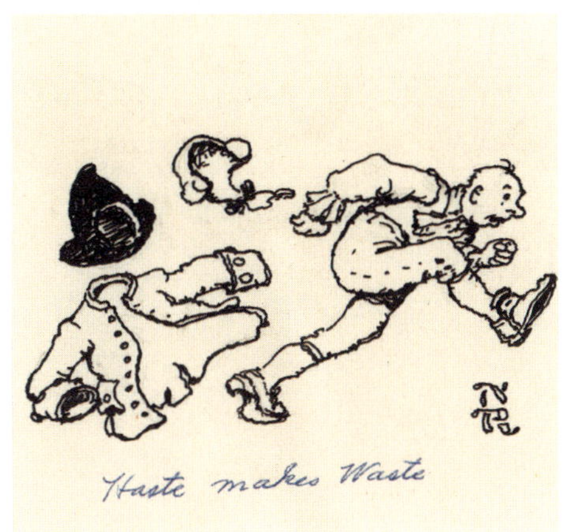


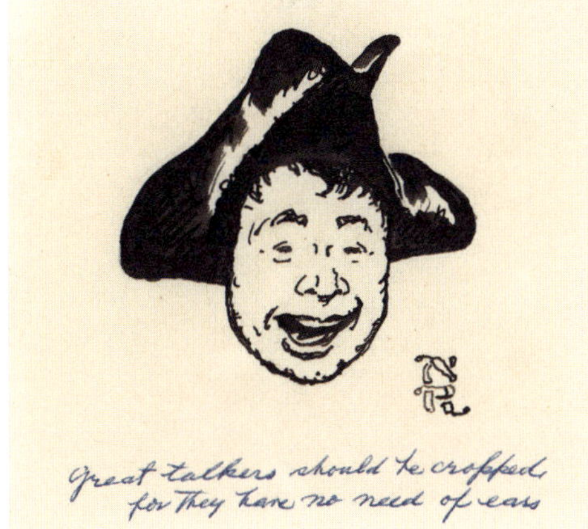


LEFT
8.28. *"Haste Makes Waste,"* 1963
Pen and ink on paper, 4 × 4 in. (10.2 × 10.2 cm)
NRACT.1973.086.03

RIGHT
8.29. *"Great Talkers Should Be Cropp'd, for They Have No Need of Ears,"* 1963
Pen and ink on paper, 4 × 4 in. (10.2 × 10.2 cm)
NRACT.1973.086.15

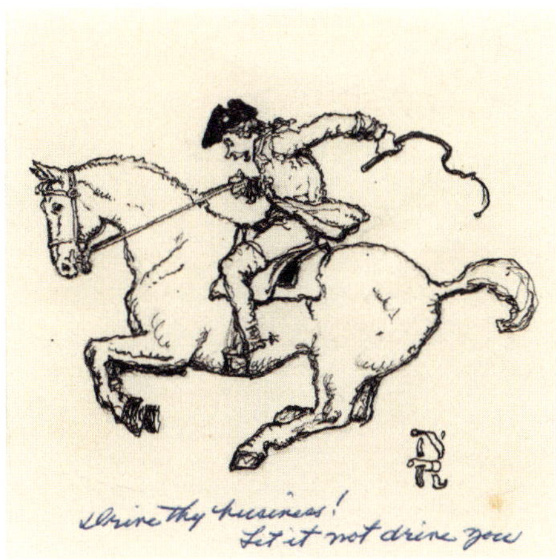


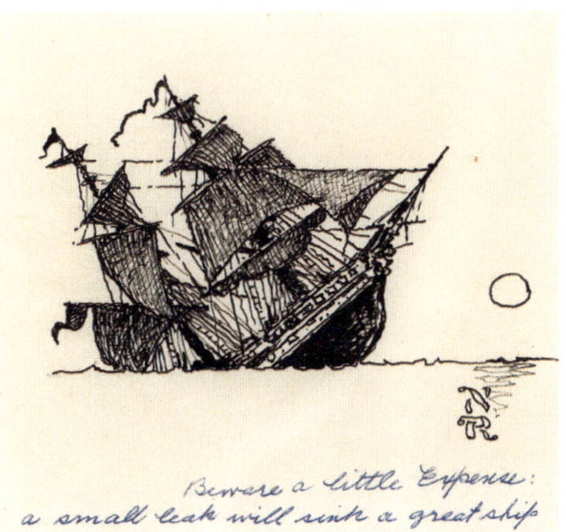


LEFT
8.30. *"Drive Thy Business! Let It Not Drive You,"* 1963
Pen and ink on paper, 4 × 4 in. (10.2 × 10.2 cm)
NRACT.1973.086.01

RIGHT
8.31. *"Beware a Little Expense: A Small Leak Will Sink a Great Ship,"* 1963
Pen and ink on paper, 4 × 4 in. (10.2 × 10.2 cm)
NRACT.1973.086.36

LEFT
8.32. *"A True Friend Is the Best Possession,"* 1963
Pen and ink on paper, 4 × 4 in. (10.2 × 10.2 cm)
NRACT.1973.086.38

RIGHT
8.33. *"A Good Wife and Health Is a Man's Best Wealth,"* 1963
Pen and ink on paper, 4 × 4 in. (10.2 × 10.2 cm)
NRACT.1973.086.17

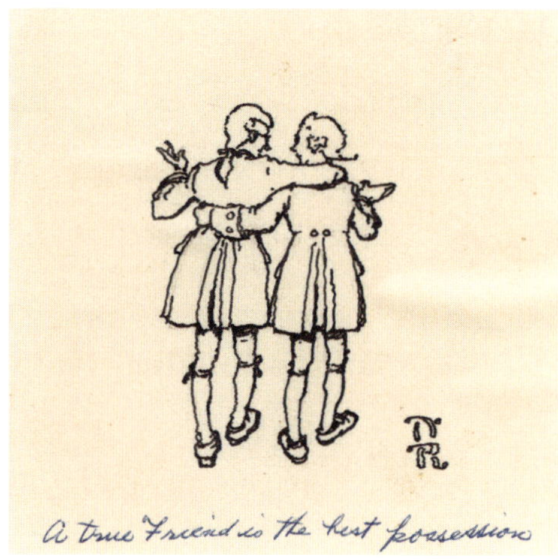


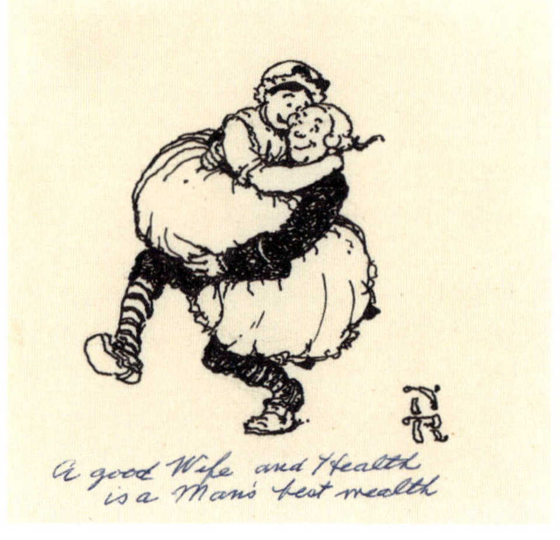


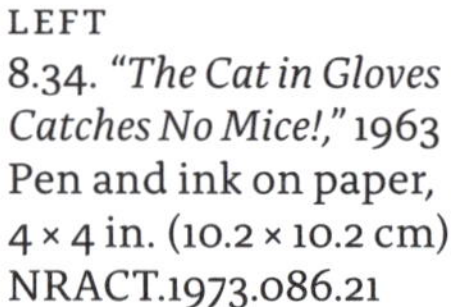

LEFT
8.34. *"The Cat in Gloves Catches No Mice!,"* 1963
Pen and ink on paper, 4 × 4 in. (10.2 × 10.2 cm)
NRACT.1973.086.21

RIGHT
8.35. *"Great Talkers, Little Doers,"* 1963
Pen and ink on paper, 4 × 4 in. (10.2 × 10.2 cm)
NRACT.1973.086.26

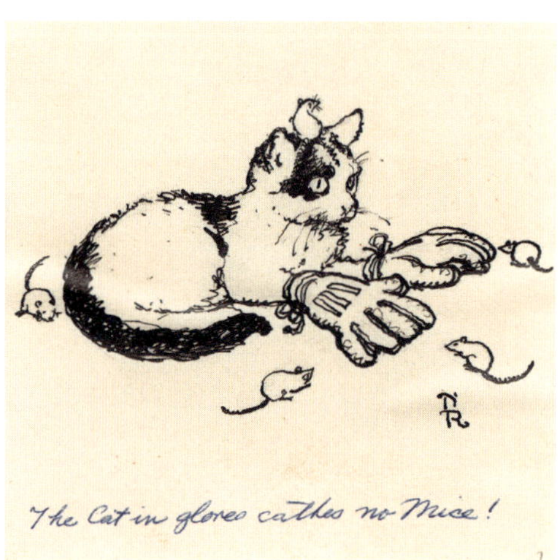


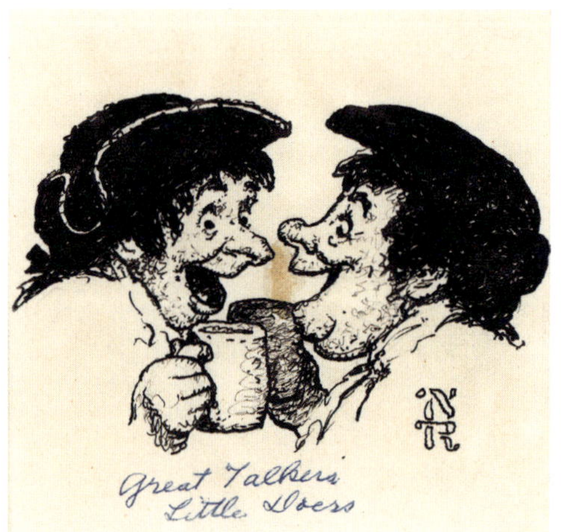


8.36. *"Lost Time Is Never Seen Again,"* 1963
Pen and ink on paper, 4 × 4 in. (10.2 × 10.2 cm)
NRACT.1973.086.37

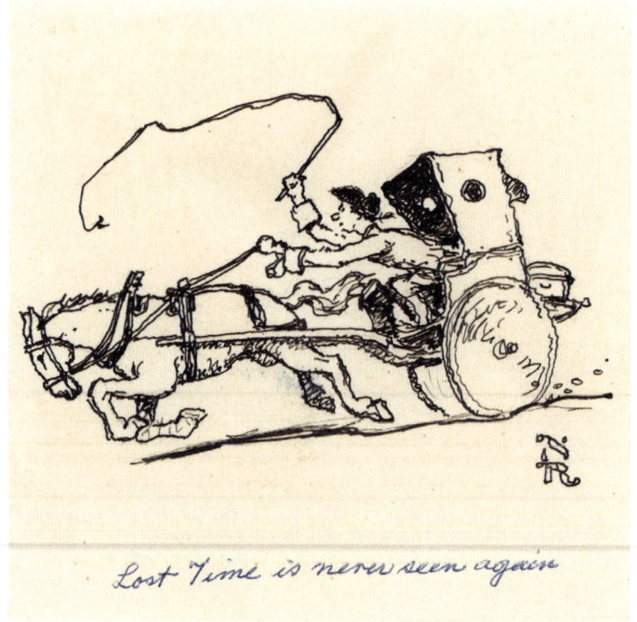

## Letters from Rockwell

Rockwell's personal correspondence often contained lighthearted notes, and would also include a doodle of a dog or a caricature of someone close to him. As seen here, even the permission slips he wrote to excuse his son's absences from school contained comical images.

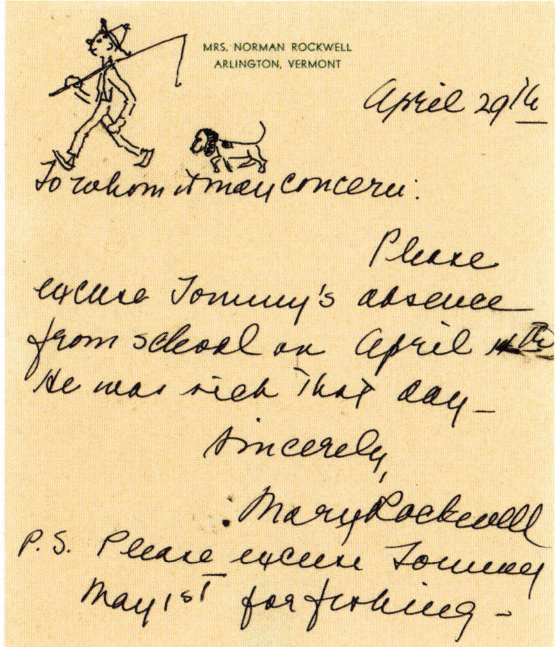

MRS. NORMAN ROCKWELL
ARLINGTON, VERMONT

April 29th

To whom it may concern:

Please excuse Tommy's absence from school on April [illegible]
He was sick that day -

Sincerely,
Mary Rockwell

P.S. Please excuse Tommy May 1st for fishing -

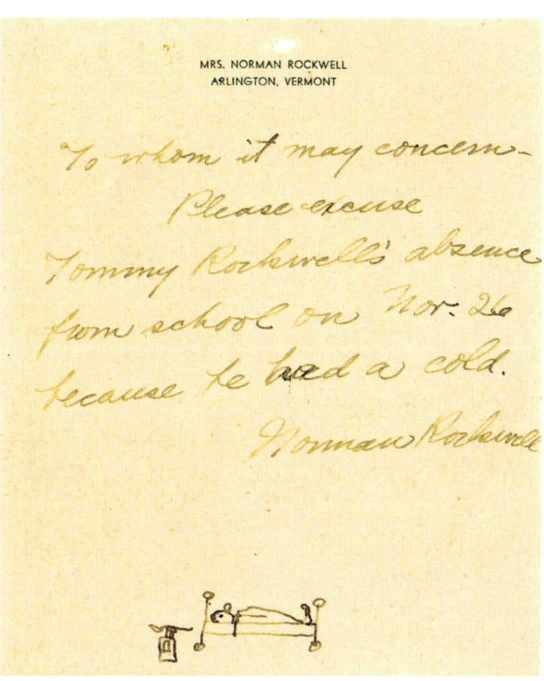

MRS. NORMAN ROCKWELL
ARLINGTON, VERMONT

To whom it may concern -
Please excuse
Tommy Rockwell's absence
from school on Nov. 26
because he had a cold.

Norman Rockwell

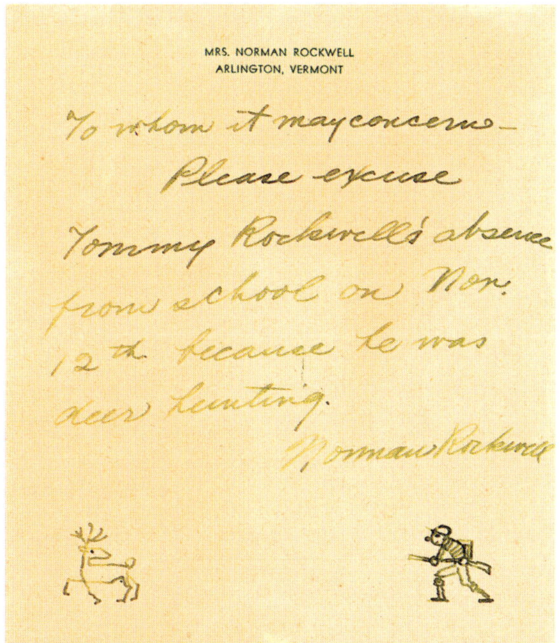

MRS. NORMAN ROCKWELL
ARLINGTON, VERMONT

To whom it may concern -
Please excuse
Tommy Rockwell's absence
from school on Nov.
12th because he was
deer hunting.

Norman Rockwell

8.37a–c. Letters from Mary and Norman Rockwell to Arlington High School excusing Tom Rockwell's absence from school, featuring related comical sketches by Norman Rockwell, 1950–51
RC.2010.12.1.23

In 1921 Rockwell rented a studio near his home in New Rochelle, New York, from George Lischke, who had two sons, George Jr. and Franklin. Franklin became the model for some of Rockwell's early paintings and assisted him with other projects. In this pictograph letter, Rockwell asks Franklin for a different model to pose for him.

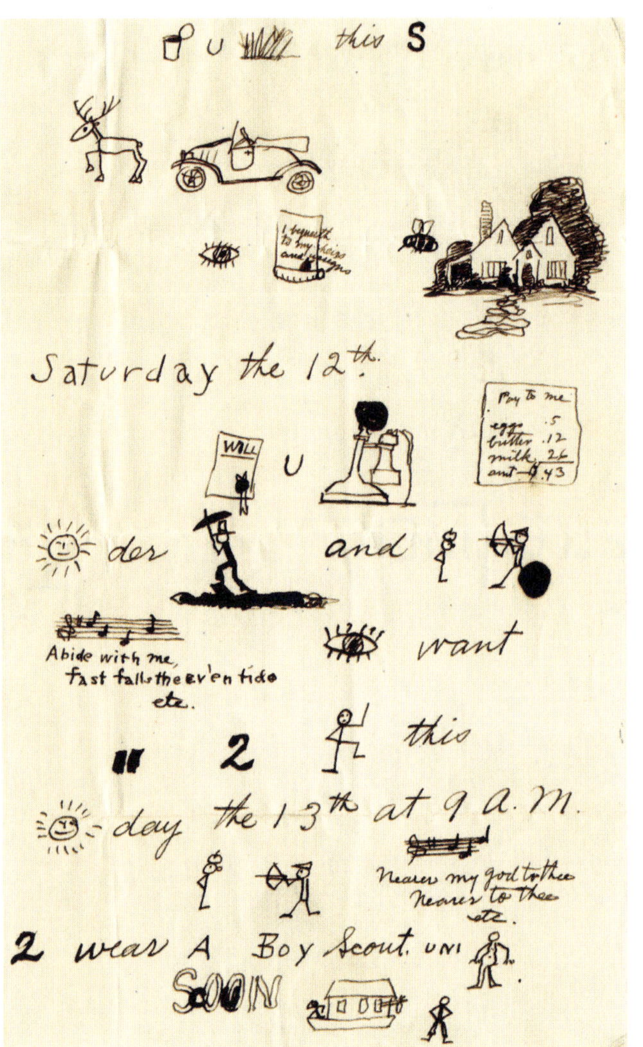


(Interpretation of sign letter)
Can you read this letter

Dear old Franklin
I will be home
Saturday the 12th.
Will you telephone Bill
Sundermeyer and tell
him I want
him to pose this
Sunday the 13th at 9 am
tell him
to wear a Boy Scout
uniform

See you in the soon

Norman.

X from Franz –
Give it to your poor.

8.38a–b. Pictograph letter from Rockwell to model Franklin Lischke, c. 1924
RC.2010.12.1.44

This is one in a series of letters written by Norman Rockwell to the Art Students League–trained artist Dorothy Humphrey (1916–2003), whom he first met when his son Tom was attending Bard College. Tom studied literature at Bard with Dorothy's husband, novelist William Humphrey (1924–1997), and introduced the couple to his father.

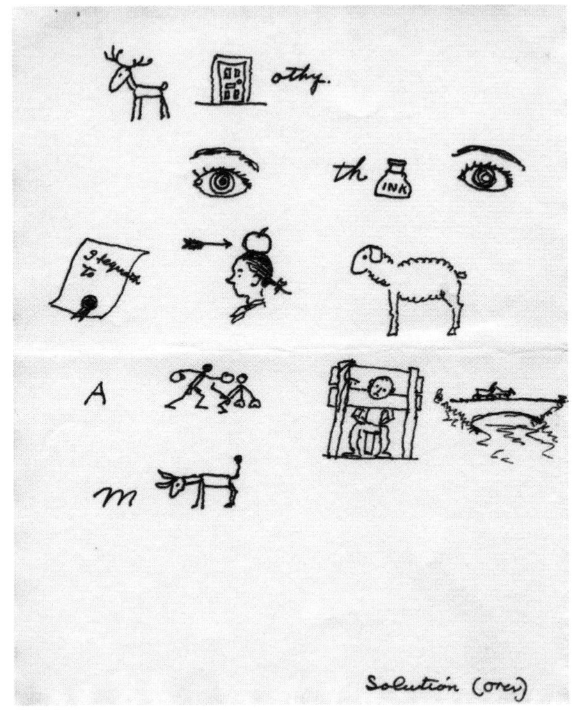


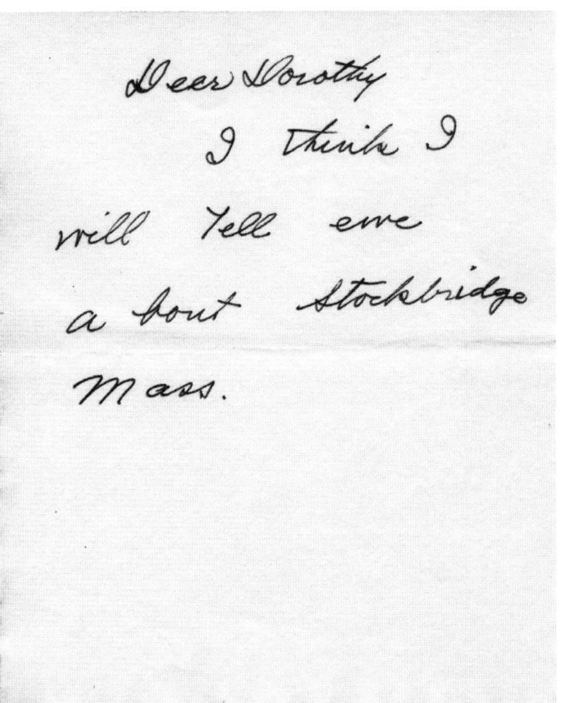

Deer Dorothy
I think I
will tell ewe
a bout Stockbridge
Mass.

8.39a–b. Pictograph letter from Rockwell to Dorothy Humphrey, c. 1955
Ink on paper, 8 × 6 in. (20.3 × 15.2 cm)
RC.1987.11.1

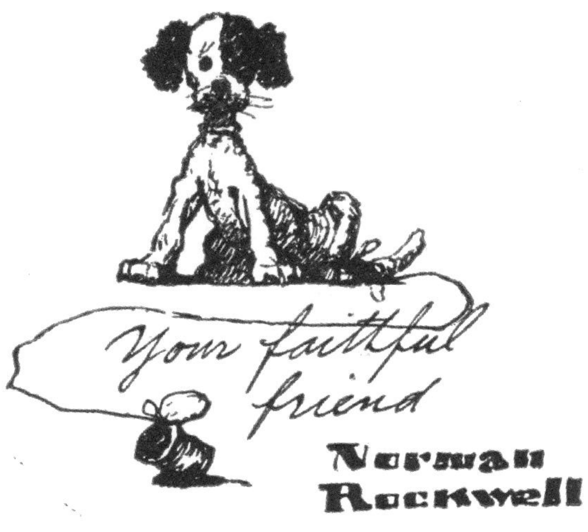


Whether stamped or hand-drawn, Rockwell used an image of a dog with a can tied to its tail on many personal letters he wrote throughout his life.

8.40. *Your Faithful Friend*, c. 1925
Stamp from metal printing block, 2 × 2⅛ in. (5.1 × 5.4 cm)
RC.1980.1 (Gift of the Estate of DeWitt D. Wise)

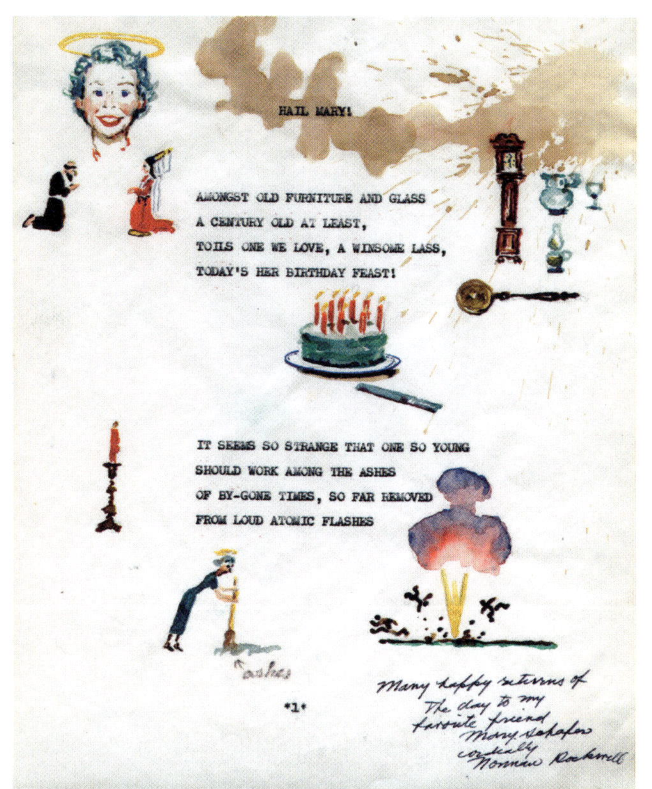


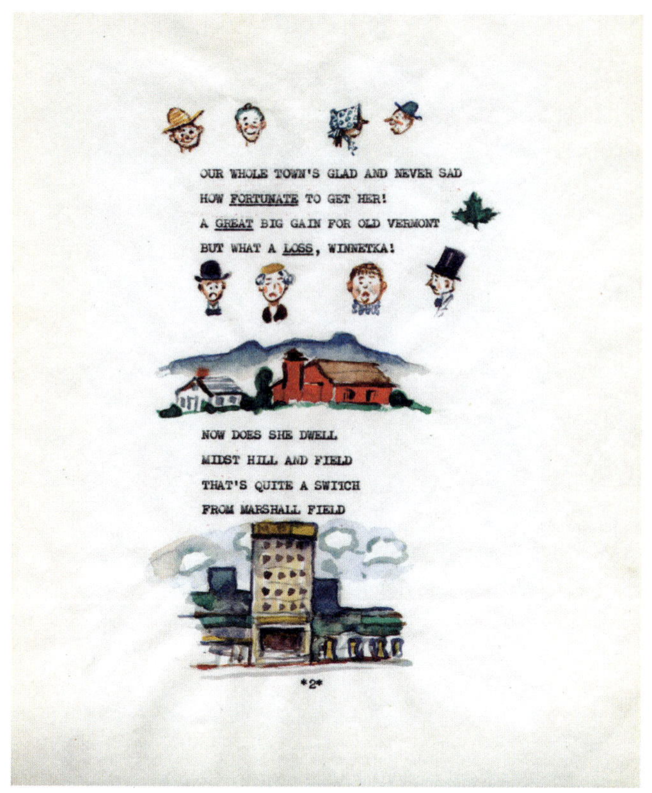


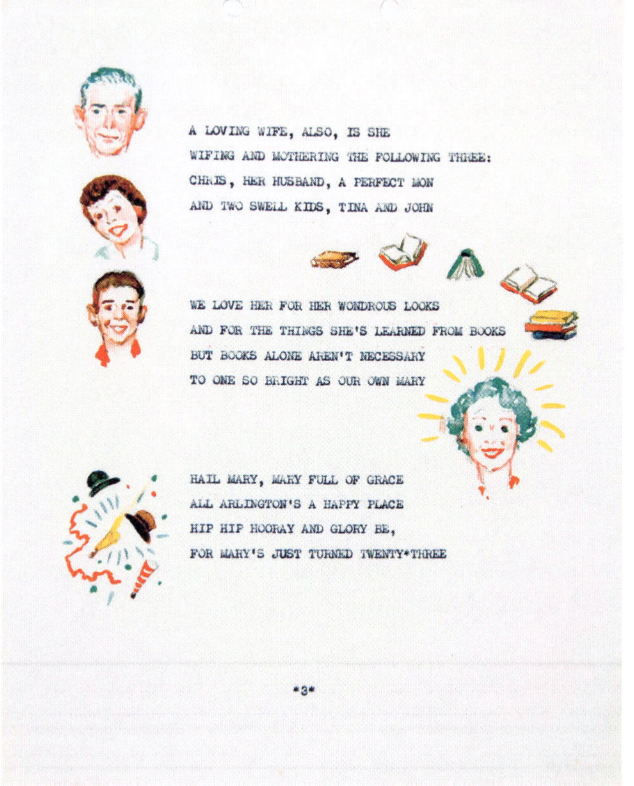


Here Rockwell illustrates a birthday poem he wrote for Mary Schafer, the wife of his bookkeeper Chris Schafer.

8.41a–c. *Hail Mary*, 1951
Watercolor on paper, 11 × 8½ in.
(27.9 × 21.6 cm) each
NRM.1988.07 (Gift of Mrs. Mary Schafer)

Rockwell illustrated this typewritten draft letter, a "tale of guts and gore," with rough pencil sketches of heroes and villains. It was intended for Steve Hibbs, the son of *Saturday Evening Post* editor Ben Hibbs.

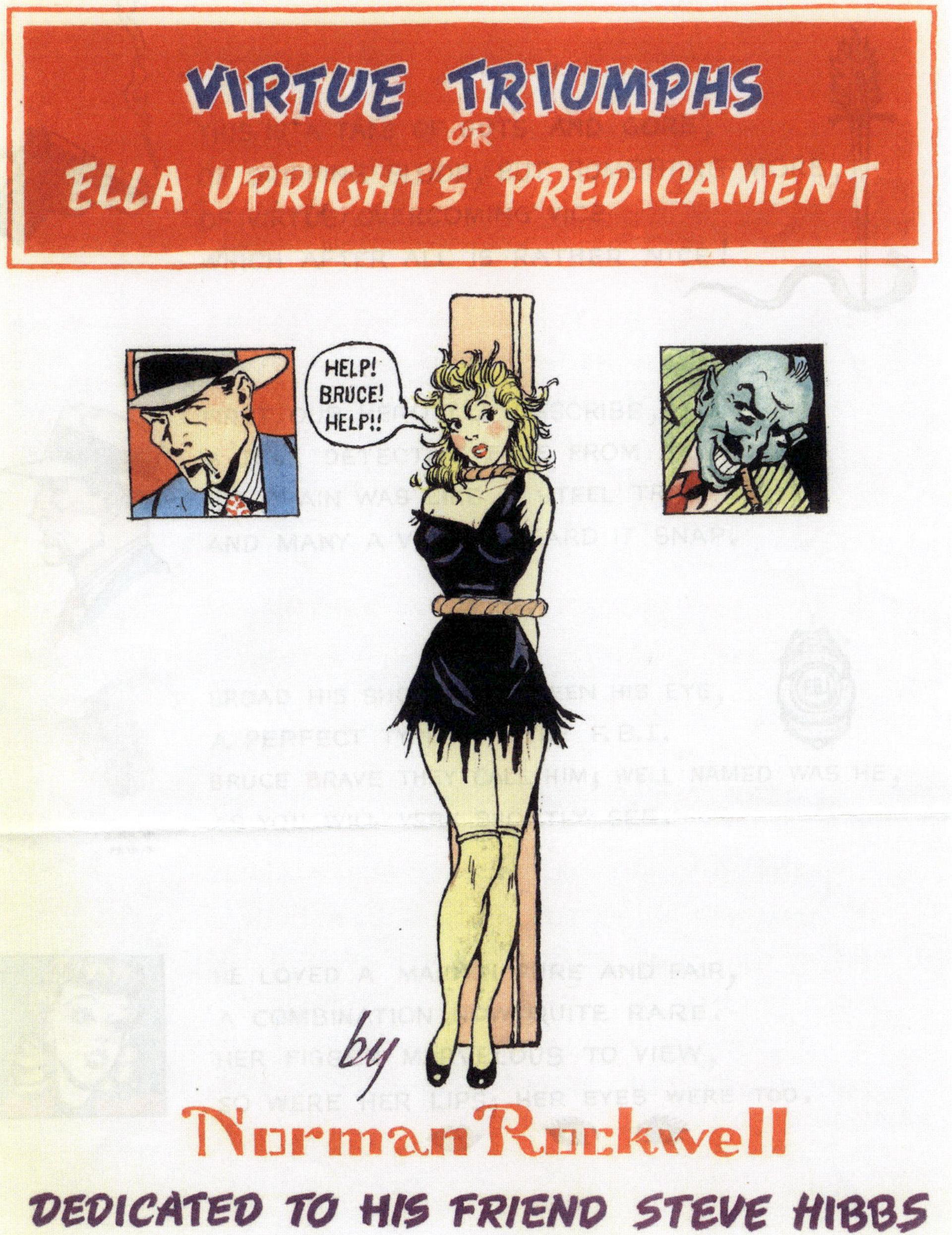


LEFT AND OVERLEAF
8.42a–e. *Virtue Triumphs or Ella Upright's Predicament*, 1946–47
Pencil and ink on paper, 11 × 8½ in. (27.9 × 21.6 cm) each
NRACT.1973.133

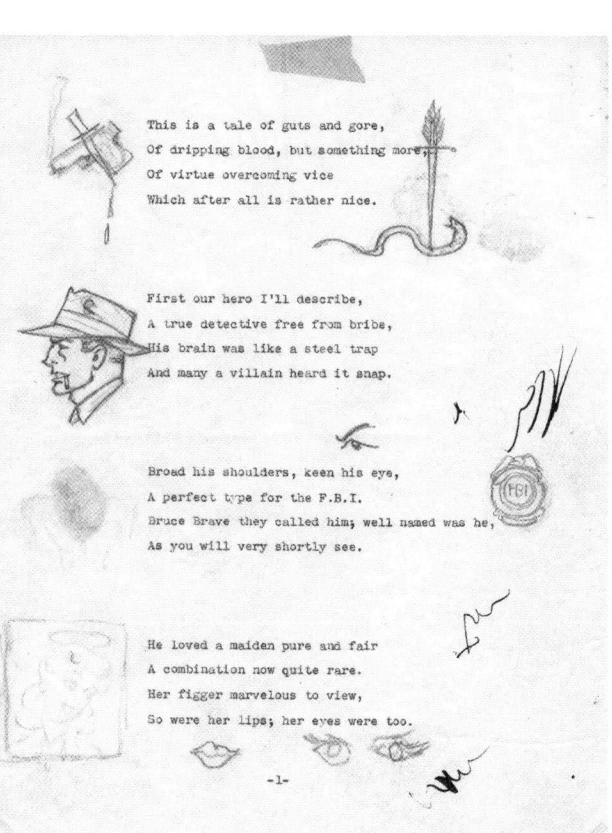

This is a tale of guts and gore,
Of dripping blood, but something more,
Of virtue overcoming vice
Which after all is rather nice.

First our hero I'll describe,
A true detective free from bribe,
His brain was like a steel trap
And many a villain heard it snap.

Broad his shoulders, keen his eye,
A perfect type for the F.B.I.
Bruce Brave they called him; well named was he,
As you will very shortly see.

He loved a maiden pure and fair
A combination now quite rare.
Her figger marvelous to view,
So were her lips; her eyes were too.

-1-



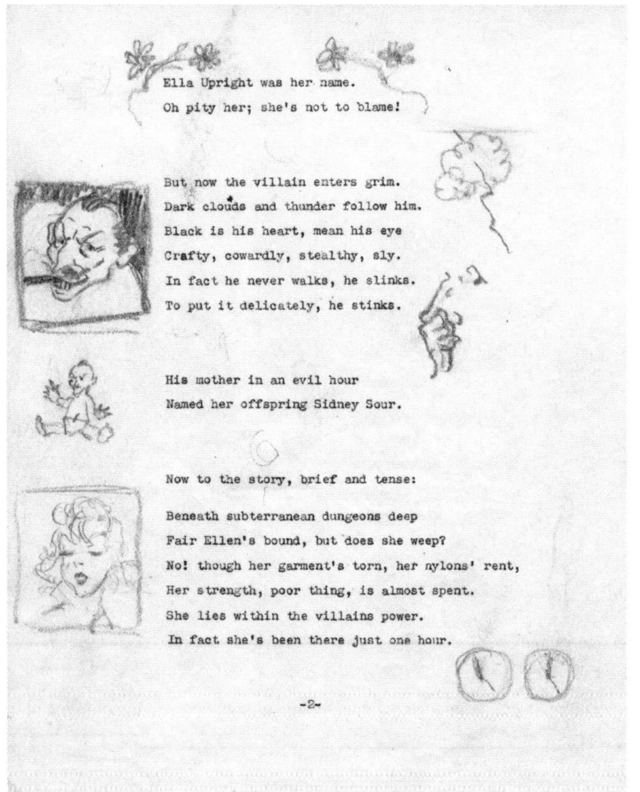

Ella Upright was her name.
Oh pity her; she's not to blame!

But now the villain enters grim.
Dark clouds and thunder follow him.
Black is his heart, mean his eye
Crafty, cowardly, stealthy, sly.
In fact he never walks, he slinks.
To put it delicately, he stinks.

His mother in an evil hour
Named her offspring Sidney Sour.

Now to the story, brief and tense:

Beneath subterranean dungeons deep
Fair Ellen's bound, but does she weep?
No! though her garment's torn, her nylons' rent,
Her strength, poor thing, is almost spent.
She lies within the villains power.
In fact she's been there just one hour.

-2-

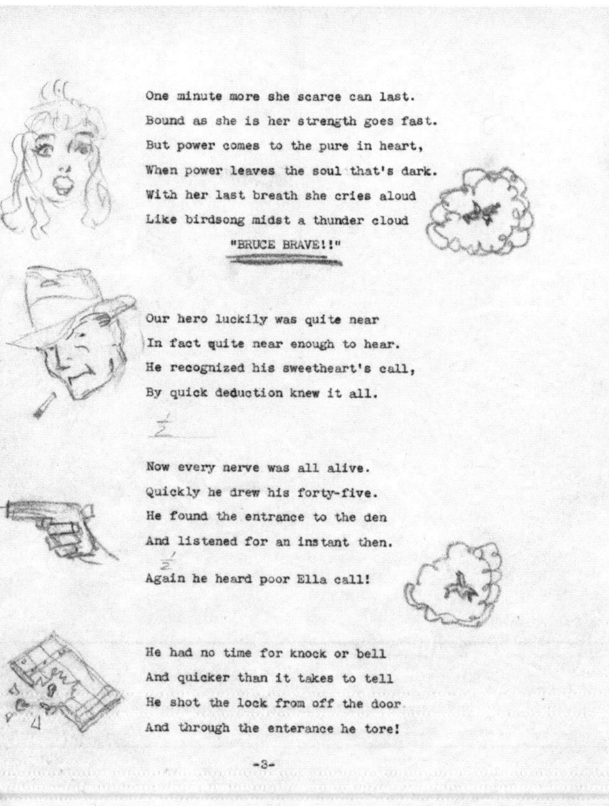

One minute more she scarce can last.
Bound as she is her strength goes fast.
But power comes to the pure in heart,
When power leaves the soul that's dark.
With her last breath she cries aloud
Like birdsong midst a thunder cloud
"BRUCE BRAVE!!"

Our hero luckily was quite near
In fact quite near enough to hear.
He recognized his sweetheart's call,
By quick deduction knew it all.

Now every nerve was all alive.
Quickly he drew his forty-five.
He found the entrance to the den
And listened for an instant then.
Again he heard poor Ella call!

He had no time for knock or bell
And quicker than it takes to tell
He shot the lock from off the door
And through the enterance he tore!

-3-

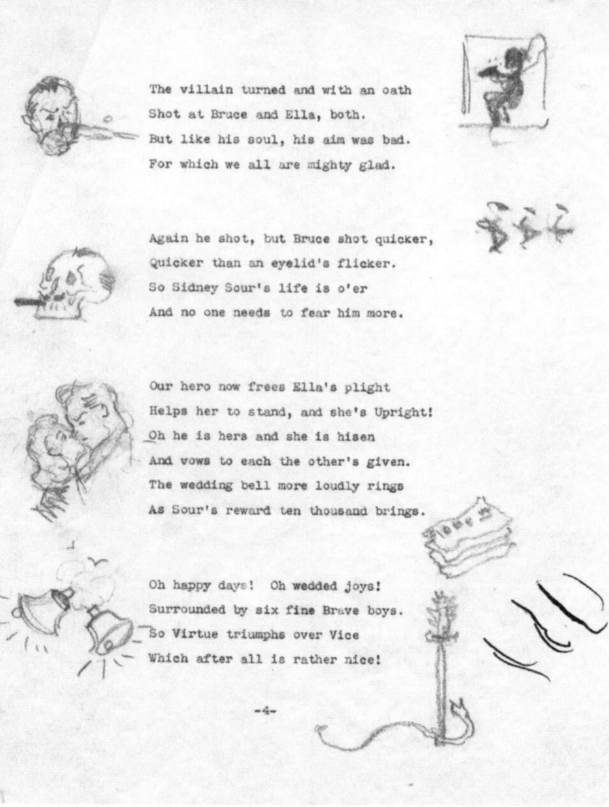

The villain turned and with an oath
Shot at Bruce and Ella, both.
But like his soul, his aim was bad.
For which we all are mighty glad.

Again he shot, but Bruce shot quicker,
Quicker than an eyelid's flicker.
So Sidney Sour's life is o'er
And no one needs to fear him more.

Our hero now frees Ella's plight
Helps her to stand, and she's Upright!
Oh he is hers and she is hisen
And vows to each the other's given.
The wedding bell more loudly rings
As Sour's reward ten thousand brings.

Oh happy days! Oh wedded joys!
Surrounded by six fine Brave boys.
So Virtue triumphs over Vice
Which after all is rather nice!

-4-

Rockwell loved to travel the world, making three trips to Europe in 1927, 1929, and 1932, and traveling extensively throughout Europe, Africa, Asia, and South America from the 1950s to 1970s. While traveling, he would mail letters and postcards back home, filled with new drawings inspired by his experiences. He created these postcards based on his 1927 trip to Europe with friends Dean Parmalee and Bill Backer. In *Norman Rockwell: Illustrator*, he notes, "When traveling, it is always fun to send mail back home. I drew these cards in ink and had them printed; then I touched them up with opaque paint."[16]

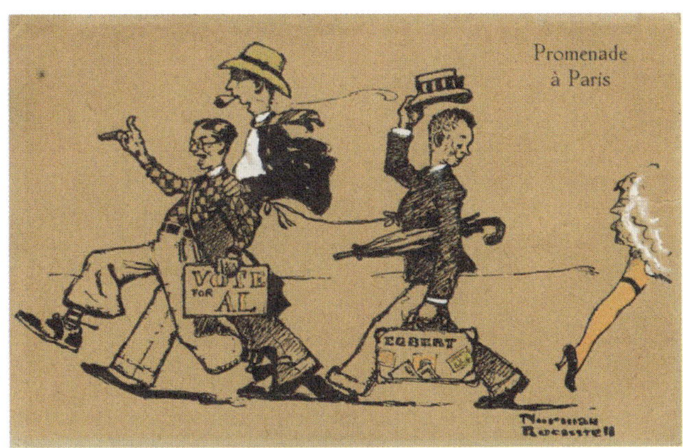


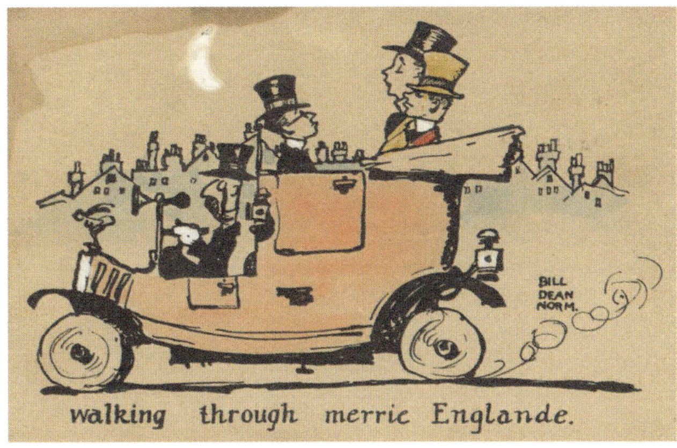


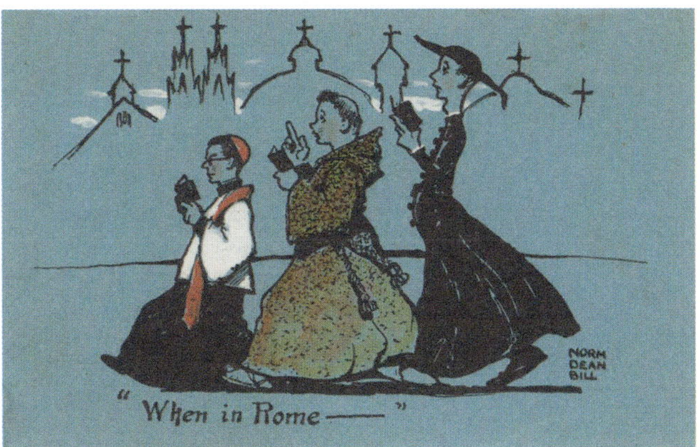


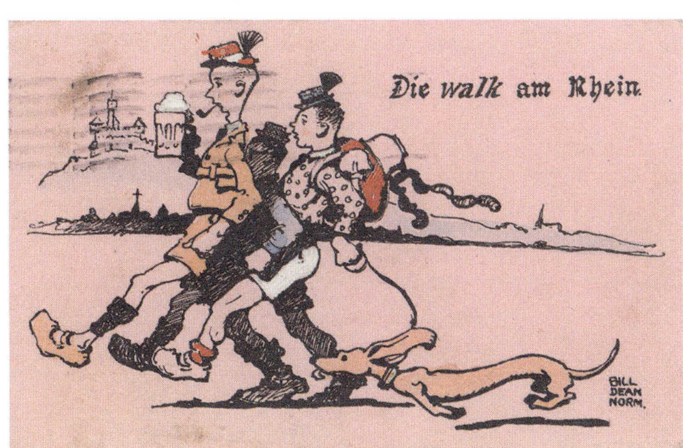


TOP ROW AND BOTTOM LEFT
8.43a–c. Postcards from Europe, 1928
"Promenade à Paris," "Walking through Merrie Englande," "When in Rome . . ."
Ink on paper, 3½ × 5½ in. (8.9 × 14 cm) each
Norman Rockwell Museum collection

BOTTOM RIGHT
8.44. Postcard from Europe, 1928
"Die Walk am Rhein"
Ink on paper, 3½ × 5½ in. (8.9 × 14 cm)
Private collection

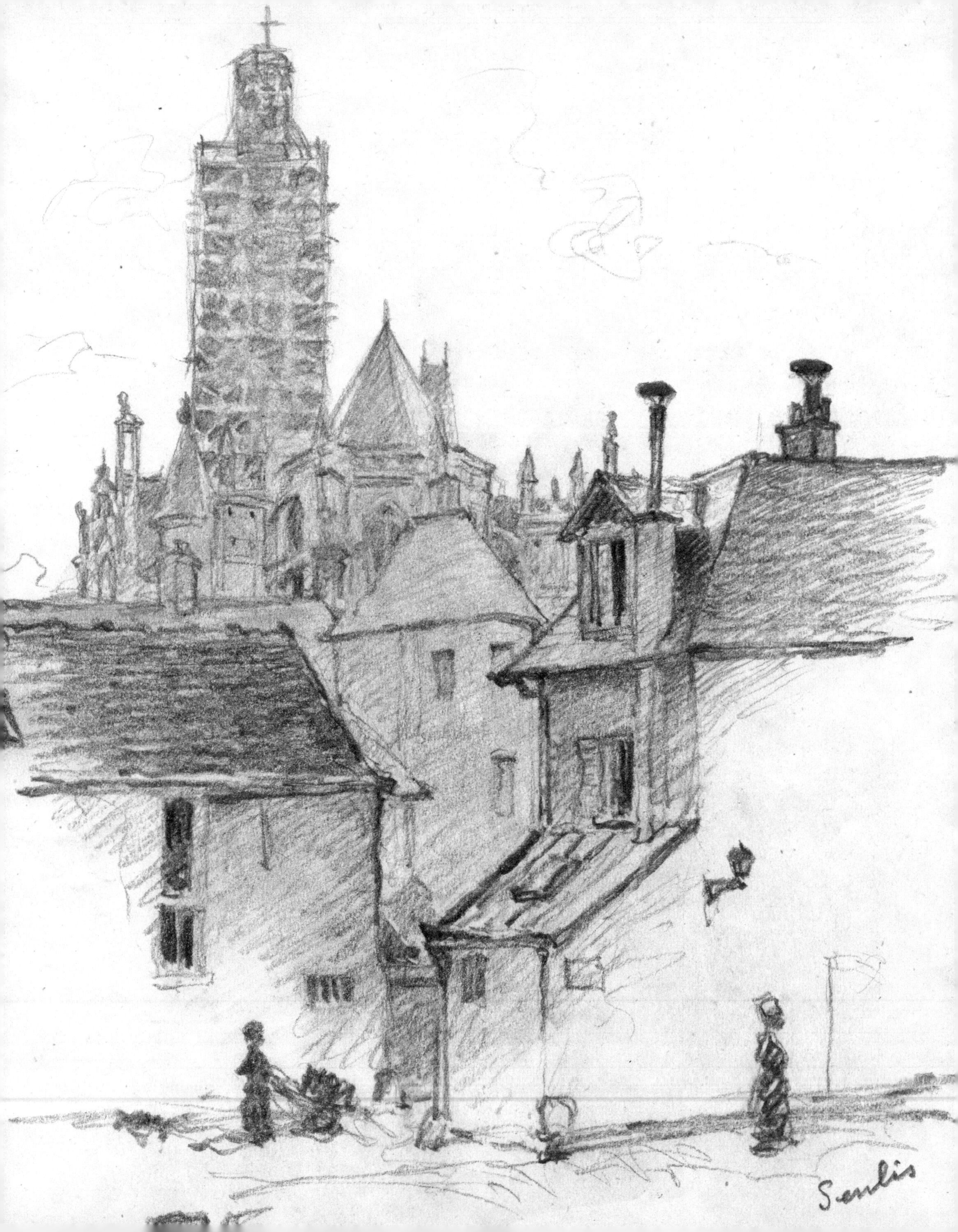
Senlis

# 9 The Artist's Sketchbooks

STEPHANIE HABOUSH PLUNKETT

Though Rockwell's deadline-driven illustration career required him to spend untold hours at his studio drawing table and easel, he always relished travel, which offered a respite from his intensive daily routine. In reflecting upon a 1921 South American expedition with Edison Mazda art director T. J. MacManus to ostensibly tour the company's agencies there, Rockwell said that the trip had inspired him to develop a case of "chronic wanderlust. A bad case—I haven't got over it yet."[1] That was the artist's first trip outside the United States, and during his lifetime,

Detail of European travel sketchbook page, 1932
See plate 9.8.

he would go on to travel frequently, capturing the sights along the way by keeping sketchbooks and creating small paintings on location until 1974, when ill-health made these excursions more difficult.

Sketching was always a part of Rockwell's artistic process when capturing the first iteration of his ideas for published illustrations, but when traveling, sketchbooks provided an unencumbered outlet for creative expression and observation. Though rare, the Norman Rockwell Museum is fortunate to feature in its collection two complete Rockwell sketchbooks, as well as a selection of loose pages documenting the artist's personal and professional travel experiences and highlighting the people and places that captured his attention. Interesting faces and figures in light and shadow are prominent in the artist's drawing books, as might be expected given his people-centric body of published illustrations. But at every opportunity, in cities and the countryside, Rockwell took time to soak in his surroundings through the act of drawing. His sketchbooks reflect his appreciation for the natural world and his interest in unique, striking architectural structures—from grand castles and bridges to picturesque shops and rural cottages.

In his 1960 autobiography, *My Adventures as an Illustrator*, Rockwell recounted the tale of a summer 1928 trip to Europe aboard the *Olympic*, the sister ship of the *Titanic*, with architect Dean Parmalee and building contractor Bill Backer, both New Rochelle, New York, neighbors and friends. A carefree adventure that Rockwell hoped would free him from "deadlines, money, bills, the right flannel trousers, and the country club,"[2] the trip presented daily opportunities for sketching, which he enjoyed. By his description, his sketchbook contained rough studies created during the day and refined, with some watercolor overlays, at his hotel in the evenings. But near the end of his trip while visiting the Prado Museum in Madrid, Spain, it tragically went missing. He recalled sketching all morning and walking directly to the gallery where a favorite painting, *The Triumph of Bacchus (Los Borrachos, The Topers)*, c. 1629, by Diego Velázquez was on view.

After sitting briefly on a settee in the gallery to rest, he got up to examine the painting more closely but left his large black thirty-by-thirty-inch sketchbook behind. When he returned to his seat, he found that his sketch-filled book was gone. "It wasn't the work I'd put in. Or lugging it all over Europe. But it was the record of our trip. . . . And I'd done it just for my own pleasure. No deadline; I wasn't planning to sell it. I still almost cry when I think about it. I've never lost anything I felt so bad about."[3] Fortunately, Rockwell would travel widely, nationally and abroad, many times thereafter. Some record of those experiences remains in the sketchbooks and sketchbook pages that are preserved for study and enjoyment in the Norman Rockwell Museum's collection.

## France, 1932

During a 1932 sojourn in France that lasted almost seven months, from February to September, Rockwell hoped to reinvent himself by breaking away from his daily work on commercial illustrations, and he took time to sketch almost every day.

This striking drawing homes in on the aspects of Rockwell's work that are particularly masterful—the distinct personal qualities of hands, feet, and faces. To carefully observe the effects of cast light on form, Rockwell hired a French fisherman as a model, but at the end of the session he realized that he had not sufficiently captured the details that he hoped for. Rockwell was particularly interested in his model's stained hat and offered to purchase it for a day's, and then a week's, wages. The fisherman declined but the drawing clearly reflects Rockwell's technical and observational abilities.

9.1. *French Fisherman, Paris*, 1932
Pencil on paper, 15 × 11 in. (38.1 × 27.9 cm)
European travel sketchbook page
NRACT.1976.111

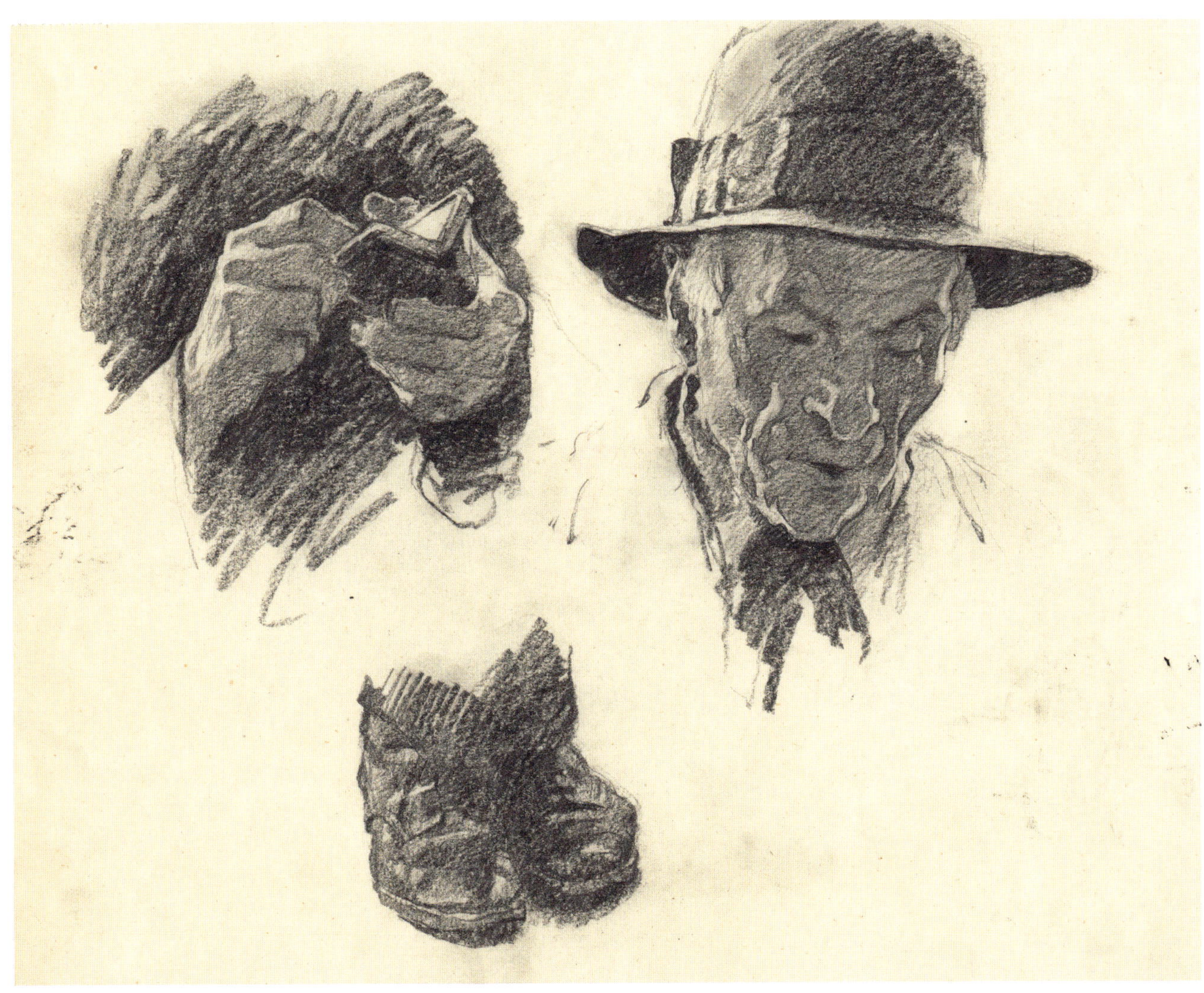

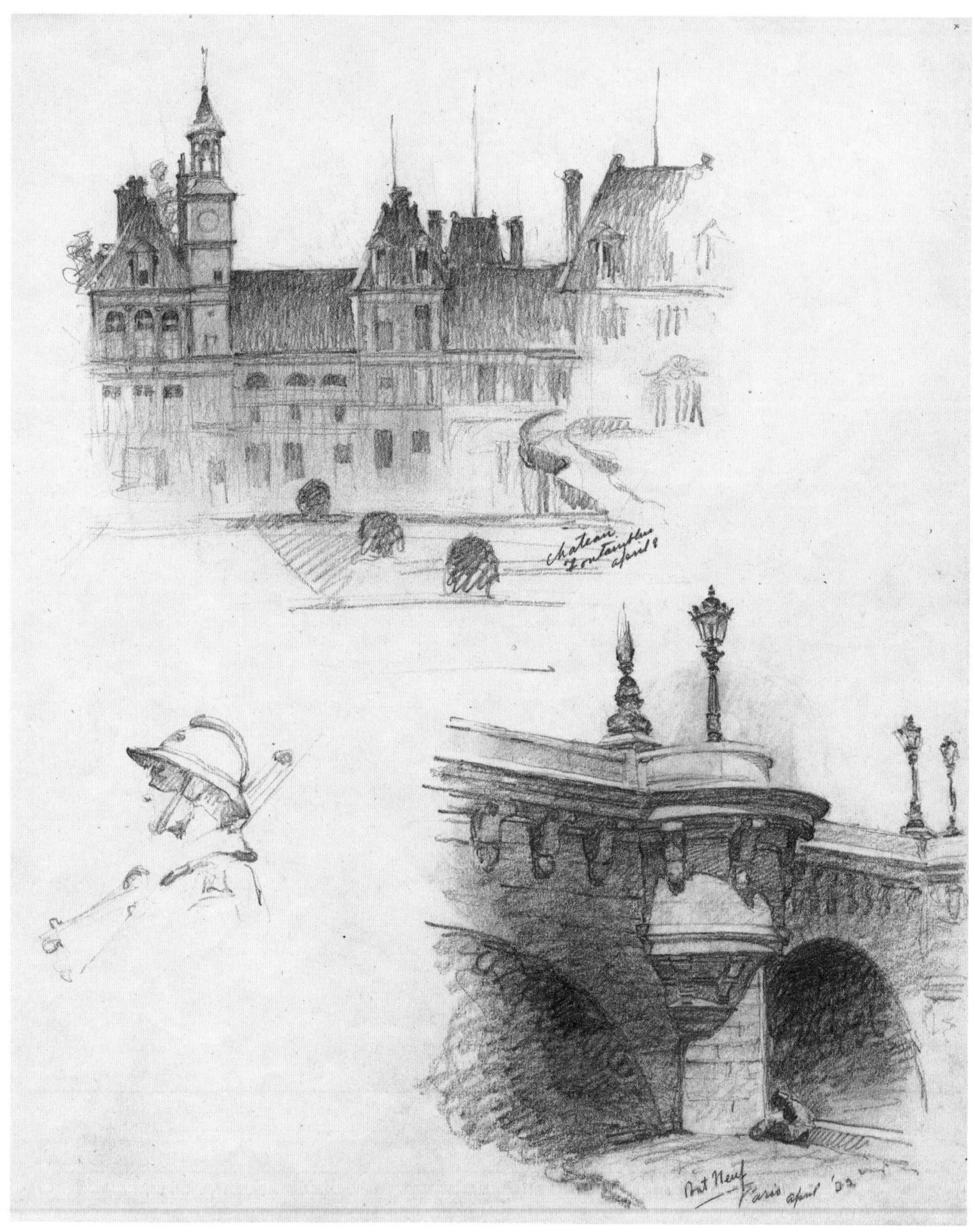
Chateau
april 8
Pont Neuf
Paris april '02

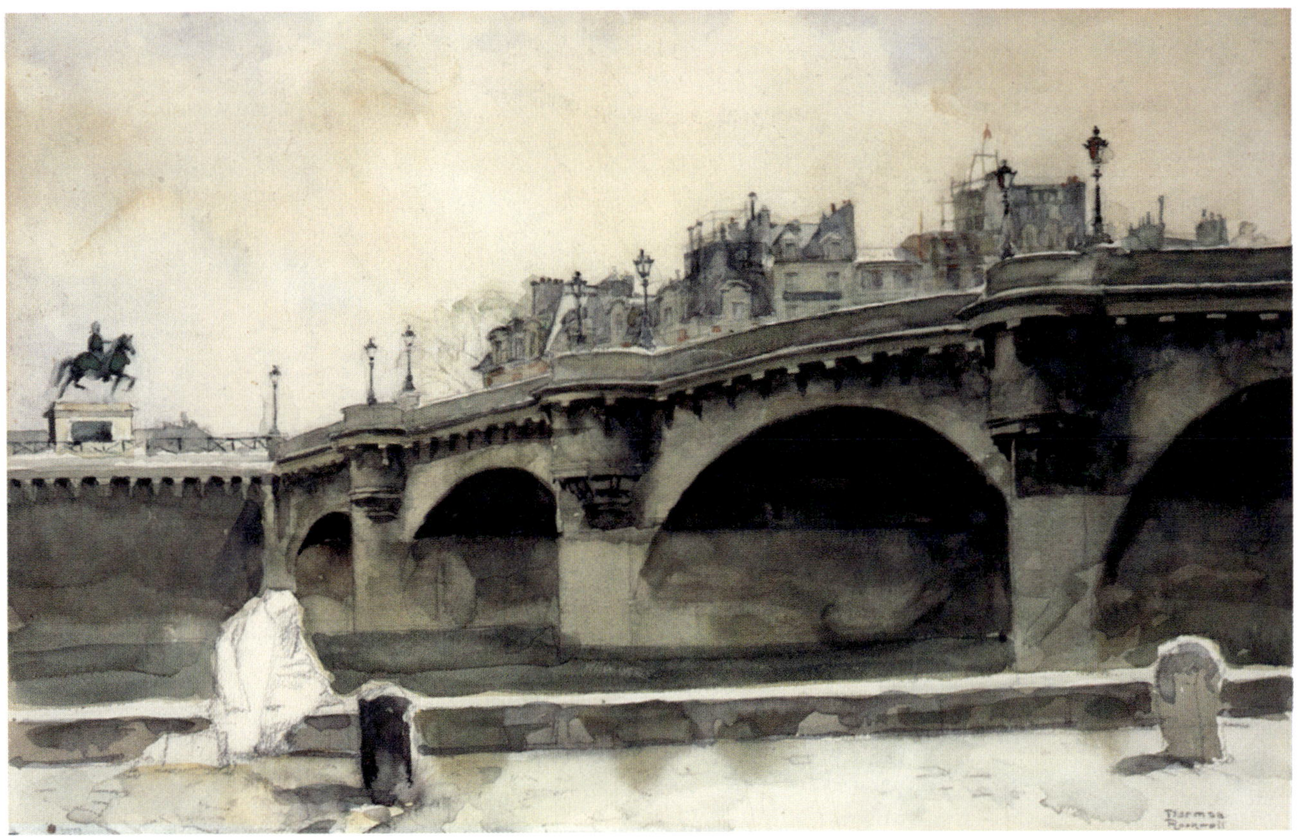

OPPOSITE
9.2. *Chateau Fontainebleau and Pont Neuf, Paris,* April 8, 1932
Pencil on paper, 15 × 11 in. (38.1 × 27.9 cm)
European travel sketchbook page
NRACT.1976.113

ABOVE
9.3. *Le Pont Neuf, Paris,* 1932
Watercolor and pencil on paper, 9 × 14¼ in. (23.8 × 38.7 cm)
Travel painting
Private collection

Rockwell would sometimes capture a variety of vignettes, including architectural fragments and figure studies, on a single sketchbook page (plate 9.2). By drawing daily on his extended trips, he was able to work rapidly, and his work had a strong graphical quality, moving from the darkest darks to the lightest lights.

While in Paris in 1932, Rockwell's studio was a short tram ride over the Seine, and the Pont Neuf, the oldest standing bridge across the river, would have been a familiar sight. Viewing art and architecture was an important component of Rockwell's leisurely retreats. In a watercolor study (plate 9.3), he captures the day's atmospheric light as well as the graceful sweep and design of the famous French bridge.

9.4. *Fontainebleau, April 9, 1932*
Pencil on paper, 15 × 11 in. (38.1 × 27.9 cm)
European travel sketchbook page
NRACT.1976.118

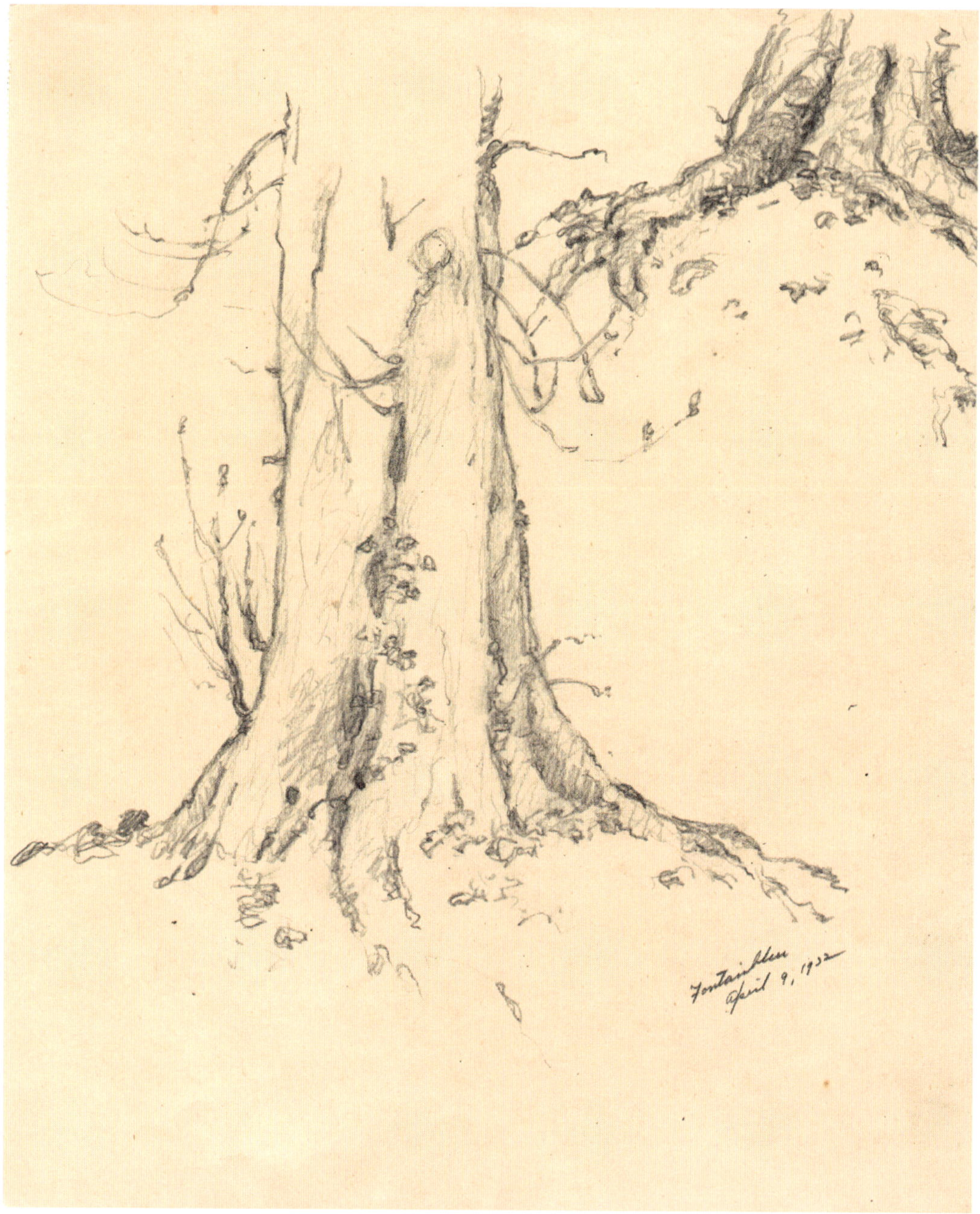


Though his focus was on people and their interactions with one another, when working outdoors, Rockwell turned his attention to nature. This sketchbook drawing explores the beauty of well-established trees in the forest of Fontainebleau, just thirty-seven miles (59.5 km) outside of Paris.

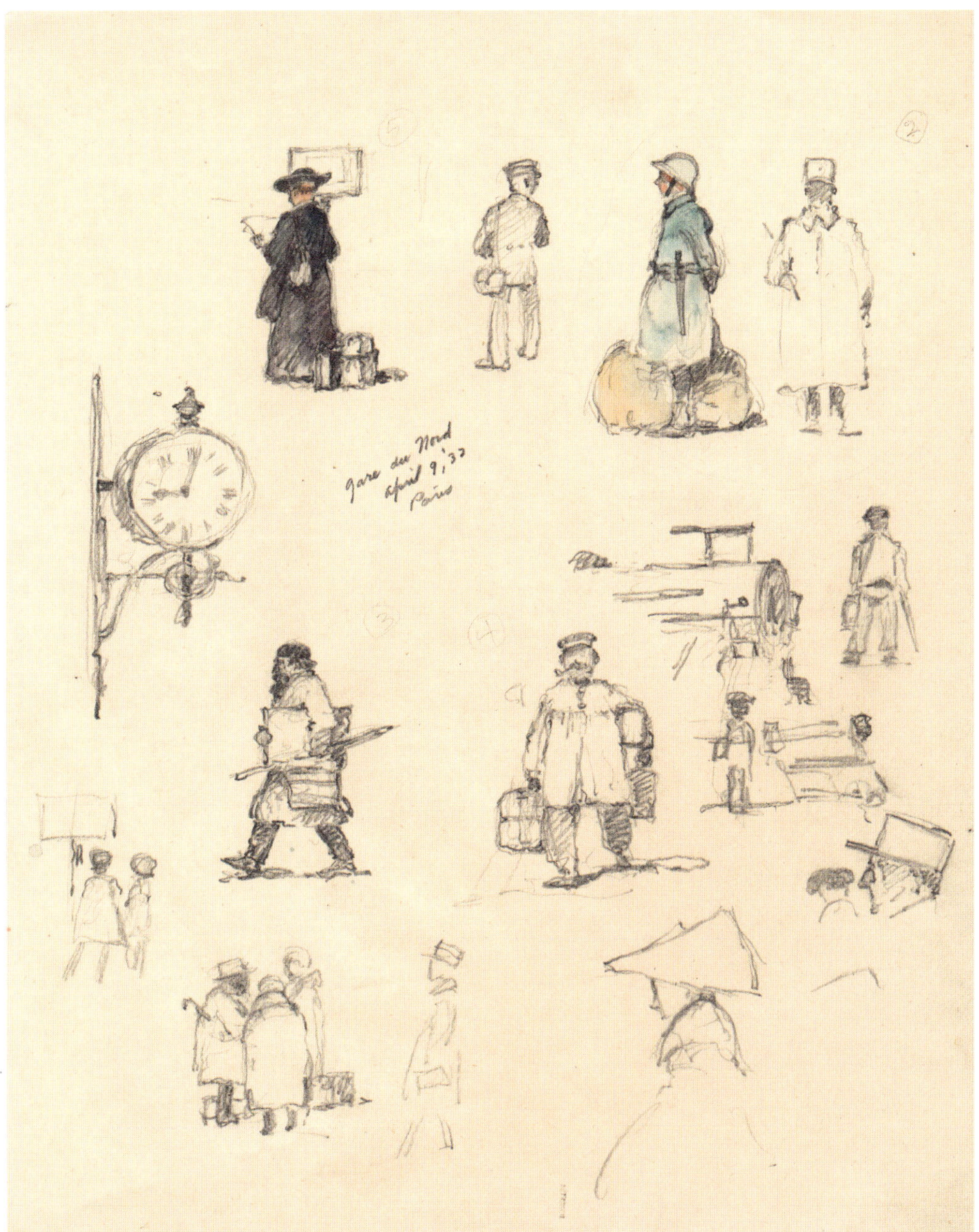


9.5. *Gare du Nord, Paris, April 9, '32*
Pencil on paper, 15 × 11 in. (38.1 × 27.9 cm)
European travel sketchbook page
NRACT.1976.107

Rockwell interjects some lighthearted humor into his sketch of the Gare du Nord, one of the six large railway terminals in Paris. The artist's loose gestural studies capture people in several types of dress—from military and clerical garb to a classic artist's smock—who carry bulky bags and wait patiently for trains.

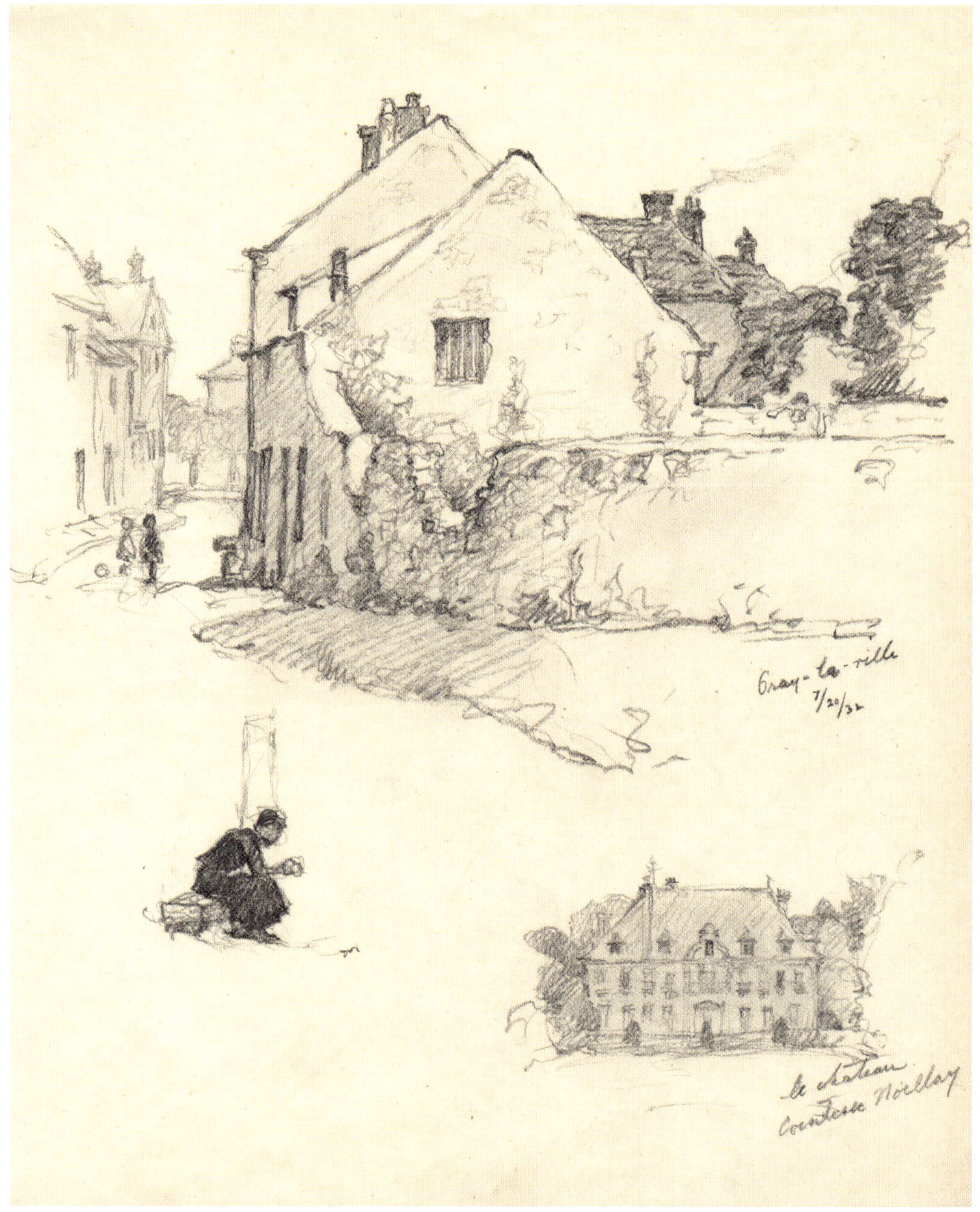


ABOVE
9.6. *Gray-la-Ville, 7/20/32* and *Le Chateau Comtess Noellay, France*, 1932
Pencil on paper, 15 × 11 in. (38.1 × 27.9 cm)
European travel sketchbook page
NRACT.1976.112

OPPOSITE
9.7. *La Coeur du Grand-Cerf, Gray-la-Ville*, 1932
Pencil on paper, 15 × 11 in. (38.1 × 27.9 cm)
European travel sketchbook page
NRACT.1976.116

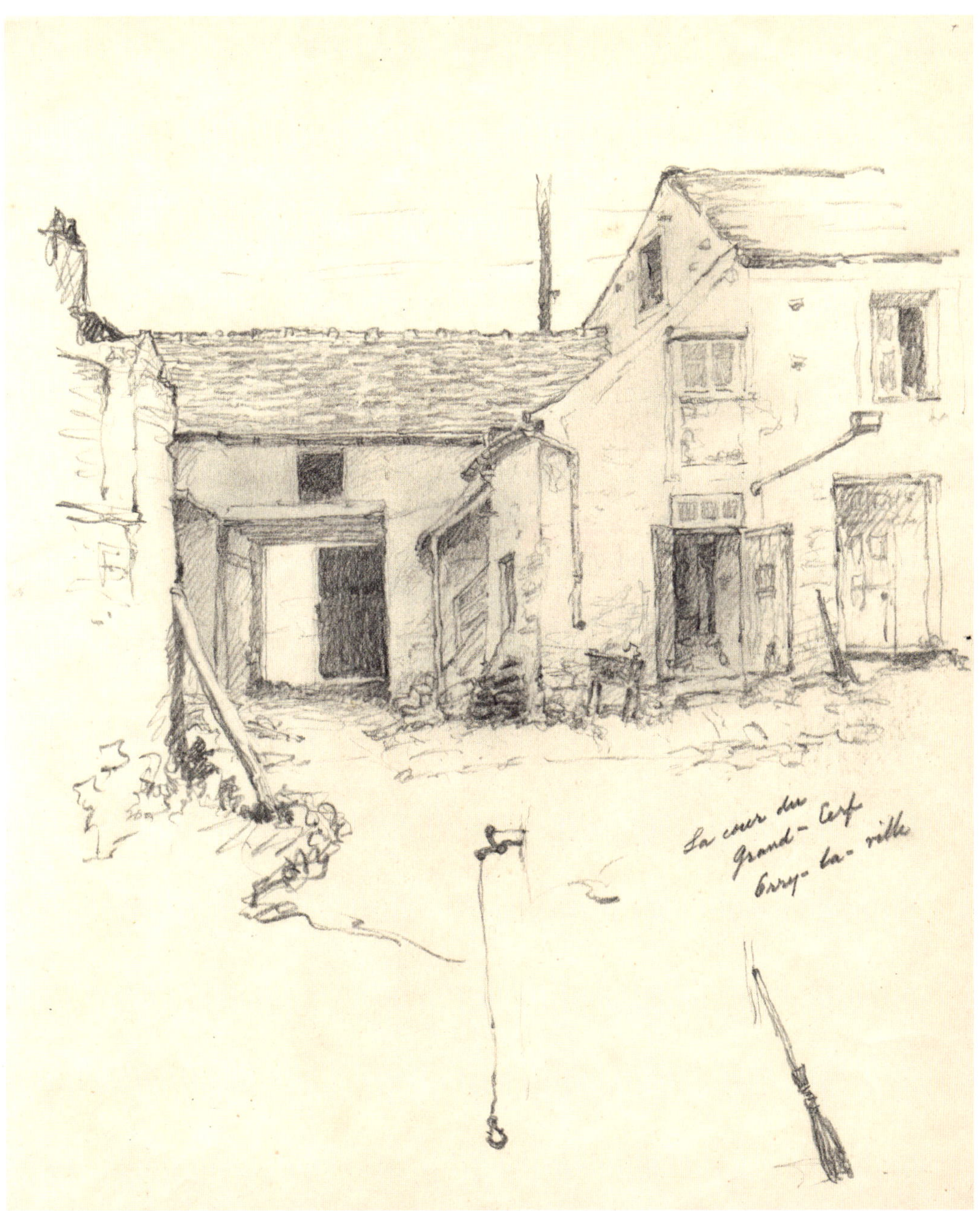


Notations on Rockwell's sketchbook drawings were helpful reminders of the location of his settings and the elements within them, as seen here. Particularly interested in unique signage such as that for a French mustard shop (plate 9.8), he often included rough indications of figures in settings to establish a sense of scale.

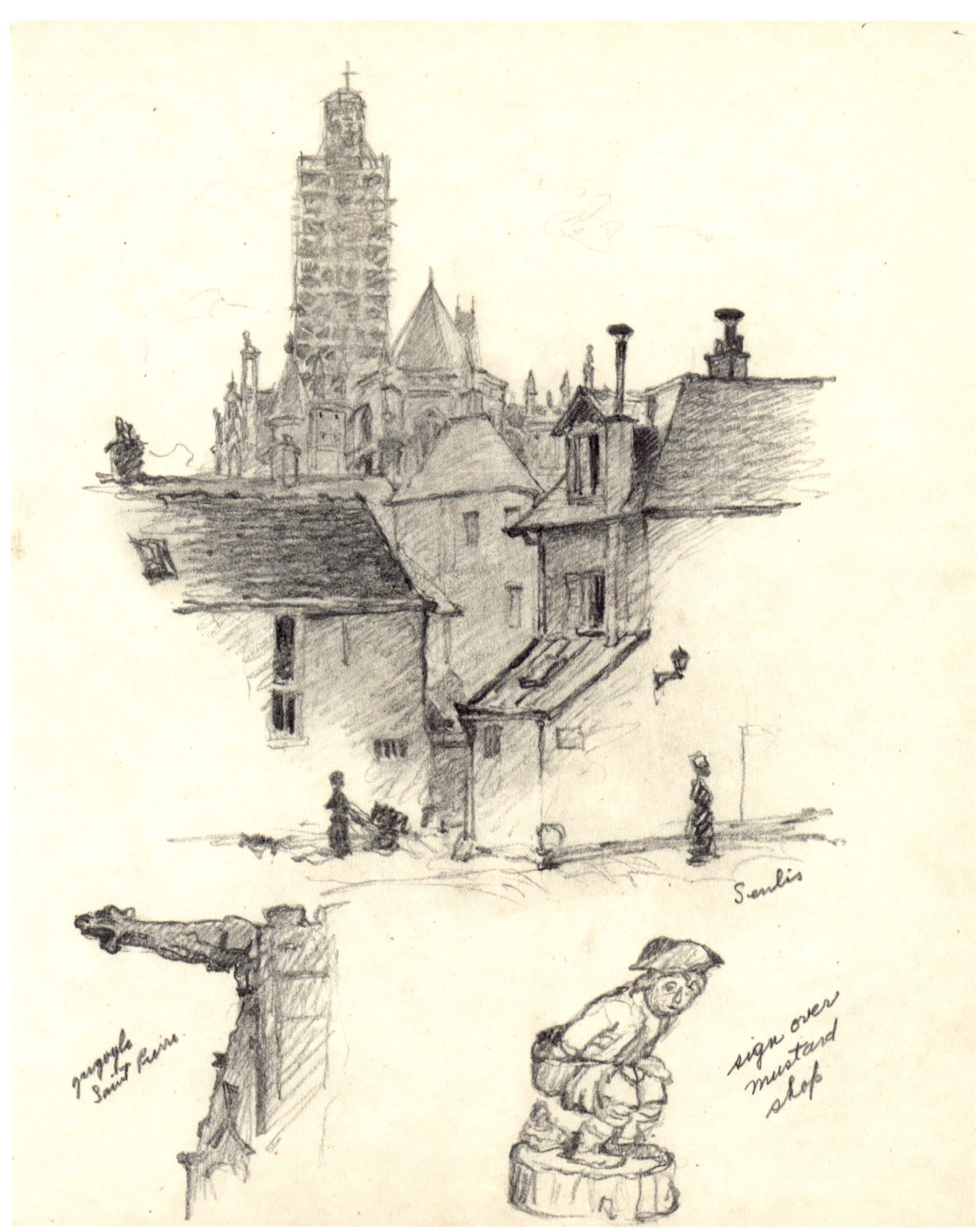


9.8. *Gargoyle Saint Pierre* and *Sign over Mustard Shop, Senlis, France*, 1932
Pencil on paper, 15 × 11 in. (38.1 × 27.9 cm)
European travel sketchbook page
NRACT.1976.117

## Canada, 1934

In September 1934, Norman Rockwell and his friend and model Fred Hildebrandt set off on a two-week Canadian fishing trip, and Rockwell carried along with him a sketchbook that he filled with memories of his experience. From Montreal they traveled north by train to the Quebec wilderness and stayed at the rustic Segouin Camp, named for its owner and operator. The camp's log cabin and adjacent tent are seen on the next page (plate 9.11).

Fred Hildebrandt was an avid fisherman who kept accurate journal entries about his catch and the weather conditions that may have affected his success or lack thereof. Hildebrandt is seen below from frontal and side views in drawings that emphasize the play of light on his face. Years later, in 1938, Hildebrandt and Rockwell fished Vermont's Battenkill River, and the beauty and tranquility of the region prompted Rockwell's 1939 move to the Green Mountain State.

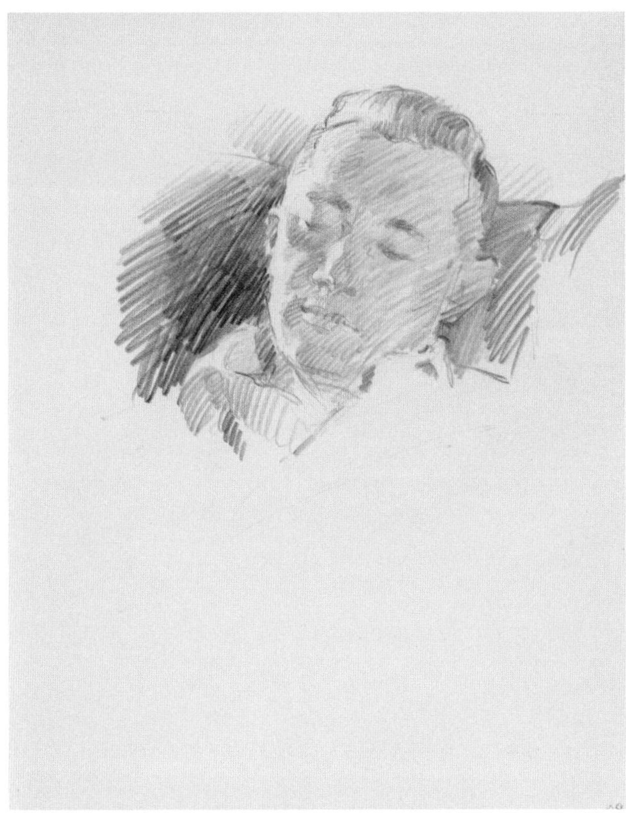

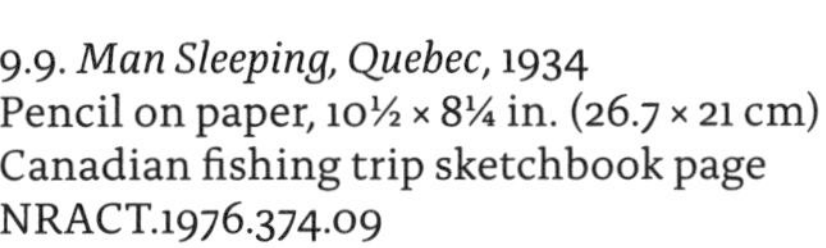

9.9. *Man Sleeping, Quebec*, 1934
Pencil on paper, 10½ × 8¼ in. (26.7 × 21 cm)
Canadian fishing trip sketchbook page
NRACT.1976.374.09

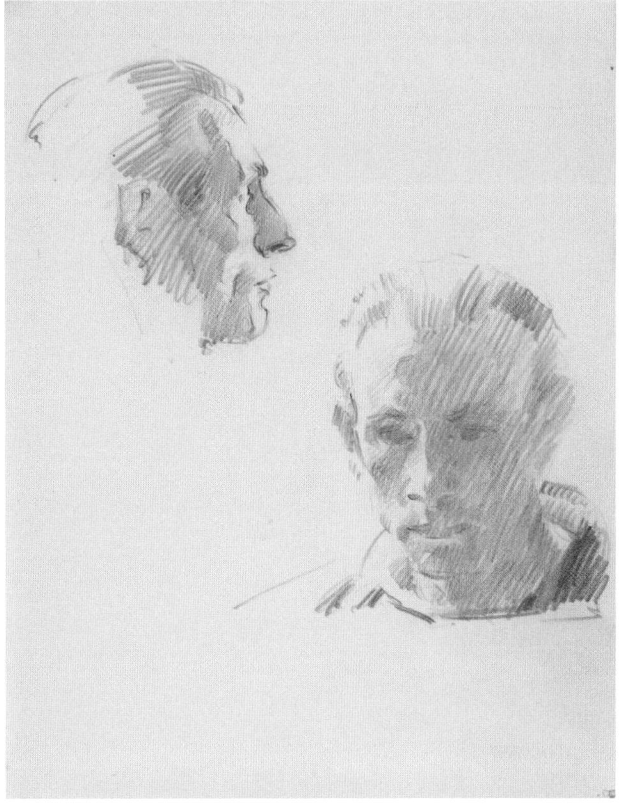

9.10. *Portraits of Fred Hildebrandt*, 1934
Pencil on paper, 10½ × 8¼ in. (26.7 × 21 cm)
Canadian fishing trip sketchbook page
NRACT.1976.374.08

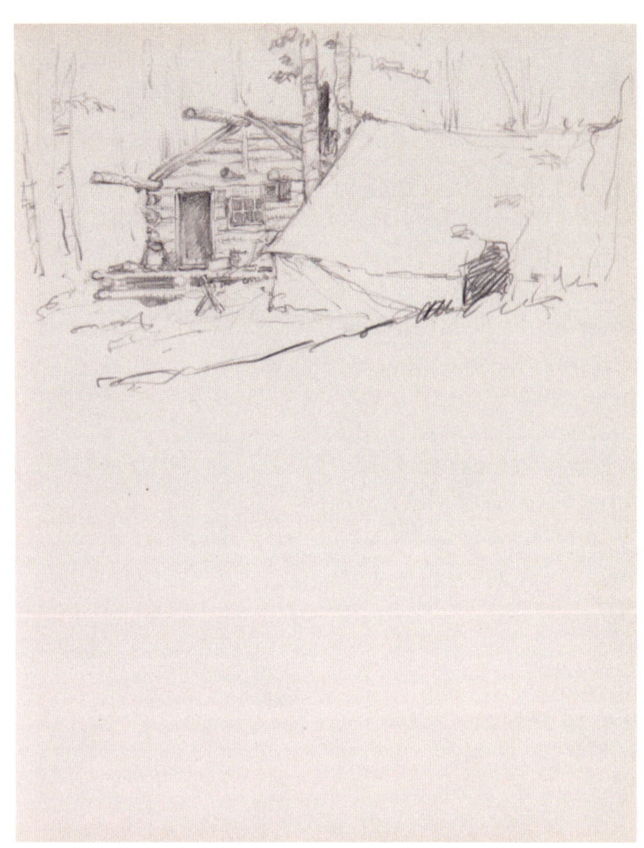

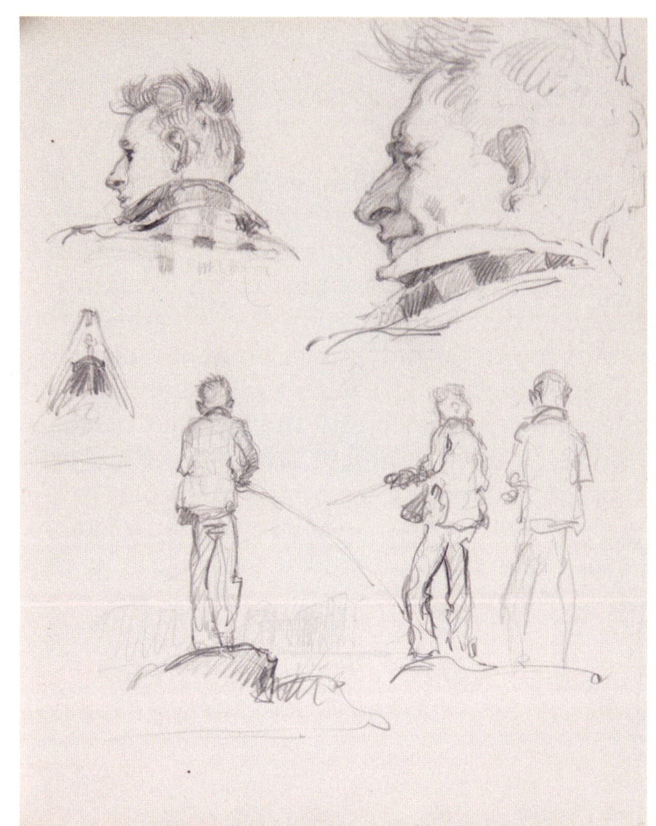

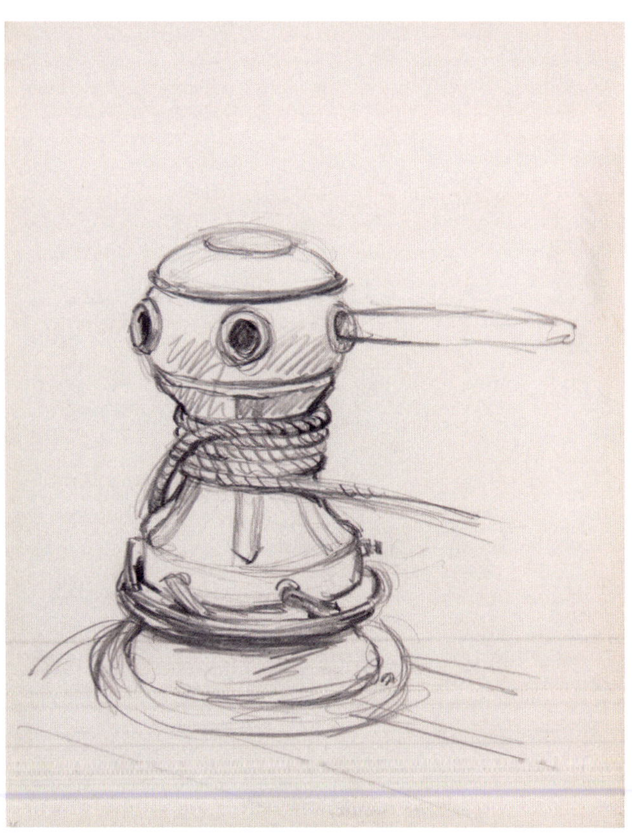

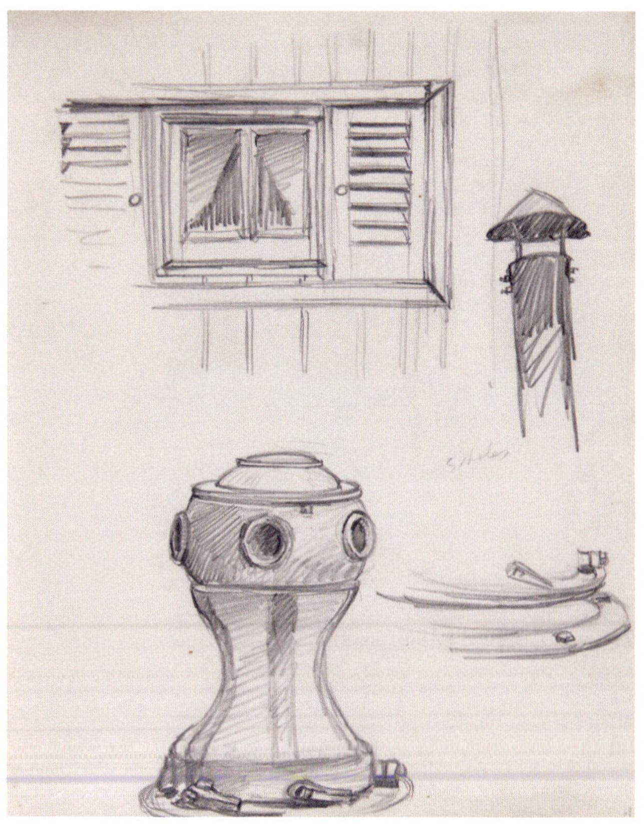

## Later Travels

Rockwell often traveled on assignment, but as he got older, he used travel to relax and rest from his demanding work schedule. When traveling for an extended period, Rockwell typically brought along a travel paint box filled with supplies. The paint box provided a means by which to store his art materials, a drawing board, and an easel for support. While working away from his studio, Rockwell's preferences varied in terms of medium, but he generally favored oil paints, watercolor, and graphite. Rockwell did not generally keep sketchbooks at home, but he brought them along on trips, though he seldom filled all their pages.

In 1955, Rockwell's wife Mary was hospitalized in Hartford, Connecticut, and while visiting her there, he stayed at the Hotel Statler in a room overlooking Bushnell Park. He commented on the city's regal architecture and created a graceful study of the park's monument for Israel Putnam, who served as a major general in the Continental Army during the American Revolutionary War (plate 9.15). The seated figure at the sculpture's base adds a less formal human element and a sense of the monument's scale.

9.15. *Sculpture of Israel Putnam by John Quincy Adams Ward, Bushnell Park, Hartford, Connecticut*, 1955
Pencil on paper, 11 × 8½ in.
(27.9 × 21.6 cm)
Sketchbook page
NRACT.1976.318

OPPOSITE TOP LEFT
9.11. *Fishing Cabin, Segouin Camp, Quebec*, 1934
Pencil on paper, 10½ × 8¼ in.
(26.7 × 21 cm)
Canadian fishing trip sketchbook page
NRACT.1976.374.14

OPPOSITE TOP RIGHT
9.12. *Men Fishing, Quebec*, 1934
Pencil on paper, 10½ × 8¼ in.
(26.7 × 21 cm)
Canadian fishing trip sketchbook page
NRACT.1976.374.15

OPPOSITE BOTTOM LEFT
9.13. *Mooring Post*, 1934
Pencil on paper, 10½ × 8¼ in.
(26.7 × 21 cm)
Canadian fishing trip sketchbook page
NRACT.1976.374.10

OPPOSITE BOTTOM RIGHT
9.14. *Fishing Shack Window* and *Mooring Post*, 1934
Pencil on paper, 10½ × 8¼ in.
(26.7 × 21 cm)
Canadian fishing trip sketchbook page
NRACT.1976.374.11

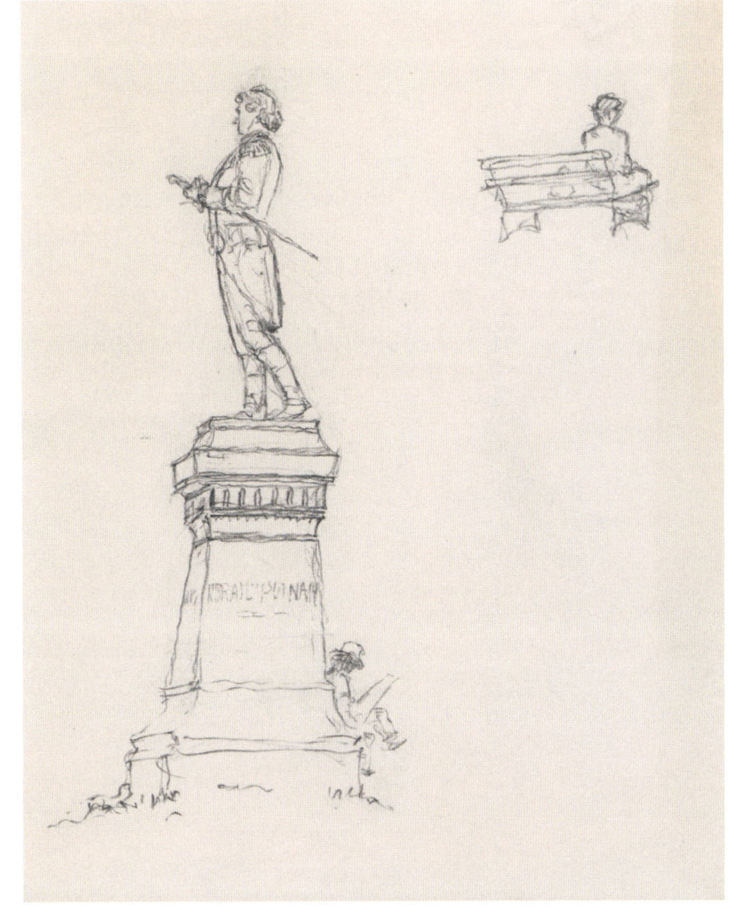

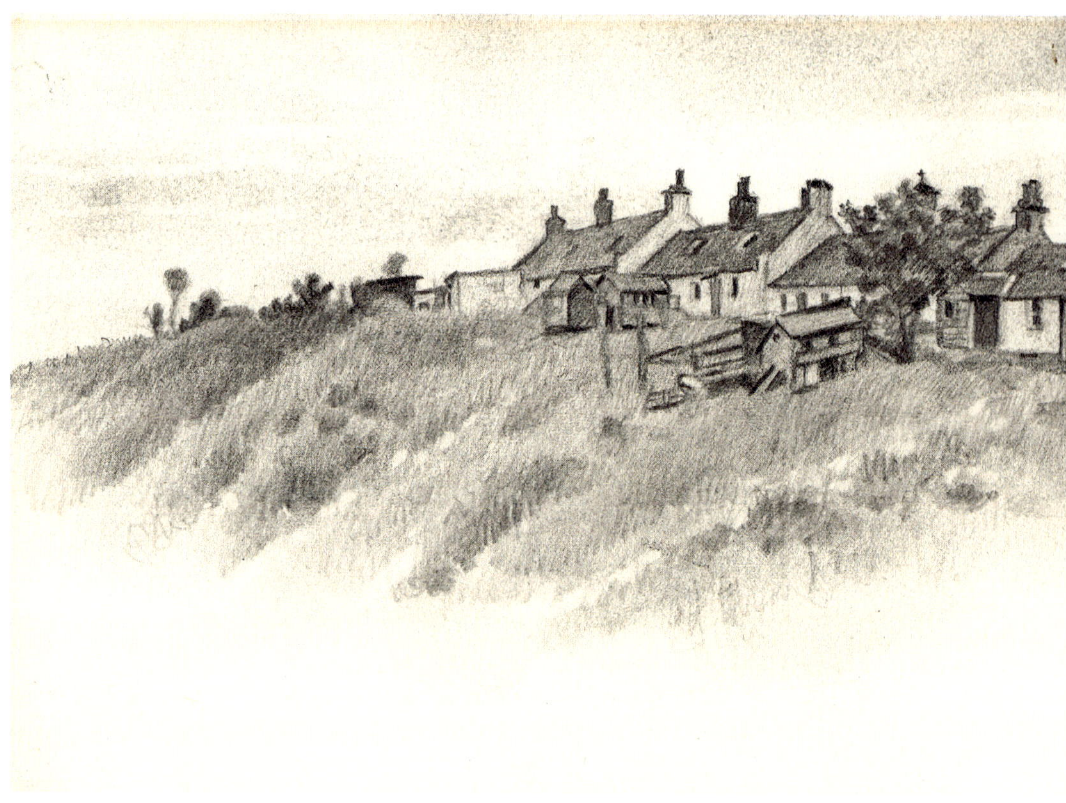

In 1969, Rockwell and his wife Molly traveled to Scotland, where he painted a fishing village in Kincardine, seen from a distance (plate 9.16), and the cliff top ruins of Dunnottar Castle, Edinburgh Castle (plate 9.17).

Rockwell's youngest son, Peter Rockwell, a sculptor and an art historian, lived in Rome from 1961 until his death in 2020. While visiting with Peter and his family in 1971, Rockwell found inspiration in a view from his hotel window (plate 9.18).

ABOVE
9.16. *Catterline, Kincardine, Scotland*, 1969
Pencil on paper, 4½ × 13 in. (11.4 × 33 cm)
NRACT.1973.125

OPPOSITE
9.17. *Edinburgh Castle*, 1969
Pencil on paper, 8¾ × 13 in. (22.2 × 33 cm)
NRACT.1973.124

OVERLEAF
9.18. *From Room 505 Balcony, Hassler Hotel, Rome, Sept. 17, '71*, 1971
Pencil on paper, 11 × 14 in. (27.9 × 35.6 cm)
Sketchbook drawing
NRACT.1976.307

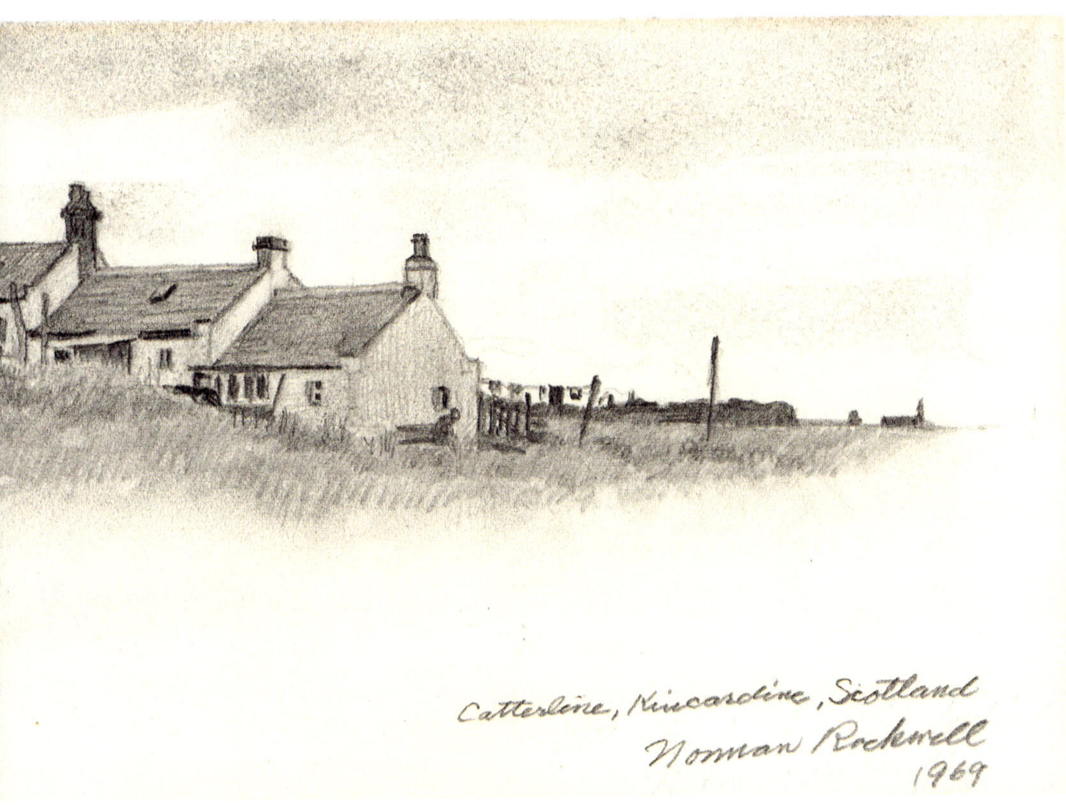
Catterline, Kincardine, Scotland
Norman Rockwell
1969

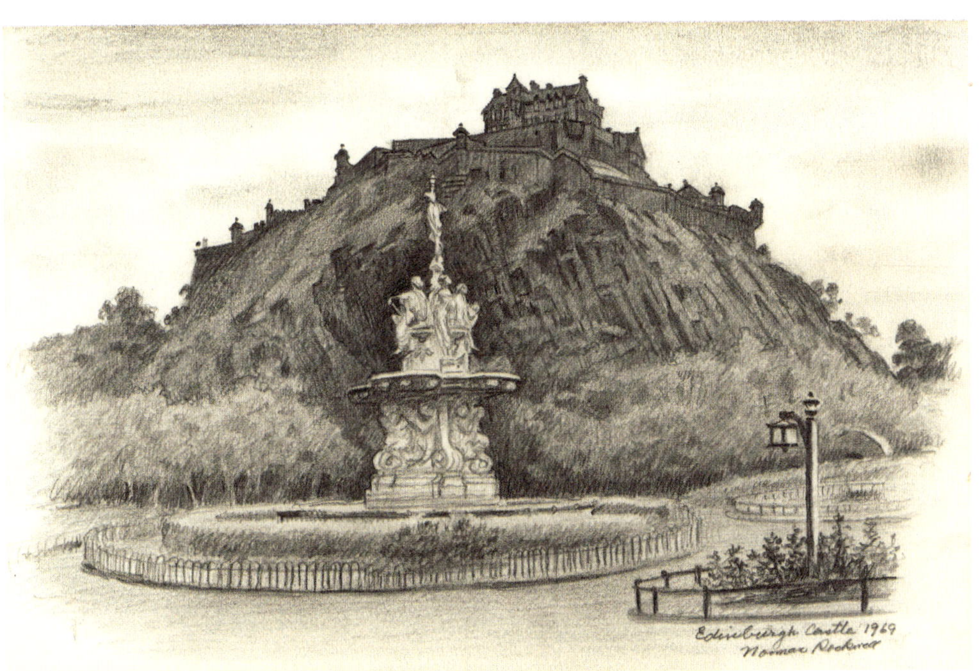
Edinburgh Castle 1969
Norman Rockwell

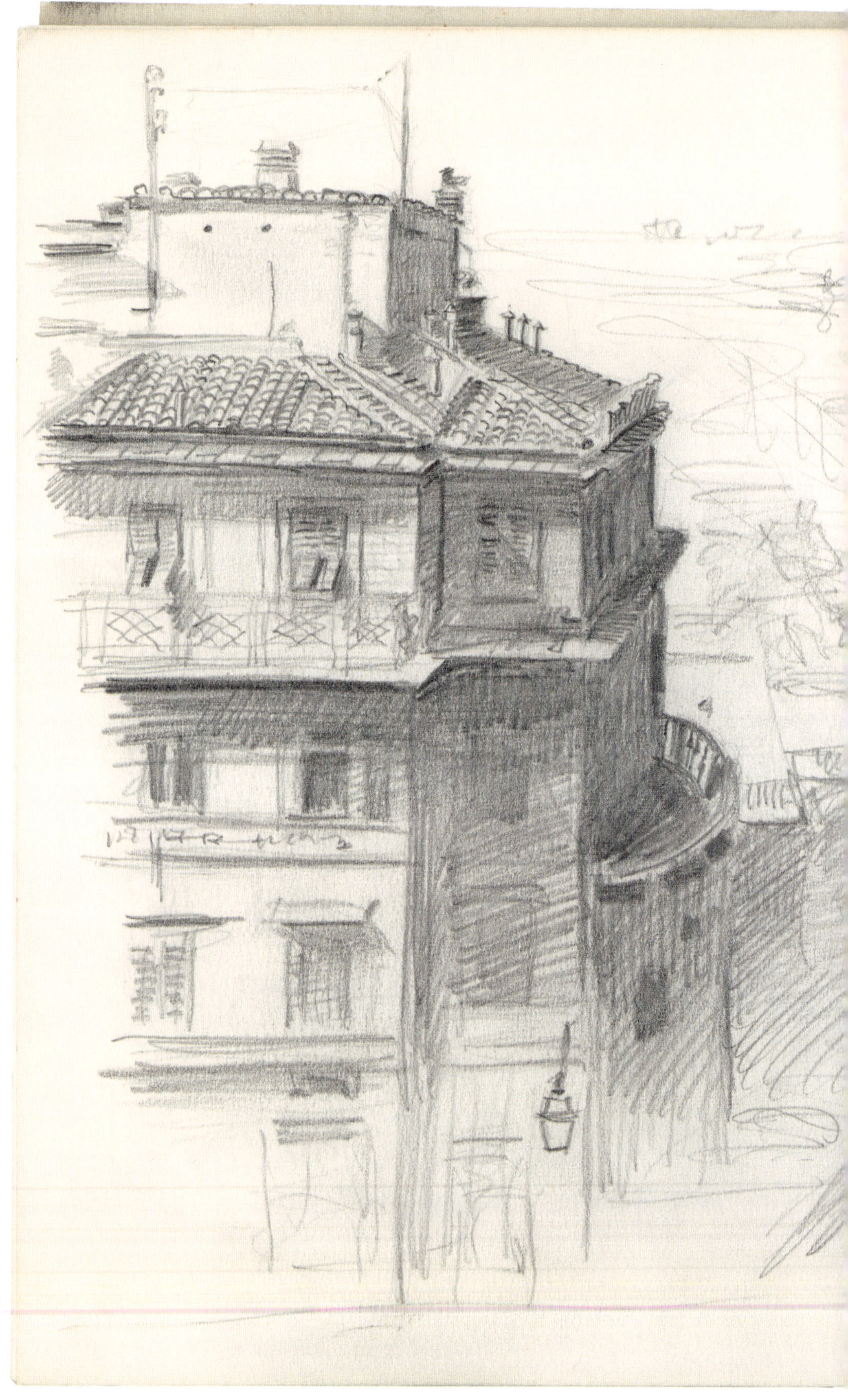

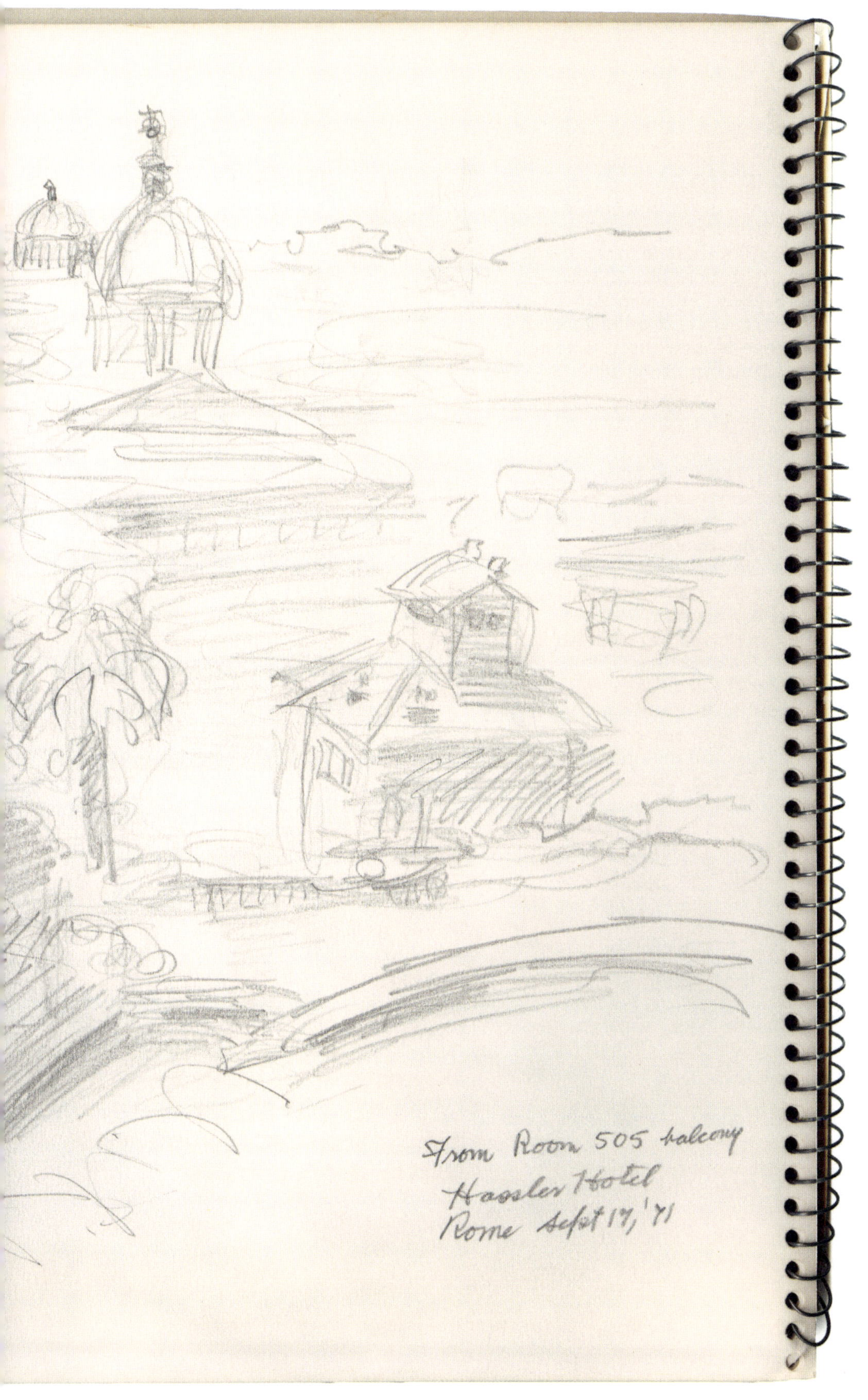
From Room 505 balcony
Hassler Hotel
Rome Sept 17, '71

# Notes

## Introduction

1. Norman Rockwell, *How I Make a Picture* (Westport, Connecticut: Institute of Commercial Art, Famous Artists School, 1948), 18.
2. Linda Szekely Pero, *American Chronicles: The Art of Norman Rockwell* (Stockbridge, Massachusetts: Norman Rockwell Museum, 2007), 167.

## Chapter 1

1. Ken Johnson, "Does Drawing Still Matter?" *New York Times*, October 10, 2003, section E, 34.
2. Norman Rockwell with Thomas Rockwell, *My Adventures as an Illustrator: The Definitive Edition* (New York: Abbeville Press, 2019), 89.
3. Herbert R. Hutter, "History of Drawing" in *Drawing*, Encyclopedia Britannica Online, July 20, 1998, https://www.britannica.com/art/drawing-art/History-of-drawing.
4. *The Making of an Artist*, National Gallery of Art, Italian Renaissance Resources, 7, https://www.britannica.com/art/drawing-art/History-of-drawing.
5. Rockwell, *My Adventures as an Illustrator*, 89–90.

## Chapter 2

1. Norman Rockwell with Thomas Rockwell, *My Adventures as an Illustrator: The Definitive Edition* (New York: Abbeville Press, 2019), 32.
2. Ibid., 42.
3. Ibid., 55.
4. Ibid.
5. Ibid., 70.
6. Ibid.
7. Deborah Solomon, *American Mirror: The Life and Art of Norman Rockwell* (New York: Farrar, Straus and Giroux, 2013), 40.
8. Rockwell, *My Adventures as an Illustrator*, 83
9. George B. Bridgman, *Constructive Anatomy* (London: The Bodley Head, 1920), 8.
10. Rockwell, *My Adventures as an Illustrator*, 82.
11. Ibid., 89.
12. Ibid., 92.
13. Ibid., 93.
14. Pamela Whiteley McLaughlin, "Syracuse University Libraries' Special Collections Research Center Uncovers Early Norman Rockwell Illustrations," *Syracuse University News*, March 7, 2017, https://news.syr.edu/blog/2017/03/07/syracuse-university-libraries-special-collections-research-center-uncovers-early-norman-rockwell-illustrations.
15. Rockwell, *My Adventures as an Illustrator*, 73.
16. Heather Campbell Coyle, "Howard Pyle's Illustrations of Black Figures in American History," *Imprinted: Illustrating Race* (Stockbridge, Massachusetts: Norman Rockwell Museum, 2022).
17. "The Collection: The Strawberry Girl," The Wallace Collection, https://wallacelive.wallacecollection.org/eMP/eMuseumPlus?service=ExternalInterface&module=collection&objectId=64930&viewType=detailView.
18. Rockwell, *My Adventures as an Illustrator*, 92.
19. Ibid., 42.

## Chapter 3

1. Arthur L. Guptill, *Norman Rockwell: Illustrator* (New York: Watson-Guptill Publications, 1946), 204.
2. Ibid., 109.
3. Norman Rockwell with Thomas Rockwell, *My Adventures as an Illustrator: The Definitive Edition* (New York: Abbeville Press, 2019), 352.
4. Ibid., 353.

5. History.com Editors, "Ruby Bridges Desegregates Her School," History (website), A&E Television Networks, March 2, 2021, https://www.history.com/this-day-in-history/ruby-bridges-desegregates-her-school.
6. Deborah Solomon, *American Mirror: The Life and Art of Norman Rockwell* (New York: Farrar, Straus and Giroux, 2013), 368.
7. Ibid., 371.
8. Chester Martin to Norman Rockwell, January 6, 1964, Norman Rockwell Museum, ST.1976.20030.5.13.
9. David J. Malarcher to Norman Rockwell, c/o *Look Magazine*, February 12, 1964, Norman Rockwell Museum, ST.1976.20030.5.14.
10. G. L. LeBon to Norman Rockwell, c/o *Look Magazine*, January 6, 1964, Norman Rockwell Museum, ST.1976.20030.5.12.
11. Rockwell, *My Adventures as an Illustrator*, 415.
12. Ibid., 416.
13. Ibid., 352.

## Chapter 4

1. Norman Rockwell with Thomas Rockwell, *My Adventures as an Illustrator: The Definitive Edition* (New York: Abbeville Press, 2019), 138.
2. Ibid.
3. Ibid., 451.
4. Ibid., 453.
5. Ibid., 250–51.
6. Ibid., 42.
7. Margaret Rockwell, *Norman Rockwell's Growing Up in America* (New York: MetroBooks, 1998), 78.
8. Deborah Solomon, *American Mirror: The Life and Art of Norman Rockwell* (New York: Farrar, Straus and Giroux, 2013), 261.
9. Ibid., 362.
10. Norman Rockwell to Asger Jerrild, New York, NY, September 9, 1963.
11. Rockwell, *My Adventures as an Illustrator*, 426.
12. Ibid., 449.
13. S. Lane Faison Jr., Kenneth Stuart, and Thomas S. Buechner, *The Norman Rockwell Album* (Garden City, New York: Doubleday, 1961), 142.
14. Ibid.
15. Rockwell, *My Adventures as an Illustrator*, 453.

## Chapter 5

1. Norman Rockwell, *How I Make a Picture* (Westport, Connecticut: Institute of Commercial Art, Famous Artists School, 1948), 13.
2. Norman Rockwell with Thomas Rockwell, *My Adventures as an Illustrator: The Definitive Edition* (New York: Abbeville Press, 2019), 333.
3. Norman Rockwell Museum, *American Chronicles: The Art of Norman Rockwell* (Remastered), December 12, 2017, YouTube video, 11:46, https://www.youtube.com/watch?v=qcV-b2aSt_I&ab_channel=NormanRockwellMuseum.
4. Rockwell, *My Adventures as an Illustrator*, 337.
5. Ibid., 142.
6. *The Free Library*, "Norman Rockwell in Black and White: Drawings for Classic *Saturday Evening Post* Covers," *USA Today*, July 1, 2008, accessed May 18, 2022, https://www.thefreelibrary.com/Norman+Rockwell+in+Black+%26+White.-a0181757190.
7. Rockwell, *My Adventures as an Illustrator*, 340.
8. Katharine Anthony, "The Most Beloved American Writer," illustrated by Norman Rockwell, *Woman's Home Companion*, December 19, 1937, 9.
9. Rockwell, *My Adventures as an Illustrator*, 334.
10. Alison Wyrley Birch, "Richard Wyrley Birch of Kent Once Was the Photographer Behind the Artist's Brush," *Sunday Republican* (Waterbury, Connecticut), November 17, 1974, xv.

## Chapter 6

1. Norman Rockwell with Thomas Rockwell, *My Adventures as an Illustrator: The Definitive Edition* (New York: Abbeville Press, 2019), 223.

2. Ibid., 427.
3. Ibid., 430.
4. Norman Rockwell to Erik Erikson, 1955, the Hotel Montalembert, Paris, in *Erikson Papers* (Stockbridge, Massachusetts: Austen Riggs Center).
5. Stephanie Haboush Plunkett, "Peter Rockwell: A Life in Art," in *The Fantastical Faces of Peter Rockwell: A Sculptor's Retrospective* (Stockbridge, Massachusetts: Norman Rockwell Museum, 2009), 21.
6. Philip Cohen, "Family Diversity Is the New Normal for America's Children" (briefing paper, Council on Contemporary Families, September 4, 2014), https://familyinequality.files.wordpress.com/2014/09/family-diversity-new-normal.pdf.
7. U.S. Bureau of Labor Statistics, "Changes in Women's Labor Force Participation in the 20th Century," *TED: The Economics Daily*, February 16, 2000, https://www.bls.gov/opub/ted/2000/feb/wk3/art03.htm.

## Chapter 7

1. Laurie Norton Moffatt, *Norman Rockwell: A Definitive Catalogue*, vol. 1 (Hanover, New Hampshire: University Press of New England, 1986), 301.

## Chapter 8

1. "Closing Scene," *Sullivan's Travels*, directed by Preston Sturges (1941; New York: The Criterion Collection, 2015), Blu-ray.
2. Pablo Picasso, "The Wisdom of Pablo Picasso," *Playboy* 11, no. 1 (January 1964): 97.
3. Norman Rockwell with Thomas Rockwell, *My Adventures as an Illustrator: The Definitive Edition* (New York: Abbeville Press, 2019), 148–51.
4. Ibid., 151.
5. Deborah Solomon, *American Mirror: The Life and Art of Norman Rockwell* (New York: Farrar, Straus and Giroux, 2013), 86.
6. Rockwell, *My Adventures as an Illustrator*, 122.
7. Arthur L. Guptill, *Norman Rockwell: Illustrator* (New York: Watson-Guptill Publications, 1946), 38.
8. Guptill, *Norman Rockwell: Illustrator*, dust jacket.
9. Jack Alexander, introduction to *Norman Rockwell: Illustrator*, by Arthur L. Guptill (New York: Watson-Guptill Publications, 1946).
10. Guptill, *Norman Rockwell: Illustrator*, 177.
11. Ibid., 71.
12. Ibid., 101.
13. Ibid., 129.
14. Solomon, *American Mirror*, 323–28.
15. Guptill, *Norman Rockwell: Illustrator*, dust jacket.
16. Ibid., 127.

## Chapter 9

1. Norman Rockwell, *How I Make a Picture* (Westport, Connecticut: Institute of Commercial Art, Famous Artists School, 1948), 231.
2. Norman Rockwell with Thomas Rockwell, *My Adventures as an Illustrator: The Definitive Edition* (New York: Abbeville Press, 2019), 263.
3. Ibid., 304.

# Selected Bibliography


Guptill, Arthur L. *Norman Rockwell, Illustrator.* New York: Watson-Guptill, 1946.

Faison, S. Lane Jr., Kenneth Stuart, and Thomas S. Buechner. *The Norman Rockwell Album.* Garden City, NY: Doubleday, 1961.

Saunders, Richard (pseud. Benjamin Franklin). *Poor Richard: The Almanacks for the Years 1733–1758.* Illustrated by Norman Rockwell. Introduction by Van Wyck Brooks. New York: Heritage Press, 1964.

Rockwell, Molly, and Norman Rockwell. *Willie Was Different: The Tale of an Ugly Thrushling.* New York: Funk & Wagnalls, 1969.

Buechner, Thomas S. *Norman Rockwell, Artist and Illustrator.* New York: Harry N. Abrams, 1970.

———. *Norman Rockwell: A Sixty Year Retrospective.* New York: Harry N. Abrams, 1972. Catalogue of a traveling exhibition organized by Bernard Danenberg Galleries, New York.

Finch, Christopher. *Norman Rockwell's America.* New York: Harry N. Abrams, 1975.

Pitz, Henry. *200 Years of American Illustration.* Foreword by Norman Rockwell. New York: Random House, 1977.

Meyer, Susan E. *America's Great Illustrators.* New York: Harry N. Abrams, 1978.

Walton, Donald. *A Rockwell Portrait.* Kansas City: Sheed, Andrews and McMeel, 1978.

Buechner, Thomas S. *The Norman Rockwell Treasury.* New York: Galahad Books, 1979.

Finch, Christopher. *Norman Rockwell: 332 Magazine Covers.* New York: Abbeville Press/Random House, 1979.

Reed, Walt. *Great American Illustrators.* New York: Abbeville Press, 1979.

Rockwell, Norman. *Rockwell on Rockwell: How I Make a Picture.* New York: Watson-Guptill, 1979.

Bauer, Fred. *Norman Rockwell's Faith of America.* Carmel, NY: Guideposts, 1980.

Norton Moffatt, Laurie. *Norman Rockwell: A Definitive Catalogue.* 2 vols. Stockbridge, MA: Norman Rockwell Museum at Stockbridge, 1986.

Stoltz, Donald, and Marshall Stoltz. *The Advertising World of Norman Rockwell.* New York: Harrison House, 1986.

Rockwell, Thomas. *The Best of Norman Rockwell.* Philadelphia: Courage Books, 1988.

Cohn, Jan. *Creating America: George Horace Lorimer and The Saturday Evening Post.* Pittsburgh: University of Pittsburgh Press, 1990.

Goffman, Judy, ed., with Davide Faccioli and Manuela Teatini. *Norman Rockwell.* Milan: Electa, 1990. Catalogue of an exhibition at the Palazzo delle Esposizioni, Rome.

Hughes, Robert. "Norman Rockwell." In *Nothing If Not Critical: Selected Essays on Art and Artists,* 230–33. New York: Alfred A. Knopf, 1990.

Meyer, Susan E. *Norman Rockwell's World War II: Impressions from the Homefront.* San Antonio: USAA Foundation, 1991.

Murray, Stuart, and James McCabe. *Norman Rockwell's Four Freedoms: Images that Inspire a Nation.* Stockbridge: Berkshire House Publishers, 1993.

Norman Rockwell Museum at Stockbridge, The. *Norman Rockwell: A Centennial Celebration*. San Diego: Thunder Bay Press, 1993.

Bogart, Michele. *Artists, Advertising, and the Borders of Art*. Chicago: University of Chicago Press, 1995.

Cohn, Jan. *Covers of the Saturday Evening Post: Seventy Years of Outstanding Illustration from America's Favorite Magazine*. New York: Viking Studio Books, 1995.

Rockwell, Margaret. *Norman Rockwell's Chronicles of America*. New York: MetroBooks, 1996.

Cohen, Joel H. *Norman Rockwell: America's Best-Loved Illustrator.* Danbury, CT: Franklin Watts, 1997.

Ermoyan, Arpi. *Famous American Illustrators*. New York: Watson-Guptill, 1997.

Marling, Karal Ann. *Norman Rockwell.* Library of American Art. New York: Harry N. Abrams, 1997.

Sonder, Ben. *The Legacy of Norman Rockwell.* New York: Todtri Productions, 1997.

Rockwell, Margaret. *Norman Rockwell's Growing Up In America*. New York: MetroBooks, 1998.

Hart Hennessey, Maureen, and Anne Knutson. *Norman Rockwell: Pictures for the American People*. New York: Harry N. Abrams, 1999. Catalogue of a traveling exhibition organized by the Norman Rockwell Museum at Stockbridge and the High Museum of Art, Atlanta.

Heller, Steven, and Marshall Arisman. *The Education of an Illustrator*. New York: Allworth Press, 2000.

Claridge, Laura. *Norman Rockwell: A Life.* New York: Random House, 2001.

Reed, Walt, and Roger Reed. *The Illustrator in America, 1860–2000*. New York: Society of Illustrators, 2001.

Halpern, Richard. *Norman Rockwell: The Underside of Innocence*. Chicago: University of Chicago Press, 2006.

Rivoli, Kevin. *In Search of Norman Rockwell's America*. New York: Howard Books, 2008.

Csatari, Joseph, and Jeff Csatari. *Norman Rockwell's Boy Scouts of America.* New York: DK, 2009.

Edgerton, James A. "Buddy," and Nan O'Brien. *The Unknown Rockwell: A Portrait of Two American Families.* Essex Junction, VT: Battenkill River Press, 2009.

Schick, Ron. *Norman Rockwell: Behind the Camera.* Boston: Little, Brown and Company, 2009. Published to coincide with a traveling exhibition of the same name organized by the Norman Rockwell Museum at Stockbridge.

Szekely Pero, Linda. *American Chronicles: The Art of Norman Rockwell.* Stockbridge, MA: Norman Rockwell Museum at Stockbridge, 2009. Catalogue of a traveling exhibition organized by the Norman Rockwell Museum at Stockbridge.

Goffman Cutler, Judy, and Laurence S. Cutler. *Norman Rockwell's America . . . in England.* Newport, RI: American Civilization Foundation, 2010. Catalogue of an exhibition shown at the National Museum of American Illustration, Newport, RI, and Dulwich Picture Gallery, London.

Mecklenburg, Virginia M., and Todd McCarthy. *Telling Stories: Norman Rockwell from the Collections of George Lucas and Steven Spielberg*. New York: Abrams, 2010. Catalogue of an exhibition shown at the Smithsonian American Art Museum.

Haboush Plunkett, Stephanie. "Chasing the Muse: Norman Rockwell and the Legacy of Howard Pyle." In *Howard Pyle: American Master Rediscovered*, edited by Heather Campbell Coyle, 156–65. Wilmington, DE: Delaware Art Museum, 2011. Catalogue of an exhibition shown at the Delaware Art Museum and the Norman Rockwell Museum at Stockbridge.

Homer, Susan. *Norman Rockwell's Spirit of America*. New York: Abrams, 2011.

Rubenstein, Bruce. *The Rockwell Heist: The Extraordinary Theft of Seven Norman Rockwell Paintings and a Phony Renoir—and the 20-year Chase for Their Recovery from the Midwest through Europe and South America*. St. Paul: Borealis Books, 2013.

Solomon, Deborah. *American Mirror: The Life and Art of Norman Rockwell*. New York: Farrar, Straus and Giroux, 2013.

Petrick, Jane Allen. *Hidden in Plain Sight: The Other People in Norman Rockwell's America*. Miami, FL: Informed Decisions, 2014.

Goffman Cutler, Judy, and Laurence S. Cutler. *Norman Rockwell and His Contemporaries*. Newport, RI: American Civilization Foundation, 2015. Catalog of an exhibition at the National Museum of American Illustration, Newport, RI.

Haboush Plunkett, Stephanie, and Magdalen Livesey. *Drawing Lessons from the Famous Artists School: Classic Techniques and Expert Tips from the Golden Age of Illustration*. Beverly, MA: Rockport, 2017.

Lach, Will. *Norman Rockwell's A Day in the Life of a Boy*. New York: Abbeville Kids, 2017.

Lach, Will. *Norman Rockwell's A Day in the Life of a Girl*. New York: Abbeville Kids, 2017.

Doyle, Susan, Jaleen Grove, and Whitney Sherman, eds. *History of Illustration*. New York: Fairchild Books, 2018.

Haboush Plunkett, Stephanie, and James J. Kimble, eds. *Enduring Ideals: Rockwell, Roosevelt, and the Four Freedoms*. New York: Abbeville Press, 2018. Catalogue of a traveling exhibition organized by the Norman Rockwell Museum at Stockbridge.

Burleigh, Robert, and Wendell Minor. *Hi, I'm Norman*. New York: Paula Wiseman Books, 2019.

Rockwell, Norman, as told to Tom Rockwell. *My Adventures as an Illustrator*. The Definitive Edition. Edited by Abigail Rockwell. New York: Abbeville Press, 2019.

Twain, Mark. *The Adventures of Tom Sawyer and Huckleberry Finn*. Illustrated by Norman Rockwell. Introduction by Stephanie Haboush Plunkett. New York: Abbeville Press, 2020.

Rockwell, Margaret. *Faithful Friends: Norman Rockwell and His Dogs*. New York: Abbeville Press, 2022.

# Index

Page numbers in *italics* refer to illustrations.

# Author Biographies

STEPHANIE HABOUSH PLUNKETT is Deputy Director and Chief Curator of the Norman Rockwell Museum. She currently leads the Rockwell Center for American Visual Studies and has organized many exhibitions, including *Imprinted: Illustrating Race; Inventing America: Rockwell and Warhol; Rockwell and Realism in an Abstract World; The Unknown Hopper: Edward Hopper as Illustrator; William Steig: Love & Laughter; Ephemeral Beauty: Al Parker and the American Women's Magazine, 1940–1960*; as well as the international traveling exhibition *Enduring Ideals: Rockwell, Roosevelt & the Four Freedoms*. Her publications include *Drawing Lessons from the Famous Artists School: Classic Techniques and Expert Tips from the Golden Age of Illustration*.

JESSE M. KOWALSKI, Curator of Exhibitions, joined the Norman Rockwell Museum in 2015. Since coming on board, he has curated *Enchanted: A History of Fantasy Illustration; Hanna-Barbera: The Architects of Saturday Morning; Inventing America: Rockwell and Warhol; The Art & Wit of Rube Goldberg; Superheroes and Superstars: The Art of Alex Ross*; and *Never Abandon Imagination: The Fantastical Art of Tony DiTerlizzi*, and is currently preparing additional exhibitions. Prior to joining the Norman Rockwell Museum, Kowalski served as Director of Exhibitions at the Andy Warhol Museum, where he curated many of the museum's popular traveling and in-house exhibitions.

LOUIS HENRY MITCHELL is the Creative Director of Character Design for Sesame Workshop, where he directs and oversees all aspects of character art. He designed Julia, the first *Sesame Street* character on the autism spectrum, from initial character illustration to final sculpted Muppet. Mitchell studied at the School of Visual and the Art Students League, and credits Norman Rockwell as a major inspiration in his desire to become an artist.

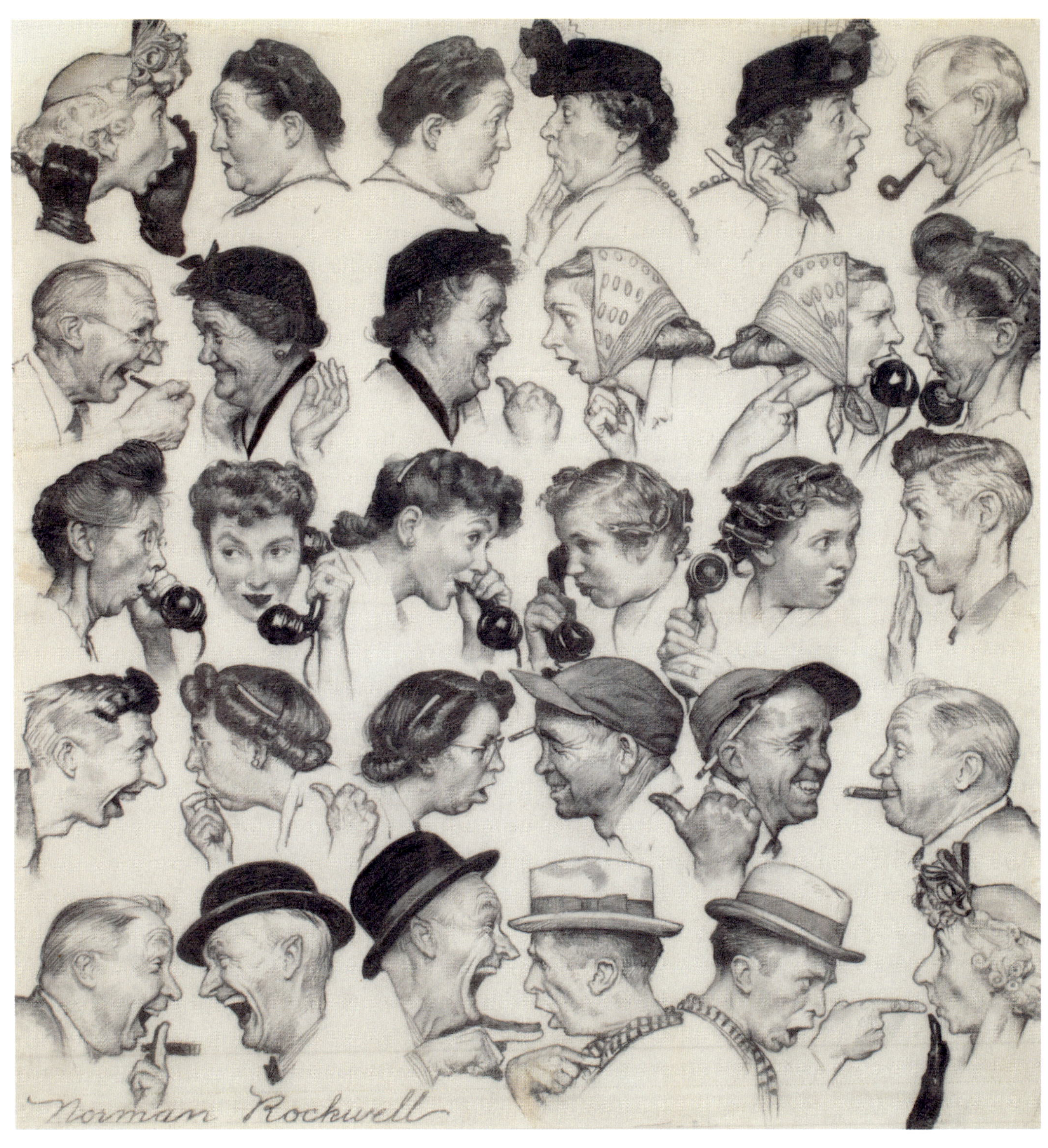
Norman Rockwell